RAUL H. YZAGUIRRE

SEATED AT THE TABLE OF POWER

ALSO BY STELLA POPE DUARTE

Fragile Night

Let Their Spirits Dance

Women Who Live in Coffee Shops:
And Other Stories

If I Die in Juarez

Writing through Revelations, Visions and Dreams:
The memoir of a writer's soul

Essays, articles, and anthology collections
are accessible online or at author's website:
stellapopeduarte.com

A BIOGRAPHY BY

STELLA POPE DUARTE

RAUL H. YZAGUIRRE

Seated at the Table of Power

Latino Book Publisher
Mesa, Arizona | 2016

First Edition | 2016
Book design: Yolie Hernandez
Front cover photograph: Felipe Ruiz Acosta (NCLR Archives)
Author photograph: Francesca Elena Garza
Family and early life photos courtesy of Yzaguirre family archives.
All other photos courtesy of NCLR, unless otherwise noted.

Latino Book Publisher
An imprint of the Hispanic Institute of Social Issues
PO Box 50553
Mesa, Arizona 85208-0028
(480) 646-9401 | hisi.org | info@hisi.org

Pope Duarte, Stella
Raul H. Yzaguirre: Seated at the Table of Power / Stella Pope Duarte
Copyright © 2016 by Stella Pope Duarte
1st. ed. xvii, 424 p.
ISBN-13: 978-1-936885-21-3

Includes bibliographical references.
1. Yzaguirre, Raul H. 2. Civil Rights Leaders—United States—Biography. 3. Mexico—
United States—Race Relations—Border Issues. 4. Chicano Movement—History.
5. Mexican Americans—Latinos—Politics and Government. 6. National Council of La
Raza—United States—Nonprofit Institutions.

The publication of this book was made possible in part by support from the National
Council of La Raza (NCLR) and its affiliate, the Raza Development Fund (RDF).

No part of this book may be used, saved, scanned, or reproduced in any manner
whatsoever without the written permission of the author and/or publisher, except
for brief quotations embodied in cited articles or reviews.

All Rights Reserved.

Manufactured in the United States of America.
1 2 3 4 5 6 7 8 9 10

Dedicated to the memory of
Graciela Gil Olivarez,
affectionately known as Amazing Grace.
You were there when we needed you the most.
Gracias.

ACKNOWLEDGEMENTS

TRULY, I CANNOT ADEQUATELY EXPRESS what it has meant for me to tell the story of a man whose love of community has influenced the workings of our government, from the halls of Congress and the Senate in Washington, D. C. to states and cities across America, as well as to countries beyond our borders. I am indebted to Raul Yzaguirre for trusting me to tell his story with all the dilemmas, joys, triumphs, losses, successes and unforgettable moments lived in the rich tapestry of America's historical landscape. His journey has been our journey, the coming together of America's Latinos, and the removal of the cloak of invisibility, once and for all.

I THANK RAUL for his patience with my hundreds of questions, the probing questions that were more tasks than simply questions, the emails, phone calls, the clarifications given, and insights offered, and the memories shared, warm, homespun stuff, and hard, brittle points along the way, some of them humorous, life-empowering, and always richly, uniquely his own. Transcribing his words into hundreds of pages of narrative was a prodigious task, and one that produced a treasure, a living memorial of a man, born and raised in the Rio Grande Valley, whose courage in confronting America's often biased and rigid beliefs led to his discovery that common ground is possible even in the most volatile situations. He has proven that there can be an end to distorted perspectives if we work together to solidify our common beliefs in freedom, equality and fairness under the law.

TIME. How valuable time is to us all, and yet Raul was generous with his time, listening to every question, and searching his memory for answers, always ready to tell the stories of those he loves and esteems, beginning with his family. My thanks to his wife, Audrey, for her indomitable spirit, her charm, kindness, and absolute loyalty to the man she loves; and to their children, especially Raul, Jr., Becky and Ben who allowed me to see their father through their eyes—thank you. Raul's brother Ruben, and his sisters, Alma "Loly" and Maria Teresa, "Tere," bid me enter the world of their childhood, and it was delightful to listen to the tales of their grandfather Gavino Morin, and Elisa, "Mama Licha," his wife, and their own parents, Rubén and Eva Linda, "Evita" Yzaguirre. Raul's cousin, Gavino, and his mother, Guillermina, "Mina," also added their own memories of Raul's favorite uncle, Pedro Morin. Precious memories all of them, and surprising, unbelievable moments, some tainted with pain or loss, and still alive with the love that bound the Yzaguirres and Morins together.

I AM INDEBTED TO ALL WHO GENEROUSLY GAVE of their time to answer interview questions. The National Council of La Raza (NCLR) family, Raul's friends and associates and the numerous interviews conducted enriched this work, adding valuable insights and making it what Raul wanted: the story of others as well. Janet Murguia, current President and CEO of NCLR graciously offered a closer understanding of what it meant for Raul to step down from his thirty-year tenure with La Raza, and graciously hand over the reins of power to her. "He did something very different," she relates. "He knew how important it was not to look back, not to become a fixture." In this way Yzaguirre allowed unencumbered time for Janet Murguia to make her own mark on the organization.

OTHERS INTERVIEWED WERE: former Arizona Congressman Ed Pastor; Mari Carmen Aponte, Ambassador of El Salvador; Cecilia, Muñoz, Director of the Domestic Policy Council for the Obama Administration; Roberto Reveles, founder of Somos America; attorney Ernie Calderon, former member of ASU's Board of Regents; David North, U.S. Immigration Specialist; Jorge Ramos, journalist and anchor for *Univision*, and Steven Reinemund, former CEO of PepsiCo.

I AM ALSO GRATEFUL for interviews from those who worked closely with Raul for years. Emily Gantz Mckay, one of NCLR's first VP's, my thanks to her for sending along *The National Council of La Raza: The First 25 Years*, (1993) and for adding insights to Raul's role as a Latino leader. And to Charles Kamaskai, the VP who played devil's advocate for Raul, and shared valuable information on NCLR's Policy Analysis Center. The numerous leaders who enlarged Raul's mission to community are many and the reader will meet each one in this work. Their worth cannot be overemphasized; it is real and without their help, I would have never completed this manuscript.

LET ME MENTION more interviewees, and if anyone has been left out, please accept my apologies. Ramon Murguia, Lisa Navarette, Danny Ortega, Tommy Espinoza, Mark Van Brunt, Pete Garcia, Ronnie Lopez, Alfredo Gutierrez, Joe Eddie Lopez, Rosie Lopez, Dr. Belen Servin, Tony Salazar, Dr. Michael Cortés, Dr. Hector F. Aldape, Armando de León, Rick Bela, Juan Gutierrez, Olga Aros, Helen Cavazos, Helen Coronado, Fabiola Rodriguez-Ciampoli, Hilario Diaz, Francisco Ivarra, Dr. Cordelia C. Candelaria, Moctesuma Esparza, Luis Valdez, Frank Barrios, and two sisters, Leticia and Delia de la Vara.

A SPECIAL THANKS to Alex Perilla who took over as Director of ASU's Center for Community Development and Civil Rights (CDCR) when Raul was appointed ambassador to the Dominican Republic in 2010. Alex provided vital information, along with the Center's Administrative Assistant, Patricia "Pat" Bonn, who has worked tirelessly in gathering information for ASU's archives from NCLR and numerous literary and global news media outlets. Thanks to both for their insightful interviews. I am indebted to the CDCR Center for allowing me access to literary articles, news reports, congressional testimonies, and NCLR historical facts and photos, which provided valuable information. A salute to James Garcia for the audio conversations with Raul Yzaguirre he collected for the ASU archives. They added a layer of understanding to the current work.

Rosa Cays edited early drafts of the manuscript, and with her expert skills, helped me envision the tone and style of the work. Raul Jr., former Principal of the Raul Yzaguirre School for Success in Brownsville, Texas, gave me access to the video, *Raul Yzaguirre: American Hero*, (2010), which contributed quotes from U.S. Senator John McCain; Dr. Henry G. Cisneros, 10th U.S. Secretary of Housing and Urban Development (HUD) from 1993 to 1997, and Texas State Senator, Rodney Ellis. A special thanks to my editor, Dr. Christine Marin, Professor Emerita, Arizona State University, whose expertise as an historian, writer, editor and community activist, has been invaluable in completing this work. Kudos to Yolanda "Yolie" Hernandez, Hispanic Institute of Social Issues Production Director, for her belief that Latino literature is American literature at its finest.

Funding for this five-year project was provided by two sources: NCLR's one-time seed grant, and funding from the Raza Development Fund (RDF). The monies allowed me to travel to the Dominican Republic to complete interviews with Raul at the American Embassy, and to travel to the Rio Grande Valley to visit Raul's birthplace in San Juan and other sites crucial to the work. Funds also provided time for writing, researching, conducting interviews, and final publication of the completed work.

For my family and friends in Arizona so close to my heart who had confidence that I would complete this project—my thanks! Without their funny stories, and loving smiles, especially from my children and grandchildren, I might have lacked the courage to carry on. I am an *aficionada* of St. Anthony, patron saint of my childhood parish, whose ability to help humanity find things, helped me find my way to the end of this work.

The mythical, mysterious and spiritual are part of my everyday life, and I would be remiss if I did not thank my Heavenly Father who did not spare me trials and tribulations along the way. Yet, there were always His everlasting arms, and the enigmatic, precious smile from the Patroness of the Americas— La Virgen de Guadalupe. Gracias, mil!

TABLE OF CONTENTS

i

PART TWO: MY SON, THE ACTIVIST

PART FOUR: IF WE BUILD THEM...

INTRODUCTION:
SERVANT LEADERSHIP

*Edward James Olmos and I were both waiting for Raul, and I thanked
him for what he had done for the Chicano community. Olmos
looked at me and said, 'What I do for the Chicano community is
nothing compared to what your brother does. He is the man.'*

—Ruben Yzaguirre

"Do you know Raul Yzaguirre?"

THE WOMAN ASKING THE QUESTION was standing before me as I sat
with friends at a table at El Portal, a popular restaurant in Phoenix
owned by Earl Wilcox and his wife, former Maricopa County Supervisor, Mary Rose Wilcox. "Yes, I do," I answered hesitantly. Of course I knew
of Raul Yzaguirre. The whole community was aware of his arrival in Phoenix in 2005 at the bequest of the president of Arizona State University, Dr.
Michael Crow. In fact, publicity had been widespread throughout the nation.
Yzaguirre, one of the nation's most renowned Latino leaders, was to serve
as the founding executive director of ASU's Center for Community Development and Civil Rights (CDCR), a prestigious first for ASU. Yzaguirre's
thirty-year tenure as President and CEO of the National Council of La Raza
(NCLR) from 1974 to 2004 firmly grounded NCLR as the largest Latino civil
rights, nonprofit organization in the nation. Under Yzaguirre's leadership,
NCLR grew from 15 affiliates to over 300 service providers, making it the
largest constituency-based Hispanic organization in the nation, with total
assets of $100 million and a net worth of approximately $80 million at the
end of Yzaguirre's term.

Yzaguirre's new position at ASU included serving as Professor of Practice in ASU's College of Public Programs and also serving on the Board of the North American Center of Transborder Studies (NACTS), which engages university professionals in educational and business-related endeavors, with an emphasis on incorporating North American content into college and university courses. The CDCR became a part of ASU's downtown New American University and was established to implement projects on community development, civil rights, leadership, education, media, and one of Yzaguirre's favorite subjects; the mentoring of young Latino males.

My hesitant response to the question posed was based on the fact that I knew who Raul Yzaguirre was, but had not had any personal communication with him. "He'd like to speak with you," said the woman, pointing to a table on the other side of the busy restaurant. I followed her to the table and stood before Raul Yzaguirre, who was surrounded by several of his friends.

"You're Stella Pope Duarte," he said.

"Yes."

"I've heard about you, read about you, and have seen one of your interviews on T.V., but now I know who you are." His blue-gray eyes looked warmly into mine. His gentle smile set me somewhat at ease as I stood there, half-embarrassed, wondering what this was all about. He continued, "I read your book, *Let Their Spirits Dance*. You're a gifted writer."

"Thank you," I managed to mumble.

"Are you still working?"

"Working?" My mind went into a flurry of commitments I had in the community, which included teaching, presenting, and working as an artist in residence, all part of an extensive schedule. "Yes, I'm still working."

"No," he said, firmly, "You should only be writing, the community needs you."

I was stunned by his words, and simply thanked him, not knowing that his frank analysis was something Raul Yzaguirre was famous for. His ability to mentor others, to see in someone else what they might not be able to see within themselves, has impacted thousands, perhaps millions of aspiring leaders over the years. Many have assumed leadership positions in politics, education, government, private industry, and a host of national and international organizations that have played key roles in evolving the role of Latinos in a world of changing cultural perspectives and challenging policies, often discriminatory ones, which have taken their toll on generations of Latinos who have struggled to attain the American dream. He asked if I would be interested in working on a writing project with him, and I agreed to talk about the project, not knowing that Yzaguirre meant business. Within a couple of weeks he contacted me through his administrative assistant at the CDCR Center, Pat Bonn, for a luncheon meeting.

This time we met at El Comedor Restaurant, a favorite spot on South Central Avenue on a hot, sweltering day in July 2010, and we discussed current issues affecting the community of Latinos in Phoenix. "Texas, like Arizona, has a long history of immigrant abuse and hardships shared by Mexican Americans throughout its history," he explained. "I'd like to document events that reflect that struggle in Texas, including my own family's experiences living close to the border and confronting injustices, prejudice, and discrimination."

As a native resident of Arizona, I had never thought to write a history of Texas, yet the idea intrigued me. I knew the story of Mexican Americans, identified as Chicanos and Hispanics living in Texas, would in many ways reflect the experiences of other Mexican American communities in the Southwest and other parts of the nation, as well as communities of Puerto Ricans, Cubans, Central Americans, South Americans and other ethnic groups from Spanish-speaking nations who share common traditions, values, and beliefs. All these groups have confronted the same social issues in the U.S. related to education, jobs, housing, health, immigration, negative media exposure, and voting rights. I was to learn later that Yzaguirre's insistence on the unification of these widely dispersed groups into one powerhouse under the banner of the word "Latinos" was the hallmark of his success at NCLR, and will remain the cornerstone of his legacy. His ability to unite groups, to compromise, negotiate, listen to opposing and often radical views, and move forward for the good of the community has been a complex and despairing task. "The only way for us to achieve power is for us to be united," Raul explained. "The way I understand it, we're the race, *la raza*. I talked to Puerto Ricans and Cubans and explained what *la raza* meant to me and they were comfortable with it."

"Has a biography of your life ever been written?" I asked. He gazed briefly into the distance, as if something invisible had suddenly taken form.

"Not yet," he said.

Those two words, *not yet*, had a prophetic ring to them, and even before the waitress took our order, I knew what my response would be. "Would you like me to write your biography and include the history of Texas?" By this time, my mind had shifted from thinking of a project in which I would simply add my two cents to one that would document the life of one of America's premier Latino leaders. I sensed adrenalin flowing through my body as excitement filled me and my senses came alive, rising as they do when I am in the presence of a powerful story.

The larger-than-life scope of this project did not hit me until later, as I read through hundreds of pages of notes I had transcribed word-for-word from numerous interviews conducted with Raul Yzaguirre both here in Phoenix, and in Santo Domingo after he became ambassador to the Dominican Republic in October 2010. I discovered there was no single source of information gathered about Raul, yet references to his life and work abounded in an enormous collection of magazines, newspapers, periodicals, books, essays, documentaries, and dissertations.

As a historical novelist, I am adept at gathering research, visiting sites related to my work, and conducting numerous interviews. However, Yzaguirre's "larger-than-life" existence, his brand of "servant leadership," his tenacity, passion, and absolute resolve in overcoming difficult obstacles for the betterment of the Latino community, tell an expansive story that seems boundless and has challenged me at levels I could have never imagined.

"I am a great believer in servant leadership," Yzaguirre related in one of the interviews. "You're not there to order people around, you're there to serve them. You're not the *cacique,* or the knight on a white horse, the juvenile idea I had when I was a boy. Later, I found out that was the wrong paradigm. I wanted to be someone who empowered others, who was a servant." This attitude is pivotal to Yzaguirre's deep sense of commitment to community and a dedication that goes deeper than position, power, or prestige.

Further information gathered at the luncheon made me aware that Raul Yzaguirre is a descendant of Basque immigrants who made their way to the Gulf of Mexico from northern Spain. They are a land grant family related to Juan Pantaleón Yzaguirre, who arrived in northern New Mexico, circa, 1743. Born on July 22, 1939 in San Juan, Texas in the Rio Grande Valley, Yzaguirre joined a long line of ancestors who have subsequently lived in three countries on the North American Continent: Spain, Mexico, and the U.S.

Throughout his childhood, Yzaguirre lived with his maternal grandparents, Gavino and Elisa "Licha" Morin in San Juan. His grandparents became his parents when Raul was left quite unexpectedly at their home at the age of five. He was not told that his parents, Rubén Antonio and Eva Linda Yzaguirre, would not be coming back for him, although they lived close by and he, at times, stayed at their home to spend time with his siblings, Maria Teresa "Tere," Ruben Antonio, Alma Elodia "Loly," and Aileen Delia. As the oldest son, he would eventually become a father figure to them.

Yzaguirre's grandparents took on the role of parents in the close-knit barrio community of San Juan, and his Uncle Pete became more like a brother. It was his relationship with his grandfather that would become most significant for Raul. Tall, dark, and illiterate, Gavino Morin's life had been one of struggle and determination. He worked as a laborer in the early 1900s clearing fields for local Texas ranchers. His grandfather described living in a tent along the Texas border when he left Monterrey, Mexico to seek his fortune in America. He married one of his Benavidez cousins, Elisa Espinoza de los Monterros, and although opposites in personality and thinking, their marriage lasted a lifetime. Their love story involved intrigue and the murder of one of their relatives by a Lieutenant Yzaguirre; yet their dynamic relationship forged the beginnings of life for Raul, and instilled in him ethics, morals, and a sense of pride in honest labor.

As Raul described his grandfather, I noted our conversation shifted to a new level of intensity. His face changed visibly and his eyes took on a look of deep caring as he began to relate some of his adventures with his grandfather. "I called my grandfather Papa, and my grandmother, Mama Licha. I even thought of changing my name to Raul Morin," he fondly recalled. In an interview with his sister, Tere Tijerina, she agreed that, "Hands down, our grandfather was the biggest influence in Raul's life. He was so compassionate and considerate. He believed we had an obligation to help people in need."

Yzaguirre's relationship with his grandfather deeply influenced him, and led him step by step into the development of a social conscience that would inspire generations of young leaders, and bring visibility to Latinos who had once been part of a vast, invisible minority. The memory of his grandfather's near lynching by Texas Rangers during a time when Mexicans in Texas were restricted by a curfew law, would add fuel to the fire already burning in a young Raul Yzaguirre as he observed the oppression of Mexican American communities.

Eventually, his grandfather opened his own business in San Juan, Morin's Ice House, and became a prosperous and respected member of society, often posting political signs on the pick-up truck he used to deliver ice throughout a segregated community—the north side for Mexicans and the south side for Anglos. Candidates running for office recognized the influence Gavino Morin had on Mexican Americans, and although he never became a registered voter, it was an honor to have their political signs posted on his pick-up truck. It was riding alongside his beloved grandfather as they delivered ice that led Raul to esteem him for the kind and caring person he was. They had long conversations together, both sharing their deepest thoughts.

In his teens, after his grandfather's death, Yzaguirre was to meet another man who would continue guiding him to maturity: Dr. Hector P. García, founder of one of the most powerful civil rights organizations in U.S. history,

xiv | RAUL H. YZAGUIRRE

the American G.I. Forum, launched in 1948 in Corpus Christi, Texas. Yzaguirre's first contact with Dr. García would take place early in his life, at age thirteen when he ran away from home to seek an adventurous life as a sailor. Hitchhiking to Corpus Christi, Yzaguirre experienced a series of "miraculous" events while suffering hardships and hunger on the streets of the city that would put him in direct contact with Dr. Hector P. García and change his life forever. "It was the greatest lesson in character building of my life," recalled Yzaguirre as he described in detail his turmoil and success as the youngest sailor on board the *Barbee Nell*, a schooner owned by Captain J. L. Murrell. "I could have called my dad or grandfather to come pick me up, but I was determined to prove to myself that I could complete this quest on my own."

The stage was set as the drama began to unfold in the lives of García and Yzaguirre, two men who would directly impact American history and create a courageous, new voice as civil rights advocates for Mexican American communities. Dr. García's role in Raul's life was to continue molding the young runaway, teaching him what it meant to sacrifice all for love of community. Reminiscent of his long rides with Grandfather Morin delivering ice as a teen, Yzaguirre drove Dr. García in his stylish Cadillac up and down Texas roadways and byways, visiting the poor, administering medical aid, and attending numerous meetings with men who would become famous in their own right. Gus Garcia, Ed Idar Jr.. "El Chicote," (The Whip); George I. Sánchez; Vicente Treviño Ximenes, and Senator Dennis Chávez of New Mexico were among the most prominent men who helped develop the ideals of the American G.I. Forum. During those long hours with Dr. García, Yzaguirre learned to know the heart of a man who would be described as a fearless reformer, passionate and relentless in his resolve to secure rights for Mexican American veterans and their families. At times, García's explosive nature would earn him enemies, even among Forum members; yet his integrity and vision for the rightful inclusion of Mexican Americans at every level of American life was never questioned.

John Gardner, who served as president of the Carnegie Corporation and as Secretary of Health, Education and Welfare (HEW) under President Lyndon Johnson and who spoke Spanish well, was Yzaguirre's third mentor, a first-class example of what it meant to serve the public. "He motivated me to enter into public life and helped me to think through a lot of public policy issues. He had an ethic of service to others and of trying to make society better. I found him to be very inspirational." In 2004, Yzaguirre was awarded the prestigious John W. Gardner Leadership Award, founded by Gardner himself to honor an individual whose leadership in or with a nonprofit community has been transformative, and who has mobilized and unified people, institutions, or causes that improve people's lives.

Researching my historical novels for years at a time before publication, I have been unafraid to tackle research—until I began Raul Yzaguirre's biography. In an e-mail message, I chided him for his humility, wishing he didn't have so much of it! I wanted a central location where I could have access to his testimonies before Congress; the history of his early life; dedication to his family and his lifelong marriage to an extraordinary woman, Audrey Bristow; and more about their six children, Regina, Raul, Jr., Elisa, Roberto, Rebecca, and Benjamin. How did his role as a father to six adventurous children influence his own perspectives on family and the role of men in our society? I wanted to know more about his college days and his early involvement as a passionate student activist. I wanted to know more about his military service in the Air Force Medical Corps, and his thirty years of leadership at NCLR and a host of other organizations, boards, and panels, including his work in founding the American Latino Media Arts Award, or ALMA. What was his role in the Chicano Movement, as well as in protests and school walkouts, and what was his relationship with the great farm labor union organizer Cesar Chavez? I knew he had been involved both locally and nationally in events that had rocked the foundation of American ideals, challenging the reality of what it meant to achieve the American Dream. I wanted to know about all his distinguished awards and unforgettable speeches, and the huge political and social issues he has concerned himself with his entire life. Yet, I was to discover that very little had been preserved, filed, or categorized. Over a thousand boxes are stored in the archives at Stanford University recounting the history of NCLR, including board decisions, meetings, notes, and agendas; however, much of it is not necessarily specific to Yzaguirre, his thoughts, and personal concerns.

Pat Bonn, Administrative Assistant at ASU's CDCR Center in Phoenix, came to my rescue with information she had collected over the years and bound into notebooks. It was a start, a launching pad. It helped me focus on writing the biography of a man who has stood at the forefront of sweeping changes in national and international policies affecting the lives of millions of Latinos and many others, as he gathered all under an over-reaching umbrella that prepared the way for greater equality and advancement in business, education, health, housing, immigration, media, leadership, and the arts.

Much of this biography will be centered on a most valuable treasure—Yzaguirre's own words. Transcribed into hundreds of pages of written narrative, he reveals for the first time the depth of his thoughts on every facet of life: politics, leadership, public service, community, social issues, family, segregation, discrimination, life, love, death, religion, and spirituality. This is a comprehensive work celebrating the life of an American civil rights leader. It is written in a style Raul Yzaguirre prefers, a narrative in story form, rich with history, culture, turmoil, hidden dreams, joys and struggles of a complex people, America's Latinos, brought to life in its pages, side by side with the stories of others who, through sharing Raul's journey, inspired him to fully grasp what it means, not only to serve people, but to love them as well.

El Comedor Restaurant filled with more people as I completed my first interview with Raul Yzaguirre. Men in shirts and ties; women in business attire; families from the South Phoenix community; young parents with children; Anglos; Latinos; African Americans, and others of mixed nationalities were coming in for lunch. I wondered if any understood that the man who sat across from me in a nondescript polo shirt and black trousers was someone who had put his life on the line over and over again for the sake of others, for people like those I observed around us enjoying their food, conversing and at ease with one another.

I noted Raul's trembling right hand. The Parkinson's disease that had invaded his body was obvious, yet he seemed to be totally at ease with himself and unconcerned about any physical weakness. "It started in 1999 with the thumb on my right hand twitching," he said. By 2001, it was confirmed that he had Parkinson's disease. As the disease has progressed, Yzaguirre has opted to undergo a series of treatments to help relieve its symptoms. He admits his mind remains clear; however, over the years, his speech and writing ability have been impaired.

My initial interview at El Comedor Restaurant in Phoenix opened the door to my understanding of a man whose worth in the Latino community cannot be accurately measured, and whose legacy as an "institution builder," a title he uses to describe his own contributions to those he serves, will long be a model for civil rights leaders worldwide. Ernie Calderon, a prominent attorney in Phoenix and formerly a member of the Arizona Board of Regents for ASU, aptly describes Yzaguirre as "someone who speaks for the powerless in such a way that even their enemies will listen." Janet Murguia, Yzaguirre's successor as CEO and President of NCLR, views him as a leader who "built NCLR into an American institution with staying power." Former Arizona Congressman, Ed Pastor, relates, "Raul stayed the course, and took us to places we've never been to before." And in the view of Yzaguirre's longtime colleague, Mari Carmen Aponte, Ambassador to El Salvador, his greatest contribution to the world is "his unyielding and sustained advocacy on behalf of our community for over four decades, no matter what the personal cost." And the cost at times would be brutal: time away from his loved ones; contention within the ranks of NCLR, and dealing with American presidents, legislators, and the biased views of critics who would see the strides made by Latinos as threats to America, the "undocumented" winning an unmerited place in American society.

Yzaguirre's brother, Ruben, remembers meeting actor and community activist, Edward James Olmos, at an NCLR conference in D.C. "Edward James Olmos and I were both waiting for Raul, and I thanked him for what he had done for the Chicano community. Olmos looked at me and said, 'What I do for the Chicano community is nothing compared to what your brother does. He *is* the man.'"

Without further ado, I would like to begin the story of "the man," as described by Edward James Olmos, a leader who has powerfully impacted the history of America's diverse Latino population. Beginning as an organizer for the American G.I. Forum Juniors at the age of fifteen, he has continued a life-long career of courageously taking on the challenges set forth by those who practice racism and segregation. He has worked diligently to change rigid attitudes while claiming new perspectives for Latinos worldwide. In this way, he has demonstrated his intense love for *la raza*, "*la raza cósmica*," the term used by Mexican philosopher José Vasconcelos to indicate a people, *mestizos*, who share bloodlines with Europeans, Africans, Asians and ancient, indigenous tribes, creating an exuberant and exhilarating history, brilliant light piercing the dark horizon. This is the story of Raul Humberto Yzaguirre.

Stella Pope Duarte
Phoenix, Arizona

*It became clear to me that if we are not at the table
where decisions are made; we get the scraps.*
—Raul Yzaguirre

PART ONE

Rio Grande Valley, South Texas

1

THE BORDER CROSSED US

*Flat land, no mountains, and the wonderful fragrance of citrus trees, orange,
lemon and grapefruit, permeated the air. The trees are long gone, and
Highway 83 became the demarcation point between Anglos and Mexicans.*

—Raul Yzaguirre

THE YELLOW SCHOOL BUS

IT'S A BRIGHT MORNING in September 1948, and Raul Yzaguirre is sitting
in a school bus, bumping along the road singing with other children. *"For
we love our Valley home, upon the Rio Grand, land of yours and land of mine,
land of the palm trees and the bright sunshine..."* The students are traveling over
U.S. Highway 83, one of the longest main streets in America running east to
west from Brownsville, Texas to Rio Grande City. The highway crisscrosses
over twenty towns that flash by in seconds under the dome of a clear, blue
Texas sky. Palm trees, not native to Texas, bring to mind a desert landscape
offering dates to assail hunger, shade for nesting birds, and a sense of remote
desert islands where palm trees once provided material for homes, roofing,
and household necessities.

The bus driver is friendly, and enjoys the children singing as they make
their way to Vida N. Clover Elementary School, one of the schools on the
north side of San Juan, Texas. It's for the Mexican kids. He knows that. The
children don't really care. They're supposed to stay there until they learn English. It's always been that way in San Juan—segregation runs deep; Mexicans
on the north side, Anglos on the south. Raul Yzaguirre is light years away
from what he will do. He'll become one of the Mexican American activists
who will lead the struggle against discrimination and segregation in the Valley; but on this day he's only a second-grader, excited about starting a new

school year. He smiles, his blue-gray eyes darting everywhere as he watches the countryside roll by, and catches the eye of a pretty little girl sitting across the aisle. He punches his friend, Armando Sloss, playfully on the arm because they're buddies and live close to each other, and they'll be friends for life.

From the open bus windows he smells the fragrance of citrus trees, grapefruit and orange trees, rows and rows blooming in huge orchards. Young Yzaguirre doesn't know it, but it was a Mexican woman, an early pioneer named Carlota Vela, daughter of Macedonio and Mercedes Vela, who planted the first orange seeds given to her by a Spanish priest travelling through from Brownsville. The seeds sprouted in her front yard in 1871 in a region called Laguna Seca (Dry Lagoon), part of the Santa Anita Land Grant in the Rio Grande Valley.

BASQUES JOURNEY ACROSS THE SEA

The Yzaguirre's come from northern Spain. They are Basques, an ancient, fearless ancestry that time and again challenged Spain's rule. The Basques struggled for centuries to have their own country. Fiercely independent, they held onto part of the Basque Country in northern Spain as an autonomous community that was finally granted the status of "nationality" as part of the Spanish Constitution of 1978. Raul Yzaguirre recalls the use of the letter "I" in the initial spelling of the name Izaguirre, reflecting a Basque influence. "There was a little town called Yzaguirre in Hidalgo, and a ranch by the same name. On one side of the road the name of the ranch was spelled with a 'Y,' and on the other side it was spelled with an 'I.'"

Once arriving in New Spain, part of the Yzaguirres chose to venture into the coastal region bordering the Gulf of Mexico and settled in Tamaulipas. Others settled in a region that would one day become the State of New Mexico. Anxious to colonize the isolated region north of the river the Spaniards had named, el Río Bravo del Norte, the King of Spain made generous offers of land grants to Spanish families, and Mexico would follow suit after the Mexican War of Independence in 1821. Originally, the Spanish Crown set a plan in motion to expand New Spain, making it an extension of the motherland; but like all plans involving human destinies, the King of Spain could not have foreseen what would really happen. The conquistadores would intermarry with the indigenous people and create *los mestizos*, (the mixed race), a blend of ethnicities—European, Indigenous, African, Asian, and South American.

The King of Spain would never see the enormous expanse of lands claimed by Spanish explorers in New Spain, and over the centuries *los mestizos* would break away from his rule and become masters of their own fate.

THE VALLEY BECOMES HOME

Raul Yzaguirre's birth on July 22, 1939, in San Juan, a city in the Lower Rio Grande Valley in South Texas, signaled a new generation of Yzaguirres.

"My paternal grandfather, Antonio Yzaguirre, was born in Rio Grande City, and all his lineage was from Texas. We were a land-grant family related to Juan Pantaleón Yzaguirre who came into {what would become} northern New Mexico State in about 1743. My grandfather owned property on both sides of the border. He came from a wealthy family and was well educated, attending college for a year in San Antonio. He was also an alcoholic and eventually he lost all his money, and died very poor."

Raul Yzaguirre never got to really know his paternal grandparents, as they died when he was still young. However, he does recall hearing Grandfather Yzaguirre telling him stories. "He told me when my father brought me to him after I was born and he said I was a boy, my grandfather didn't believe him. So he had to take my diaper off and show him I was a boy."

A hub for early settlers, Rio Grande City was originally the property of Hilaria de la Garza Falcón, heiress of the region that would become the birthplace of Yzaguirre's grandfather, Antonio Yzaguirre. Falcón married an Anglo soldier, Henry Clay Davis, and for a while the city was known as "Rancho Davis." Located in Starr County, Rio Grande City was eventually connected to Camargo, Tamaulipas, its neighbor south of the border, by the Rio Grande City-Camargo International Bridge.

Camargo was the first settlement to be established in the Lower Rio Grande Valley on March 5, 1749 by the Spanish, and it became the ancestral home base for the Yzaguirres. Rubén Antonio, Raul Yzaguirre's father, was born in Camargo and eventually found work as a customs officer on both sides of the border, often traveling from Matamoros, Tamaulipas to Brownsville, Texas. He made it to the sixth grade in school, and later in life took a liking to raising cows, did some farming and established his own ice delivery service in Alamo.

Refusing to follow the example of his own father, afflicted by alcoholism, Rubén Antonio Yzaguirre resisted the lure of alcohol and chose a sober lifestyle. "My father was big on morals, honesty and living a decent life. He was a man of his word, *un hombre de su palabra*," Raul Yzaguirre says, describing his father's staunch determination to reverse the cycle of drinking that plagued his own father.

Laying down roots on both sides of the border, the Yzaguirres were among thousands of families who crossed the Río Bravo del Norte on a regular basis, not knowing that one day, *el norte*, would neither be part of Spain nor Mexico, but would be Texas, USA. The muddy river, el Río Bravo del Norte, would simply be called the Rio Grande by American colonists claiming Texas as their own, and native tribes, prominent among them, the Lipan Apache and Comanche, would face great losses of their ancestral lands in battles fought with Spain, France, Mexico and the U.S.

Segregation of Mexicans enforced by Anglos through racism and discriminatory laws gained a strong foothold after the Mexican-American War (1846-1848) and the signing of the Treaty of Guadalupe Hidalgo on February 2, 1848, which set the boundary between Texas and the U.S. at the Rio Grande. The Valley's rich, fertile land would one day bloom with citrus trees and crops of every kind, just as Raul Yzaguirre remembered it as a young boy: "Flat land, no mountains, and the wonderful fragrance of citrus trees, orange, lemon and grapefruit, permeated the air. The trees are long gone, and Highway 83 became the demarcation point between Anglos and Mexicans."

The ancient word, *táysha,* meaning "friends," or "allies," in the Caddoan language of the Hasinai, became the name for the entire region north of the Rio Grande River. In Spanish, the word is, *Tejas,* and centuries later Anglos would rename the area in their own English diction—Texas.

Without moving from their front porches, north of the Rio Grande River, a good number of Raul Yzaguirre's ancestors found themselves living in the United States of America. "We didn't cross the border, the border crossed us," Yzaguirre says, reflecting on what it meant to own land along the Texas border.

I WANT MY QUARTER BACK!

Standing in her high school classroom, Raul Yzaguirre's mother, Eva "Evita" Linda Morin, was angry one day, and wanted her quarter back. She was one of the targets of destructive stereotypes, a carry-over from early frontier days in Texas. Her high school class was planning a swimming party and only the Anglo kids were allowed to use the swimming pool. Mexicans were not allowed access. Eva Linda Morin was the only Mexican student on the list of invitees. "Everyone had to pay a quarter to get into the pool, and my mother soon found out that only the Anglo kids were going to the party," Yzaguirre says. "Then she discovered that the teachers thought her last name, Morin, was an Anglo name, and that's why she got on the list for the swimming party. 'I want my quarter back!' were my mother's words. She was so mad."

Raul Yzaguirre's determination to change destructive stereotypes afflicting his own family members and striking hard against Mexican American communities throughout South Texas, began at the early age of thirteen when he ran away from home to try his luck as a sailor. As a teen, he embarked on a quest, an ambitious adventure, but one not uncommon for the Yzaguirres who had the courage to traverse thousands of miles from the Basque country in northern Spain to find a home in a new land. As a young visionary, Raul Yzaguirre would begin a quest for equality that would last a lifetime.

2

THE LITTLE HOUSE ON MAIN STREET

At school we were fed this stream of images that Mexico was poor and no good, and Mexicans were a bunch of losers.

—Raul Yzaguirre

WHAT MY FATHER KNEW

"MY TEACHER TOLD US that Texas went into the Mexican-American war for good reasons," Raul Yzaguirre explains to his father one afternoon after listening to his social studies teacher reveal the "truths" she says were part of Texas history. The two are sitting at the kitchen table. The kitchen's walls are painted bright yellow with red Venetian blinds hanging at the windows. Raul lives with his grandparents, but often visits at his parent's house. Today he's helping his father with chores and with ice deliveries. Rubén Antonio is in the ice business like Raul's grandfather, Gavino Morin.

Rubén Antonio looks steadily at his son, their faces appear almost as duplicates—one older, one younger—blue gray eyes, light skin, strong handsome faces. Raul's father shakes his head. He knows his son is intelligent and destined to pursue a college degree, while he only got as far as the sixth grade; but today, his son needs a lesson on what really happened in Texas, and Rubén Antonio is an expert on that.

"*Hijo, nos robarón la tierra,*" his father says emphatically. "Son, they stole our land. Someday, you'll learn the truth."

Undaunted, Raul begins, "But my teacher said there were reasons...there was Manifest Destiny, and the Treaty of Guadalupe Hidalgo, and..."

"All lies! Mexico should have never signed that treaty. We settled this land; they threw us out. We had our own heroes and battles, and our own government. Mexico got weak and gave up. We should have never signed our land away. We would be living in Mexico right now." His father stands up and says, "Let's go, it's getting late. Don't believe *los gringos*, they only tell their side."

Raul follows his father to the pickup truck they will use to make ice deliveries. He's used to clashing with his father. They're both fiery and able to stand their ground. At Pharr-San Juan-Alamo Independent School District, (PSJA) Raul will one day earn first place in his high school's debate team and develop skills as a formidable opponent, able to spontaneously produce an argument and follow it logically to the end. But today, his father's words trouble him. He knows his father's right.

"At school we were fed this stream of images that Mexico was poor and no good, and Mexicans were a bunch of losers. My father would refute what I was learning in school. He had a lot of insight, and was proud, a real *macho* in a positive manner, with a true sense of honor and always proud to be Mexican," Yzaguirre says, recalling his conversations with his father.

Rubén Antonio didn't exaggerate in his comments to his son that day. Information at school often lacked the true story of Texas, a story of bloodshed and battles over land, slaves, water rights, oil wells and control of an area so vast, it covered over 268,000 square miles. Over the course of its history, Texas would change governments like a chameleon absorbing colors from its surroundings, each time taking on something new as populations rose, at times violently, one against another. It would take personal commitment, courage and fortitude to explore the twisted tales of conquest, control and exploitation that cast dark shadows over South Texas.

THE OLD THREE HUNDRED

Hoping to use Anglos to help fight warring Indian tribes and establish settlements in the Lower Rio Grande Valley, the King of Spain decided to grant one of the Crown's first *empresarios* in March of 1821, a tract of land measuring 200,000 acres, to a non-Spanish citizen, Moses Austin, an American settler from Missouri.

The plan was that Anglo Texans would live as Spanish colonists in independent states, and protect New Spain from hostile Indians while cultivating vast tracts of land for cotton and other crops. Green DeWitt became another early grantee of an *empresario*, and soon word spread like wild-fire across the Texas plains that land was there for the taking. American settlers, not blind to all that Texas offered, started making plans to form their own government and establish Texas as a slave state, taking control of the land and subduing Spaniards, Mexicans, and Indians by any means in their power.

Austin's land grant was located along the Brazos River near San Antonio and was meant for the settlement of Austin's 300 Catholic families, later known as the Old Three Hundred, although initially, there might have only been 100 total families.

After his death in June 1821, the *empresario* was inherited by his son, Stephen F. Austin, who would one day become known as the "Father of Texas," although at the time, he and his followers had to pledge allegiance first to the Spanish Crown, then to Mexico, and commit to obeying the laws of the land as stipulated by their new rulers. The area settled by Stephen Austin became known as San Felipe de Austin.

Not long after the founding of the American colony, Stephen F. Austin enlisted small groups of men to protect American citizens from Indians and "Mexican bandits." In early frontier days, the great majority of Mexican men were considered bandits, unless there was a White man to vouch for their integrity. In 1823, Austin stated that he wanted to "employ ten men to act as rangers for the common defense." The "common defense" was whatever Stephen Austin thought it should be. The men's uniforms consisted of a light grey duster and badges made from Mexican pesos. Their monthly wages were $15 paid in property. They were to "range" over the countryside, acting as an arm of the American military. Soon, their numbers rose to over 300. The Mexicans called these Texas Rangers the *Rinches Tejanos*, or simply *los rinches*, and quickly learned that these rough-riding gunmen used brutal means, including lynching their victims while dragging them from horses as they prepared to hang them. Many years later, Raul's grandfather, Gavino Morin, suffered a direct confrontation with the Texas Rangers that would nearly cost him his life, during the Texas Race War, a time when the color of a man's skin could mean the end of his life.

As *empresarios* of Anglo colonists increased in Texas, the need for more slaves to work the cotton fields owned by wealthy Anglo ranch owners grew by leaps and bounds. "Mexico was against slavery, and that became a problem for the Anglos in Texas," Yzaguirre says. "There were *peones* (poor laborers) and *braceros* (contracted labor) who crossed the border from Mexico to work the fields, but in those days Anglo settlers depended on Black slaves for picking cotton, and working in the tobacco fields. It was big business."

In 1829, the president of Mexico, Vicente Ramón Guerrero, a *mestizo* of African descent, was appalled at the growing slave trade and further enraged Texas slave owners by issuing the Guerrero Decree, prohibiting slavery in any form. It was southerners against northerners and Texas was divided on the issue of slavery. A grab-bag of Anglo settlers emerged in Texas who wanted to keep their Black slaves. They armed themselves to the teeth for war against the Mexicans who were pushing in the opposite direction. In the meantime, America was on the march for more states that would join the Union, as more immigrants moved into South Texas by the hundreds from Mexico, Europe, Africa and Japan. To add fuel to the fire, the concept of Manifest Destiny surfaced during President Andrew Jackson's administration, (1829-1837) asserting that expansionism was an American right—period.

By 1836, Anglo Texans defied Mexican President Antonio López de Santa Anna, also referred to as the "Napoleon of the West," by signing the Texas Declaration of Independence at Washington-on-the-Brazos, and General Sam Houston became president of the Republic of Texas. He was now the president of his own country, but would face stiff competition from other Texans who also coveted the position. The site for the capital city would be disputed between Austin and Sam Houston, who at the time was living in the city that now bears his name. In the end, the city of Austin would be designated the Texas state capital.

Over the years, France, Spain and finally Mexico gave up the fight for the Texas territory; but for Moses Austin and his 300 Catholic families, the "Old Three Hundred," Texas was fair game, and they were onboard.

WHERE DID ALL OUR HEROES GO?

"The Alamo was covered in our history classes, but there was no mention of Juan Seguin, who also rode with Sam Houston," Yzaguirre says. "Mexicans were divided in their allegiance during the Texas Revolution because some had strong ties with Anglos and thought it would be better to align themselves with them and save the whole region. There were some good alliances made between Anglos and Mexicans, but those were few and far between."

Yzaguirre's fascination with the Mexican heroes of the old west began with the story of the first Mexican American mayor of San Antonio, (1840-42), Juan N. Seguin, born in San Antonio in 1806, a captain in Sam Houston's army. He fought with Anglo forces during the Texas Revolution against Santa Anna at the battle of the Alamo in San Antonio, and at San Jacinto in present-day Harris County on April 21, 1836.

As a teen, Seguin disapproved of Santa Anna's repeal of the Mexican Constitution of 1824 that joined Texas with Coahuila, forming the state of Coahuila y Tejas, and opening the door for Texas to become its own state under Mexican rule. Seguin's narrow escape from death at the Alamo was nothing short of a miracle. He had been sent on a secret mission through enemy lines to deliver a message to Houston's military officials, advising them that the Americans would not surrender at the Alamo. By the time Seguin arrived at the Alamo, Santa Anna's forces had won the battle. This served to ignite Seguin's determination to continue fighting with American forces for what he thought was a just cause.

It didn't take Captain Seguin very long, after the battle of San Jacinto, to analyze the situation, and understand that he had made a huge mistake in aligning himself with Houston's forces. Land grant families, as well as Mexican *rancheros*, businessmen, and laborers were being driven out at gun-point from Texas cities and rural communities and their land and wealth confiscated by Anglo Texans who now governed the state using their own brand of frontier justice—the Texas Rangers. Seguin tried in vain to protect Mexican families brutalized on a daily basis, and bring sanity to a world gone mad with rage and revenge on both sides of the border.

Seguin's term as mayor of San Antonio ended abruptly in 1842 as he fled with his family into Mexico after receiving numerous death threats. His allegiance switched from time to time between Mexicans and Anglos who both viewed him with suspicion. In the end, Seguin stood his ground for the rights of his fellow countrymen, forever ending his commitment to Houston's forces. After Seguin's term as mayor ended, San Antonio would not have another Mexican American mayor until 1981 with the election of one of Yzaguirre's close friends, Henry Cisneros, a popular, three-term mayor who successfully negotiated peace between warring factions of 20th century Tejanos and Anglos.

After his defeat to Houston's forces at San Jacinto, Santa Anna was captured and forced to sign two documents known as the Treaties of Velasco, in Velasco, Texas (now Freeport, Texas). Santa Anna, along with interim president of the Texas Republic, David G. Burnet, agreed, among other things, to end all hostilities, mutually exchange prisoners, and set the southern boundary of Texas at the Rio Grande River. The treaties were never observed, and eventually U.S. President James K. Polk would use nonobservance of the treaties as one of the reasons for invading Mexico.

Annexed as the 28th State, on February 29, 1845, Texas entered the Union as a slave state, nullifying the Texas Declaration of Independence and the Lone Star's status as an independent republic. Upon annexation, Mexico declared war on the United States. For two years, from 1846 to 1848, the Mexican-American War exploded on both sides of the border.

The treaty that Raul Yzaguirre's father said should have never been signed, was signed on February 2, 1848, ending the Mexican-American War, one of the bloodiest wars fought along the Mexican border. The Treaty reshaped the state of Texas and the greater part of the American Southwest, setting the boundary between Texas and Mexico at the Rio Grande, and ceding to the U.S. the states of California, Nevada, Utah, New Mexico, most of Arizona and Colorado and parts of Texas, Oklahoma, Kansas and Wyoming. In return Mexico was paid $18,250,000 in U.S. dollars. The U.S. also agreed to assume $3.25 million in debts that the Mexican government owed U.S. citizens. Mexicans who chose to stay in the U.S. were guaranteed the right to become American citizens, and were to be "protected in the free enjoyment of their liberty and property." The treaty's articles were challenged by members of Congress, changed, reworded and parts entirely stricken from the original document, until nothing was left but the reality of broken promises, increased racism, discrimination, and the deportation of Mexican Americans from their homeland in Tejas to Mexico, which was now situated south of the Rio Grande.

WALL TO WALL HEROES

"There was a little house almost a shack on Nebraska Avenue, San Juan's main street, where there were classes run by these two ladies who had been teachers in Mexico and had left due to the Mexican Revolution. They couldn't find work so they set up this private school. I never went to that school but every one of the kids who went there had a very positive concept and tended to be leaders. That made an impression on me. The school had horrible conditions hot, dusty, dirty, and the classrooms were very noisy. They only taught in Spanish and it cost you a quarter a week to go to the school. But they made an enormous contribution to the students of San Juan. They were teaching history and pride in our own heritage."

"The ladies would gather kids from San Juan and surrounding barrios and teach them folklore dances, the meaning of Cinco de Mayo, and the 16th of September. I learned about those things in the 3rd grade because we were overcrowded in our elementary school where we were also segregated. The pretext was that we had to learn English before we could be transferred to an English-speaking school. In the 3rd grade, the school district rented the hall of the *Sociedad Mutualista Obrera* (Mutual Aid Society). This was the *mutualista* movement that was big in our community for many years. It started around 1920. On the walls, the Mexican teachers had literature and pictures of all the Mexican heroes and about Mexico's struggle for independence. And because the district was renting the place, they could not move the pictures, only use the space. So, it was very fortunate that I got that exposure as a primary grade student."

Sitting in the rented hall of the Sociedad Mutualista Obrera was when Raul Yzaguirre had his first look at true Mexican history. He strategized, putting two and two together: there was another side to history. He had never heard talk of pioneers Moses and Stephen Austin or Green DeWitt, nor of slave traders, Sam Houston, James Bowie, Davey Crockett and William Travis at his house. Instead, the guitars would come out at family parties and he would hear *corridos* (ballads) sung and stories told of swashbuckling heroes, *muy machos*, (very manly) who devised ways to resist Anglo occupation and regain the self-respect they had once had in a land they had lived on for centuries. They could outrun and outdo the Texas Rangers, and like Juan Seguin, the first Mexican mayor of San Antonio, ended up racing across the border when they had to, only to return again. They disappeared for months in the mountains and valleys of Mexico, and played guerilla warfare to stay alive. There was Juan Nepomuceno "Cheno" Cortina, born in Carmago on the south side of the Rio Grande, known as the "Red Robber of the Río Grande," who warred against Anglo occupation; his nephew, José "T.J." Canales, a member of the Texas Legislature from Brownsville, who filed formal criminal charges against the Texas Rangers on January 31, 1918, and Gregorio Cortez, who, because of a faulty interpretation by a sheriff's deputy, became one of the most hunted "bandits" in Texas history. And, of course, there were stories galore of the great revolutionary leader, Francisco "Pancho" Villa who was both the hero of the poor, and at times their worst nightmare, stopping at nothing to destroy those who got in his way. There were women like the two ladies from Mexico who worked with mutual aid societies and overcame incredible obstacles to teach young *Tejanitos* their own heritage. Their stories were absent from the history books in Texas.

"I wanted to become among other things, a scientist, cowboy, lawyer, or a president," Yzaguirre says, reflecting on his childhood aspirations. "I was all over the place. I also wanted to go to sea and sail the world." Harry Belafonte's role as a freedom fighter in the film *Island in the Sun*, coupled with the good guy roles of Mexican film stars, Pedro Infante and Jorge Negrete, and the loving guidance of Gavino Morin began to create in him a desire to fight for those whose voices might not be heard in the daily rush and grind of American society. His pledge to "leave the world a better place" was born at a young age, and it became real—something he could sense in the air he breathed.

"I loved Mexican movies. The good guys always won and justice was carried out. The men on the screen were not abusive; they were responsible.

They had fun, and they were not afraid to cry. They were positive role models. So I had this script in my mind that said that it is okay to be a man, a real *macho*, in the positive sense of taking care of others."

The heroes and role models talked about at Raul Yzaguirre's house were never mentioned in school. Their names sounded like people who could be his next-door neighbors. They could be sitting at his grandfather's house, laughing and sharing stories, but they weren't anywhere near Vida N. Clover Elementary or any other school in the Valley. If they were mentioned it was always to tell that they were on the wrong side of history; a history that also belonged to him. In his mind, Raul matched his heroes' stories with the pictures he saw on the walls in the rented hall and it was a comforting feeling, like having a bowl of hot soup served up on a cold, rainy day. "I loved to read, and I would go to the library and check out books on the Mexican heroes. They weren't just myths or words sung in Spanish songs, they were real, and that gave me the courage to believe that there would be a time when they would have their stories told in our schoolbooks."

HIS FATHER'S HISTORY LESSONS fresh in his mind, young Raul Yzaguirre listened to his social studies teacher at Edison Middle School, where he attended after "learning English" at Clover Elementary and satisfying the district's language requirements. His teacher knew nothing about the secret missions Grandfather Morin had taken, risking his life during the Mexican Revolution so Mexico would be free of tyrants, or the death of his great-grandfather Morin at the hands of an Yzaguirre ancestor. It was the quick thinking of his grandfather that saved another murder from happening on the day his mother and father announced they would be wed.

Raul was to learn that the Yzaguirres were part of the Mexican heroes whose stories had never been told. He was to discover that blood ran thick in the early frontier days of Texas, while death, with a stealthy eye, watched on the sidelines—eager for victims.

3

DEADLY ENCOUNTERS

In the Race War, as many as 5,000 Mexican Americans were killed or lynched. I have a book on it. It's all documented. I can say it's true, aqui esta (here it is).

—Raul Yzaguirre

THEY LOOKED LIKE US

ACROSS MEXICO'S COUNTRYSIDE in cities, villages and small *jacales* (huts) in the country's most remote, rugged terrain, the Mexican Revolution erupts in 1910, and rages on for a decade, sparing no one. The Morins and Yzaguirres are eyewitnesses of the revolution. Families are forced to choose between the Mexican Revolutionists or the Federales under the direction of tyrants like President Porfirio Diaz or Victoriano Huerta, or whoever happens to be in power in Mexico City. Pancho Villa commands a military division in the northern state of Chihuahua and Emiliano Zapata, commands a division to the south in the state of Morelos. They're raising armies to oppose the Federales, determined to stand up for the poor and downtrodden of Mexico.

Loyalties are all over the map, tearing families apart and making enemies of friends. It's hard, at times, to distinguish revolutionaries from Federales— they are all Mexicans. They look like fathers, brothers, uncles and cousins who could sit at your kitchen table and share a cup of coffee and a plate of enchiladas and beans with you.

A certain Lieutenant Yzaguirre, loyal to the Federales, sets out on a mission one day to rid the countryside of known revolutionists who oppose General Porfirio Díaz. One of his targets is Raul Yzaguirre's great-uncle, Pablo Morin.

"There was a Lieutenant Yzaguirre who was with the Federales. He went looking for my grandfather's uncle, named Pablo Morin who was a leader in the Mexican Revolution. He couldn't find Pablo Morin, so he interrogated my great-grandfather, who told him nothing about his brother. So this Lieutenant Yzaguirre killed him. Pablo Morin came to the scene, and tried to find the lieutenant but by the time he found him, he had already been killed by someone else. Years later, my mother fell in love with my father, Rubén Antonio Yzaguirre, a descendant of Lieutenant Yzaguirre. She didn't know anything about this story and neither did my father, but my grandfather and his brother knew the story well. So, when they were courting, my grandfather, Gavino Morin, took my father to meet some of the family, one of which was his brother. He opened the door and his brother had a gun pointed at my father. And he said, 'I'm going to kill you.' My father didn't know what the hell was going on. So Grandfather Morin stepped in front of my father. He said, 'You're going to have to kill me first. I know how you feel, but if I can accept him, you can accept him.' My father said, 'What the hell are you guys talking about?' He had no idea what it was all about. It was kept as a family secret for a long time. Lieutenant Yzaguirre shot my great-grandfather. That made my grandfather an orphan. This was during the Mexican Revolution around 1910. Shortly thereafter, Grandfather Morin crossed over the border and settled in Texas."

Opposites Attract

Coming into manhood in El Catán, a ranch close to Monterrey in Nuevo León, Mexico, Gavino Morin falls in love with one of his cousins, most likely a descendant of Sephardic Jews, although she will hesitate to admit that in the future. Elisa "Licha" Espinoza de los Monterros is from a small town, Los Herreras, also close to Monterrey. Gavino's known her all his life, and one day makes up his mind to marry the petite, fair-skinned beauty. He proposes marriage and both families agree.

Although the cousins are from a large closely-knit family, they are opposites in many ways. Gavino Morin is a hard worker, tall and dark, *moreno*, with the quiet presence of a man who observes life, considers his choices carefully, and is unafraid to stand up for the things that matter. He's never been able to pursue an education as his life has been one of hardship and toil—farming, taking care of horses, milking cows, and harvesting corn and other crops. He's a humble man in constant motion, working from dawn to dusk. His cousin, Licha Morin, also a hard working woman, is only 4' 11", a fiery, outspoken woman unafraid to voice her opinions and exert her will on others. She is well-educated and can read and write, unlike her husband-to-be, Gavino

Morin, who is illiterate. She is able to sew and do the things ladies of her day were expected to do—and she boasts that she is a descendant of royalty.

Reflecting on his grandmother's claim to royalty, Yzaguirre says, "My grandmother used to say she was Espinoza de los Monterros to signify she was some kind of royalty. In fact, my grandmother's descendants may have been Jewish immigrants who made their way to Monterrey, the city of her birth, during the Spanish Inquisition." Yzaguirre attributes his grandmother's custom of covering up mirrors when someone died, and placing stones on graves as Jewish traditions.

In spite of major differences in her grandparents' personalities, Yzaguirre's sister, Teresa "Tere" Tijerina recalls, "My grandfather was totally devoted to my grandmother, and she adored her husband. She repeatedly reminded him she was royalty and had 'blue blood' to which he responded she was probably a fountain pen."

"I knew my maternal grandparents best. They were related to each other, they were cousins, both were Benavidez," Yzaguirre says in describing his relationship with the grandparents who were more parents to him than his own biological parents. "The Benavidez is important because they were related to Gavino Morin Benavidez and my great-grandmother Espinoza Benavidez. The family was also directly related to Colonel Santos Benavidez, a colonel in the Confederate Army. They named a small town in Duval County, Texas after him. My family history reflects the ambivalence Mexican Americans had about the American Civil War. I once asked Mama Licha how our ancestor could be on the side of the slave masters and she replied, 'How else could a Mexican get paid to shoot Anglos?'"

"My grandfather was easy-going, cursed constantly, was philosophical, generous, affectionate and warm," says Tere. "The motto he lived by was that everyone deserved to be treated with respect. He taught us that material things were not as important as humility and the ability to forgive, and that what is in your heart is, and will always be of utmost importance. Hands down, he was the greatest influence in Raul's life. My grandparents were complete opposites, and yet I never heard a discussion about it. Grandpa put it this way, he was the boss, but he always did what Licha wanted so as not to fight."

The tall, dark man with the gentle smile, and the petite fair-skinned beauty marry and begin a life that will lead them across the border into the Rio Grande Valley. With very few possessions between them, they embark on a dangerous journey, traveling north in the highly charged border region where both Mexican Revolutionists and Federales ride side by side. With no formal education, Gavino Morin is considered illiterate and poor, a *peon* as identified by local descriptions of the time period. The word would later change to *bracero*, indicating a seasonal worker who was allowed to come into the U.S. to pick crops and do all sorts of menial, backbreaking work with no guarantee of citizenship.

"My grandfather lived a rough life as a laborer clearing fields when they first got to Texas," Yzaguirre says. "They lived in a tent and my grandfather had to teach my grandmother how to cook, wash and do all sorts of things while living in primitive conditions."

Gavino Morin had no use for tyrants, nor for the rich who took advantage of the poor. His was a philosophy of justice for all. The wealthy should not grow so rich that they would forget their duty to those who were struggling each day to make a living. But the stakes were high, and to defy the Federales meant a man could swing by the neck on a tree, be ambushed on a lonely mountain pass, suffer execution by a firing squad, or even worse, have his entire family wiped out. Those were the risks, and there was more. He knew the story of a certain Lieutenant Yzaguirre, aligned with the Federales, who had murdered his own father—and this wound Gavino Morin suffered, even as he made his way to the border with his new bride. But he was firm in his decision; he would follow one of the country's most daring revolutionists—Pancho Villa, General of the *División del Norte*, based in Ciudad Juárez in the state of Chihuahua.

Gavino Morin's plan was to reach el Río Bravo del Norte and cross over into los Estados Unidos. He and his new wife, Licha, would be safe in South Texas from the relentless pursuit of Porfirio Díaz's Rurales, a force of Federales determined to rid the countryside of President Díaz's enemies, although soon enough, he would come face-to-face with America's own brand of the "Rurales," the Texas Rangers—*los Rinches Tejanos*. Gavino had heard of *los rinches*, and knew the danger they posed, but there was hope. Texas had once been Mexico, and Mexicans had been living there for centuries. They had thrived and built cities, churches and homes. He had heard the stories of valiant Mexican heroes who had challenged *los gringos*, pressing for justice and equality for Mexicans living north of the river the Americans called the Rio Grande. He could find a job in Texas as a laborer, not earning much, of course, but it was a chance to make a decent living, and besides that, he could continue to serve Pancho Villa's forces. It was in Texas that Gavino Morin's allegiance to Pancho Villa would be tested. The coastline was ideal for smuggling arms that could be loaded into rail cars for transport to Villa's forces hiding in the mountains of Chihuahua. Gavino was conscious that he had to protect his young bride at all costs, and he began by telling her nothing about his allegiance to Villa. If he was captured, she would be innocent of all charges.

Describing Gavino Morin as "a man of strong principles and very interested in justice," Yzaguirre recalls stories of his grandfather's mysterious disappearances. "My grandfather would disappear for days at a time and he would come back and say he had been on a drunk. In fact, he wasn't on a drunken spree. The legend was that he was really running arms for Pancho Villa. He was part of the Mexican Revolution from Chihuahua."

Villa's military campaign ended on March 9, 1916 when he crossed the Río Grande and waged an attack in Columbus, New Mexico. Recognizing Venustiano Carranza as the rightful President of Mexico, President Woodrow Wilson sent General John "Black Jack" Pershing into Mexico to capture Villa. The expedition failed, as Mexicans were opposed to any American invasion of Mexico and fought off American efforts to capture Villa. On May 21, 1920, Carranza was assassinated by Álvaro Obregón, which opened the way for Villa to negotiate with interim President, Adolfo de la Huerta. In negotiations with de la Huerta, Villa was allowed to retire from military service and given land and money; however, this was to be short-lived.

In July 1923, Villa was assassinated while driving back to his ranch in his 1919 Dodge roadster. Tere recalls seeing her grandfather become teary-eyed when he remembered Pancho Villa, and would call him *"mi general"* (my general). Villa's death served to strengthen Gavino Morin's search for equality for Tejanos and an end to the racism that labeled Mexicans as a caste minority. His moral convictions and beliefs formed the basis for how he lived his life and deeply influenced his young grandson.

Over the years, the dark story of the murder of Yzaguirre's great-grandfather ceases to plague family members. Somehow, the Yzaguirres and Morins come to terms with the violence and are able to put it behind them. One day, Raul's parents, Rubén Antonio Yzaguirre and Eva Linda Morin will be allowed to wed in peace, and the disastrous tale of Lieutenant Yzaguirre will be all but forgotten.

FACE TO FACE WITH LOS RINCHES TEJANOS

Rushing home one dark night, Gavino Morin has only one thought in mind: get home as quickly as possible to avoid meeting *los rinches*. He's settled in San Juan and bought a couple of lots not far from Nebraska Avenue. He plans to build a house for Licha and his young family. He acquires a franchise for his own ice delivery business in San Juan and soon rents a building to expand his new enterprise. Over the years, Morin's Ice House will thrive and be quite lucrative. But on this night it's still a young enterprise, and struggling to stay in competition with other ice houses that supply needed ice to homes and businesses. "In an era of no refrigerators, ice was big business," Yzaguirre recalls, "and the franchise my grandfather owned reaped a good profit. Trucks lined up for two blocks waiting to get ice during the cotton picking season so they could give water to their workers."

Working from the ground up to make his ice business a success, Gavino Morin finds he must get a second job. That's easily done, as ranchers are in constant need of laborers for harvesting grain, hauling produce and doing a hundred other things to keep a ranch going. But there's a problem. New trouble has erupted in the Valley. There's a curfew on Mexicans in South Texas. The Anglos governing Texas have decided that it's too dangerous to allow Mexicans on the streets after dark—after all they're horse thieves, cattle rustlers and drunks who parade around town looking for trouble, drinking, singing and whooping it up at saloons. A local judge rules in favor of the Anglos and declares that there will be a curfew of all Mexicans beginning at sunset. It will keep the cities of South Texas safe, is his reasoning. Let the Texas Rangers patrol the streets at night and make sure Mexicans are in their homes and not out at meetings planning protests and developing campaigns against the segregation prevalent in the Valley. The curfew will also put a lid on Mexican Americans moving up in Texas society, demanding back their land and opening up private businesses that compete with Anglo-owned enterprises.

But a hard-working man has to make a living, and a Mexican man, faced with discrimination and working at the lowest paying jobs must work extra hard. Before long the day is gone, and night falls, and still there's not enough food on the table. Gavino Morin is one of the men caught in this trap. He needs a second job to make ends meet. There's nothing he can do but disobey the judge's order and take his chances on meeting *los rinches* some dark night on the streets of San Juan. He does not have long to wait.

LOS RINCHES AND WHISPERING TOM MAYFIELD

"As a child I remember the Texas Rangers as mean looking, and wearing Stetson hats," Yzaguirre says, reflecting on his childhood memories of *los rinches*. "One night my grandfather came close to being lynched by the Texas Rangers, which meant death by hanging. His work went past the curfew hour for Mexicans and the Texas Rangers were patrolling the streets, looking for Mexicans to lynch when they confronted Grandfather Morin. The constable who intervened that night on my grandfather's behalf was named Whispering Tom Mayfield because it was said his vocal cords had been damaged when a mob of Mexicans caught him and proceeded to hang him. That was when he was still a member of the Texas Rangers. According to legend, Pablo Morin, my grandfather's uncle, saved him. My grandmother also told us about one of her relatives confronting the Rangers, crying and cursing at them because they had killed her son, and the Rangers just staring and saying nothing."

Chicano scholar and civil rights activist, Dr. Julian Samora, the first Mexican American to receive a doctorate in 1953 in Sociology and Anthropology at the University of Wisconsin, along with Texas civil rights activists Bexar County Commissioner, Albert Peña and Texas state senator Joe Bernal, summarized the violence waged by the Texas Rangers in 1979, describing the Rangers' execution of justice as one of "operating without restraint and with unchecked power." Their research concluded that the Rangers' abuse of power was disguised as "maintaining law and order."

Dr. Américo Paredes, born in 1915 in Brownsville, Texas during the traumatic years following the Mexican Revolution, described the Texas Rangers' brand of law and order as one of "ambush, surprise, and shooting first." Paredes became one of the first to establish a body of knowledge of Mexican folklore, ballads, *corridos* and the understanding of border stereotypes that opened the way for modern Mexican American Studies at Texas universities.

Raised in the heart of the discrimination and segregation experienced by Tejanos, Paredes earned a doctorate from the University of Texas in folklore and English. In 1958 he wrote a dissertation immortalizing the South Texas folk hero and outlaw, Gregorio Cortez, entitled: *With His Pistol in His Hand: A Border Ballad and its Hero.* Death threats by a Texas Ranger against Dr. Américo Paredes for blemishing their reputation were never carried out, and on May 5, 1999, *Cinco de Mayo*, Américo Paredes died in Austin, a courageous Tejano who had survived racism as harsh as the one inflicted on Gregorio Cortez.

Many years later, Raul Yzaguirre had the opportunity to turn the story of his boyhood hero into a full-length motion picture. "Moctesuma Esparza came to me and said he'd like me to help him do some film projects," Yzaguirre says in describing NCLR's early sponsorship of Esparza's film project. "So we created a task force of writers and intellectuals and decided to pick five stories that best described our experience. Our first choice was the *Ballad of Gregorio Cortez*. We went to the Corporation for Public Broadcasting, and we got the money to do the film in 1981, starring Edward James Olmos. It was Olmos's first big break. We showed it on PBS, and in theatres, and it was very successful."

Yzaguirre's description of Moctesuma's epic film on the life of the South Texas folk hero, Gregorio Cortez, is based on the dissertation written by Dr. Américo Paredes. Charged in the murders of Karnes County Sheriff W.T "Brack" Morris, Gonzales County Sheriff Glover, and Constable Henry Schnabel, Cortez's life hung in the balance as he fled for his life pursued by one of the largest posses in American history, 300 strong, made up of Texas Rangers and state officers. The relentless pursuit extended over four hundred miles of rugged terrain with no success. Cortez's adeptness at survival in the remote, wild landscape kept him alive for ten days before he was apprehended.

Mexicans throughout Texas, and Anglos who marveled at Cortez's ability to survive insurmountable odds, banded together to demand his release, citing the attack on his brother, and the faulty translation by a sheriff's deputy as his defense. It was the word, *yegua* (mare) that the sheriff's deputy didn't understand on June 12, 1901, as the sheriff paid a visit at Cortez's ranch, determined to arrest him as a horse thief. The deputy who acted as Sheriff Morris's translator, asked Cortez if he had bought a stallion that day, to which Cortez responded, that he had not bought a stallion, *era una yegua* (It was a mare.) Not understanding the word, *yegua*, the deputy reported to Sheriff Morris that Cortez was lying. Already prepared for the Anglos once he had seen them approaching his ranch, Cortez pulled out his forty-four pistol hidden under his shirt, and as the sheriff turned and shot his brother, Romaldo, then wildly shot at him, Cortez responded with a volley of shots that killed the sheriff.

Cortez escaped the scene, securing his wounded brother, Romaldo, onto a horse as they made their way to Kenedy for help. The wounded Romaldo kept falling off his horse, and Cortez ended up carrying him by nightfall into Kenedy. Leaving his brother in Kenedy, he made his way to Gonzales on foot, over fifty-five miles from Kenedy, to the house of Martín Robledo. There, he was surrounded by a posse led by Sheriff Glover, one of Morris's best friends, and Constable Schnabel. A hail of shots were fired between Glover and Cortez, and in the aftermath, Sheriff Glover lay dead. Constable Schnabel, it was discovered later, suffered death at the hands of one of his own comrades whose gun may have misfired in his direction. No members of the Robledo family were armed, yet a woman and a boy were wounded, and thirteen year-old Encarnación Robledo was hung from a tree until his tongue protruded and he was near death, and still he had nothing to report about what the posse described as the "Cortez gang," as there was no gang and the boy knew nothing.

Falsely accused of being a horse thief, Gregorio Cortez became for South Texas Mexicans a symbol of the resistance against Anglos who encroached on the land that had once belonged to them. Cortez had often asked that he be tried under Texas laws, fairly, and not judged by racists as a Mexican who deserved to die. Cortez's pardon was finally issued by Governor Oscar Colquitt in 1913. Not long after his release, Cortez died at his family ranch, some say, due to being poisoned in his last meal at the prison facility.

Gavino Morin, an ardent admirer of Gregorio Cortez, had no idea that one day, his grandson would be the first to put his hero's story into a major motion picture that would inspire young Tejanos for generations to come.

SAN DIEGO IN TEXAS: THE RACE WAR

"In 1915 maybe before that, a group of Mexican American lawyers got together in a little town called San Diego, Texas. They wanted to deal with the oppression being imposed on *Mexicanos*. So they drew up a plan of insurrection called el Plan de San Diego. They were organized to drive off all Anglos out of Texas. One of the people tipped off the police, and they started to hunt them down, enlisting the Texas Rangers for help. The one who captured the leader of the Plan de San Diego was Whispering Tom Mayfield, the same constable my grandfather knew.

The infamous Race War (1915-17) in South Texas was a veritable blood bath for murders committed against Mexican Americans by the Texas Rangers and their vigilantes. The numbers of those killed reached five thousand, as Mexicans fled the fury of *los rinches*, who joined forces with local officers to mete out their own brand of justice. Gavino Morin, caught in the Texas Race War, escaped death by the Rangers on the night Whispering Tom Mayfield stood up for him against his former allies.

"The Rangers terrorized Tejanos well into the twentieth century without legal repercussions," Yzaguirre says. "They were regarded as the Ku Klux Klan of Texas for their disregard of justice under the law and the brutality inflicted on their victims. Their plan for establishing a curfew in San Juan and other cities was to keep Tejanos off the streets so they wouldn't be out raiding ranches of Anglos or anything like that. I have a book on the Texas Race War. Fortunately, it was all documented. Before, people would say, ah, he's just an activist, but now I can say, *aqui esta*, here's the truth."

Yzaguirre's memories of what he had heard about the Plan de San Diego and the Texas Race War correlates with information gathered by Texas historians in describing the unity Tejanos sought as a way to combat the growing escalation of discrimination, prejudice and blatant attacks on Mexican American communities. A radical plan to strike out at the relentless oppression by Anglo Texans came to a head in the city of San Diego, Texas in Duval County, and an uprising was planned for February 20, 1915 by a Mexican army formed in Texas, the "Liberating Army for Races and People."

Joining the Tejano seditionists were Blacks, Japanese and Indians who gathered to boldly demand an end to injustices and crimes committed against Tejanos. The Plan de San Diego proposed to rid Texas of all the *gringos*, specifically males over the age of sixteen, and form a new republic consisting of Texas, New Mexico, Arizona, Colorado, California and parts of Mississippi and Oklahoma. The group went as far as asserting that they would force the return of Indian lands to the tribes and open the region for creation of a Black nation. Labeled as "bandits" by Anglos, the group's major assaults consisted of derailing trains, burning bridges and sabotaging irrigation facilities.

The Texas Rangers, and local posses entered the fray and burned down ranch homes of Tejanos, relentlessly pursuing suspected sympathizers, and not hesitating to shoot at will, as Anglo land speculators moved in to claim ownership of deserted homesteads. Many Tejanos fled across the Rio Grande, never to return, but many others sought help from Anglo *patrones*, refusing to abandon their small *jacales* for an uncertain future in Mexico. A high number of Anglo Texans made the longer journey to Corpus Christi, or San Antonio for safety. Close to 30,000 people, Anglo and Mexican combined, vacated the Lower Rio Grande Valley, leaving the region half-deserted.

After a lull in the confrontations, Tejano raiders once again renewed their attacks on May 5, 1916, prompting a coalition of approximately 50,000 men, including Army troops and Texas Rangers to be dispensed to the Valley to protect Anglo citizens. This proved to be a fatal blow to the Plan de San Diego, and the raids finally ceased, with the death of Mexican Texans, according to Ranger historian Walter Prescott Webb, rising to 5,000, while only 62 American civilians and 64 soldiers were killed. Webb admits that many innocent Mexicans were unjustly treated, and that there were many members of the Rangers who were ashamed of the bloodshed they had caused.

"The Plan de San Diego proved that Tejanos were able to organize themselves and wage war against injustice," Yzaguirre says. "The fact that they failed to reach their goal means little when you look at the big picture and see how much they risked to fight for what they believed was a just cause."

THE STAKES WERE HIGH in South Texas, and would move several notches higher as Yzaguirre took an early interest in righting the wrongs suffered by Mexican Americans living in the Rio Grande Valley. By the age of 16, he would face a panel of arrogant school board members and district attorneys, all of them bent on "beating the Valley kid at his own game." Had they looked into the future, they would have seen that the unassuming "Valley kid," had the stamina not only to endure hardships, ridicule and scorn, but to beat them at their own game.

4

YZAGUIRRES MAKE GOOD HUSBANDS

War is like a blind man touching an elephant. The side is like
a brick wall, the leg a tree trunk, the tail is like a snake, and
the blind man still doesn't know what he's looking at.

—Ruben Yzaguirre

OMINOUS TRAIN RIDE

RUBÉN ANTONIO YZAGUIRRE and Eva Linda Morin meet while traveling on a train. Neither one expected to fall in love while riding a rail car speeding along the tracks close to the border between Mexico and Texas. Surrounded by fellow travelers, Rubén Antonio and Eva Linda are in a time warp, aware only of one another. They will mark this time as the day they fell in love. Eva Linda's only eighteen, and Rubén Antonio is twelve years older; but that is of no consequence to them. It will not be long before they marry, and Eva Linda's father, Gavino Morin, will step in front of his daughter's fiancé as his own brother threatens to shoot him dead.

In this way, Gavino Morin will end the vendetta started so long ago by the murderous Lieutenant Yzaguirre. The wound over the loss of his own father, murdered at the hands of the lieutenant, has slowly healed, as Gavino has chosen the path of forgiveness. After a time of courtship, Rubén Antonio proposes marriage to the slender, dark-haired girl. Gavino Morin will not hesitate in granting his daughter her wish, and his wife, Licha, will follow suit. Evita's wish is a simple one: she wants to marry Rubén Antonio Yzaguirre.

25

EL OTRO LADO

Matamoros, on the Mexican side of the border, was a place of rich colors, busy open-air markets, delicious smells of food simmering in huge pots, and comical performers who juggled and jostled their way through the streets. Moving between the port cities of Matamoros and Brownsville while he still lived with his parents, young Raul Yzaguirre recalls going to traveling shows housed in tents and watching Mexican circus performers. The tango was very popular, and there were many sing-a-longs with local musicians who played guitars and violins, uniting barrio neighborhoods with traditional Spanish songs, *corridos*, rowdy Tejano (Tex Mex) tunes, and heart-wrenching love songs. Fish, grilled meat, *frijoles de la olla* (whole beans simmered in a pot), freshly-made tortllas and tamales, fruits, Mexican candy and big avocados you had to pull out the pits to eat, were daily fare in Matamoros. Noisy crowds, busy shops and people walking up and down the streets were the visions of Matamoros, only one short bridge away from Brownsville, Texas.

"All the tastes were delicious and the days beautiful," Yzaguirre recalls. "There were always festivities going on, but I never saw Anglos at our celebrations; we were isolated from their communities, yet we had lots of fun, and were united in living out our traditions."

Action-packed Mexican movies were Rubén Antonio's favorites and he often took Raul with him, giving him a close look at dramas produced by early Mexican film-makers who perfected their craft while creating celebrities as popular to Mexican Americans as their Hollywood counterparts were popular to American audiences. "My father and I loved Mexican movies and we went to local theatres. We got to see Tongolele, a Cuban dancer with a white spot in her black hair. Once my dad took me to the beach and I almost drowned at Boca Chica. I was only four years old, and I had gone crabbing with him. I was walking along the beach and this big wave came, and my father grabbed me just before it took me off to sea."

There were times when young Raul slept between his parents on cold nights, wrapped in a warm Mexican quilt made of soft wool. Early memories of his parents left him with a sense of enduring family love he treasured for the rest of his life. "Being in the middle of them, I remember feeling so loved," Yzaguirre fondly recalls. It became a wondrous place for him, a world of hearts beating close, and warm arms embracing him. Many years later, one of the most precious memories of his life as a young father was holding his sleeping infants up to his bare chest. "I would hold them close and watch them sleep. It was a feeling of love I will never forget."

The peaceful scenes of Raul's early childhood days later erupt in violent encounters with his father, as he grows older. As the first-born of four siblings—Maria Teresa "Tere," Ruben Antonio Jr., Alma Elodia "Loly," and Aileen Delia, Raul's the one who endures his father's anger more than the others. "Dad would lose his temper," Yzaguirre says, "and some of that is in me. Over the years I've learned to curb it. At times, my dad would hit me hard, so there was tension between us. As I got older, he totally favored my brother Ruben. My brother looked like him when he was young, but now I look more like my father than my brother does. There was distance between my dad and me. And when he got angry, I usually became his target. One time I ran out of the house with my dad after me. There was corrugated sheet metal for roofing on the ground, which I didn't see. So I cut my feet and left bloody footprints all over the place. Still chasing after me, my dad begged me to stop. I didn't feel the pain in my feet, I was so scared."

Rubén Antonio's temper, coupled with his work as a customs official in Matamoros and Brownsville, may have been reasons for leaving young, five year-old Raul with his Morin grandparents in San Juan. "After a while, I had two families. I called my grandparents Mama and Papa. My brothers and sisters called my grandmother, Licha, her nickname. They didn't like her. She was mean to all and was not the kind to show much affection. My grandfather was her opposite, easy-going, carefree and kind to all. He became my authority figure."

Linked by four bridges built over the Rio Grande, Brownsville and Matamoros are strategically located along major waterways. At one time or another, both cities were valued by Mexican, Confederate, Union and American military forces as ideal spots for shipping ammunition, food, cotton and other goods to the United States and other parts of the world. Matamoros, the oldest of the two cities, was founded in 1686 by Spanish explorer, Captain Alonso de León. By 1774, the city had been named San Juan de los Esteros Hermosos, and later the name changed to Matamoros. Established as a camp near Matamoros, Brownsville evolved into a base for military operations under the command of General Zachary Taylor. The city was named for the fallen fort commander, Major Jacob Brown, and was incorporated as an official city of Texas in 1853.

In his role as a customs official between Matamoros and Brownsville, Rubén Antonio Yzaguirre made friends easily, while his wife, Eva Linda, had a tight circle of friends. "Dad was more shallow, he had relationships with lots of people," Yzaguirre says. "He wasn't a joiner in the community. He wanted us to do okay. He wanted us to grow up safe and sound. Like some of my teachers, he wanted me to become a mechanic or a carpenter. My mother was his opposite, she never doubted I would go to college—it was a given in her mind. My father's idea was to let me get a piece of land, some cows, and let me go out and get all the leftovers from the fields and feed the cows, then sell them. That's not the way to make money, that's subsistence living. I had to help support my dad most of my life. When I was in the service I sent him money. And when he died I pitched in for his funeral expenses."

Four years go by before, Yzaguirre's parents move from the Matamoros-Brownsville area to San Juan, and take up residence only three houses down from the Morins. His parents' house was in Yzaguirre's mind "more like a shack," compared to the larger, more stylish house of his grandfather. "I remember one time we were at a school picnic and we ran out of something and the teacher was going to drive me home to get it, and I didn't want him to see my parents' house, but my grandfather's because it was nicer and bigger."

Yzaguirre describes his father as a product of the Depression, not a risk-taker, and one who held onto his money. "I lamented that my father wasn't a risk-taker. He was always trying to find a deal in flea markets—treasures of some kind, and there were hardships for him in supporting the family. He was not adventurous. Mom was more a spendthrift, and more adventurous. One thing I did admire about my father was that he was an honest man, a man of his word."

"There is a saying in our family—*Yzaguirres make good husbands*," Raul's brother, Ruben Yzaguirre says, confirming the honesty and integrity of his father's life. "Dad didn't go to church but he was very moral and never cheated. I remember when I found an envelope with six hundred dollars in it. I showed it to him and he said, 'Turn it in. That's wages for working men.' He never took a penny of the money."

Machismo, the idea that men are superior by the mere fact that they are men, was not something demonstrated either by Gavino Morin or Rubén Antonio Yzaguirre. Both allowed their wives freedom to carve out a special place for themselves in the family and community. "My grandmother was a strong woman, and strong willed," Yzaguirre recalls, describing the fiery personality of Mama Licha. "My grandparents played games with me. '*Quien manda, tu abuelo o tu abuela?*' (Who rules, Grandpa, or Grandma?) I would look from one to another and say: "Papa rules but if Mama doesn't want to do what he says, Mama rules."

One favorite family story coveted by Raul Yzaguirre involves his father's quick wit in describing Licha Morin's habit of over-dramatizing everything. "My aunt's husband, Ray, was Anglo and didn't speak Spanish and Dad spoke broken English. My grandmother was very dramatic at times and my dad would say she was putting on an act, '*Esta haciendo papeles.*' She put on this tirade of rants and angry words and my aunt's husband couldn't understand what was going on and my dad would say. 'Papers.' Her husband said 'What?' And so 'papers' became a family joke...anybody faking it was 'papers.'"

It would be his father's adherence to a code of honesty and his mother's dramatic, playful nature that would help mold a young Raul into someone who would stand solidly behind the things he valued. Still, his "banishment" to his grandparents' house remained throughout his lifetime, an unsolved mystery.

FATHER FIGURE

Cows lounged on the grassy pasture just outside the Yzaguirre home in San Juan, close to rows of orange trees that filled the air with a sweet, sticky fragrance when the trees were in full bloom. Dotting the landscape, here and there, palm trees grew, laden with dates. The cows were a challenge for the Yzaguirres. They had to be taken care of daily, milked and led in and out of the fields. The milk was collected to sell locally. "We had duties and chores. My dad had cows. I was horrible at milking," Alma Yzaguirre recalls. "Mom took care of putting the milk in containers. We delivered the milk before we went to school."

The Yzaguirres raised chickens too, selling eggs as another way to make money. Both Alma and Ruben remember they always had food to eat and their dad always had a vehicle, a pick-up truck he used for his ice business in Alamo. Another money-maker were beer bottles they collected, littered along the alleyways and tossed into garbage cans from beer joints off San Juan's main street. "A whole case was worth fifty cents," Ruben recalls. "It was another way for us to make some money that we could spend on things we wanted. We lived on the north side of San Juan and were divided from the affluent Anglo community on the south side. I remember going to the Anglo side of town one day with some childhood friends from school and walking for the first time into a two-story house. It had carpet and an air conditioner. I went to get something from the refrigerator and it had a freezer. I saw a difference in the way they lived and was impressed."

Both Alma and Ruben agree there were no friendships made with Anglos, except at school. Swimming in canals and living in the segregated barrios was something the Yzaguirre's accepted as a way of life. But there was a closeness in the Yzaguirre home, and in spite of the house's shabby appearance, Alma says, "We were close to one another and spent lots of good times together. Mom was a great cook, and we girls learned from the best."

"One rare exception to the stereotypical ethnic segregation in the Valley were two Anglo doctors who served the community faithfully," Yzaguirre says. "I remember Dr. Reed and Dr. Mock. They were Seventh Day Adventists. They took care of Mom and delivered me, and my brother and sisters. Mom always came to San Juan to have her children."

Playing the role of father figure, over the years, in the lives of his younger siblings, Raul Yzaguirre's strict rules were not always welcome. Alma got a taste of her brother's vigilance at the age of fifteen while visiting him and Audrey and their two young children Regina and Raul, Jr., in Washington, D.C. Planning to go with them to Ocean City, she decided to wear a two-piece bathing suit.

"Where do you think you're going with that thing on?" Raul asked.

"Swimming, where else?" Alma answered.

"That's indecent and I won't have you wearing that! You better go change into something else if you want to come with us."

Alma's tears did nothing to sway her brother. She was a young teenage girl, and saw no problem with the bathing suit; but looking at her brother, she knew he wouldn't budge an inch, so there was nothing left to do.

"I borrowed a one-piece suit that was too big for me, and I cried and cried. I was crushed."

It would not be until years later that Alma would learn to appreciate her brother's vigilance and his absolute dedication to family. "Later, I saw how much Raul loved all of us. It was hard for him to be away from the family. By far, this was one of the greatest sacrifices my brother had to endure to serve the community he loved so well."

HAUNTED BY WAR

1968. The war in Vietnam is escalating, and there is no end in sight. Ruben Yzaguirre is in his junior year at the University of Texas-Pan American (UTPA), and for reasons unknown, the university fails to process his Fall registration. This makes Ruben an open target for the draft. "Let me get it over with," he remembers telling his family and friends. There was nothing his parents could say about his impending service in a region of the world that had exploded in a new wave of violence, claiming thousands of American lives. Of these thousands, a high percentage, were Latinos coming from every corner of the U.S. Warriors at heart, Mexican Americans were looking forward to service, in spite of the fact that military training was a rushed few weeks, then they were sent off to war, most of them landing by Hueys in the battle zones of Vietnam. Ruben joined the Army and trained as a paratrooper for the 101st Airborne Division.

Raul Yzaguirre's service in the Air Force had started just before the war in Vietnam became a major battleground for the U.S., and his request to serve abroad in Vietnam or Japan never materialized; however, his brother was caught in the middle of the Vietnam War's escalation in 1968-1970. "I was afraid that Ruben would become a Prisoner of War. I felt guilty because I didn't go, but my little brother did. It was tearing us apart. I told him if you become a prisoner, I will come and get you. I was determined that if my brother was held as a POW I would go to Vietnam and not return from the country without him."

The war divided the U.S into camps of Americans, some standing with President Johnson, and backing the war, while millions protested, and burned their draft cards. "Then, the demonstrations came, anti-war sentiment," Yzaguirre says, "and I was against it. I thought it was bad policy. We didn't make a distinction between the soldiers who were doing their duty and the politics, and that bothered me a lot because my brother was there, and I wanted to support him. I valued what he had done as opposed to blaming him for the atrocities. When he came back he was a changed person. He used to be very out-going and friendly, and still remains, but he wasn't quite the same. He got married immediately afterwards, and probably shouldn't have, because he divorced later. He would not talk about the war. He also had lots of injuries as a result of Agent Orange and it took years to put his claims through. Many years after the war, he told me things he had never told anyone else. He poured his heart out to me about things he had experienced in Vietnam."

In Vietnam, Ruben assumed dangerous duties in reconnaissance missions for the Army. "I didn't know how little I knew about the geography of the places where we would be deployed, Vietnam, Thailand and Laos. I was in regular infantry for a while and stayed out three weeks at a time in the bush with about one hundred other guys. I trained for a month to be a paratrooper. We wore camouflage out in the jungles, no showers and everything was dirty. We got to Hue City, and I saw grubby dirty men everywhere. I was fascinated by war, duty, honor and fighting for my country. We were on our own looking for the enemy. We learned to take care of each other. I never knew how hard things could be. During monsoon season, we were eating and sleeping in the mud. I was so grateful for a bunker, a candy bar or a cigarette."

The destructiveness of war haunted Ruben, "War is like a blind man touching an elephant," he says. "The side is like a brick wall, the leg a tree trunk, the tail is like a snake, and the blind man still doesn't know what he's looking at." The thought of going home kept him strong through the hardest times in Vietnam. "When two years were over, on July 3, 1970, I was in the jungle and by 5:30 in the afternoon of the next day, I was in Seattle, Washington. I got home to San Juan that same night, and fireworks were going off for the 4th of July celebrations. It was scary. Dad was sleeping on the front porch. He woke up when I walked up and he said 'Okay, *mijito*, (my little son) see you in the morning.'"

Rubén Antonio's greeting was said as if his son had never been gone. In fact, the whole family followed Ruben to Vietnam, via their love, so the greeting was entirely correct.

HOAGIE AND HIS GRANDFATHER

Tears are running down Rubén Antonio Yzaguirre's face as he looks tenderly at his grandson, Raul, Jr. The year is 1973. The tears are heartfelt. His oldest son, Raul Yzaguirre, is moving his family from Texas to Mt. Airy, Maryland. Raul, Jr., nicknamed "Hoagie," had been destined to bear his grandfather's name, but his grandfather had told him, "Every man I ever knew who was named Raul, was very smart." So, at his grandfather's request, Hoagie was named, Raul, Jr.

"I turned to look at my grandfather and tears were running down his face. His hand was stretched out to give me a goodbye hug. Then he looked into my eyes, and for the first time in my life, he used my nickname. He said, 'Hoagie.'" The memory of this loving encounter remained with Raul, Jr., and prepared the way for his final farewell with his grandfather in December 1984, after his sister Lisa's 15th year birthday party (*quinceañera*). At that time, a more grown-up Hoagie said goodbye, and this time, he lovingly used his grandfather's first name. "Adios, Rubén," were the last words he said to his grandfather. Rubén Antonio Yzaguirre died on January 16, 1985.

For his father's funeral, Yzaguirre, thinking to comfort his son, bought him a pair of new boots to wear, not understanding the "double-identity" his son felt. "I didn't want to be a Mexican, after Grandpa died," Raul, Jr., recalls. "I hid the boots, and my dad yelled at me, 'Where are those boots I bought you, boy?' I broke down and told him they made me think of my grandfather. Dad made me wear them anyway. Then Mom told me to think of the boots as the last gift from my grandfather. Mom was like that, she could turn things around and make me see things differently."

MY SON THE LAWYER

Eva Linda had high aspirations for her son, Raul, and expected him to go to college. Graduating from high school, she attended one semester of college before marrying, and considered education essential for all her children.

"Mom took it for granted that I would be educated and go to college. There was never a question about it. I don't understand when kids say they don't know if they're going to college. I was raised with the mentality that I was going to college. No questions, no debate, you will do this. My mother expected great things from me, and so I expected great things from myself."

Eva Linda wanted her son to become a lawyer. In fact, she claimed he *was* a lawyer. "I hired lawyers and taught in law school," Yzaguirre explains, "but I never became a lawyer." Still his mother would put him on the phone when she was grappling with a legal question. "My mom would say, 'Here's *mi hijo, el licensiado,* (my son the lawyer). Talk to him.' And she would put me on the phone. So I had to fake it. She was very proud of me."

An incident, involving a young, jealous Eva Linda is still something Yzaguirre laughs about. "I was a little boy when my father gave a ride to one of his co-workers. We rode in this old Ford car and I sat on the lady's lap, and he said, 'Don't tell your mother or she'll spank you.' When I got home, my mother asked me, '*Se portó bien tu papá?'* (Did your father behave himself?) I told her we had picked up this lady and I had sat on her lap, and sure enough she spanked me for sitting on the lady's lap. Instead of beating up on Dad, she beat up on me."

Eva Linda is described by family members as very emotional, and a "drama queen." She loved to make her wishes known, and often challenged everyone to meet her expectations by saying, "You're not invited to my funeral!" The words became something everyone expected to hear from her at one time or another, and knew she never meant them at all. In the end, everyone attended her funeral.

"My mom was very smart, things came easy to her," Raul Yzaguirre says, describing a trait he himself inherited from his mother. Although quick-minded, and talented as a cook and seamstress, Eva Linda was a casual housekeeper. "My sister, Alma was very fastidious about her house. She always kept a very clean house. My mother, on the other hand, was not as good a housekeeper as my sister. My sister came into town after she got married, and my mother asked if she would like to stay at the house and she said no. Mom asked her why, and she said, 'Because you don't keep a clean house.' Mom was very offended. It grew on her. My sis went back to her home in a town four hundred miles away. My son would go visit there, and we were planning a trip. My mom said, 'Take me with you.' It was a long trip with three guys, but she insisted. I took her to my sister's and she told her, "I just came here to tell you, I'm not going to stay at your house either." And we drove all the way back, four hundred miles, so my mom could get her point across."

Alma, a graduate of the University of Maryland in Business Administration, upset her mother when she married a Baptist man. Enraged when she found out Alma was attending services at the Baptist Church, her mother hid out in a barn for hours, until a neighbor, Mr. Calhoun, reported to the family that he had seen her go into the barn, but not come out. Eventually, all was cleared up, and over the years, Alma remained a devout Catholic. When Alma's daughter was born she and her mother agreed she should be named after Yzaguirre's wife, Audrey, someone whom the entire family admired.

Eva Linda's sense of humor and love of the ridiculous are traits Yzaguirre exhibits in his dealings with associates, friends and family. "Mom would kid around with me, 'Don't smoke marijuana, but if you do, give me a call,'" Yzaguirre reminisces. "She took life easily, and was very compassionate." Raul, Jr., recalls times when his grandmother would barely speak to his father when she saw him. Then when he was gone, she couldn't stop talking about all his accomplishments. "We were riding around one day, and she looked out the car window. She pointed at a school and said, 'Look at that school over there, it should be named after your father!'"

Alma said her mother always told her Raul had a way with words. She felt her son would make his mark on the world *con el sudor de la lengua* (by the gift of speech, or the "sweat of his tongue").

"When I started in the movement, Mom thought I was overdoing it, and she threatened to lock me up unless I went on dates," Yzaguirre says. "She wanted me to drink and party and date like the other guys, but I wanted to organize. She said I was obsessed with it. I even sold beer bottles to get gas money so I could keep organizing. A whole case would get me fifty cents. 'You're not maturing normally,' Mom would say. But later she was proud. My family thought I was crazy. *Los Mexicanos nunca se van a unir*, (Mexicans will never unite). This was before Chavez. Mom was more a friend, than an authority figure."

Yzaguirre recalls worrying about his mother's health. She didn't like hospitals and refused to go to one. "Mom had cardio vascular disease, and had gone through a quadruple bypass. I remember she was so sick and stayed with my sister. "Mom, go to the hospital right now, I said, *Mamá insisto*. (I insist) And she said, '*Tu quien eres para insistir?*' (Who are you to insist?) Then she died a couple of days later. My mother knew she was dying, and a hospital is where you go to die. She died at the hospital and is buried in Pharr, next to Dad."

Spanning centuries of frontier history and finding roots in Texas, the Yzaguirre family tree grew hundreds of branches that would include ancestors from numerous frontier families, many of them original settlers who risked everything they had to venture to a vast, wild continent that would one day become America.

And in the city of San Juan, the story of a mysterious lady whose history reached back to the early 1600's, would dramatically impact the lives of the Yzaguirres and Morins. The mysterious lady crossed the border into San Juan, and things took a turn for the better. She set up a permanent abode in the barrio not far from the Morins and Yzaguirres, and her motherly affection breathed life into a community that would stand the test of time.

5

SAN JUAN AND THE MIRACULOUS STATUE

All religions say the same thing; be kind to your fellow human beings, treat them as you'd like them to treat you. Work for justice and compassion and honor a higher power. It's all part of making this world a better place.

—Raul Yzaguirre

LEGEND OF THE FLYING ACROBATS

A FAMILY OF ACROBATS flies through the air, swinging gracefully from one small wooden platform to another. Down below, the audience gasps in fear. The acrobats' aeronautical flights will meet with instant death if anyone of the performers falls down on the bed of sharp spears lining the ground below. These are the chances the performers must take to earn their daily bread. They are Nahuas from one of the native tribes who have lived for centuries in small villages outside of San Juan de los Lagos, a town in the region of Los Altos in Jalisco, Mexico. They often visit busy towns to awe townspeople with their dangerous acrobatic feats. The year is 1623.

The acrobats sail through the air, as many in the crowd hold their breath while others clasp their hands over their mouths to stifle screams as they watch, relieved each time one of the family members makes it over the bed of spears. Ooo's and ah's follow after each successful flight. Then suddenly, it happens—close to the end of the act. One of the youngest family members, a seven year-old girl, a fragile looking creature that resembles a butterfly flitting through the air, takes hold of the swinging rope and is ready to take another flight. The crowd has exploded in shouts of praise the two previous times she has flown over the sharp spears, and now her last attempt is about to happen.

Scoffers below have wondered if the bed of spears the Nahuas use is made of *real* spears, or if it is only a circus prop. They are about to find out. The tiny girl glides effortlessly through the air, and whether it was a gust of wind that unbalanced her, or her own childish error, no one knows for certain. Later, some will say it was to remind them that God is the one who has the power to give life, or take it away.

Suddenly, the young girl's flight ends in mid-air and she falls headlong onto the bed of spears. The sight is indescribably gruesome and the audience below gasps in horror. Panic strikes, people scream, and mothers hold their hands over their children's eyes. The young girl, now on the bed of spears, shows sharp points protruding through her body. Scoffers have their answer. The native acrobats were genuine, and not swindlers after all.

The grieving parents have no choice but to pick up the body of their dead child and prepare her for burial. As a last resort, they take the body to the chapel of Our Lady of San Juan de los Lagos located in the center of the plaza. There, they meet the aged Ana Lucia, wife of the church caretaker Pedro, who is custodian of the beloved statue of Cihuapilli, *la Gran Señora*, (The Grand Lady), also known as Our Lady of San Juan de los Lagos. Ana Lucia assures the parents that Cihuapilli, the Mother of God, is truly miraculous and will surely take pity on their daughter even now, in the hour of death. She takes the small statue, dressed in a cloth garment from its altar, and lays it on the child's dead body. Suddenly, they see movement under the burial shroud, as the girl returns to life. It is a moment that will change the course of history for the small town, and for the state of Jalisco. The Lady's miracles over the centuries will astound the world and the city will become a site of great pilgrimages. Cihuapilli, the Grand Lady, centuries later, will cross the Rio Grande, and reside in a Texas town of great importance to the Yzaguirres—San Juan, the birthplace of Raul Yzaguirre.

THE LADY CROSSES THE RIO GRANDE

The mysterious healing of the young acrobat through faith in Our Lady of San Juan de los Lagos in Jalisco, Mexico becomes a legend told over and over again by storytellers who then add their own encounters with the miraculous statue. Over the years, immigrants crossing the Rio Grande into Texas, among them some of Yzaguirre's ancestors, carry with them loyalty and faith in Our Lady of San Juan de los Lagos. In 1949, a Basque priest, Father José María Azpiazu, serving his parish in San Juan, Texas becomes aware of the people's devotion to the miraculous statue and has a replica of the statue installed in the parish church in San Juan.

"Before La Virgen de San Juan came into town, we had a priest, Father José, a Basque Spaniard, very conservative," Yzaguirre recalls in describing the church's history. "He was only a part-time priest at the time, serving in a small, frame church. Father José and two or three others went to Mexico to San Juan de los Lagos in Jalisco to see about getting a replica of La Virgen de San Juan de los Lagos to San Juan, Texas. They were going through the mountains and their car was derailed off the road, and was hanging over the edge of a mountain, about to go off a canyon. Father José, prayed to la Virgen de San Juan de los Lagos, and said: 'If you save us, I'll bring your statue to San Juan, Texas.' Immediately after he prayed, some people showed up and they pulled them right out, and everyone was saved, so he brought a replica of la Virgen de San Juan de los Lagos to San Juan, Texas."

The statue, three feet tall and wearing traditional robes, is initially installed in a small, frame church built in 1920 under the direction of Father Alfonso Jalbert, a member of the order of the Oblates of Mary Immaculate (OMI), on the corner of Nebraska and Second Street in San Juan, Texas. The church, originally a mission of St. Margaret Mary's Church in Pharr, is eventually re-located to Lopezville, once the new church is built. "They just picked up the old church and took it to the new location. My parents were married in that little church in St. John's Parish. They celebrated their 40th anniversary there."

Over the years, the miraculous statue attracts thousands of pilgrims from all over the world, and causes major changes to occur in the small town of San Juan. "All of a sudden people started coming from all over the country, literally from all over the nation," Yzaguirre says. "We had a fire hazard because they were buying candles and putting them in the altar and there was wall to wall candles that burned forever; so I told the priest we should put them out, and put some more wax and another wick and resell them. And he bought the idea and to this day, I think they still do that. So they made a lot of money with the candles. We had so many donations, so quickly, we didn't know what to do with all the money. We set up a radio station. I was an altar boy so I was close to the Church, and witnessing all this firsthand."

Active as an altar boy, and later in the Catholic youth movement in his teens, Yzaguirre meets the first of many valued community mentors who will dramatically influence his life. Father Francisco of Belgium, assigned to the San Juan parish, becomes one of his most coveted relationships. "He and I were very close and we talked a lot. I was president of the Catholic Youth Organization (CYO). Father Francisco was my counselor and confidant and we talked about everything. The beauty of that was that years later he was assigned someplace else, and later came back to San Juan, and mentored my son, and at the end of my mother's life he officiated at her services."

As the years go by, pilgrims journeying to the church to venerate the statue now named, Our Lady of San Juan, increase dramatically, and plans for a new church become urgent. The Yzaguirre's and Morin's are present at the elaborate ceremony in 1954, attended by thousands of pilgrims in which the first church of Our Lady of San Juan del Valle, a huge shrine seating over 800, is dedicated as a permanent home for the beloved statue. The church becomes an important community center for locals living in the numerous Mexican American *barrios* that dot South Texas. Segregated from the more affluent Anglo communities, the Mexican communities thrive on values, traditions and beliefs that unite them in the daily struggle against poverty and discrimination. The shrine is an open door to international visitors, arriving by the thousands, weekly, to pay their respects to the statue of La Virgen de San Juan de los Lagos, now renamed, Our Lady of San Juan del Valle.

KAMIKAZE SKY DIVE

Frank Alexander, a World War II fighter pilot, has his heart set on serving impoverished communities in South Texas. Imagining himself a do-gooder, he moves into the Rio Grande Valley in 1970 determined to help migrant youth achieve their educational goals through his work as a teacher and self-proclaimed minister. He's hired by the Pharr-San Juan-Alamo Independent School District (PSJA) and begins a game plan to inspire groups of needy youth, while offering the community one of his areas of expertise: he can fly planes. Alexander becomes a local flight instructor, and his skills are welcomed by all, until a fatal day when the shell of protection he's lived in for years shatters, leaving in its wake, destruction.

"I was already organizing in D.C. when Frank Alexander came to town. He tried to set up a congregation in San Juan, and he didn't have any luck," Yzaguirre recalls. "He got very depressed, and one day he got in an airplane and called the police and said, 'I'm going to fly into the church.' But he didn't say which church. He was planning a kamikaze suicide flight."

Yzaguirre's memory of the tragic event of October 23, 1970 is an accurate account of Alexander's death dive into the shrine of Our Lady of San Juan del Valle. Priests and worshippers were gathered in the church, and children were on their lunch hour at the school adjoining the church when the plane, frantically tracked by air controllers at Miller international Airport close to McAllen, made a deadly nosedive into the shrine. The plane crashed into the roof of the church, but was prevented from falling into the sanctuary by a steel beam that supported the structure. Everyone was able to escape before a fire broke out. Both the church and school were burned to the ground, however the statue of Our Lady of San Juan suffered no damage. Frank Alexander was found, still strapped to his seat. His suicide attempt had proved fatal.

"The steeple was the only thing that remained of the church," Yzaguirre recalls. "The bishop of that area took over the church, and built a bigger church that accommodated thousands of people. The most important change that resulted from the burning of the church was that the whole character of the church changed. It went from traditional Gothic architecture with dozens of hand painted frescos on the ceiling walls owned by the local parish, to a large basilica more suited to accommodating the public at large. A small chapel built on the grounds of the burned church was constructed for the parish and the much larger basilica was now the property of the diocese. The churchgoing habits of the congregation changed. More established or Americanized Catholics tended to attend the more cerebral local parish churches, whereas newer immigrants and tourists tended to attend the Mariachi masses at the new basilica. The diocese set up very lucrative enterprises that sold a variety of religious objects at the basilica. There was actually a counter complete with a cash register that sold CD's of religious music including songs by the Mariachi that people could buy as they exited the church. It reminded me of the money changers outside the temple area referred to in the Bible."

It takes ten years for the San Juan community to rebuild the shrine. By April 19, 1980 the new shrine, an immense basilica with seating for 1,800 is dedicated by Bishop John J. Fitzpatrick and Cardinal Humberto Medeiros, who officiate at the solemn ceremony. In spite of the deep devotion of the majority of Tejanos in San Juan, and their loyalty to the Lady of San Juan, Gavino Morin was at odds with the Catholic Church. He lived out Christian principles on a daily basis, yet did not attend mass on Sundays. "My grandfather hated the Church. He hated organized religion," Yzaguirre says, recalling his grandfather's on-going dislike of the Catholic Church. "He kept quiet about it, but he made jokes about the priests. He'd tease my grandmother and tell her Father José was a drunk and she would deny it. He would say '*Dale jocoque al cura, que tambien cuida las chivas.*' (Give yogurt to the priest who also cares for the goats.) It means give everybody their due. It was his way of putting down priests—give them something for their labor. It was also his way of telling us it was dinnertime. I've never heard anyone else say this."

"In those days they would announce what everybody gave on Sundays, and they would announce my grandfather as the biggest contributor, but it wasn't him who was giving money to the Church, it was his wife, my grandmother. He never went to church, and that is consistent with the Mexican Revolution. Benito Juárez was a mason."

Yzaguirre's own relationship with organized religion takes on symbolic meaning in his life, as he learns to tackle problems, looking within himself for the same innate Christian principles that marked his grandfather's service to his community. As a child, Yzaguirre often thought about the existence of God and the meaning of life. "I had a sense very early of wanting to make a difference. At times, I couldn't relate to any of my peers. I wanted to talk about why we were here. I thought about priests and how they served God, but decided celibacy was an impediment. An image comes to mind, when I was maybe seven years old. I was riding in the back of a pick-up truck with the wind hitting my face, thinking of the topic of eternity. What does existence mean? Why are we here?"

Later, Yzaguirre would face doubts about organized religion, seeing more negatives than positives in the way religions expounded their beliefs. "All religions say the same thing; be kind to your fellow human beings, treat them as you'd like them to treat you. Work for justice and compassion and honor a higher power. It's all part of making this world a better place. I am against all theocracies. Islam is a doctrine based on the Koran, but when a country adopts religious beliefs as laws, they may turn to things like stoning and oppressing women. The Catholic Church has the right to expound its religious beliefs, but it cannot be the law of the land. Secular government is the only liberating way to truly enjoy freedom."

In his personal struggle to develop a relationship with God, Yzaguirre relates going through "phases" in which prayer and religious rites become an important element in his life, and "stages where I'm not into it and go through the motions." Finding a personal relationship with God is something he does not believe he has achieved. "God remains *the* Man. I envy people who say they have a personal relationship with God. God's too far removed from where I am. I'm an insect in comparison, but I want to be close. I'm not one of those people who say I've talked to God and he told me what to do. Somebody tells me what to do sometimes, maybe it's not God, maybe it's one of his lesser angels who stops by to tell me."

Yzaguirre's brother, Ruben, developed a lasting connection with the Church after his time in Vietnam. He became active in lay ministry in the Church, and described his service as a belief that "something good comes out of something bad." His war years taught him to be thankful for legs and hands and whole bodies coming home. Gratitude was part of faith in God and Ruben was impressed by the courage of one of his buddies who related to him that he had come back home—except for his legs. His wheelchair had taken the place of his legs. "A certain amount of how we live is choice," Ruben says, reflecting on his own personal commitment in seeking wholeness after his harrowing experiences in Vietnam.

TRANSFORMED BY THE STATUE of Our Lady of San Juan, and populated by immigrants who crossed the Rio Grande, and those who sailed over the Atlantic, San Juan was to be the internal compass by which Raul Yzaguirre navigated between two worlds, the north side for Mexicans and the south side for Anglos. The hard work, daily struggles, poverty and discrimination faced by San Juan residents were eased by faith in God's protection, and La Virgen de San Juan del Valle's motherly care.

Gavino and Licha Morin, two opposites, who settled in San Juan, now take center stage in the drama that will unfold in Raul Yzaguirre's life, giving their young grandson a first-hand view of what it means to enter both worlds—north and south, seeking the best in each, and forging bridges that many years later will earn him the title, "Uniter."

6

LA CASA DE MORIN

Lo cortés no quita lo valiente. (Being courteous and having good manners signify strength and strong character, and should never be confused with weakness.)
—Elisa "Licha" Morin

ICE MAN

HE BOY AND HIS GRANDFATHER get up early every morning. The boy is weary but uncomplaining. He drinks his cup of coffee, eats a burrito his grandmother offers him, and is ready to take off with his grandfather even before the sun rises. Raul Yzaguirre is in the ice delivery business, and works for his grandfather, Gavino Morin, who sees in his young grandson natural abilities, courage and determination. When Raul is only seven-years-old, his grandfather decides to teach him how to drive his pickup truck. Raul's feet can barely reach the pedals, but he manages, and has full control of the vehicle. His grandfather nods his head and smiles, and tells him he's doing a good job, "You can move the truck from house to house," he says, and Raul does just that, proud to be working like a full grown man alongside his grandfather.

Residents in San Juan are used to seeing Gavino Morin's pickup truck making its way through the city's streets. At his side sits "Little Gavino," as some folks in San Juan call Raul. The pickup has wooden panels installed on either side for advertising Gavino Morin's choice of political candidates—the best candidates, the ones that will help Mexican Americans with the hard struggles they face. Gavino listens closely to the political hopefuls and chooses those who are fair, who won't make their lives miserable and always side with Anglos who want to make up more rules that will keep the barrio people down. The political candidates believe in Gavino Morin's power.

They've already seen it in action. They're not blind to the influence this one man has over the voters of San Juan—especially the increasing numbers of Mexican American voters. They know Gavino Morin is not a registered voter himself, and probably doesn't even have citizenship papers, but never mind all that, the man's influence and power in the community is deeply felt, and they can make something of it during election time...and they do.

But every morning, it's the ice business that propels Gavino Morin out onto San Juan's deserted streets, while overhead, the moon begins its ancient descent, grasping the fringes of night's dark shroud as it disappears over the horizon. A few brave stars shine dimly, but they too will soon fade away. In the early dawn he watches, half-amused, as his truck moves a few feet forward as he hoists another block of ice onto his shoulder and delivers it up to another front porch. He can barely see the top of Raul's head as the truck moves in perfect unison with his deliveries. It's a good day, the sun is glowing orange in the distance, the town is coming alive, slowly, and his grandson is learning how to be a man.

Big Mexica Heart

City limits blur as a maze of small towns appear abruptly, one ending as a new one begins. Alamo's to the east of San Juan and Pharr is to the west. "Highway 83 runs east and west through San Juan. It's been called one of the longest main streets in the world, the reason being that over twenty towns have that highway as the main street. Nebraska was the main drag going north and south, and Highway 83 was the main road going east and west," Yzaguirre says, explaining the layout of San Juan. "Martin's Drugstore was a big store on the south side, on the corner of Nebraska and Highway 83. Right next to it was Polk's Grocery Store, and on the Mexican side was Rodriguez's Grocery Store. There was a big yellow store called La Tienda Amarilla on the north side by the railroad tracks for the Mexicanos and a Mexican family owned that. My grandfather's house was almost in the middle of Mexican town on 4th street, close to Nebraska and Highway 83, but his ice business was on the south side, which was the Anglo part of San Juan. I grew up multicultural, comfortable with other cultures, but not really feeling I belonged to either one. No culture defined me; I found I could feel comfortable in both."

Two exceptions to the strict separation of Anglos and Mexicans during Raul's childhood resulted in marriages for the Morins and Yzaguirres. "My aunt, Maria Elodia, married an Anglo and their son, Robert Ray, often stayed with us. And on my father's side, his brother, my uncle Roberto, married an Anglo woman named Maude. They had a wonderful life together. He moved to Ohio and tried to sell his business of making parts to improve airplane performance, but he had no success due in part to the Depression. Later he got a job as a dishwasher at a restaurant, and years later he owned the restaurant. Uncle Roberto and Maude had three children, Anthony, Lowell and Charlotte. Lowell was my age and we had a long-term relationship. We joined the Air Force at about the same time. It was said that Aunt Maude talked about my uncle as if he was a Gatsby-type hero. He was an incredibly handsome man who dressed well and sported 'spats' on his shoes. They traveled around the world together and had a storybook marriage."

Three to four thousand people lived in San Juan during Yzaguirre's childhood, yet interaction between Anglos and Mexicans was most likely to happen in middle school, high school or as part of business or farming. "The north side of town was the Mexicano side and there was an Anglo-owned plant for metal works, and a concrete mixing plant, also Anglo-owned. The junkyard was called 'the Iron' because owners wanted to be sure people didn't think it was Jewish. All the dirty industries were on the north side of town. All the nice stores were on the south side of town. There were two movie theatres, a Mexican one called the Murillo, and an Anglo theatre called the Rex. I enjoyed them both. There was a continuous loop of the movies. You could come to the theatre in the middle of the movie and stay, as the movie would start all over again. I would stay and watch the movie twice. My grandfather would come into the theatre to get me. One of my favorite actors was Pedro Infante. His character was sensitive yet masculine. You can imagine my delight when he came in person to the Murillo. I can claim that I met Pedro Infante."

A maze of dirt alleys ran through the barrio on the north side, while across the railroad tracks on the south side of town stood the San Juan City Hall. On the south side, the roads were paved and well-lit, with sturdy block and concrete houses, some built as two-story residencies surrounded by grassy lawns and decorative fencing. Parks, libraries and other amenities were available to local residents on the south side. San Juan's cultural divide did nothing to deter the north side Mexicanos from relentlessly pursuing the good life America promised. A drum beat sounded somewhere in invisible time, as *los mestizos* struggled, a caste minority, unnamed, unseen, harboring revenge for the exploitation by the Anglos, yet loving the land they lived in and refusing to leave no matter what the cost.

A big Mexica heart—partly wild, partly tame reminiscent of the ancient ancestors, the Mexicas, (Aztec)—emerged each day as *el Quinto Sol* (the Fifth Sun) rose, at times fitfully, in the eastern sky. Each new day meant they had gained another foothold in Texas. They weren't foreigners on the land as the

Anglos wanted them to believe. Theirs was a history spanning centuries, time-less and expansive, like the vast plains of Texas, and as grueling and exacting as the White man's rigid "rule by conquest." The Mexicans on the north side labored hard each day even though their future at times was only an illusion. Work, family, church, festivals, birth and death—their lives were spent in sweat, anguish and laughter for life's ironic beginnings and puzzling endings. They were part of a greater identity, hidden, a pulse beating announcing a new day, another time, another chance on this side of the Rio Grande. This was the reality Raul Yzaguirre lived each day, a reality that would make him a believer in the goodness of life.

PAPA AND MAMA

"I called my grandfather, Papa and my grandmother, Mama. At first I would work with my grandmother raking leaves and cleaning the yard and then one day, my grandfather said, 'You're going to go with me to work.' And I was delighted. We got into his pickup truck and I rode with him most days deliv-ering ice, even in the winter when it was cold and dark. It was a thrill. We'd go to the restaurants and have coffee. We went to the bars and I'd get a Grapette in a little bottle. Some Anglos used to call me "Little Gavino." It made me feel good to be associated with my grandfather. I even thought of changing my name to Raul Morin, I identified so much with him. We would talk about milking goats and things like that. We had a good time. At first I didn't do anything but sit in the pickup truck, then at seven years old I got to drive the pickup from house to house, even though my legs barely reached the pedals. Later, I started to lift the ice and deliver it myself, learning how to work hard at a very young age. My grandfather and I got to know each other very well. He would tell me things he wouldn't tell anyone else. He would never admit he was sad to anyone else but me."

When you carry ice you are prone to get rheumatism, was something Yzaguirre heard from his grandparents. "My grandfather carried ice against his leg or shoulder, so he got rheumatism very early in life. He was always trying to find a cure. Somebody told him that if you steal a potato and put it in your pocket until it's so hard it's like a rock, it will cure you. He would do that. He would steal a potato, cut it up and put it in his pocket and he would tell people about it and everyone would laugh. And he'd laugh, and he kept on doing it for a long time, hoping for a cure."

Gavino Morin loved to work from dawn to dusk. Once in a while, young Raul would convince him to go to a movie, and they would go to McAllen to the Spanish language theatre. On Friday nights, they would watch the detective series Dragnet on T.V. His grandfather referred to the gavel pounded on a judge's desk at the end of the show as "*el chingazo*," (hit).

"His children did not resent me for being there. My uncle Pete was like my older brother. He got me my first BB gun. I would sleep in a storage shack that had netting to keep mosquitoes out. My uncle would come home late at night, drunk, and my grandmother wouldn't let him inside. He would crawl over to my little shed and try to sleep in my little bed, and I'd kick him out and we'd have a fight. But it was more fun than violent. He was a good man."

Gavino Morin had friends on both sides of San Juan's segregated communities. His philosophy of hard work, responsibility, humility and taking pleasure in simple things won him the esteem of everyone he met. "He loved iced tea, and creamed carrots, sliced with white sauce, upside-down pineapple cake, and the usual meat, rice beans and tortillas. He'd go to the corner to tell stories, and wasn't known for drinking or womanizing. Having friends, and appreciating the simple things in life were important to him."

Fiestas and family gatherings, most of them based on religious beliefs, and attending services at Our Lady of San Juan Shrine, were common events for the Yzaguirres and Morins. "We weren't big on Thanksgiving, but we celebrated Christmas for a long time. We actually celebrated Christmas twice, once on Christmas Day and again on January 6, Dia de los Tres Reyes (Three Kings). So that was a big deal. We had the regular Christmas tree and decorations, a nativity scene, and a statue of El Santo Niño de Atocha (Christ Child). We called him Santo Niño. As a child I had both beliefs—one American and one Mexican. I believed in Santa Claus and in Los Tres Reyes, and it all stopped by the time I turned eight or so, first Los Tres Reyes, then Santa Claus went away. Church was very important, and midnight mass was a big deal. We would fast all day, then come back after midnight mass and eat. We had tamales and as kids drank champagne cider from Mexico pretending it was real. As we got older, it was less of a big deal."

Not part of mainstream America, Mexican American families like the Morins, weren't big on celebrating the 4th of July or other national holidays. For Yzaguirre and his grandfather, the 4th of July was just another hot day to sell ice to customers who were on their way to picnics and fireworks shows.

"One year, my uncle Pete bought me a bike for my birthday. I was so thrilled. At birthdays, we had Mexican bread, *pan dulce*, Mexican chocolate, watermelon, and of course presents. I don't remember blowing out candles, but piñatas were a big thing, and swats for how old you were, and one for good measure."

Yzaguirre also recalled home remedies as a way to cure illness, as the tradition of *curanderismo* (use of natural healing herbs and spiritual beliefs) was prevalent in the Valley. Oppressed by poverty and lacking doctors, especially in small rural communities, Tejanos often took medical matters into their own hands, relieving illnesses with herbs, homemade poultices, prayers and rituals. Raised in a traditional Mexican American home, Yzaguirre was exposed to traditional rituals and beliefs, some based on superstition and fear.

Mal de ojo, (evil eye) was believed to be a hex or evil thought sent to someone through an unfulfilled desire or a wish to do another harm. *Mal de ojo* could start by someone simply desiring to touch or hold an infant seen resting in its mother's arms. Not touching or holding the infant would constitute an "unfulfilled desire," and would work somehow against the child, making the child ill. At other times, a person, thinking evil thoughts or actually using black magic to conjure up a hex, could bring on the "evil eye," in the form of negative energy reaching an unwary victim and creating an illness. In traditional medicine, envy, hatred, anger, bitterness, and many other destructive human emotions are often thought to be the cause of illness, and the job of a *curandero/a* is to uncover the roots of the illness lodged in the soul. *Curanderismo* offers a holistic approach to healing, encompassing body, mind and spirit.

"As a cure for *mal de ojo*, my mother would pray for me and make the sign of the cross over my body with a fertilized egg. She would break the egg in a cup that was put under my bed. In the morning, she'd check to see if there was a sign of an eye, and that would put an end to the illness. *Empacho*, which was a stomach ache, she would cure by massaging the area with olive oil, and giving me a tea made with *yerba buena*, a healing, aromatic herb."

Yzaguirre never recalled seeing an eye in the cup underneath his bed, but he did recall enjoying the attention paid to him by his mother and grandmother that, more than likely, were major factors contributing to his recovery. Whether illness was cured by fertilized eggs or massaging the stomach, or the use of herbal teas was not as important to Mexican American families as was the urgency of curing an ill family member through a system of traditional beliefs in the absence of modern medical care. What was important to Tejano families like the Morins was that they were together, living out their daily triumphs and woes as one. The heart of community, and strong family ties centered on age-old religious beliefs such as those revealed in the story of Our Lady of San Juan del Valle, were valued traditions of the Mexican American communities and proved to be stabilizing factors when war, the Great Depression and numerous political and economic set-backs confronted the segregated communities.

WHO IS RAUL MORIN?

Gavino Morin's house stood on two big lots. It was built of clapboard with a screened front porch, a large kitchen, dining room, living room, four bedrooms and one bath.

"It was a big, beautiful gingerbread house with high-end furnishings from the tapestries to the dishes," recalls Tere. "For the small town of San Juan their home was certainly extravagant."

Yzaguirre remembers his grandmother, Mama Licha, as a "bundle of energy," working from early dawn until late to keep the house so clean you could eat off her floors. "The laundry was not only clean," he says, "it was boiled and sanitized." Mama Licha's indomitable spirit was present in all she did, and her dedication to her husband was something she lived out on a daily basis in a house that boasted polished wood floors. "The smell of pine oil was in the air," remembers Alma. "They had beautiful antique furniture, some upholstered in maroon velvet."

Near the Morin's house was Vida N. Clover Elementary School, part of the PSJA School District. "The principal, Vida Clover, taught my mother, my aunt and me," Yzaguirre says. "The school had fifteen classrooms, offices, and a nice play area." Yzaguirre remembers it as the school where Mexican children were forced to attend while they learned English. "We were labeled as Caucasians, which meant we were only separated from Anglo students on the pretext that we needed to learn English. It was the District's excuse for keeping us segregated."

On the fringes of the San Juan community, Yzaguirre remembers there were colonias, with no water, and no electricity for the majority of its residents who were migrants traveling from town to town to harvest crops. "Land was sold to the poor for building their homes, with no sewage, water or electrical power. The migrants would run electrical lines getting what little electricity they could from city electrical poles. Inevitably, city officials would find out, and disconnect their dangerous, hand-made electrical connections. By summertime, the migrants would go up north to pick crops. The whole area was agricultural and had more farm workers than any other part of Texas."

Moving back and forth across the border was common for both Mexican and Anglo Texans as business was shared, crops harvested, and commerce shipped back and forth between the U.S. and Mexico on a daily basis. "My father worked for customs on both sides of the border. It could have been my grandmother insisted on it, but my mother left me with my grandparents when I was five years old. She told me to go to the bathroom and when I came out I knew something was wrong. She was gone, so I was raised by my grandparents. Later on my parents moved to San Juan when I was nine years old, but I continued to live with my grandparents. No explanation, but that my mother wanted me to be in school and not have to move around, but it didn't sound right—there was more to it than that. I was very lonely and sad, and my grandmother didn't treat me like a mother, she treated me like my boss."

Later, Yzaguirre would come to know the deep love Mama Licha had for him that went beyond her seemingly harsh nature. "She was critical of all of us, but when she paid me a compliment it was like gold. Maybe only twice in my entire life with her, she said two words that made me go to tears, she would say, *Raulito bonito* (beautiful Raul). She hated to be loving."

Gavino and Elisa Morin had a total of six children, and only three survived. They had one boy, and a set of twins, also boys, who died in infancy. "My aunt, Maria Elodia was the oldest who survived and went to college. She married an Anglo, had a son, then she came home and {eventually} died of tuberculosis. Her son was a few months younger than I was. My mother, Eva Linda, was the second child to survive. My uncle Pedro 'Pete' was the youngest, and he died in 2011, a good man, Pedro Angel Morin."

The Morin's named their oldest boy who died in infancy, Gavino, but after that no one in the family bore the name until the birth of Uncle Pete's son, named "Gavino" who was destined to grow up in South Texas, graduate in 1993 from the University of Texas School of Law, and become an attorney, eventually setting up his own Video High-Tech Company.

Yzaguirre remembers his grandfather chewing tobacco and smoking cigars, usually wearing khaki pants and shirts, a hat and work boots. "My grandmother absolutely hated the chewing tobacco and she would tell him not to get near her, and he'd say, 'Give me a kiss.' And she would say, 'Get away from me!' If my grandfather didn't want any dinner, my grandmother wouldn't cook for anybody. Everything circulated around my grandfather. We learned how to cook because she wouldn't cook if my grandfather didn't want dinner."

A storyteller at heart, Gavino Morin would make up stories to tease his wife. Yzaguirre recalls his grandfather's mischievous smile as he would accuse his wife of having a secret lover. "He would make up stories about my grandmother's lover, but it was all in fun. He loved to play practical jokes on people. He was happy. To the outside world he was always happy, kidding, being friendly, an incredibly brave man. Anglos treated him like a funny, Black man—they liked him, but they had a way of dismissing him. When he died the whole town closed down, and 3,000 people, Mexicans and Anglos came to his funeral in a town of 4,000."

"My grandfather had no education, but he learned to speak English and my grandmother, who was educated, never learned English," Yzaguirre says, noting educational differences between his grandparents. "The wooden panels my grandfather used to advertise political candidates on his pickup truck gave him notoriety and local politicians would come to see him to ask for his endorsement. He never became an American citizen, so he couldn't vote but they wanted his endorsement. It was a big deal to get your poster on that truck and get his endorsement. So he became a political leader. It was funny that the endorsement of a non-voter mattered so much."

Yzaguirre's memory of his grandfather's political endorsements formed in him an early impression of the importance of voting rights, which over the years were threatened by Jim Crow laws in Texas that, among other things, required a poll tax from Texas voters, targeting poor Black and Tejano voters who had no money to pay the tax.

One story that stands out in Yzaguirre's mind, was told to him by Mama Licha about her own mother. "She told me about her father having a *casa chiquita* (second family), and her mother going over to her husband's mistress and bringing food to his illegitimate children. One of them was named Raul. It may have been her half-brother. My great-grandmother would come back and beat up on my great-grandfather and say 'You're not feeding your children. You're not taking care of your house.' So instead of beating him up for having a mistress, she would beat him up for neglecting his second home."

Mama Licha didn't stop at scrubbing, scouring, cooking and tending to her family. A shrewd business woman, she used her Mexican education to bring in money. "My grandmother tutored at home," Yzaguirre says. "She read in Spanish and taught skills that women learned in her day. She read a lot and liked to talk about stories, and politics. I remember her reading to my grandfather about the war. Let me explain her personality this way. I have one brother and three sisters and I am the only one who speaks fondly of my grandmother. On the one hand she made my life miserable and on the other hand she made me who I am today. She was mean, she was rough, she was vindictive, and fiery, but you could eat off her floor. She worked from early in the morning to late at night. She would cook for us at the ice house when we were working. She was a firecracker. She was a strong-willed woman but she had her little quirks. She loved to go shopping, and not buy anything. She would lend money out at high interest. I think she broke the usury laws of Texas everyday. She was a loan shark but mostly with the family."

Tere's memories coincide with her brother's in her remembrance of Mama Licha's overpowering personality. "I remember that my grandfather would give me money and my grandmother would take it away. Sitting in the front pew in church was vital to her. She was also very sanitary and hygienic and employed two or three housekeepers and had them continuously cleaning at all times washing down walls and boiling dishes and laundry. All in all, I remember my grandmother was often annoyed and irritated at us and my memories of my grandfather were always as a loving full-of-affection grandfather, therefore, I can easily say we favored him."

Tere recalls that work at Morin's Ice House began as early as 4:30 AM. "Raul was hardworking. He was up at 4:30 AM, so he could be at work at 5 AM, even on school days. As a teen, he helped our grandfather deliver fifty to one hundred pound blocks of ice he would carry on his shoulders. He was also very protective of me, at times to a fault. I remember him buying me comic books every week as we both loved reading."

Entering the world of work at an early age, Yzaguirre later discovered that the labor was backbreaking and the rules were rigid. "I worked with my dad and my grandfather in the ice business, and sometimes took care of my dad's cows. At times, I felt overworked and underpaid. The family business was lots of hard work. I got an allowance but no salary. In winter we also did farm work. I picked cotton, but was not good at it. We got a penny a pound for the cotton. One hundred pounds equaled one dollar. I was not a good cotton picker. I found out that no matter how hard life is, it's better than picking cotton!"

One story Tere vividly remembers illustrates how hard-working and enterprising Yzaguirre was, even as a child. "When Raul was about six years old, he convinced our cousin, Neri, that they were going to become very rich by developing a formula to take away the odor of skunks. They hunted and killed skunks. Then, they spent the night outside because my aunt wouldn't let them in the house. As far as I know, he never developed the formula."

A model of what it meant to work hard, Mama Licha's talent for keeping a clean house was legendary, but her work didn't stop at the back porch. In her backyard, she cultivated her garden year-round. She used huge bins she would store carefully under the house to stew tomatoes, and also ground fresh corn in the traditional *metate*, (grinding stone).

"She taught me how to garden. She had a beautiful garden and took care of it until she couldn't do it anymore. It breaks my heart to see the lot now full of weeds," Yzaguirre says, describing fond memories of his grandmother's gardening skills. The most profound message she left him, and one that has made a lasting impression on his life was his grandmothers *dicho* (wise saying), *Lo cortés no quita lo valiente*. (Being courteous and having good manners signify strength and sound character, and should never be confused with weakness). Later, Yzaguirre would prove the truth of his grandmother's words over and over again, as complex problems and conflicts stole his peace of mind. Those who, over the years, would come into the presence of Raul Yzaguirre, spoke again and again of being impressed by his humble, unassuming and quiet ways. His personality at times was described as "shy" and "quiet."

Helen Coronado met Yzaguirre in Washington D.C. in 1985 shortly after arriving in the city with her husband Gil Coronado, a USAF colonel who had been assigned to the Inter-American Defense Board. Living overseas as a military wife, Helen had never heard of NCLR. As fate would have it, Yzaguirre hired Helen to assist his own administrative assistant. And when his assistant vacated her position, he asked Helen to become his new administrative assistant. Coronado's long years of service with NCLR brought her in close contact with Yzaguirre. Her first impression of him would certainly have brought a smile to Mama Licha's face, although her show of affection might have taken her by surprise. Her words, uttered so long ago with great conviction, "*Lo cortés no quita lo valiente,*" had lived long after her death in the life of her grandson.

"My first impression of Raul was that he was a very humble, mild mannered, and polite individual," says Coronado. "He was extremely dedicated and devoted to the betterment of the Hispanic community, working very long hours. When one carried on a conversation with him, he would devote all his attention to that person. Raul was also a very cheerful and happy person, always wanting to make people comfortable around him."

Emily Gantz McKay, working in 1970 in Washington, D.C. with the BLK Group, an African American consulting firm, came to know Yzaguirre when he was head of Interstate Research Associates (IRA). Invited by Yzaguirre to join his staff at NCLR, McKay became indispensable to him as a technical assistant, writing grants and contracts with funding agencies. Eventually, she became an executive vice president, serving in high-level capacities for NCLR. McKay's description of Yzaguirre's innate ability to make himself invisible—in a sense forgetting himself for the sake of others—captures the Morin spirit inspired by his grandparents.

"Raul lived for many years in a small town in Maryland {Mt. Airy}, where apparently almost no one, not even neighbors and church members realized he was a civil rights leader," recalls McKay. "I believe a lot of them thought he was an interpreter and translator or something like that. It was quite a shock in his community when his picture was on the front page of the Washington Post for the first time. While attending his daughter Elisa's *quinceañera,* I discovered that many of her friends and their families had no idea what Raul did for a living. His family life tended to be somewhat apart from his work, probably because Mt. Airy was a long trek from D.C., though Audrey and the children often came to NCLR conferences."

Caught between the opposite personalities of his grandparents, Yzaguirre inherited both the fiery, fierce determination of his grandmother and the humble, caring ways of his grandfather. The combination empowered him to fearlessly confront his greatest opponents, while holding the door of peace open for some of the most volatile and destructive forces he would ever encounter in his long career as an advocate for human rights.

Tony Salazar met Yzaguirre in 1977 while serving as Executive Director of the Guadalupe Center in Kansas City, Missouri. "I was very intrigued by Raul's vision to create a national membership organization comprised of independent Latino- serving non-profit organizations," Salazar says. "As a result, my first impression was one of a modest man with great vision. Raul was fearless, he was willing to go anywhere and speak to anyone about Latino issues. He showed me how to find the common thread that bound people together."

The common thread, crucial for the unification of diverse groups, would be stretched to the limit, and Yzaguirre would fall prey at times to those waiting to cause havoc for the sake of personal gain. Salazar described Yzaguirre's ability to bring peace to the most hostile confrontations in the following manner: "He challenged you to be a better person. He brought out the best in you. It was his hard work and perseverance that brought organizations, elected officials, and community leaders together to speak with one voice."

Lo cortés no quita lo valiente, survived a lifetime.

A Tale of Whispering Tom Mayfield

Whispering Tom Mayfield, San Juan's constable, was a man who could play the role of friend, or foe, defending those he valued and taking revenge on those who opposed him. On the night of Gavino Morin's encounter with *los rinches* it was Mayfield who was the reason Gavino Morin wasn't lynched; yet Mayfield's role as a Texas Ranger put him in a hostile position with the Mexican American community. Yzaguirre witnessed the good and bad of Whispering Tom Mayfield through his grandfather's relationship with him over the years.

One story told of Mayfield, involved a peaceful meeting of Mexicanos sometime in the late 1940's. Gavino Morin was among a group of locals who gathered in San Juan for the purpose of nominating another candidate who would run for constable and hopefully win, thus replacing Mayfield in the upcoming election. Mayfield and his Mexican deputy decided to take matters into their own hands that night, and forcefully end the meeting. "They came in," Yzaguirre says, "and beat up everybody and tore up the meeting."

In another incident, Whispering Tom Mayfield took a solid position against another Mexican American deputy in defense of Gavino Morin.

"Whispering Tom Mayfield had a deputy constable, a Mexicano who was a gangster. He owned the local bar and had a gambling operation in the back. He had this Mexican patrón mentality that he didn't have to pay for anything because he was a cop. He took what he wanted. His family lived across the street from us. He and his brother-in-law had eight or nine kids between them. My grandfather delivered ice to them for weeks and they wouldn't pay him so he stopped delivering ice. One day, I was at the ice house. We were crushing ice for customers, and my grandfather had an ice pick in his hand. When ice got stuck in the crusher, we had this baseball bat we would use to push it through. Sometimes it would get caught and crack. I was sitting in the back with the baseball bat when the Mexican deputy walked in with his brother-in-law. He was a big guy. He walked up to my grandfather and said, 'You have insulted me. You have failed to deliver ice.' My grandfather said, 'You haven't paid me for weeks. I can't afford to do that anymore.' 'Nobody does that to me,' the guy said. So he took out his night-stick. And my grandfather had the ice pick. The deputy was about to start beating up on my grandfather when a guy came out of a meat-packing place and saw the whole thing. I got up and started to swing the bat, but my grandfather turned around and looked at me and said, 'No. Go get your uncle.' He would not let me hit the constable with the bat. He acted with so much dignity, not scared at all. The deputy and his brother-in-law had guns. My grandfather was thinking of me that day, not about himself. This was what the man was about. When they saw they were being witnessed, the deputy and his brother-in-law stopped. This went to trial and the Mexican deputy was acquitted but Whispering Tom Mayfield said, 'You're out of here.' The guy left town and nobody ever saw him again."

Yzaguirre recalls that, "Throughout my youth, Whispering Tom Mayfield was very cordial to me and my family, in sharp contrast to the way he treated other Chicanos. I still have this indelible image of Whispering Tom directing traffic and taking off his hat as the hearse carrying the body of my grandfather passed him by. I think I saw tears in his eyes."

A GREAT MAN DIES

January 1956, winter settles over South Texas. An immense gray sky meets the Texas horizon, disappearing into the distance, forming a landscape of unseen shadows, foreboding and threatening. Early Sunday morning, dawn appears over San Juan, mincing its way into winter's hard, cold calculating hand. Fifteen year-old Raul Yzaguirre and his best friend, Armando Sloss are planning to go duck hunting, and pack the pickup truck with their guns and gear. Just before they leave, Yzaguirre gets a call from his grandfather asking him to go to Alamo to pick up some ice. His ice machine is broken down he says and he's brought in a mechanic to check the apparatus. The trip the boys make to Alamo and back to San Juan to deliver the ice will be one they will never forget. That day, the hunting will never be done and Raul Yzaguirre's world is about to be shaken to its foundation. Life's cruel reality will bludgeon its way into young Yzaguirre's life, leaving painful scars that will fade over time, but never truly disappear.

"My grandfather called me on a Sunday around noon in January 1956 before we left to go hunting. The refrigeration in the ice house had gone down and he couldn't store any ice. I was going to go hunting with my friend, Armando. 'I need you to go get me some more ice,' he said to me. He didn't want to close the ice house because the refrigeration was down. He wanted to keep enough ice to take care of his customers. 'Go to Alamo and get me one hundred pounds of ice.' Alamo was the town next to San Juan so it didn't take us long to get there. As we drove back on Highway 83 heading west to San Juan, there was an explosion, and we heard sirens and saw police and fire trucks as we got closer to the ice house. A crowd of people had gathered on the street, and ambulances were waiting. Ammonia in the cooling apparatus had exploded in the iron container making it shoot up like a torpedo as the mechanic was fixing it. I saw some people pulling my grandfather out on a stretcher. I ran to him. He had a huge gash on the back of his neck. I knelt down and looked into his eyes. He had a blank look, but somehow he knew I was there. He took his last breath and died in my arms. I heard the mechanic who had been working on the machine yell, '¡Saquen a mi compadre primero!' (Take my compadre out first!) Apparently, he did not know that my grandfather had already been taken out of the ice house. The mechanic also died on the spot that day. My grandfather was taken away in the ambulance. I walked down seven blocks to my house. My grandmother was coming out of the house. She saw me with blood all over my shirt. She screamed and ran to the ice house. She sensed he was gone. I lay down on my bed and cried. It was the most painful day of my life."

In recalling the day of her grandfather's fatal accident, Tere, describes the devastating effects his death had on her brother. "The most heartbreaking moment in Raul's life, I believe, was when our grandfather died. Raul was 15 years old at the time. My grandfather was in excellent health; he didn't even have a cavity and had all his teeth. He had never been sick a day in his life. He didn't need glasses as he had 20/20 vision. His death caused great sorrow and grief not only because we loved him, but because his death was so unexpected."

Mexican American traditions were observed as plans unfolded for the services and burial of Gavino Morin. "There was a viewing of my grandfather's body at home for three days," Yzaguirre says. "There was a *velorio* (wake) every night. I just stood and watched him in my living room. For three days this went on. He would go back to the mortuary, then at night he would come back home for three or four hours—coming and going. They shaved off his moustache, and he seemed strange. I stood and watched him and remembered him wearing his hat, his khaki brown pants, long sleeve shirt and work boots."

GAVINO MORIN WAS BURIED IN PHARR, alongside other family members. Yzaguirre remembers his grandmother "putting her hair up in *trenzas*, (braids) and wearing black forever and ever, *de luto*," without ceasing, mourning her husband and her daughter, Maria Elodia. "My grandfather was the anchor for our family. Everyone revolved around him, his authority was unquestioned."

As time passed, Yzaguirre's uncle Pete worked the ice house with him. Later, Uncle Pete's son Gavino Morin, who had never met his grandfather, would recall his father telling him how the explosion that killed his father had rocked the town, breaking windows for blocks. The McAllen Monitor ran the story on the front page, announcing the sad news of the loss of Gavino Morin, a man esteemed by thousands in San Juan and the surrounding communities.

Raul's close relationship with his grandfather brought him into a man's world that would, in later years, begin a series of relationships with men who would serve as his mentors, men who would, through their activism, spark in him a commitment for community and ignite his passion for organizing. What he received from his grandfather—the ability to listen attentively and to use silence at times to encourage another's confidence, was something Yzaguirre would eventually pass on to thousands of young Latino males through creation of the Young Latino Male Symposium, one of his most coveted programs during his term as director of the CDCR Center at ASU. He envisioned a national Clearing House of information and statistics related to young Latino males. "There are serious problems in our educational system for young Latino males. The symposiums were set up to find interventions on how to make a difference. Why do so many young Latino males quit school? We needed to find causation."

Gavino Morin's legacy lives on in the thousands of dedicated young leaders Raul Yzaguirre has mentored over the years, those he has worried over, loved and defended as his own, serving them unselfishly and challenging them to achieve their highest goals.

7

THE BARBEE NELL

*I was almost starving to death in Corpus Christi and all I had to
do was pick up the phone and call home and say, come and get me.
Sleeping under a warehouse with rats and snakes and just having
the determination to do what I wanted to do. I finally succeeded at
it. It was the most important character development of my life.*

—Raul Yzaguirre

THE RUNAWAY

THERE'S DANGER ON THE HIGH SEAS, but thirteen year-old Raul Yzaguirre isn't worried about it. He's heard of sailing and has listened to
fishing stories all his life. He's heard news reports of hurricanes that
have hit the Gulf of Mexico with a vengeance over the years causing damage and destruction to fishing vessels and cities along the coastline. He's read
stories of offshore oil drilling gone wrong, spewing tons of oil into the sea,
polluting the water and causing havoc for marine life and fishermen dependent on the ocean's bounty—still the ocean is there, over a hundred miles
away from San Juan, a startling truth, something he can't get out of his mind
since his 7th grade class visited Corpus Christi on a school field trip.

The prospect of an adventurous life onboard a ship, and earning a good
sum of money as a fisherman, tempts young Raul Yzaguirre. Season after season, fishermen have ventured into the treacherous gulf waters to fish for red
snappers, swordfish, gag groupers, yellowfin tuna (ahi), sea bass and a variety
of other sea creatures. Besides that, bay shrimping and the harvesting of oys-
ters has been going on for centuries on the gulf, guaranteeing a good profit
for enterprising fishermen. It's hard work, but Yzaguirre is familiar with hard
work. He can't resist the sea. Fast money is the lure, but it's the sea that's the

mysterious magnet, an internal fishhook young Yzaguirre can't get out of his system. He'll make money, of this he is sure, and it won't be delivering ice or picking cotton.

He invites his best friend, Armando Sloss, and a few other guys he knows to go with him and they all turn him down. Too risky, they say, besides that, their parents won't let them go. He tries to explain the freedom they'll have, the right to do what they please as sailors and hang around with men who know what life is really all about. But they shake their heads, and tell him he's got to be kidding, he won't ever get hired as a fisherman, he's too young, then what? Besides that, they're starting high school—their freshman year looms ahead and that's important. Doesn't he care about that? "We'll come back with a sack full of money," he tells them, pressing his point, "then you'll be glad you went." Already, he imagines himself on a schooner, plowing through the ocean's waves, working side by side with men just like he's worked at his grandfather's side for years. It can't be that hard. But the guys don't want to take a chance. Alone, Raul Yzaguirre considers his next step. None of his friends want to take a chance, but in his mind, his desire to go to sea becomes a passion, his own quest—a mythical dragon he must slay, or die trying. It doesn't take him long to make up his mind; he will go alone.

Lured by the Sea

The Spanish explorer, Alonso Álvarez de Pineda, set sail along the Texas coastline in June 1519 on the feast day of the Body of Christ and spotted a small settlement nestled in the lush, tropical bay area. He named it Corpus Christi (Body of Christ) in honor of the sacred feast day. Corpus Christi was destined to become one of the largest port cities in the nation and would one day play a key role in the life of a young thirteen year-old runaway looking for adventure on the high seas.

"We had a school trip that took us to Corpus Christi when I was in 7th grade," Yzaguirre says, remembering his adventures as a young sailor. "We went to an aquarium and I fell in love with the city. I saw the ships in the bay and I said, this is where I want to be. The city was about one hundred-twenty miles away from San Juan. Just that one trip made me fall in love with it."

For a boy who had not developed "sea legs," the desire to become a sailor proves to be a quest that matures a young Yzaguirre, building in him a resolve to follow through on his plans and succeed at all costs. And the costs will add up: hunger, sleepless nights, homelessness and despair. The thoughts of home will take hold of him, especially when he's at his most vulnerable, only to quickly disappear as he wrestles with fate, seeking his place in the world and not willing to quit until he finds it.

"I ran away from home at the age of thirteen. Actually, I left in late May, right before my birthday on July 22, so fourteen is more accurate," Yzaguirre recalls, explaining his abrupt decision to leave home. "I was mad, so I made up some excuse, but the real excuse was I wanted to leave home. I wanted to be my own person. I wanted freedom and adventure, and I thought I should be allowed to do all the things I wanted to do. I was working with my father at the time and we had a fight or something. He came in and woke me up to go to work and I said, I'm not going to go to work today. He said, 'What's happening?' I'm leaving home, I told him. And he said, 'Do what you need to do. I'll see you at dinner tonight.' But he said it in a kind way, meaning you're free to do what you want to do. He gave me the license I needed. I didn't tell my grandfather. He waited for me on the porch every night, my grandfather, waiting for me to come home."

Once his decision is made, there's no turning back. Grabbing a Boy Scout backpack he had bought at a surplus store, Yzaguirre promptly starts packing his clothes. Mexican boys were not allowed to join the Boy Scouts in those days as discrimination against Mexican Americans included segregation and exclusion from Anglo-led organizations, yet Yzaguirre had always dreamed of joining the Boy Scouts, going on camping trips and learning how to survive in the wild. He now stuffs the backpack with a pair of jeans, assorted shirts and underwear and what little money he has saved. In his mind is the mental image of Corpus Christi, the city he had seen on his 7th grade school trip, with its harbor overlooking the Gulf of Mexico. He had been fascinated by the schooners and huge ships that docked in the harbor, the hustle and bustle of sailors and the ocean's waves splashing against the shoreline as the ships pulled in and out of the bay. What lay beyond the harbor? What could he experience as a sailor? These thoughts are deep in Yzaguirre's mind, although they do not form a clear picture for him until after he goes to an unlikely place—a movie theatre.

Hitchhiking to nearby Edinburgh, Yzaguirre decides to go to a movie theatre in town and watch *Island in the Sun*, starring Harry Belafonte, who plays a crusader on a Caribbean Island fighting for his people. As he sits in the dark theatre watching Belafonte take on the island's enemies, Yzaguirre becomes conscious of the struggle between good and evil, and of one man's battle to win justice for his people. The movie touches into the fabric of his ideals: justice for all, and fighting for the most vulnerable among us. Leaving the theatre, Yzaguirre feels renewed and inspired to continue his quest, setting his sights on Corpus Christi. Many years later, he will tell Belafonte about the impact the movie had on his life.

On his way to Falfurrias, Texas, Yzaguirre meets a man by the name of Gonzales who offers to take him to his home in Falfurrias. The man lives on a street called Noble. "Why don't you stay with me in my home with my wife and two girls?" Asks Gonzales. Yzaguirre thinks that's a good idea considering he has nowhere to go and no definite plans, except that he's headed for Corpus Christi to find a job. He stays on with Gonzales for a few days, doing odd jobs, and is welcomed by his wife and girls, yet he knows he will not be there long. After three days, he tells Gonzales he has to move on, and the man generously pays him for his services. Now, he has a bit more money he can use for the next leg of his journey to Alice, Texas.

Hitchhiking to Alice takes persistence and nerve as Yzaguirre often finds himself sleeping in ditches and seeking out a crevice on a hillside or by the canal bank where he feels safer, even though he shares the space with field mice, snakes and spiders. Once in Alice, he rents a cheap hotel room, giving his age as 16. The hotel desk clerk doesn't care if he's lying, he's paying for the room and times are rough. Raul's glad the desk clerk didn't make a big deal about it, he's weary and in need of a hot shower and a good night's rest.

"In the middle of the night, someone knocked on the door. It was the hotel owner with a policeman. They wanted to know who I was. I showed them my Texas identification, a blue laminated birth certificate card with no photo on it. The policeman wanted to know where I was going and I told him I was going to Corpus Christi to find a job. May I ask why you are interrogating me? I asked. The policeman said, 'A young man fitting your description killed somebody.' It's not me, I said. I realized they would take my name and call my parents, so I left early the next morning and hitch-hiked from Alice to Corpus Christi."

Realizing he was in danger of being found out as a runaway, Yzaguirre wastes no time in making the decision to keep moving toward his goal. Early the next morning he packs his clothes as quickly as possible, stuffing everything again into his Boy Scout backpack, and slips away from the hotel to begin the long trek to Corpus Christi.

RED SNAPPER FISHERMEN

Arriving in Corpus Christi, Yzaguirre walks to the docks and looks over the vast harbor where the ships are anchored. He sees a big schooner docked at the bay and is impressed by its beauty and the sense of adventure it holds out to him. "That's what I want to do," he says to himself as he walks to the schooner that he later learns is called, the *Barbee Nell*, a shortened version of the names of the captain's wives and daughters. From his vantage point on the dock, he observes the sky's blue horizon in the distance, the smooth, glassy ocean waves blinking back bright sunlight and the schooner's sails waving in the breeze. He takes a deep breath of the salty sea air, imagining himself sailing away on the elegant schooner. The schooner has three masts and is seventy feet long with two powerful engines and equipped with sonar. It carries a crew of seven men, and has captain's quarters at the helm.

Climbing on-board the schooner, Yzaguirre asks a couple of sailors, "What do you guys do?"

"We're red snapper fishermen. We go way out into the deep sea and we fish for red snappers," one of the men says.

"How do I get a job here?"

"You wait twenty years and come back!" The second man says, handing a steel fish hook to his fellow crewman. Both men laugh out loud and Yzaguirre good- naturedly, joins them.

"I don't have twenty years to spare," he answers.

Unwavering, once his decision is made, Yzaguirre stubbornly refuses to give up his dream of sailing on the *Barbee Nell*. His connection with the sailing crew has only just begun, and his determination to join them on their fishing expeditions kicks into high gear.

"I just stuck around talking to them for a while, then the captain came by in a big Cadillac with his wife, Margie I think was her name, a red-headed, younger woman. J. L. Murrell was the captain's name. He was wearing a captain's cap, and looked like a Hemingway sort with a square jaw and a cigar in his mouth."

Captain Murrell's from Oklahoma, but speaks with a distinctive Texas drawl. He looks half-amused at the young boy and asks.

"What is it you want, son?"

"I want a job on the *Barbee Nell*."

"Sorry, I can't hire you. Besides we're full, but you seem like a nice kid, you can hang around if you want to. You can sleep in that lifeboat if you don't have a place to stay," the captain says pointing to a lifeboat bopping in the water close by.

A few days later a truck comes by and fills the ship with ice and groceries for the crew. In a few days they set sail, and Yzaguirre finds himself alone on the dock wondering what to do next.

EATING TOO MUCH

Deciding to look for a job in Corpus Christi, Yzaguirre walks around the streets early the next morning, getting hungrier by the minute, often looking into dumpsters for any scraps of food he can find. He sleeps in an old warehouse under the building's foundation, crawling into a space where he sees straw and a place where he can sleep with some sense of security, although he shares the space with rats, snakes and spiders. "I was getting hungrier and hungrier and dirtier as well, and now I was desperate for a job," he recalls. "I finally found this restaurant owner who would give me a job as a dishwasher. I didn't know how to wash dishes, and burned myself several times, but I finally learned how to do it."

Yzaguirre's grateful for the owner's offer of two meals a day, plus the two dollars or so he is earning daily. Trying to satisfy the needs of his starving body, he eats ravenously at the restaurant. After only a few days, the restaurant owner says to him, "Son, I like the way you work, but you're eating too much. I gotta fire you."

Once again, Yzaguirre is faced with the need to make a new plan for himself, always keeping in mind his ultimate goal, which is to get onboard the *Barbee Nell*.

Desperate for another job, he roams the docks, looking for anyone who will offer him employment. He finally comes upon an enterprise he thinks has something he can do.

"There was a fish house on the docks where lots of women were employed, mostly Mexican women, to head shrimp. You pinch off the shrimp heads and cut the tail and that's what you eat. You do that as fast as you can because you get paid a penny a pound for the heads, some heads are very small, so you have to have a lot. There's a lot of chopping and cleaning to do to make any money. I started working there and got pretty good at it, and the women treated me like their own son, but it was very hard work for only pennies. I got pretty good at it, but after a while bay shrimping opened up for me."

Catching sight of a fisherman casting his nets along the bay, fishing for the smaller variety of shrimp that swim close to the shore, Yzaguirre decides to try his hand at bay shrimping. It's a one-man operation but he takes his chances and offers the man his help.

"I'd like to work for you," he says to the fisherman.

The man looks him over and sees a rather scrawny kid, but one who seems sharp and ready to take on any task he's given. "Sure, I'll take you on," he says, "you can sleep on the boat too if you don't have a place to stay."

Within a few days, Yzaguirre's collected enough money to buy himself a pair of work pants, boots and fishing gear. By the time the *Barbee Nell* returns to the harbor, he is set up in his shrimping job, and now sails casually by the big schooner in his little boat, waving at the sailors on board. The sailors know who he is and wave back at him, amused at his tenacity and determination to become a sailor.

"In the afternoon after we came back from shrimping, I would go back and talk to the guys on the *Barbee Nell*, so they got to know me, and got to feel comfortable with me and the captain saw me on the ship, saw me with my work boots and all my fishing gear. I wanted him to get the idea that I was comfortable walking on the boat and had skills as a fisherman."

Yzaguirre's goal to get on-board the *Barbee Nell* seems closer than ever to him, and he once again looks for an opportunity to become a member of the crew.

Captain Murrell's Offer

"By luck, two of the deck hands left the *Barbee Nell*, a dentist and another professional who had been fleeing from someone or something," Yzaguirre recalls. "Captain Murrell was two people short, and he was hurting for deck hands. I want to work for you, I told him. I know I can do this job. So he said, 'Okay son, go get your gear.' And that's how I made it onto the *Barbee Nell* as a deck hand. I was the first Mexican American the captain had ever hired."

Yzaguirre finds out that Captain Murrell sleeps in his room in the captain's quarters by the wheel and navigating equipment. Four men sleep up front in the bow, and two sleep in the rear engine room. He ends up sleeping in the bow where there were two bunks and one little board separating a crewman from his shipmate.

"I had a shipmate nicknamed Cowboy who snored badly all night. The space was so small, Cowboy kicked me in his sleep all night long. One thing about Cowboy was that when we docked at port he was an alcoholic, but out at sea you could trust him with your life. I didn't want to bunk in the engine room, it was too smelly, and another option was to go to the stern (rear) of the ship, it was smelly too but there was more room. The ship sailed two hundred to three hundred miles from shore and the sonar equipment told the captain what was at the bottom of the ocean. The crew used steel hooks about an inch and a half long dangling from steel wires three inches long weighing about fifteen pounds and bicycle pedals for the rods. The red snappers weighed from twenty-five to forty pounds. Sometimes we would catch a monster sea bass weighing three to four hundred pounds. Bass meat sold for only ten cents a pound verses forty cents a pound for red snapper, so we saved only a small portion of the sea bass because we had limited space in the ice-filled hold of the ship."

Yzaguirre discovers on the first day of sailing that he has no "sea legs," and his adventures as a hard-working crew member start with miserable seasickness.

"The first day out I got sick as a dog. I got sea-sick on every trip we made after that. I never got over it!"

Making allowances for his youth and inexperience, the crew of the *Barbee Nell* put up with Yzaguirre who recalls he was "stumbling all over the place, a danger to everybody." The men ignore his failings teaching him how to submerge big steel fishing hooks into deep water. Then, an idea begins to form in his mind: *What would I do if I were a fish?*

Carefully studying how the men fish as they sink huge hooks into deep water, he begins to formulate a plan of action that will reap the biggest results. "I would bait the hooks in such a way that I thought would make the fish want to bite, using baits with different smells. The schooner rolled back and forth when they stopped, and for gears, the sailors used the bicycle pedals."

Yzaguirre puts two and two together as he watches the ship roll over the waves and observes the bait go up and down several feet under the water. He develops a technique that makes him the most successful fisherman on board the *Barbee Nell*. "I adjusted the movement of the hooks and imagined how the fish would look at the bait. I imagined I was a fish, and it worked." Patience and a knack for sensing what the fish are doing deep under water is Yzaguirre's method for reeling in red snappers. "Somehow, I had the tactical ability to feel the nibble of the fish and would hook them just as I imagined they were nibbling, and when they took a big bite, I would reel them in." The method he uses is quite successful, and as a result Yzaguirre catches more fish than anybody else, impressing the captain and putting his mind at ease about hiring a teenager to do the work of a full-grown man.

At night, on the bow of the ship, Yzaguirre watches in amazement at the sky's dark canopy overhead glittering with thousands of stars that seem to reach to eternity. "The ocean's waves would splash water on my face and sometimes I would see porpoises playing as the ship was coming through the water. I saw beautiful blue flying fish glowing in the moonlight, and sometimes they would land on deck."

The beauty of the night scenes on board the *Barbee Nell* many years later play vividly in his mind as he sees, for the first time, Iguazu Falls, bordering the countries of Argentina and Brazil. The falls rising over 260 feet, divide the Iguazu River into upper and lower regions, and were first named in 1541 by the Spanish conquistador who would later explore South Texas, Álvar Núñez Cabeza de Vaca.

"When you go out for the first time, they call you a greenhorn, and you only get one half of the share that others get, or four percent of the profits," Yzaguirre says, describing the business end of the fishing expeditions. "The captain earned 10% of the profits plus a share. The owner of the ship got 40% of the profits, and since the captain was the owner, he made out pretty good unless the trip was a bust (loss). He also assumed all risks and took all the liability. The crew was not liable if there was a loss. On my first trip, after seven days, I made ninety dollars and that was a huge amount in those days. Then the crew voted to give me a full share because I had caught more fish than anyone else. I came back in victory. It was a big triumph for me."

As the summer months slip by, Yzaguirre finds himself living a life of freedom and excitement. Now he has money, and the men take charge of him, inviting him to local bars to shoot craps and to nearby hideaways at county fairs to watch cock fights. They teach him the rough, hard-working world of a man and to quell his natural curiosity, they explain the facts of life.

"The first time I saw a guy smoking pot it was on the ship. I was afraid he'd turn into a monster. That's where I had some wrong-headed ideas. My parents scared the hell out of me. 'If you take drugs you're going to turn into a monster. You're going to lose your mind. You're going to get addicted imme-diately.' And I believed it. When I first saw that guy smoking pot I thought he was going to turn into a monster, but he was just happy."

Life at sea offers a thrilling experience for Yzaguirre, but once on shore, he turns to his favorite pastime—roller skating. He's still a kid, and finds ways to play games that his shipmates find boring and childish. His work on the *Barbee Nell* goes on for weeks and weeks, extending into his first semester at high school, and eventually, the rough life of a fisherman starts to catch up to him. He begins to dislike the cramped quarters, the men's sweating bodies, their loud snoring, the alcohol and the hard grind of a fisherman's life.

"Then two things happened. The captain gave me more and more things to do. He would even let me take the ship out of the harbor, which is a big deal. And he would teach me how to navigate."

Then the day comes when Yzaguirre navigates the *Barbee Nell* out of the harbor all by himself, and Captain Murrell says, "Look, Raul, my second wife, Margie, has two children, one is male the other is female. I don't have any children of my own. The male is very sickly and he's not going to be able to take over my ship. I want you to be my son, and I want you to take over my ship. When you get to be twenty-one, we'll get your captain's papers."

Surprised at the captain's proposal to adopt him as his son, Yzaguirre doesn't respond to his offer until a day or so later. Their conversation makes him realize that his plans for staying on as a sailor are changing. He realizes that his family, parents and grandparents are where he belongs. His focus now turns to ending his time on the *Barbee Nell* and returning to San Juan, but unknown to him, there's one more thing he has to do—possibly the most important reason fate led him to Corpus Christi in the first place.

THE AMERICAN GI FORUM

It's a community room close to downtown Corpus Christi, not anything fancy, but there's a table in the center with several Chicanos sitting around it, some wearing business suits, some with briefcases open and all of them talking about the community and how they plan to change things to better the lives of Mexican Americans. They've got concrete plans, and are not just spewing out arguments. They've collected data, and are staring at statistics and information. Their passionate voices reach Raul Yzaguirre as he walks into the room with José Rodriguez, a fellow sailor. The men acknowledge him, some looking his way and nodding their heads or smiling in greeting. They know José, and greet him by name. As they listen to the discussion, José explains to Yzaguirre, "Dr. García isn't here tonight, but you'll get to meet him soon." Already, Raul has heard Dr. García's name mentioned several times in the men's conversations. He's curious about him.

That evening, he learns that Dr. Hector Pérez García is the founder of the American GI Forum. He's a World War II veteran, earning the Bronze Star with six Battle Stars. He has served in the Medical Corps, and is one of the most respected activists in the community. He's got brains and guts and doesn't hesitate to take on Anglo racists. His ultimate goal is to equalize the playing field and advance human rights for Mexican Americans who continue to suffer oppression, unfair treatment and Jim Crow laws meant to dismantle their participation in a democratic society. His activism has ignited nationwide publicity and he has now acquired a most valuable and powerful friend, then Texas State Senator Lyndon B. Johnson, who will one day welcome García, Yzaguirre and many of the Mexican American activists sitting around the table in the humble community room in Corpus Christi to a place they would have never dreamed they would ever go—the White House.

DR. HECTOR P. GARCÍA: MEETING AN ICON

José Rodriguez comes onboard the *Barbee Nell* as Yzaguirre begins plans to go back home. The Anglo crew of the *Barbee Nell* now feels comfortable with

Mexican Americans, thanks to Yzaguirre, and Captain Murrell has no problem in hiring another Mexicano for the second time in the history of the *Barbee Nell*. José Rodriguez, who is destined to change the course of Yzaguirre's life, comes on board as a deck hand.

"José took me to cock fights, dances and barrio events when we came on shore. He belonged to the American GI Forum. He took me to some of their meetings and told me all about Dr. Hector P. García who had been a captain in the Army, serving as a medical doctor during World War II. Now he was fighting discrimination facing Mexicano vets coming home from the war. He was organizing the community to fight for equality. I remember walking into this community room with José, and I saw all these Chicanos, some of them dressed in business suits. They were sitting around a table making plans for pursuing litigation for the Mexican American community. And I said to myself—that's what I want to do. That's what's going to give my life meaning."

Unbeknownst to Yzaguirre that night, the founder of the GI Forum at Corpus Christi, Dr. Hector P. García, along with many other famous members of the GI Forum, were to become his mentors, and the men who would inspire him to realize his true destiny.

"I first saw Dr. García talking to a group of men, and to me he was like a god. I thought he was incredible, very knowledgeable, very funny and he liked to tell jokes. He had chapters of the GI Forum he was organizing into districts. He was a medical doctor who could practice medicine and didn't need to do this. He wanted to recapture our history so we would be proud of who we were. I wanted to emulate his passion and commitment for the community."

An immigrant from the region known to Yzaguirre's father, Tamaulipas, Mexico, Dr. García's family was also a land grant family who had arrived in the North American continent from Spain. Fleeing from the Mexican Revolution in 1917, García's family settled in Mercedes, Texas. Even though both his parents, José García García and Faustina Peréz García were schooled in Mexico as educators, their credentials were never recognized once they crossed the Rio Grande into the U.S. Growing up, García experienced discrimination from Anglos in South Texas and also felt the backlash of revolutionary battles fought in Mexico as the country struggled to stabilize its government against foreign invaders and warring factions of Mexican liberals and conservatives. Dedicated to education as a way to improve their lot in life, García's parents set high standards in education for their ten children.

Struggling to make a living among the segregated communities of South Texas, García's father had to cash in his insurance policy to finance his son's education. Graduating as one of the top ten students in 1932 from the University of Texas at Austin with a degree in Zoology, García went on to earn his medical degree from the University of Texas at Galveston in 1940. Due in large part to his parents' insistence on higher education, García joined five of his other siblings as they attained their medical degrees and also became physicians. While serving in Italy, he met Wanda Fusillo in Naples, and they were married in 1945, sharing a lifetime together. Returning to Corpus Christi in 1945, after earning the rank of major in the Army, García and his brother José Antonio opened a private medical practice in Corpus Christi, and offered medical services to anyone in need, regardless of ability to pay. Much later, in 1984, Dr. García would be honored with the Presidential Medal of Freedom by then President Ronald Reagan, and posthumously, in 1998 he was awarded the Order of the Aztec Eagle, Mexico's highest award granted to foreigners. "Dr. García was an avid scholar," Yzaguirre says, describing his mentor's high intellectual abilities. "He was interested in proving that Mexican Americans deserved fair treatment in this country. He made us sensitive to our history and why we were where we were."

It did not take Yzaguirre long, after meeting Dr. García, to make up his mind that his stint as a fisherman was over. "I told Captain Murrell I was sorry that I couldn't accept his offer to become his adopted son. I had been out at sea six months and it was now Christmas time. I bought myself a suitcase and new clothes, a vest sweater, white shirt, bow tie, dress slacks and a bus ticket to San Juan. My grandfather's house was only four blocks away from the bus station, but I rode back home in a cab with one thousand dollars in my pocket. I wanted to come home as a success. I was determined not to go back with my tail between my legs. They were very happy to see me."

The family story was that Yzaguirre's grandfather would sit every evening on the front porch waiting for him to come home saying, "Raul is coming home tonight." Ironically, the night Yzaguirre came home, Gavino Morin was not on the front porch. He was down the street talking to friends.

"I opened the front gate at my grandparents' house and walked in, and called out, Mama, and my grandmother screamed and came up and hugged me. My sister, Tere, called my mother, then my grandfather and uncle got home and everyone was very happy and impressed with all they saw. I was hugged and scolded by my mom and grandmother, and my grandfather asked me, 'Did you get it out of your system?' Next time I went to sea, they gave me their permission."

Things were different for Yzaguirre for a few months as he settled into life in San Juan. "I used to have to ask permission to go everywhere, but now they gave me more freedom. I used to have a bad temper before running away, but now I was more in control of my feelings. For a while I was treated differently. My parents were embarrassed because I had run away from home. Only my close friends knew. At school, my teachers thought I was a migrant worker who wouldn't come to school until January. I had seen the educated men of the GI Forum and realized, I had to finish school."

Yzaguirre had taken on a new purpose and his life seemed to be moving in the right direction, even though around him the Mexican American community was struggling to survive in a world dominated by segregation and discrimination.

"I bought the whole story, you can do anything you want to do within your grasp. I really believe that. Some kids nowadays don't believe that. I had invited my friend Armando Sloss to go with me, but he didn't want to go. None of the other kids I knew left home to go on a quest, but it seemed real to me. I had to make it real. And in a way it's stupidity, but I believed what I saw in the movies that you could do all these things. And I thought, if they can do it in the movies, I can do it in real life. I remember I had always kept a dime in my pocket in case I needed to call home, but I never used it. In terms of spiritual and character transformation, those few days when I was almost starving to death in Corpus Christi and all I had to do was pick up the phone and call home and say, come and get me. Sleeping under a warehouse with rats and snakes and just having the determination to do what I wanted to do. I finally succeeded at it. It was the most important character development of my life."

During the months of Yzaguirre's adventure in Corpus Christi, Tere and her mother kept the midnight oil burning. "Mom and I would cry and pray for him every night. To this day, I really believe that God answered our prayers and that was why he returned," Tere says.

The amazing timing between Yzaguirre's quest in 1953, and the formation of the GI Forum in Corpus Christi in 1948 is nothing short of a miracle. The memory of the Chicanos he saw that night in the community room assembled around a table discussing issues facing Mexican Americans, was to fire up his desire to imitate their passion and follow the pattern forged by the GI Forum's enigmatic leader, Dr. Hector P. García.

GI FORUM IDEALS IN ACTION

One of Yzaguirre's major goals as the founding Executive Director of the CDCR Center at Arizona State University in 2005, was to build links between university resources and community needs. Yzaguirre's premier leadership skills, and his knowledge of issues impacting the Latino community opened the way for the formation of two highly successful programs that focused on empowering young Latino/a students in their quest for a higher education.

And, in keeping with Yzaguirre's own relationship with powerful mentors as a youth, he established the Young Latino Male Symposium with a grant from the W.K. Kellogg Foundation. The problem of young Latino males failing in school in far greater numbers than young Latinas, became something Yzaguirre was determined to address. "What was causing young Latino males to fail in school? This was a question I took to outside research agencies to gather information and filter the results through a clearing house and back to the community."

The symposiums brought together local and national leaders in discussions directly impacting young Latino males. "Latino males often lack good role models, and don't have a script for defining themselves. This is where mentors lead the way to offer scripts that make sense to them."

Remembering the chapter in his own life when he ran away from home at age thirteen to search for adventure as a sailor, and instead, found himself captivated by successful Latino leaders of the GI Forum, inspired Yzaguirre to focus on the critical needs of Latino male students who, of all ethnic groups, continue to exhibit one of the highest high school drop-out rates in the nation.

YZAGUIRRE'S EXPOSURE TO DYNAMIC LATINO LEADERS as a youth, turned his life around, and set him on a life-long commitment to the Latino community. His desire to sail on the *Barbee Nell* set in motion a response to a world community that resonates to this day through the Young Latino Male Symposium, as well as his mentorship of young leaders working in NCLR's extensive non-profit network, and his leadership in a host of other national and international programs in which he has played a major role. His determination to work for equality and human rights has mapped out a new way for Latino youth to "sail the world" and discover for themselves, the meaning of life.

Captain Murrell's generous offer to adopt him as his son, ignited Yzaguirre's own loyalty to his family, and a sense of empowerment—he had proved to himself that he could tackle a difficult job, earn the respect of those in authority, and thanks to his grandfather's life lessons, come out a winner. It was one of many experiences that would prepare him for the battles that were soon to appear—fast, and furious.

8

SPANISH FORBIDDEN HERE

I was involved in debate groups. Raul could have beat me anytime. That's where he learned his negotiating skills. He seemed very sure of himself, and stood his ground firmly.

—Helen Cavazos

LOUDER THAN WORDS

VIDA N. CLOVER is the elementary school that's supposed to give San Juan's north side Mexican American students a "head start" on the English language. Anglos have officially declared that it's only language that separates them from their Caucasian counterparts. Only language. Let the Mexican kids stay at Vida N. Clover, then after they learn English, say by the fifth grade, they can join the English fluent students at Edison Middle School in Pharr, and then if they can make the grades, they can go on to high school in San Juan, which is all part of the PSJA School District.

For years, San Juan's Mexican Americans accept this set-up, until they begin to see the truth; the plan is nothing more than another way to segregate them from the south side community, and keep them in a sub-standard school setting that doesn't offer the programs and advantages given to Anglo students. Awakening to this fact has taken time, and two world wars, to convince the barrio people that the sacrifices made by their fathers, sons, uncles and cousins on the bloody fields of America's wars are just as valuable to the struggle for democracy as sacrifices done by Anglos. Blood speaks louder than words, and armed with this reality, the Mexican Americans of San Juan declare war on the injustices that have forbidden them from taking their rightful place as Americans.

DE FACTO SEGREGATION

Elementary school begins for Raul Yzaguirre in 1946, eight years before the United States tackles the volatile issue of segregation by race *(de jure)* and by fact, *(de facto)*. Early in its history, PSJA solidly defended *de facto* segregation of Mexican American students basing their decision on the "fact" that students needed to learn English in primary grades in order to function in middle school and high school where they would intermingle with Anglo students. Unlike African American students who suffered *de jure* segregation through the enactment of laws that racially separated them from White students, citing the premise that school facilities were "separate but equal," Mexican American students were considered Caucasian and separation was done only as a way to allow students time to learn English.

"We were segregated in elementary school," Yzaguirre says, "and bussing was done from one area of town to the other. If you were Mexicano, you went to Vida N. Clover or one of the other schools on the north side of San Juan. In rural areas there was less segregation. Mexican American students who happened to live on the south side of San Juan were bussed to the north side where the majority of Mexicanos lived to attend school. It was hard-core, *de facto* segregation. We were supposed to learn English in Kindergarten through fourth grades, then change to an English speaking middle school and then on to high school."

The United States Supreme Court in *Plessy v. Ferguson* (1896) upheld separate facilities for students as long as they were equal and did not violate the Fourteenth Amendment. In 1951 a class action suit was filed against the Board of Education of the City of Topeka, Kansas by twenty African American parents who claimed that separate facilities for their children were not equal to their White counterparts, and in fact were grossly inferior. In a landmark decision on May 17, 1954, the United States Supreme Court, officiated by Chief Justice Earl Warren, ruled unanimously in *Brown v. Board of Education* that state laws establishing separate public schools for Black and White students were unconstitutional, and violated the Equal Protection Clause of the Fourteenth Amendment. The case was future justice, Thurgood Marshall's big win, and one heavily funded by NAACP.

By 1956, while serving as an active member of his high school's student council, a young Yzaguirre, inspired by the Court's decision in *Brown v Board of Education*, got a resolution passed to desegregate the school. "There were only a few Black students in the school system at the time. One became a friend of mine, Johnny Harper. We corresponded for a long time over the years. We sent a letter to the school board asking for desegregation throughout the school for Blacks. The Blacks were totally segregated. They were bussed all over the place. We were a little bit ahead of all the other schools in the Valley."

Standing up against segregation of Black students as a teen makes Yzaguirre aware that Mexican Americans in San Juan have been treated with just as much disdain. Although outlawing separate schools for Black and White students, *Brown v. Board of Education* does nothing to address the day-by-day reality of Mexican American students segregated in schools on the basis of language. PSJA's stance on segregation of Mexican Americans is nothing new. It's something alive and well in the U.S. and as a student leader, it is something Yzaguirre will meet head-on. He will ride the tide of civil rights now budding throughout the Southwest, and will soon begin to strategize on ways to equalize the playing field on his high school campus.

A CLASS APART

Exploding on the national scene is another landmark decision that will turn things around for Mexican Americans and foster an understanding that, although referred to as "Caucasian," Mexican Americans are not considered equal to Anglos but are thought of as inferior and not seen as part of mainstream America. "Growing up in the 1950's, I remember seeing signs in Texas and other regions of the Southwest posted outside restaurants or public buildings that read, NO MEXICANS, NIGGERS OR DOGS ALLOWED," Yzaguirre says, reflecting on the blatant racism that was an obvious fact during his childhood.

Ready to take on a case that will make national news is an unshakable Texas team of attorneys: Gustavo "Gus" Garcia, Carlos Cadena, and John Herrera, along with James de Anda and Chris Aldrette, who would assist with extensive research. Their goal was to challenge the widespread discrimination of Mexican Americans in Texas and begin litigation that would address not only the needs of Mexican American students, but of whole communities divided by abusive laws that denied basic civil rights as defined by the Constitution of the United States.

The case begins with a murder committed in 1950 in Edna, Texas a small community of Jackson County. Pete Hernández, a migrant cotton picker gets into a heated argument one day with an acquaintance, Cayetano "Joe" Espinosa, and in a violent rage shoots him dead. Gus Garcia, a tall, green-eyed Texan who grew up in the battlefields of hard-core discrimination against Mexican Americans, takes on the case pro bono, seeing it as an opportunity to point out a serious breach of civil rights. No person of Mexican descent has ever served on a Texas jury as far as Gus Garcia or anyone else can remember, and Garcia identifies this as a deliberate violation of an American's right to be judged by his peers. Pete Hernández is judged by an all-White jury and is convicted of his crime. When Garcia accuses the court of violating Hernández's civil rights, the state of Texas refutes his argument by stating that the Fourteenth Amendment protects the rights of Whites and Blacks and that Mexican Americans are Caucasian—so what's the problem? Garcia argues that the Fourteenth Amendment guarantees protection not only on the basis of race, Caucasian and Negro, but also on the basis of *class*, a term that is soon to make its way into the annuals of American history.

The team of attorneys, Garcia, Cadena and Herrera work diligently on *Hernández v. Texas* and on October 8, 1951 present their findings in the Jackson County Courthouse. The attorneys confront the reality of class discrimination in the county courthouse as they make a trip to the men's room, only to be told by a Mexican janitor that they can't go into the regular "Men's Room." They must walk downstairs to the door with the sign COLORED MEN, HOMBRES AQUI (Men Here), it is the bathroom facility for Mexican and Black men. The attorneys come to the conclusion that they share more in common with Pete Hernández than they do with fellow Anglo attorneys who don't consider the signs offensive. If Mexicans are Caucasian, then they should be allowed to use the Anglo bathrooms. The team of Mexican attorneys joke about it, seeing it as another opportunity to turn up the heat in the case.

As they walk into the courtroom to present their case, the first thing the judge asks them is, if they need an interpreter, to which the witty Garcia responds articulately, in perfect English, "No sir, if you can't understand English or Spanish perhaps one of my colleagues can interpret for you." During their presentation, the team passionately argues that their litigant, Pete Hernández, accused of murdering Joe Espinosa, has not been tried by a jury of his peers, but by an all Anglo jury that does not reflect his Mexican American heritage. Their goal is to allow testimony from witnesses and introduce statistics that will show the court a general pattern of discrimination of Mexican Americans. Several witnesses are sworn in, and tell of specific times they, or their children, were treated unfairly. Their testimony boils down to the fact that they have all been victims of blatant forms of discrimination; their very identify is now on trial.

Initially, the Texas judge overrules the team's request for a new jury for Pete Hernández, only to be overturned by the Supreme Court three years later. The opportunity to present the case before the nation's highest court is a first for Mexican Americans and many feel there is little hope of victory. Word that the Supreme Court of the United States is willing to hear the case spreads quickly by word-of-mouth and Spanish radio and newsprint to the Texas barrio communities. Dr. Hector P. García gets into the action, and speaking from his own radio program, he pleads for needed donations, and the League of United Latin American Citizens (LULAC) follows suit, asking for monetary support from its many councils.

Once Mexican American residents learn that their own team of Texas attorneys is scheduled to argue *Hernández v. Texas* before the Supreme Court of the United States, donations pour in to help them with living and travel expenses, and court related fees. Sometimes the donations come in the form of nickels and dimes saved in coffee cans by poor migrant farm workers and mailed to the attorneys' offices in envelopes smudged with sweat and traces of mud from the fields. "These were people who couldn't afford it {donations}, but couldn't afford not to," recalls Carlos Cadena.

The team pledges to prove to the Court that Mexican Americans are not foreigners, nor are they Caucasian, but are indeed, *a class apart*, deserving protection of their civil rights as outlined by the Fourteenth Amendment. On the flip side of the team's argument stand Mexican Americans afraid of *not* being considered Caucasian. If labeled *colored*, they'll have to endure discrimination reserved for African Americans and suffer Jim Crow laws that will further oppress them. It's a dilemma that will split Mexican American communities, leading to volatile confrontations.

Adding to this dilemma, the team has another problem that will plague them even as they put together a brilliant case. Gus Garcia, the lanky, green-eyed Texan who could be mistaken for a movie star, has a drinking problem and he's hard to control. In fact, his actions on the night prior to their oral argument before the nine Supreme Court Justices, puts all their months of hard work in jeopardy. Garcia somehow escapes, after a raucous party he decides to throw in their suite. No amount of lecturing from the serious, hard-working Carlos Cadena seems to help him. He disappears to continue his mayhem, and appears drunk out of his mind at the suite only hours before they must present themselves before the Court. The men are so angry with him, they throw him into a cold shower with his clothes on, and order up strong, black coffee to sober him up.

On January 11, 1954, the Texas team heads for the Supreme Court, with Gus Garcia, now dressed and dealing with a major hangover. As Carlos Cadena begins the opening argument, Garcia, barely mentally present, suddenly stiffens when he hears one of the Justices identify Mexican Americans as "greasers," and asks Cadena if they are real Americans, and do they speak English. Now awake and indignant, Garcia begins a brief but dynamic historical account of who Mexican Americans are, insisting in a voice rich with passion and conviction, "My people were in Texas before Sam Houston, that wetback from Tennessee." Garcia spins a tale that holds the court in rapt attention, even after the red light goes on, signifying that the team's oral argument must end. It is Justice Earl Warren who leans across the bench, and says, "Continue, Mr. Garcia."

On May 3, 1954 the United States Supreme Court, once again officiated by Chief Justice Warren, rules in *Hernández v. Texas*, that the litigant, Pete Hernández, will get a new trial before a jury of his peers. The Texas team successfully convinced the nine Supreme Court Justices that Mexican Americans are a "class apart" and a population that requires protection under the Equal Protection Clause of the Fourteenth Amendment. It's a victory for Mexican Americans throughout the nation, and the first time Mexican Americans are seen as a distinct group with a history extending many centuries to the founding of America. As a result of the Court's decision, Pete Hernández gets a new trial, and is judged by a jury of his peers. His reconviction was expected, but his case made history—Mexican Americans are a *class apart*.

The Texas team is hailed as heroes throughout the U.S., yet Gus Garcia, plagued by alcoholism and mental problems, eventually loses the confidence of his fellow team members and ends up destroyed by his addiction. On June 3, 1964, forgotten and homeless, he dies alone on a park bench. Still, his passion and love for his people led the way for the Supreme Court's reassessment of Mexican Americans, and the founding of a new era of protest and activism that will engage a young Raul Yzaguirre in a face-off with school administrators.

INSTRUMENT OF TORTURE

Punishment for speaking Spanish is swift and painful at Vida N. Clover for Yzaguirre and his fellow classmates who don't comply with the school rules. The goal of making Mexican American students "mainstream Americans" is something adhered to by PSJA. Although labeled as "Caucasians," under Texas law, Mexican American voices are nonetheless effectively silenced in school by *de facto* segregation.

"First they told you not to do it anymore, then they stopped you from playing outdoors and brought you into the classroom and made you sit in your chair by yourself," Yzaguirre says recalling in detail the humiliating process of shaming done to those accused of speaking Spanish. "The third grade teacher had a very powerful weapon, she had this stick that had holes drilled into it. It was an instrument of torture. She spanked us on the behind. I don't know if she ever asked for parental permission, nobody stopped her. As we got older the punishment was more relaxed. They found it harder to suppress us. I think the practice of *de facto* segregation had more to do with justification. Civil rights leaders had won several cases in desegregation by that time and the research showed they had to have a rationale not based on ethnicity. The rationale was we didn't know how to speak English. We were not segregated by ethnicity but by our ability to speak English. I knew some English, but they didn't put me with Anglos, they put me with Mexicanos. Some kids who didn't know Spanish at all were put in with us too. We spoke Spanish on the playground anyway. Teachers couldn't see us or hear us there. Those who didn't speak good English sat in the back of the room."

An intelligent student, Yzaguirre didn't consider himself studious and often saw school as a time to have fun and develop friendships. There were times he had to fight for survival against local gang members who would lie in wait for him outside of school. Unwilling to report their threats, he learned how to fight—a quick learner, his skill at throwing punches and kicks proved to be one of his best assets.

"There was a little gang close to where I lived, and the guys wanted me to be part of the gang, and I didn't want to, so I had to fight. Los Martinez brothers were the gang members, maybe they were *pachucos* (distinctive clothes and use of slang). It was a big family of migrant workers, and they lived in *las colonias*. This went on from the third grade to the ninth. I never told any teachers. Six years I had to put up with them. It was my own world."

At Clover Elementary, Yzaguirre recalls Mrs. McCafferty, a fourth-grade teacher, announcing a district-wide writing contest. To everyone's surprise, he submitted a story and won 2nd place, thus garnering the attention of teachers and administrators early on for his skills at using, of all things, the English language. "I think I wrote about a bear, or something like that. Mrs. McCafferty kept mentioning it to everyone. They made a big deal about it because no Mexicano had ever won a district-wide writing contest."

Yzaguirre's passion for learning was voracious, extending to all subjects and most specifically to science and history. "My worst subject was band. I was last chair for four years in a row on trumpet. I had no musical talent whatsoever but I enjoyed being in band." Later, his interests shift to baseball and football and he meets Coach Cheney, nicknamed "El Viejo," (old man) who also functions as the high school driving instructor.

Walking to nearby Clover Elementary only six blocks away from his grandfather's house with friends Armando Sloss and Ted Treviño, allows Raul time to cultivate neighborhood friendships at an early age, which in high school will prove vital as he begins to organize Mexican American students in protests against unfair school policies. "We would fight with each other at times, and do all kinds of things together like swim in canals and play baseball. There was an older kid who had polio, Eli Sanchez. Eli was very interesting. He spoke perfect English, but he couldn't do the work because he had been in the hospital so many times. Eli had to drop out of school. His upper body had lots of strength and he could sing and do lots of things, but his legs were withered."

Throughout his school years, Yzaguirre continues to work at Morin's Ice House, and later any spare time he has is taken up by his work as a Junior GI Forum organizer. "After school, I'd go to the ice house and take care of customers. They would come by and want twenty-five pounds of ice or crushed ice for parties and I would sell it to them." By 1956, Yzaguirre's work at the ice house takes on new demands after the death of his grandfather; still he hangs on, stabilizing his life around his grandmother and Uncle Pete.

"I think in some ways we were insulated because my grandfather had business on the Anglo side of town. My closest cousins were half-Anglo, so we didn't see as much discrimination as other folks did. I do remember one time I was helping someone with ice. The lady turned around and said to me, 'You're very nice. You speak English. You're not like those other Mexicans.' She meant to pay me a compliment, but I realized it wasn't a compliment at all."

Inspired to think about his future for the first time in middle school, Yzaguirre remembers his fifth-grade teacher walking around the classroom asking the students what they wanted to become. "I said I wanted to become a scientist and she said 'Great, but you have to improve your math.' And I thought I don't like math. I'm okay in math, but I don't like it, so I guess I won't be a great scientist because I'm not fond of math. She made me think of what I wanted to do with my life."

An incident of racial discrimination in sixth grade causes Yzaguirre to realize that the way people think about one another ethnically is something at times bred from within and acted upon unconsciously. Fellow Anglo classmate, George Morley, taught him a lesson he would not soon forget. "If we finished our work early, we were allowed to go out to the playground. One day, I was there with my friends George Morley and the twins, Melissa and Melinda Hudson. George had a crush on one of the twins and asked one of them 'Who do you like?' And she said, Ricky Cavazos, or something like that and George said, 'Oh my God, how could you possibly want to be with a Mexican?' And then he realized I was there, and he apologized. My reaction was to ask him. What are you talking about? What's wrong with you? Later he moved to an adjacent school, and I saw him in my senior year, playing football. He was center and I was inside linebacker. The center has his head down to get the ball down center, and the inside linebacker positions himself with his head up and hits him. I hit him a lot that night. George, remember me? He said, 'Yes,' and I said, yeah, but you're going to remember me a lot more before the night is over."

The George Morley story ended on a good note. Years later he contacted Yzaguirre through the alumni email. He had become a school principal and they conversed as friends, never once mentioning the beating George received on the football field, nor George's comment to the Hudson twins.

THE FIVE MINUTE BOOK REPORT

"Some very specific things happened to me in high school. One of them was a teacher, Mrs. Brooks, who said I should learn a trade because that's all I could expect to become, a mechanic or carpenter," Yzaguirre says in describing how most teachers at his high school felt about Mexican American students. Attending high school alongside her brother, Yzaguirre's sister, Tere, remembers the derogatory remarks made by many teachers at PSJA. "When we were in high school teachers were very discriminatory towards Mexicans. We were often insulted by our teachers, as they knew there would be no repercussions."

One year ahead of Yzaguirre, Helen Cavazos, active as the head cheerleader of the school and a member of several school organizations, recalls the difficulty students had in connecting with the majority of Anglo teachers.

"Discrimination was the sign of the times," Cavazos says. "I remember one teacher, Emma Martinez, the only Hispanic teacher at the school who looked after me. She was the Spanish teacher and sponsor for the cheerleaders. Most of the other teachers favored Anglo students, and gave good grades even to the Anglo trouble-makers. At times, we were called 'Latin Americans,' because 'Mexicans' was considered a dirty word. Our history teacher was biased. We asked how come there was no history of Mexican Americans. We knew the information was skewed."

The first time Yzaguirre encounters teachers of color is on a high school campus. "We had a band teacher, Mr. Gamboa. And we had two young ladies from the community who worked at the school. They both lived a couple of blocks from where I lived. They would see me coming down the hall and they would turn around and go the other way. They were interested in keeping a certain professional distance. These were ladies that I grew up with and we kidded around a lot, but they didn't want to kid with me at school, so they would avoid me."

Making plans to pursue a college education, Yzaguirre is disappointed by the behavior of high school counselors who do nothing to help Mexican American students navigate through the maze of scholarships and information needed to pursue a college degree. Instead, they steer them towards vocational careers, bypassing vital college information. "All the counselors did was give everyone forms to fill out for applications to colleges. There was no counseling whatsoever. As a matter of fact, I'm arrogant enough to think I could have made the Merit Scholarship but I had no idea how to apply for it. Even though in my sophomore year I got one of the highest scores they had ever seen on the college tests, I was not offered the Merit Scholarship. It was not for me or any other Latinos."

The same discriminatory attitude exhibited by the school counselors and the majority of Anglo teachers was practiced by Mrs. Brooks, Yzaguirre's English teacher, who soon finds herself embroiled in a battle of wits with a young Yzaguirre who challenges her classroom policies.

"Mrs. Brooks was very tough on everybody. She was very precise about teaching us to express ourselves and I did well in her class. I had her for two or three classes in my four years in high school and in my senior year, she taught English Literature class. She started the year by saying that ten percent of our grade would be based on book reports we would be required to submit."

An avid reader, Yzaguirre found the works of Hemingway especially engaging in high school. "He represented a man's world to me, depicting strong male characters who lived up to their highest ideals." Attracted to historical works, he read books on the lives of Thomas Jefferson, Lincoln, Napoleon, Alexander the Great, Julius Cesar, Benito Juárez, Emiliano Zapata and Eleanor Roosevelt. Also of interest were *A Tale of Two Cities* by Charles Dickens; and *The Economic Origins of the Constitution* by James Beard. Anything on history and government caught his eye, and helped to establish a foundation for understanding the workings of government, rule of law and how ordinary people can impact change.

"Mrs. Brooks had a list of books we had to read, and I realized that nobody was seriously reading the books, just copying from each other or reading a synopsis. Nobody was reading three hundred to four hundred- page books. It was all a charade; nobody did the book reports honestly. They went and bought either comic books of the books or the Cliff Notes or copies from somebody else. It was all hypocrisy, and I didn't want to participate in it. As a matter of fact, I did some of the reports for some of my friends. So I knew it was a charade, and they got good grades on the book reports that I did for them, but I wasn't going to turn my own in. So I decided not to participate in the charade."

"The book reports in their totality represented ten percent of the grade. I didn't do the book reports and expected Mrs. Brooks to take off ten percent of my grade, ten points off, so that would make a ninety percent; but she gave me a zero, and flunked me. She wasn't playing by her own rules. My grades were very good, high A's, but at the end of the semester, she gave me an 'F.' I always thought if I paid the consequences, then she shouldn't change the rules on me. English was a required course to graduate, and mind you I had quite a personality in school by that time, because I had already organized a walkout and things like that. So, the principal Mr. Henderson called me in and said, 'I understand you flunked a course.' I was stunned because it was a large school and how would he know one of his pupils failed one semester. I said yes, and he asked me what happened and I told him what I did and why I did it and he said, 'Let me talk to Mrs. Brooks,' and pretty soon he came back and said, 'It's very interesting to have a dispute between a teacher and a student. There are always two sides to a story, but in this case the facts are all the same, there is no question as to why you did it and what you did and what the result was. But I've got good news for you, Mrs. Brooks will let you do the book reports, and if you do them in the next two weeks you'll pass the course.'"

"I said, you don't understand, I'm not going to do that. You lay down the rules, so I should at least get an A- or a B+. Book reports were only ten percent of the grade, and that was the deal. Stick to it. He tried to convince me to take the deal, and I wouldn't do it and told him to do whatever he needed to do. So he said, 'Let me talk to Mrs. Brooks again.' He called her back in and she walked into his office and said, 'Okay, here's what we're going to do. You have one week to do one book report.' And I knew this was the last deal, and I wasn't going to get another chance. I said, okay, give me a pencil and paper, and I will give you a book report in five minutes. I gave them a book report in five minutes. And that was the end of that for the time being. I felt good because I had won, but I felt bad because I had had to compromise."

The internal conflict Yzaguirre experiences over the "five minute" book report done to satisfy Mrs. Brooks' class requirements, haunts him as graduation day approaches, and at the same time gives him the fuel he needs to continue organizing student protests, setting him up for more serious confrontations with school officials. Many years later, he faced Mrs. Brooks again for the last time, and his encounter with her was not what he expected.

"Fast forward to years later. I was now the program director for the Southwest Regional Office of Equal Opportunity and we had a big grant, for the state of Texas. The governor of Texas at that time had asked the president of the United States, LBJ, for some money. He was granted fifteen million dollars for the state of Texas. The district hadn't been evaluated for two or three years, and I was in charge of going out and visiting all the districts we were funding and I went to my own school district. I told the superintendent I was there to evaluate the school system. It was the same superintendent I had sued and petitioned before as a student. He recognized me and was very surprised. He said I had a *carte blanche* to go to any classroom and any school that used materials and programs that were federally funded. He found someone to escort me, and when I walked out the door I asked him to take me to Mrs. Brooks' classroom. I didn't know what I was going to say. I just wanted her to know that this kid she had counseled to go into carpentry or auto mechanics had not done that, and had made it. So I walked in and surprised myself because I thought I would lay it on her but instead, I ended up telling her that in spite of all our differences, I wanted to thank her because she was tough on me and made me a better writer, and I appreciated that. I was sort of watching myself go through this and didn't know what to expect. In the end, I decided that rather than lower her, I would be nice to an old lady who probably did what she thought was best for us. I thanked her. I thanked Mrs. Brooks for her craft as a teacher. She made sure students had the right tone and style for their writing, and that the style was rich and vibrant and disciplined."

As president of the science club, Yzaguirre took on another leadership role during his high school years and it brought him face-to-face with another set of rigid classroom expectations. Unknown to him at the time, he would spend most of his military career in a lab, meet his wife in a lab, and excel in science. High school provided him his first look into the intricate world of science, enabling him to nurture a life-long dedication to the study of scientific disciplines.

"The biology teacher and I got off on the wrong foot. She started the course by saying we had to go out and catch butterflies, chloroform them and mount them on boards. I said I'm not going to do that, so she gave me an 'F' for the first six weeks. But then she said, 'I see something in you, so why don't you come and sit up front from now on.' She took me and other students on trips that were very interesting, and kept us after class. She taught me about biology, a lot about parapsychology, hypnotism, rocketry, and I became president of the science club. We worked on space research in 1956 before Sputnik.

Everybody laughed at us, and when Sputnik came on the scene, everybody thought we were ahead of our time. She became very important to me and was someone who led me to do some serious studies in biology."

Deciding to try his luck in the arts, Yzaguirre next joined the drama club and was given a lead part in one of the dramatic performances; but due to his work at the ice house he was unable to attend rehearsals and dropped out of the club. He went on to join the Literary Society and at times members published their works for the campus literary magazine; but the prospect of publishing held little interest for him at the time. It would be many years before Yzaguirre gained a true appreciation for arts in the world of education.

"I started out as a civil rights activist, my focus was on jobs, housing, civil rights, education, what I call the hard stuff, and I had a disdain for the arts. I thought it was for people who didn't have anything else to do, it was a diversion from the real issues. I have now come to believe just the opposite and I think through this change of mind I've become a convert, like Paul on his way to Damascus. I am now an advocate for the arts, because the arts capture our souls and define who we are, where we've been and where we want to be in a way that can't be done through anything else as effectively as the arts."

One night, while playing trumpet in the school band, Yzaguirre finds himself aggravated at the football team who seem to be doing everything wrong that night. Not particularly interested in joining the football team, he crosses another threshold before the game is over, and soon finds himself playing on the team.

"They were the Bears, and we had a bad team that year. I got into the emotion of the game and I started yelling, come on guys get on with it. You can do better than that, and words like that. A guy next to me, said, 'You know if you think you can do better why don't you get out there yourself?' I said, you know what, you're absolutely right. So I joined the football team. My grandmother didn't want me to be on the team and came to my practice and embarrassed me by pulling me out of the football field by the ear in front of everybody. It embarrassed the hell out of me, but I went back. My uncle Pete, who was like my older brother, conspired with me. We kept it a secret until I was well-entrenched in it. My grandmother never came to the football games, but my mother and father did. They were okay with me playing."

SUSPICIONS COME TRUE

Excited to begin her work as a high school teacher, Laura Pollard arrives in the Rio Grande Valley from Kentucky. She's a speech teacher and is looking forward to a year of setting up debate teams, and watching students learn the challenging world of argument, debate and sticking up for their ideals. She's heard the students at PSJA are tough, some are Mexican Americans from poor barrio communities—maybe even gang members who will disrupt her classes. She's prepared to take on the impossible. An idealist at heart, she is slim, attractive, and has a knack for engaging even the most obstinate students in the thrill of learning and expanding their minds.

Mr. Henderson, the principal at PSJA, is suspicious of the young teacher with a heart for students. There are walkouts going on at PSJA and protests, most of them led by a student who has proven to be quite a challenge for administrators—Raul Yzaguirre. They can't quite get a handle on him, and he's obviously skilled as a leader. Maybe Ms. Pollard will back up the kids—make them think about justice and liberty and they'll get stronger in their protests. The media loves conflict and will jump on the story, and the result will be that the students will be harder to handle and parents will come to board meetings and demand answers. The whole country was on the move; civil rights issues were exploding everywhere. Keeping his doubts to himself, Mr. Henderson hires Ms. Pollard anyway, and the school board approves his decision; but in the back of his mind, his suspicions remain on edge about what she might do. Mr. Henderson's suspicions are about to come true.

LEGACY OF A TEACHER: LAURA POLLARD

"The teacher who had the most influence on my life was Ms. Laura Pollard, an attractive and vivacious young woman who was newly married and was the wife of the chorus director. I signed up for debate in my sophomore year, the same year my grandfather died. They put me in her class with all Anglos and seniors. I was the only Mexicano, and the only sophomore. Ms. Pollard worked us to death. We did Shakespeare, extemporaneous speaking and debate, in class and statewide. I found myself competing with the best folks in the state. That gave me the self-confidence to tackle other things. We entered every debate contest, and everyone in the class was well-educated in speaking and in parliamentary procedure. I learned parliamentary procedure, and that has helped me all my life. I became the captain of the debate team and we won contests all over the state. I came to realize that the students in the class were the valedictorian, salutatorian, the senior class president, all the beautiful people, all the smart people in the entire school were in that class, and I could pin them all. That made a big difference in my life."

Tere witnessed, first-hand, her brother's metamorphosis, as he took on the challenges of debate and social issues oppressing the Mexican American student population. "Raul excelled at speech and placed in state competitions while at the same time becoming a community advocate and seeking change in policies that were unfair and discriminatory. His speech teacher was dismissed as a consequence of his excelling in his work of advocating as he became skilled due to her teaching."

"I was involved in debate groups," recalls Helen Cavazos. "Raul could beat me every time at debate. That's where he learned his negotiating skills. He seemed very sure of himself, and stood his ground firmly."

In spite of his success as an expert debater, Cavazos saw the other side of Raul—the quiet listener. She could have never imagined that in the future he would become a national leader and a master communicator. "I don't remember Raul wanting to be a leader. He tended to be quiet and someone who wanted things to be right and people to be treated with dignity and respect."

Acting as the captain of the debate team that won the majority of their encounters, Yzaguirre's favorite part of speech class was extemporaneous speaking. "It felt better, thinking on your feet. It was more exciting. In debate, you had one topic and you debated that for an entire year, presenting facts and figures. The same type of debates went on all year. In extemporaneous speaking you picked out a topic from a hat. You didn't know what you would get. That was more exciting. I loved it. The 1956 debate topic was: Should the federal government provide funding for local public education? That was it. And to this day all the arguments for and against are still viable. We're still debating that issue with No Child Left Behind, and other programs. Ms. Pollard's class had a lifetime impact on me. Debating in front of one to three judges and others who wanted to be there was very challenging."

THE STORY OF MS. LAURA. Pollard, the most influential teacher in Yzaguirre's life, would end with an act of injustice. "They did not renew Ms. Pollard's contract the next year. She was the best teacher the school had ever had, but the system reacted against her," Yzaguirre says, remembering with sadness the loss of Ms. Pollard at PSJA.

Armed with the debating skills she taught him, along with his passion for tackling a variety of crucial issues, and having been influenced by such magnetic personalities as Dr. Hector P. García; Ed Idar, Jr., "El Chicote," and Bob Sanchez, Yzaguirre felt ready to take on a new level of social commitment. The year he met Ms. Pollard was the same year his grandfather died, and Yzaguirre was sorely in need of renewal. Ms. Pollard's love for students ignited his courage, inspiring him to develop skills that would launch his career as a formidable civil rights advocate.

For the rest of his high school years, Yzaguirre concentrated on organizing students to protest unfair school policies, and it all began casually with a popularity contest and voting for the Belle and Beau of the Junior/Senior Prom. Organizing his first constituency, he learned how to battle for the rights of Mexican Americans to enjoy fair treatment at school. At 16 years old, he confronted the PSJA school board, head-on, over *de facto* segregation, and asked tough questions that they found impossible to answer. The hiring of Ms. Laura Pollard had paid off—not for Mr. Henderson and the other administrators at PSJA—but for the students.

9

FIVE HUNDRED SIGNATURES

Raul led a walk out in his junior year in high school and was consequently expelled. Mom talked to the principal and he was allowed back in school. Some of the teachers loved Raul and others absolutely hated him. There were very few who were indifferent.

—Tere Yzaguirre Tijerina

TRIGGERED BY CHAOS

Yzaguirre's idea of leadership begins to take shape in childhood. He recalls an early memory that triggered a sense of responsibility and compassion for others and later inspired him to take on leadership roles in high school, military life, and in his evolvement as a civil rights leader.

"I had a recurring thought as a child. I didn't like bullies. Bullies were about taking advantage of people as I remember and they were cruel. I was maybe four years old and I remember a guy being very mean to dogs. Our dog's name was Chang Kai Check, but we called him Chow, and I remember crying and hugging Chow and saying, I'll never be that way. I promise you that I'll never be mean or cruel to animals or to people."

"As a kid, we played games and I was always testing things to do. I was always the leader, but I don't think I thought of myself consciously as a leader. It just kind of happened. When I joined the Air Force I made up my mind that I had to do this for my country, but when I got in, I didn't want to volunteer for anything. I found out later that things were going bad in basic training just like when I was in school. Things weren't going well. So I had to speak up and tell them we had to make changes. I became a flight leader in basic training, but I purposely didn't want to volunteer for anything, yet the chaos forced me to lead and I became a leader. I guess I realized I can't stand chaos, I can't understand inefficiencies. It forced me to start making suggestions and get more forceful. If all was going fine, I'd stay in the background, but if things were in chaos I intervened."

Over the years, chaos becomes Yzaguirre's adversary. It's the shadow that pursues him and makes him spring into action at the most unexpected times. It stirs in him the lessons he learned from his grandfather about decency and integrity and standing up for justice, and once he's in the midst of chaos, the battle is on, and he won't leave without a fight.

Unfair policies at PSJA stir up Yzaguirre's nemesis, as he engages in defending Mexican American students, sometimes referred to as "Americans of Mexican descent," from discriminatory school policies that keep them locked in destructive stereotypes. "We were very careful about using one of those terms. But in the barrio, the words, *raza*, Chicanos, *vatos* and Chicanada were also used. Chicanos was a slang word while *pocho* was an insult, and for *cholo*, we used the word, *pachuco*. The *pachucos* dressed in khakis and hats, and wore *cadenas* (chains). It wasn't so much the dress as the speech that set them apart, *ese ven pa ca* (Hey, dude, come here.) You became a part of their culture by using their language."

Accused of starting trouble at PSJA, Yzaguirre is blamed for leading gang members to start fights on his high school campus, and later finds out that once chaos begins, nothing but direct confrontation can resolve it.

THE POPULARITY CONTEST

Raul Yzaguirre's role as a "rebel" begins in 1956, as he enters his junior year at PSJA High. Identified as a "class apart," by the 1954 Supreme Court's ruling in *Hernández v. Texas*, Mexican Americans in San Juan now feel empowered to seek educational equality for their children. In high school, Yzaguirre is at the center of walkouts, which consist of students not coming to school on specific days, or cutting classes. The absence of the students is significant enough to make the local newspapers. Parents are stirred up by the trouble that reporters say is caused by Mexican American gang members who are starting fights on campus. The state of Texas gets on the bandwagon and wants answers for the money they're losing for students not in attendance. Overnight, Mexicans and Anglos in San Juan take opposing sides.

The school principal, Mr. Henderson, is infuriated by the reports and minimizes the protests, telling news reporters that it's a bunch of "bad apples" that are causing the trouble. He knows who's at the center of the turmoil. He has his secretary pull Raul Yzaguirre out of class. In his office he stares grimly at Raul who sits across from him, looking unperturbed. He wants the kid to know he has zero tolerance for what's going on at the school.

"Stop giving gang members orders to start fights! I know you're the ringleader," he accuses.

Yzaguirre shakes his head, "I'm not the ringleader. I'm not giving them orders to fight."

He's actually telling Mr. Henderson the truth. He's not the ringleader of the gangs, but the protests and walkouts—now that's another matter.

"The newspaper reported gang fights at the school, but did not talk about discrimination or ethnic tension. They never interviewed me," Yzaguirre says. "They had no interest in what was causing the unrest. They wanted to blame everything on Mexican gang members and avoid the discrimination going on at the school."

Polarized by years of racial tension, Anglo and Mexican American students often clashed at PSJA High. For years, Anglo students headed the yearly traditions and held the reigns of power and control over all major activities at the school. "I had been trying to organize Mexican American students, but with no success. I wanted us to make demands for more Latino teachers. I challenged history teachers. We had to change the curriculum. Texas history painted a negative image of Latinos, and specifically of Mexican Americans. But what finally got the students excited was selecting people for the popularity contest," Yzaguirre says, referring to the beginning of his involvement with students that would launch his career as a community activist.

"In my sophomore year, we elected a student council that promised to change the rules on how they would elect students for the school popularity contest. The class favorites, the Belle and Beau, were elected every year by students and crowned at the Junior/Senior Prom. Although we were the majority at eighty percent, all the popular people with pictures in the yearbook were Anglos. So we made an issue on that because we also had nominations. The Anglos would get together and find out who they would vote for, and we just voted for our friends. The Anglo strategy worked and each year the favorites were Anglo. I was the Parliamentarian of the class, and brought it up for a vote, and the Anglos didn't want to give in, so we started a fight, back and forth, we started yelling at each other. The principal, Mr. Henderson said, 'We might have to have an Anglo and Mexican American popularity contest.' And I told him we had already voted to have only one contest."

As Yzaguirre confronts school officials, tempers are roused and fights begin both in and out of school. "Anglos got together with chains and tire tools and went over to the Mexican side of town but police stopped them, so there was no big problem. Coach Cheney, "El Viejo," was one of the only ones who defended me. The Assistant Principal, Mr. Ward, would call me in and say, 'You're responsible for everything that's going on.' He felt that as the Parliamentarian of the class, I had to enforce the Robert's Rules of Order and bring the issue to the student body for a vote. Mr. Ward would call me in everyday and accuse me for all the riots and walkouts and then he would call in the gangs, and would say, 'We know what's happening, and we know Raul is your leader. And it has to stop.' And they said, 'Raul's not our leader.' Then they came to me, and said, 'Hey, maybe you are our leader, tell us what to do.' So the Latinos got together and we said, okay, we'll play the game. At the next election all Latinos were elected, and I was one of them. We had the greater vote, but we always voted our consciences. Now we had meetings, and we had a plan and a strategy. We were united. I was voted the class favorite in my junior year."

Yzaguirre's sister, Tere, remembers her brother creating quite a stir in school by standing up for the rights of his fellow Mexican American students. "Raul led a walkout in his junior year in high school and was consequently expelled," Tere says. "Mom talked to the principal and he was allowed back in school. Some of the teachers loved Raul and others absolutely hated him. There were very few who were indifferent."

Throughout this turbulent time, Yzaguirre actively worked in the community as a Junior GI Forum leader and organized a chapter of students who worked in correlation with the Forum's goals. "I started organizing for the Forum at age fifteen. We had district and state meetings, and I organized the youth conventions state-wide. We had people like Congressman Henry B. Gonzalez, Ed Idar, Jr., "El Chicote"; James de Anda, a federal judge; Chris Aldrete; Bob Sanchez, and of course, my mentor, Dr. Hector P. García. I was hungry for everything they had to say. I listened carefully, and began to form an opinion about government and the nature of discrimination in society and how people are oppressed."

On weekends, Yzaguirre took to chauffeuring Dr. García around in his stylish Cadillac. The Cadillac was a luxurious anomaly, out of place along the dirt roads of Texas's rural communities. Its sleek and fancy appearance seemed like something you'd expect in Dallas or Houston, not cruising through agricultural communities of poor Mexican Americans. Dr. García used his Cadillac to visit clients in makeshift clinics that dotted the farthest reaches of small Texas towns with no street lights, much less a major highway. He was there to ease his patients' medical needs, and to bring down fire upon them in the form of his own passionate rhetoric—a call to Mexican Americans to stand up for their rights as American citizens. And who better to chauffer him around than the gutsy Valley kid, Raul Yzaguirre?

When Dr. García spotted migrant farmworkers in the fields, he'd say, "Pull over, Raul. Let's go talk to them." Without hesitation, Raul would slow the Cadillac down, and could see far in the distance that already the bodies bent over the hard labor in the fields were standing upright, and waving their hands in greeting.

"The Cadillac was packed with medical supplies, food stuffs, water and voter registration information. Dr. García was there to unify a community living in poverty and suffering unfair treatment at every turn," Yzaguirre recalls. "The farmworkers were unable to pay the poll tax imposed on them by the state of Texas so those who could vote, had never voted. The doctor was there to make changes come true for them. He was there to rally them to join in the struggle for equality and an end to segregation and the shame of living as second-class citizens. I was proud to be in the driver's seat. It reminded me of the days I spent with my grandfather moving the pick-up truck every few yards while he delivered ice. I think my grandfather would have been proud of the driver's job I had with Dr. García."

FIRST GRASSROOTS CAMPAIGN

As tensions rise at PSJA High, Forum members decide they want nothing to do with the school walkouts. They feel the fights are getting out of hand and refuse to take responsibility for any injuries that might happen as a result of the violence. "Older veterans in the GI Forum said, 'We don't want you to associate this with the GI Forum. We don't want to be involved in your fights.' They were very cautious. Some parents supported us. They had been through it," Yzaguirre recalls.

Sensing himself at odds with members of the GI Forum who were beginning to feel uncomfortable with his leadership role, Yzaguirre had no choice but to step back a bit and reevaluate his work with the Forum. "I found myself in a dilemma. I was rising in status in the American GI Forum as a youth leader and thus competing with adults. Some of the adults resented the fact that I was a youth and a non-veteran, leading an adult veteran's organization."

Disappointed with the Forum's position on the walkouts and with the controversy sparked by his leadership, Yzaguirre, nonetheless, forges on, securing help for his next venture from attorney and Forum member, Bob Sanchez, who writes up a legal petition on behalf of parents in the PSJA School District who are seeking pre-school education for their children. The petition is a direct hit against *de facto* segregation that keeps Mexican American students isolated in primary grades until they learn English. Why not start them learning English as preschoolers? Yzaguirre asks this crucial question, and his logic makes sense; but chaos, the shadowy figure he can't seem to lose, laps at his heels.

Caught up in a busy whirlwind of attending classes, working at the ice house after school, and the usual adolescent preoccupation with sports, parties and the opposite sex, Raul still manages to continue his role as a student leader at PSJA High. Then one day, a Texas law, describing the protocol for parents to request pre-school services from Texas school districts, catches his eye.

"The State of Texas had passed a law that said that any school district that got a petition signed by fifty or more parents who had children who were five years old, could obligate the school system to implement a pre-school program. I went to Bob Sanchez, my mentor and an attorney from the GI Forum, and I told him I wanted to get a petition to get the pre-school programs implemented in San Juan. That would help our students learn English and get them started so they wouldn't be one or two grades behind the Anglo students. So he wrote a legal petition and we not only got fifty signatures, we got five hundred."

Yzaguirre enlisted his best friend, Armando Sloss and a few other friends to join him in his campaign to secure signatures. "Armando looked like Rock Hudson," Yzaguirre, says, describing his childhood friend. "We went hunting together, but mostly we chased girls. We played football together, until Armando found out he had a heart murmur and couldn't play anymore. Years later, in his mid-thirties, he died of heart complications just before a scheduled heart surgery. School came easy for me, but Armando struggled in school, and didn't graduate. I felt guilty and talked him into going with me to all the organizing. We only lived a couple of blocks from each other. He helped me get the five hundred signatures."

Together, Yzaguirre and Sloss formed an early version of M.E.Ch.A (Movimiento Estudiantil Chican@ de Aztlán) an organization officially founded in the 60's to promote Chicano unity and empowerment through political action. The word *mecha*, the pronunciation of the group's name, refers to the word "match" in English. The group's motto became, *La Unión Hace La Fuerza*, (Unity Makes Strength).

Not sponsored by a teacher, nor having official status for the school club he organized, Yzaguirre is limited by what he can actually do on the school campus, so he adjusts his campaign strategy and sets his sights on the community. His campaign for educational reform is grassroots—knocking on doors and getting support from the community. "We went from house to house and asked people if they had children five years of age. We showed them a copy of the law, and asked if they would sign the petition, and I don't recall anyone saying no. It was just a matter of finding the people. They were all Latinos."

Armed with the 500 signatures and the legal petition prepared by Bob Sanchez, Yzaguirre is now ready for the next step, which is to contact the president of the school board and get the petition into his hands. "I called up the school board president. His son was in one of my classes and I said, Mr. Gross, I have a petition to give to you. And he said, 'Okay come down to my house and I'll take it from you.' So I did. And I asked him, when I could expect an answer. And he said, 'I'll schedule a meeting and I'll call you.'"

The night of the school board meeting comes too quickly for Yzaguirre. No one else opts to go with him, and he knows that Mr. Gross has offered him no choice in the matter. If he wants to attend the school board meeting it will be on Mr. Gross's terms.

BLUE JEANS AND THREE PIECE SUITS

After a long day at school, Raul Yzaguirre still has work to do at Morin's Ice House. It's a warm spring day in San Juan, and he knows customers will want to buy ice, so the place will be busy. He's been handling things as best he can at the ice house, helping his Uncle Pete, both of them running the place after his grandfather's death. But it's hard work, and now he's worried he won't make it on time to present his case before the school board.

He has plans to present the petition Bob Sanchez drew up for the school board and then he'll hand them the 500 signatures he and his friends collected to prove to them that the community needs preschools in the PSJA School District. Of course, he knows all the parents who signed are Mexican Americans, but they are the ones targeted by the unfair practice of *de facto* segregation. It's time to start teaching English early to Mexican American students so they won't have to be separated from fluent Anglo speakers. But how will he convince the school board? The petition refers to the Texas law that permits parents with preschool children to demand a preschool from the District with only 50 parent signatures. This will put the case on the table in straight-forward, legal language. Yzaguirre's ability to sway the school board members will depend on the merits of the petition, but there's a bigger problem he has to face that night. There's no one there to back him up. He would have more clout if parents and students had filled the Board Room. Even his friends didn't want to join him, in spite of all the hard work they did in collecting the signatures in the first place. GI Forum members also declined to attend and his constituency, poor parents from the barrios, couldn't be counted on to challenge the school district. He'd have to face the school board alone.

"I didn't have time to change my clothes, so I walked into the school board meeting with a room full of lawyers in three-piece suits, and all these sixty year-old school board members and staff, wearing a T-shirt, blue jeans and my work boots. I was playing lawyer for my constituency," Yzaguirre recalls, "and I presented my case on behalf of the parents and their children, and the lawyers presented their case. They went back and forth as to why they could and couldn't do it. They were polite but hostile and called me 'son' a couple of times, patronizing me. I was sixteen years old and wasn't exactly a big figure there. Finally, they said they didn't have the budget for it and no money to do it, so they just said, 'Sue us.' And of course I didn't have the resources to sue them."

Sitting at the back of the room, three Mexican janitors listened attentively as Gavino Morin's grandson presented his petition before the PSJA School Board. "I remember they were the only Mexicans in the room besides myself," Raul recalls. The janitors had seen very few Mexicanos come before the school board to petition for anything, much less a teenager from PSJA High. Sitting side by side in their khaki uniforms, each man wondered at young Yzaguirre's courage. His voice reached them, articulate, and masterful in the way he explained the petition and the Texas law that backed it up to the stern looking school board members. There was no fumbling or pauses, only the steady cadence of his voice. The custodians knew nothing about Ms. Laura Pollard and the debating skills she had taught him. They only knew that Gavino Morin's grandson had made the school board nervous, and they watched as two attorneys held counsel among themselves before they answered him.

In their minds, the attorneys were doing exactly what the PSJA District wanted them to do. How dare this Mexican kid from the Valley think he could come into their arena and threaten them with a Texas law! The signatures meant nothing; they were from poor Mexican Americans who had no influence, so that wouldn't be a problem. They figured they'd be rid of the kid tonight and be paid for their services by the district. The attorneys had no way of knowing what would really happen. Not too far into the future, there would be schools in Texas named after Raul Yzaguirre and pre-schools operating in each one. Unbeknownst to the attorneys at the time—they had met their match.

"LATER ON, THE SCHOOL SUPERINTENDENT came into my life. 'I remember you', he said, 'you cost us a lot of money, because the school district had to retain lawyers.'"

By then, Yzaguirre had chalked up his first encounter with the powerful and pompous as, "A good experience for a sixteen year-old kid."

Later, things took a significant turn for the PSJA School Board, and the Anglo/Mexican ratio changed radically. "We were seventy percent of the population yet all the school board, school administrators and politicians were Anglo. Only a handful of teachers were Mexican," Yzaguirre recalls.

Beginning in the mid-50s Yzaguirre witnessed a shift from an all-Anglo school board to one that included Mexican Americans. By the '60s the greater percentage of school board members were of Mexican descent and eventually his brother, Ruben, would serve as school board president.

In spite of the 500 signatures, Yzaguirre had gathered, the State of Texas abolished the preschool law shortly after the petition drive, and the needs of preschool children would not be officially addressed by Congress until 1965 with the founding of Project Head Start during President Lyndon B. Johnson's War on Poverty campaign. Yzaguirre would be one of the analysts working for the Office of Economic Opportunity (OEO) to make Head Start a reality. His desire to establish preschools for Tejanitos to learn English had been one of the many factors contributing to the push for preschool education that would address the needs of millions of preschool children nationwide. His petition, presented so long ago to the arrogant members of the PSJA School Board, had come full circle.

FAMILY PHOTOGRAPHS

Rubén Antonio Yzaguirre and Eva Linda Morin's wedding
day in San Juan, Texas, September 11, 1938.

Left to right: Unknown, Uncle Pete Morin, Elisa Morin (Grandmother),
Gavino Morin (Grandfather), Eva Linda Morin (Yzaguirre), Elodia Morin
(Raul's aunt). Cinco de Mayo celebration in San Juan, Texas, 1938.

Grandfather Gavino Morin in San Juan, Texas in front of the Ice House, circa, 1955.

Laura Pollard, speech and debate teacher at PSJA
High. San Juan, Texas, circa 1956.

American GI Forum Members gather in San Juan, Texas, circa, 1957. Bob Sanchez, far left, Dr. Hector P. García in center, Raul, second from right.

Uncle Pete Morin and his bride, Guillermina, on their wedding day. Raul as best man, Maria Teresa "Tere" Yzaguirre, as maid of honor. Father Lopez officiated the ceremony. San Juan, Texas, circa, 1963.

Raul and Audrey's wedding day at St. Mary's Mother of
God Church in Washington, D.C., January 2, 1965.

Alma Yzaguirre "Loly," Raul, Raul, Jr., Audrey, and Regina at
Bristow family home in Baltimore, Maryland, 1967.

Raul and Audrey at Alma Yzaguirre's wedding,
San Juan, Texas, December 23, 1971.

Rubén Antonio Yzaguirre tending farm animal in San Juan, Texas, circa, 1975.

Raul and Audrey with son Raul, Jr. "Hoagie" in
back, front, Gina and Lisa, circa, 1976.

Raul and son Bobby on his shoulders picketing the White House
and Jimmy Carter for Hispanic appointments, circa 1977.

Uncle Pete Morin, Rubén A. Yzaguirre, Eva Linda Yzaguirre, Raul,
Alma Bristow (Audrey's mother), and Audrey in Washington
D.C. Raul was recipient of Rockefeller Award, 1979.

Raul's mother Eva Linda "Evita," and his cousin Robert Ray
"Butch" at Morin home in San Juan, Texas, 1990.

Audrey, Maria Tijerina (Raul's niece), Regina Campanile Raul's daughter – husband and children: Antonio, Maria, Mike and Raul at Father of the Year Award at the National Press Club, Washington, D.C., June 5, 2003.

Left to right: Dolores Miller (Audrey's sister), Raul, Jr., Mindy (Bobby's wife), Audrey, Ben Yzaguirre, Hillary Clinton, Bobby, Raul, Mike Campanile, Gina Campanile, Fred Hintermister (Elisa's husband), Elisa Yzaguirre and Rebecca Yzaguirre at Swearing-in Ceremony as Ambassador for Dominican Republic. Washington, D.C., 2010.

PART TWO
My Son, the Activist

10

LEAVING THE VALLEY

The next thing I knew, two armed soldiers, MP's, were standing over my head in my bunk. 'Come with us, immediately,' they said. They dragged me into the lab to face the lieutenant colonel.

—Raul Yzaguirre

WILD FAREWELL

66 AFTER HIGH SCHOOL, I was trying to figure out what to do next. I went to Pan American College and attended for about half a semester. I found the courses to be repetitious of what I had studied in high school. I specifically remember taking a test in an English course and I was the only student to pass it. I was very dissatisfied with the school and couldn't find anything else so I decided I had to get out of there. By this time I had had two to four years of intense organizing with the American GI Forum. We had a rule that stated that district councils could have a youth working with them who would have a vote equal to that of an adult. I was the youth representative and was involved in leadership positions with the GI Forum at the state level, but a lot of the adults resented me because I was a kid. I figured I had gone as far as I could go at that time in organizing my community, and felt an obligation to serve my country."

Late for his graduation ceremony at PSJA High in 1958, Yzaguirre's partner had to march in alone. He remembers a celebration for him at home, but not much else happening. His last night as a civilian before joining the Air Force more than made up for the boring graduation night. That night, Raul's taste for speeding cars would land him in jail and bring about events he'd laugh about later; but on that night, the whole thing played out like a skit from a gangster movie.

"The night I left for the Air Force was special. I was dating this girl and her mom was very strict. My uncle and I had worked very hard at the ice house and I had saved up money to buy a V8 Impala, red and white. That car could move fast. I remember my girlfriend had a curfew and we were running late. I was speeding, maybe sixty in a thirty mile zone. So, a cop stopped me. He was a little brazen and asked me if I knew how fast I was going and I told him I didn't, but that I had decided to stop as I could easily out-run him. He said, 'Well, why don't you come with me.' So I had to leave the car with the guy that was dating my girlfriend's sister. So he drove them home. They took me to the police station and gave me one phone call. I called my uncle Pete. I knew what bar he would be at, so I found him, and he said, 'Ok, I'll go get you out.' I was sitting in the jail looking out a window, and I saw my uncle, drunk out of his mind, driving up on the sidewalk."

"I thought we were both going to go to jail that night. I could hear him demanding. 'What are you doing with my nephew? You can't do that to him.' He asked what the fine was and I can't believe how he kept his senses because he was drunk out of his mind. They said there was a thirty-five dollar fine and he asked, 'Do you have a draft check?' He didn't have a bank account, but he signed the check and gave the police a bad check. I couldn't believe how he kept his senses through it all. While this was going on, in walk eight guys who drove up to the station in my car."

The eight guys were Yzaguirre's friends who were planning to charge the police station and break him out, although the scheme was more a show of bravado than a logical reality. They had plans to go out drinking in nearby Reynosa and didn't want to miss their friend's last night as a civilian. "We went to Reynosa and I got drunk for the first time in my life, and threw up. And next morning, I had to face the judge, and he let me go right away. No big deal. My girlfriend got punished and was grounded for being late but she managed to escape and met me at the bus station in Edinburg and said goodbye. Then I took off to the Air Force."

The next day, as Yzaguirre reported to Lackland Air Force Base in San Antonio, Uncle Pete returned to the police station and asked for the draft check he had signed. He settled the score that day by paying in cash. In retrospect, the two would look back and laugh about the time they could have both spent a night in the San Juan jail.

TWENTY DOLLARS

Beginning his military service at Lackland Air Force Base in San Antonio, Yzaguirre begins to make plans to take his pilot's test. "There was a draft going on. So I said before I'm drafted, I'll just volunteer. I passed the exam for pilot school but they didn't have another class until two months later so I said I want to join now. They said they could test me again for pilot training. They tested me again, and told me to go to intelligence and learn Chinese. I didn't want to learn Chinese. I went to basic training instead, and they said, 'Would you like to go to medical school?' And I said, fine. The medical training course was in Lackland, Texas which was close to home. So I could go home a lot. Whoever was first in the class at Lackland could have whatever base they wanted as an assignment. I came in first, and I chose to go to D.C. That's how I ended up in D.C. My thought was that I would do this for a little bit then go back to pilot training school."

Recalling her brother's time at Lackland Air Force Base, Tere remembers an incident that displayed her brother's style for confronting discrimination and racism. "When Raul was stationed at Lackland Air Force Base he often came to the Valley to visit us. One time during one of his visits, he was returning to the base by bus, so we went to the bus depot to drop him off. When he purchased the bus ticket the attendant, in error, gave him an additional twenty dollars in change. Raul immediately returned the overpayment, although he was broke and in spite of the fact that the attendant was very rude to us. The guy was known as a racist against Mexican Americans. I asked Raul why he gave it back to him and he responded that it was not about the other person, but about our own integrity. It was not about what other people do, it was about what we do."

Yzaguirre's commitment to integrity and living up to high personal standards, reminiscent of his grandfather's own pledge to live a righteous life, is about to be tested in the hotbed of D.C.'s political scene. Juggling military service, a part-time job at a lab, classes at George Washington University and the beginning of married life, he still has time to do what he loves most: organizing. Skills learned as a GI Forum youth organizer go into full gear in D.C. and influence his decision to pursue civil rights as a career, rather than complete a medical or law degree.

Unbeknownst to him at the time, his decision to serve in D.C. is to last a lifetime, as he establishes a career and a permanent home for his wife and young children. He will never go back to pilot training school at Lackland Air Force Base as his life's path will lead him step by step to the center of heated political debates in D.C. The "little bit" he had planned to stay on as a medical technician turned into the beginning of civil rights activism, propelling him into the national spotlight.

"When I got to D.C. they gave me further training and I didn't know how much I would love it," Yzaguirre says, describing his introduction to the Medical Corps. "I was learning new things everyday and working in different parts of the hospital—pediatrics, OBGYN, and other parts of the lab. I assisted at autopsies and the work was fascinating. So, I asked if I could go to officer's training school. They said, 'Fine, but you'll stay on the Medical Corps and we'll put you where we need you.'"

Due to his skills as an excellent lab technician, the majority of Yzaguirre's time at Andrews Air Force Base Hospital is spent working in the laboratory. Once a month, he's required to do a twenty-four hour shift, sleeping at the lab until morning and dealing with a variety of complex tests as well as emergency patients. It isn't long before he runs into a problem that will threaten his military career with a court martial.

MP's Surprise Visit

His old nemesis, chaos, begins to take its toll on Raul Yzaguirre as he observes that the lab at the hospital is over-utilized. The quality of service has gone significantly down as Air Force doctors, all higher in rank than he is, expect their orders for lab tests to be filled without delay, not considering the length of time it takes for complicated tests to be performed, nor how many previous orders they've already demanded. Working long hours and still playing catch-up on lab tests, weighs heavily on Yzaguirre and as the days go by, things go from bad to worse.

"Doctors were abusing their rights. They ordered tests for emergencies that weren't emergencies. We were piled up with routine work, and when real emergencies would come up we couldn't do them. So I decided that some of the tests were not necessary. One night I got a call for blood that a patient needed immediately. I had to cross-match the blood type, which takes about twenty minutes, and every minute counts. The uric acid test, unlike a lot of other tests that can be used for different diseases, can only be used for one test, and that is gout, and gout is not an emergency. I was trying to deal with real emergencies. Then the same doctor who had ordered the uric acid test, a captain who was my superior, came in and ordered another test on the same patient. So I said, this isn't going to fly. I called the nurse and told her I was busy and was not going to do the captain's new request. In the meantime, he wanted a third test and came running down and said, 'Are you disobeying a direct order?' And I said, 'I guess I am. You have no right to order these kinds of tests. I'm trying to deal with emergencies and you're outside your authority.' He said, 'You don't question my authority. You will do that test or else. I'll talk to the officer of the day.'"

"The officer of the day was a major. I told him what was happening. And he said, 'I'll do the tests myself.' I said, 'don't do it. I'm taking a stand on this.' But he said he wanted to pacify the situation, so I said, go ahead."

Upon finishing his twenty-four hour shift, an unsuspecting Yzaguirre writes up his report for the night, and turns in to his barracks for much needed sleep. Having achieved only Private, 2nd class at the time, he's aware he has no right to oppose a captain, and a doctor at that; but his desire to "do the right thing" is the motivation that holds sway over his logic and any consequences he will have to face for disobeying a direct order from a superior. "The next thing I knew, two armed soldiers, MP's, were standing over my head in my bunk. 'Come with us, immediately,' they said. They dragged me into the lab to face the lieutenant colonel."

Explaining to the lieutenant colonel what happened, Yzaguirre's surprised to hear him say he'll go to bat for him as he has a great work record. "But you're in trouble," the lieutenant colonel warns. "I'll work to get you an Article 15."

An Article 15 is a procedure in which a serviceman admits guilt, and thus avoids doing jail time. It's a reprimand that involves taking away one stripe and restricting the serviceman to the base for 30 days. Additionally, the infraction will not go on the serviceman's record once he leaves the base. "I told the lieutenant colonel that I would not accept an Article 15 because I was guilty. Court martial me, I said to him. And he said, 'Okay.'"

For two weeks Yzaguirre's assigned every dirty detail his superiors can come up with, from peeling potatoes to cleaning toilets; however, they can only assign the detail for eight hours. "I was used to working sixteen to eighteen hours," Yzaguirre explains, "so for me it was a vacation." The restrictions are enforced for two weeks, until his superiors make a decision to waive the punishment and end the process.

At the hospital's annual picnic of technicians, officers and doctors, two captains approach Yzaguirre. "You son-of-a-bitch, you got away with it," they tell him, laughing.

"Got away with what?"

"They're not going to court martial you. You disobeyed a direct order from an officer and a doctor and you got away with it."

"I didn't get away with anything. I stood up for what I believed and I paid the price. And I'll do it again."

Yzaguirre discovers that for the right reasons, someone can take on a big institution and win. This marks one of the greatest lessons he learned in the Air Force. "You know who your friends are too, because everybody in the military wouldn't talk to me during the time I was 'radio active.' Some civilian women were behind me and stood by me and I think it had an influence because they would speak out loud and say things like, 'It's lousy what they're doing to Raul.' It was a great character building exercise."

Yzaguirre recalls one more incident of a near court martial, and this one involved two young Bolivian children at Andrews Air Force Base Hospital. One of them in particular, was gravely ill, suffering burns throughout his body.

"There were two kids from Bolivia whose father was in the Bolivian Air Force. They had gotten badly burned when they got blown up in an explosion, particularly a little boy of twelve years old. There were burns all over his body, and the doctors tried to do skin grafts on him and they got infected all over his skin. He was in very bad shape. He spoke no English, only Spanish, so they asked me to go up and translate for him."

"The process for caring for him involved changing his bandages every day or so. He was given a sterile bath in saline, and gradually the bandages were unwrapped. He was in such bad shape that they were afraid to give him any anesthesia, so they had to do this without any painkillers. They were doing such a lousy job, finally I said, Look let me do it. So I put on my surgical gown and I would talk to him and I tried to take his mind off what was happening, and would sing songs and tell stories. This went on for several weeks. When I would finish taking off all the gauzes, I would put him on a table and the doctor and nurses would come in and put new bandages on him."

"One day I stayed in case I was needed to interpret, and the boy started crying and the nurse said to the doctor, 'Be careful you're too rough. He's hurting badly with no anesthesia.' The doctor said, 'These Latinos cry every time they see blood. They go crazy. Don't worry about it.' I knew the doctor was an officer and my superior, but I said, you son-of-a-bitch, I'll wallow in blood with you anytime. I called him a few more choice names and walked out. He threatened to court martial me, but never did. I stayed with the boy for years, because he needed a lot of treatment. He was there apparently due to an agreement between the U.S. and Bolivian Air Force."

Eventually, the boy was transferred for treatment at Bethesda Naval Hospital, and his parents came to the U.S. to take him home. "After we got him cured, the parents were very grateful and they invited me to their house to celebrate and gave me a whole box of Chivas Regal, a high quality whiskey, fifteen years old and very expensive. I had no idea what it was, so I took it to my room and put it in my locker. And every time I would get a coke, I would put a little whiskey in it and one day somebody came into my room and said,

'You're the dumbest SOB I've ever seen in my life. Do you know what you're doing?' I asked him what I was doing wrong, and he said, 'This is quality stuff. You don't put Coca-Cola in it.' I had no idea it was quality stuff. You drink it for pleasure. Years later, I saw the boy again, and he had become a teacher but he was still very badly scarred."

Yzaguirre's work as a lab technician does not end when his service in the Air Force is completed in 1963. He continues to work in laboratory settings while establishing the first of many civil rights groups he helps organize in the D.C. area. As chairman of the National Organization of Mexican American Services (NOMAS), a student organization set up to be a "funnel" of information for several Latino-based groups, he seeks to provide a uniform platform for addressing crucial civil rights issues. Already, his focus is on uniting disjointed groups that will become more effective by joining forces with like-minded people, thus producing a stronger voice for lobbying Congress. As the saying goes, "easier said than done." The road to unification is to be a bitter one, and yet one that will claim Yzaguirre's entire attention. The tumultuous years of the Kennedy and King assassinations, and the changing of the guard, first to President Lyndon B. Johnson, then to Richard Nixon, will mark a new path for Yzaguirre and his band of followers who will flock to him from all over the nation.

The times will become more chaotic, as Yzaguirre stands at the crossroads of another important decision in his life: choosing the woman he will marry. Fate sets up the perfect woman for him, and he doesn't have to look very far to find her. The urgency of completing one of his last courses in botany at George Washington University is the open door, bringing him into the proximity of the woman he will spend the rest of his life with: Audrey Helen Bristow.

11

AUDREY

Raul and I became friends first and knew each other as lab partners.
Our friendship was very important and later, we began to fall in love.

—Audrey Bristow Yzaguirre

Y<small>ZAGUIRRE'S DAYS</small> as a fiery student rebel, challenging Mrs. Brooks over book reports, leading students in walkouts and protests, and standing before the PSJA— School Board on behalf of the Mexican American community, sharpened his ability to confront things that made no sense as he sought a path of resistance that often set into motion new possibilities. In his last two years in the Air Force, his sense of getting things done in a practical, sensible manner proved to be the best route to follow. Enrolled in a botany class at George Washington University (GWU), he refused to attend the lab and lectures conducted by Dr. Margolis. His resistance would prove to be the impetus for the next path he would follow—down the aisle. He could not have imagined that this time, his resistance would win him a bride.

THE SHY LAB BEAUTY

Working at Andrews Air Force Base Hospital for the last two years of his service in the Air Force, Yzaguirre continues to specialize as a lab technician. One day, he meets Dr. Robert Ghoad, the astute supervisor of the lab, who offers him a new opportunity.

"I was working at the lab and this guy would come around and look at all of us for about two weeks, observing what we were doing, and asking questions. One day he tapped me on the shoulder and told me his name was Dr. Ghoad, and he'd been charged with starting a virus research laboratory from the ground up. 'One of my lab technicians is leaving and I want you to take his place,' he told me. 'I'm choosing you as the best technician there is.'"

"I decided to take him up on his offer and started working at the annex, not directly in the hospital, observing live viruses under a microscope. It was interesting work. We published a couple of papers and Dr. Ghoad faked my credentials. When you write a paper you list your degrees. I didn't even have a B.A. at the time, but Dr. Ghoad put one after my name and said, not to worry about it. I worked pretty much alone. I would start in the morning and I would work alone all day. I worked in hospital whites, which were laundered for me. I got housing, food, a room, and didn't have to spend any money. The last three years I think I wore my Air Force uniform maybe twice. It was strange, like not being in the Air Force at all."

Working in the lab at the Air Force base builds Yzaguirre's knowledge of laboratory procedures, including the use of laboratory instruments used for studying microscopic cells, viruses, tissues and malignant specimens that will aid in making a diagnosis and prescribing appropriate medical treatment. Completing classes first at the University of Maryland, and later at George Washington University, his pre-med focus changes to liberal arts with a concentration in business management and the social sciences. Towards the end of his college days, Yzaguirre takes a five-hour course in advanced botany that requires a lecture and a lab.

"I never went to the lab," Yzaguirre recalls. "Occasionally I went to the lecture given by Dr. Margolis who was teaching the class. He called me in and said, 'I'm going to flunk you.' And I said, but I've got A's on all the tests. And he said, 'Yeah, but you don't come to class. And I said, yes but it's not a requirement to come to class. This is what I do for a living, I don't need this class."

Worried that Dr. Margolis will flunk him, Yzaguirre asks what he can do to pass the course. Dr. Margolis quickly takes the opportunity to make Yzaguirre his lab assistant and agrees to pass him if he works for him. "He assigned me three female students who had trouble with the microscope, adjusting it, and understanding what they were seeing. One of them was this dark-haired young woman by the name of Audrey Bristow. She was shy and very good-looking, and I never thought anything would happen, we just started to be friends. It was a long class, and we'd have a break in-between. Audrey and I would go to the corner shop and get an ice cream cone, and sometimes after class we'd go have a drink. Next thing I knew we were falling in love. We dated for a year, then we got married."

Audrey remembers that friendship came first, as described by her husband. "Raul and I became friends first and knew each other as lab partners. Our friendship was very important and later, we began to fall in love."

It's the deep respect each has for the other that seals their friendship into a life-long commitment, reflecting the same dedication to marriage modeled by their own parents and grandparents. Unknown to the young couple, their marriage will produce six children, three boys and three girls, each one captivating, challenging, and uniquely able to express his or her own talents and gifts. Their relationship will endure set-backs and twists and turns that will threaten the vitality of their love, forcing them to examine their beliefs and values in the midst of Yzaguirre's swirling, maddening role as a civil rights leader.

"Audrey was the first woman who truly understood what I was doing and that's what attracted me to her," Yzaguirre recalls. "She was sincerely interested in all I was doing. It was so different from what she knew, but she organized her friends and helped me do receptions and meetings, and I shared my dreams with her. I wanted to build institutions for our community. And she was very supportive."

Honorary Latina

Audrey Helen Bristow's parents settled in Maryland, a state originally founded in 1629 by George Calvert who sailed from England with the intention of securing a safe haven for a minority of Roman Catholics of English descent. Before his death in 1632, Calvert earned the title, 1st Baron Baltimore, and named the state "Maryland," some say to honor Mary, the mother of Jesus. The state is nicknamed "Little America," for the variety and beauty of its landscape, or the "Chesapeake Bay State," for its eastern border that faces the Atlantic Ocean. It boasts a proud history of loyalty to the Union and celebrates heroes, such as Francis Scott Key who in 1812, wrote the Star Spangled Banner as the British military bombarded the port of Baltimore.

Arriving in America during early colonial days, immigrants, both Protestant and Catholic, took on jobs as indentured servants and had to labor several years to pay for their passage. The Bristows, descendants of immigrant families who settled in the Maryland/D.C. area, proved that through hard work and determination, success could be achieved in America. Living above their grocery store, the Bristows were in close proximity to their primary source of income. "I grew up in a Mom and Pop grocery store," Audrey says. "My father was a devout non-Catholic and my mother was very Catholic. My mother was at odds with my father's family because of her religion. For reasons unknown to me, they hated Catholics, but Dad was smitten enough with her to ignore all this."

Attending a Catholic school, Audrey embraces her mother's faith whole-heartedly, which will later prove to be the strongest link endearing her to the Yzaguirres. Once Mama Licha Morin and Eva Linda Yzaguirre get wind of the fact that their new daughter-in-law is Anglo, sparks fly and doubts on how this *gringa* will fit into their Mexican American family erupt like a South Texas hurricane blowing across the nation all the way to D.C. The storm doesn't quell, until the family finds out she's Catholic.

"My family did not approve of Audrey because she was Anglo and not from Texas," Yzaguirre says. "But she was Catholic. I tell people that in my family I'm not the one with the mixed marriage. My sister Alma is. She married a Mexican two blocks away, but he was Baptist. They eventually broke up."

Suffering through the Great Depression, Audrey's parents, Raymond Hayse Bristow and Alma Eder, labor long hours to provide for their two daughters, Audrey and her older sister, Dolores, nicknamed, 'Doe.'

"Father was a stern Englishman," Audrey explains, "although he never admitted to being of English heritage, but referred to himself as a 'Virginian.' My mother was German, and her mother spoke German, but her father would not allow the kids to learn it. It was hard for me to get close to my father. He was obsessed with keeping 'the store,' open for many hours. My sister and I longed for a normal family life."

The 'normal family life' Audrey so fervently longed for, continues to elude her after her marriage to Yzaguirre, whose life will be far from 'normal,' as he struggles through the lean years, when, together, they will search under the cushions of their frayed couch for change that might get them a tank of gas or bread and milk for the children who quickly become part of their household.

"Her father grew up in Virginia," Yzaguirre says. "He was one of five male siblings and worked on a ship in Baltimore. For some reason his father didn't send him to school even though his other siblings went. It was in Baltimore that he met and married my mother-in-law, Alma Eder. It was a Romeo and Juliet story. She was a staunch Catholic and he was a staunch Protestant. That used to matter a lot, but he was madly in love with her. They had two girls, my wife, Audrey and her older sister, Doe. I remember the family living upstairs on top of their grocery store and delicatessen. Audrey went to Catholic school all her life, and there were problems between her mother and father over this because it was so expensive."

Worried about their daughter marrying a Mexican American, the Bristows have a way of making their concerns known to Raul, but in a more subtle

"English" manner in comparison to the fiery passion of Yzaguirre's South Texas family members. "Her parents were gracious, not warm, but courteous," Yzaguirre recalls. "Her dad was a racist of Blacks and my mother-in-law felt the same way, but over the years they got better about accepting other races. Audrey's uncle would call me Pedro at times, like he couldn't remember my name."

Employed at the National Institute of Health (NIH) in Washington, Audrey proves to be a dedicated student, who cuts short her college career, once she makes a decision to marry. Meeting her future husband in 1964 in the GWU lab class brings her into direct contact with a man who's a natural born organizer, and is already chairman of the board for NOMAS in the D.C. area. Acting as chairman of the group, Yzaguirre spends time nurturing the student group he believes will bring together various Latino organizations into a stronger base for creating much needed change, and uses his office at the hospital as a meeting place.

Not long after Raul and Audrey begin dating, cultural differences arise between them, some of them on the serious side, others comical. Growing up around a delicatessen, Audrey's a good cook, but unfamiliar with Mexican food. Yzaguirre's sister, Alma, raves about Audrey's German potato salad, breads and desserts, but as a young wife, Audrey's knowledge of how to make spicy, tasty Mexican dishes was nil. A naturalist at heart, she later cultivated her own garden, growing herbs and spices for use in her cooking. But her first attempt to cook Mexican food to please her husband-to-be turned out to be a fiasco they would not soon forget.

"On my birthday before we were married, Audrey decided to make us a nice Mexican dinner, but she knew nothing about Mexican food, so she got a cookbook somewhere. For tortillas she got a recipe for Spanish tortillas made with eggs. She had never bought avocados for guacamole, so instead of buying green ones, she bought brown ones and didn't know they were bad. She boiled turkey and made molé sauce from scratch. All day long she cooked for me. It was a total disaster. She made a dessert that called for rum flavor, so she put in real rum and it tasted horrible, so I had to pretend that I liked it. We laugh about it now. Cornmeal and eggs to make tortillas, I said, what is this?"

Visiting for the first time in South Texas opens the way for Audrey to acquaint herself with Mexican food from the experts, Yzaguirre's mother and grandmother. At first, the Yzaguirres don't quite know what to expect from Audrey, but it doesn't take them long to set their reservations aside. She charms the family by dancing the Charleston, and doesn't hesitate to accept Mexican traditions and customs, no matter how strange they appear to her.

Eventually, she will be named, an "honorary Latina," by their son, Raul, Jr. Quickly becoming a family favorite, Audrey wins the hearts of the entire family. Her father-in-law, Rubén Antonio, affectionately called her "Audi." Yzaguirre's sister, Alma, who often spent time with them in Maryland as a young girl, decided to name her only daughter, Audrey, and it was Raul's mother, Eva Linda, who called him from South Texas to proudly tell him, "The baby's name is Audrey."

Yzaguirre's sister, Tere, best describes what Audrey's presence has meant in her brother's life. "Raul and Audrey struggled in the early years of their marriage. Audrey has always been an excellent wife and all the family loves her. I don't think Raul could have been successful in his life if Audrey had not been at his side encouraging him and standing by him."

I'll Take You to the Moon

Recalling their year of courtship, the Yzaguirre's quibble over who proposed to whom. "Actually, she proposed to me," Yzaguirre says, "At least that's the way I saw it but she doesn't like me to characterize it that way. We were dating for a while and we were at an Italian restaurant on Wisconsin Avenue having dinner after a movie and we were talking about something deep, and she looked at me and laughed and smiled and I asked her, why are you smiling? And she said, 'When you ask the right question, the answer will be yes.' I said, I think I know what the question is. I nodded and said, that sounds good to me. I just bought her a ring and put it on her finger." Audrey recalls the proposal a bit differently. "We were at a restaurant in D.C. and Raul gave me two rings, and I liked them, so I said, okay, I'll marry you."

The money for Audrey's rings materializes in a most unorthodox manner, through an accident Raul experiences while driving a motorcycle on the D.C. streets. On his way to deliver blood samples to a nearby lab; he's suddenly hit by a car. The test tubes in his backpack burst open, spraying him with blood, which horrifies the driver who hit him. The terrified driver offers to pay him a high price for all his injuries and thus, the money for Audrey's rings, and Yzaguirre's last semester at GWU miraculously appears.

Over the years, the couple will exchange gifts that reflect the abiding love and trust each has for the other. "On one of my birthdays, Audrey took a replica of my dog tags and had them redone in silver. I went out and bought her a charm bracelet and picked out charms for the places she visited in Europe and places we visited in Mexico, and one for each child. We added more charms as the years went by. Also she loved banjos, so I got her one. She didn't know how to play it, but she liked it."

Living in the D.C. area away from their hometown parishes, the young couple seeks direction from a local priest who advises them through the marital process. "Both sets of parents had reservations about our marriage," Yzaguirre recalls, "Then the priest said, 'I will only do this if you invite your parents.' So we invited them. My mother wouldn't come. My cousin, Gloria Yzaguirre Stephens and her daughter, Leslie, were the only ones from my family who came. Audrey's father, who didn't want to go to a Catholic church, didn't come either. So, the only ones there from her side of the family were her mother, her sister Doe, and her sister's husband Charles and their kids. A few of our friends showed up, including my boss, Dr. Robinson."

January 2, 1965, the Yzaguirres wedding day, turns out to be a cold, wintry day in D.C. Strapped for funds, there's little money to go around, much less enough to host an expensive reception with a long list of invited guests. Audrey's sister, Doe, is chosen as the maid of honor, and Roberto "Bob" Reveles, a native of Miami, Arizona, acts as the best man. Attending Georgetown University in the School of Foreign Services in D.C., Reveles is destined to be one of the first to join Yzaguirre's circle of student leaders and begin the dynamic work of challenging discriminatory policies that negatively affect Mexican American communities nationwide. Later, he will hold key staff positions for Congressmen Stewart L. Udall, and his brother Morris "Mo" K. Udall.

"We had no money, but we didn't want to ask our parents for support so we did the wedding by ourselves," Yzaguirre says. "Audrey wore a nice white dress suit, but not a traditional wedding dress. I remember a professional singer sang the Ave Maria. The church was in a poor neighborhood, and as we walked out of the church, one of the bums tried to kiss my wife. We went to this little restaurant/bar in the building where I worked, but it was closed so we went to the drugstore to have coffee. The wedding party waited at the drugstore, drinking coffee, then they opened up the restaurant and my boss, Dr. Robinson, donated all the liquor. My brother-in-law and sister-in-law made the cake, my brother-in-law took photos, and I paid for the food and for the lady who sang at mass, and that was it. It was all we could afford. We went on our honeymoon to Virginia and I tell my wife I took her to the moon. We went to a restaurant called 'The Moon.'"

CRAZED MONKEY ON THE LOOSE

A series of complicated twists and turns await the Yzaguirres as they begin their married life. Negotiating between two D.C. addresses is one of the first things they have to deal with. "We lived apart for six months," Yzaguirre says. "She lived in a little apartment over a Chinese restaurant about a half block from the executive office building by the White House. I lived in Bethesda, and we got together on weekends, then we got an apartment on 14th & Military. It was a nice apartment, something we could afford. I remember we had a cat and a little neighbor girl used to talk to the cat all day long through a window. Audrey took in typing and did odd jobs to help out. I was still working at the lab. She had a nice little car, a Mercury Comet, I had this old Renault which was nothing more than a clunker, so we drove her car most of time."

Keeping a clean house becomes one of Audrey's trademarks. She insists on making sure everything is washed, polished and things put away, in many ways reminiscent of Mama Licha in her diligence to her home, but that's not the way her husband understood it at one point. "Our first argument was about cleaning the house or going out for the weekend. I wanted to do the latter, and she said no she had to clean the house, wash clothes, and do all kinds of things, so I asked her if that was more important than me? I got angry because in my mind she was putting the orderliness of her apartment before me. And to me that was unthinkable."

Yzaguirre makes a quick decision to come to terms with his wife's urge to keep things tidy, attributing her passion for a clean house, in part, to her German mother's example of order and cleanliness. "I came to the conclusion that women have a different kind of logic. They're very territorial and are, at times, nest builders. When I took an apartment in downtown D.C. to avoid a three hour drive after we got our first house, I asked Audrey to come in and decorate it, then it was okay because now it was her territory."

After seven months of marriage, the couple takes time off to go on a real honeymoon, traveling to South Texas for the first time so Audrey can meet the Yzaguirres. The plan is to fly from Texas to Mexico City. On the road by rental car, Audrey remembers they listened to Bill Cosby's comedy routines, and argued at length about something that made them both angry. Taking a bus from San Antonio to San Juan, they arrive at Mama Licha's house and are greeted by her in the traditional Mexican manner. Audrey witnesses the tiny, yet ferocious grandmother, whack Raul across the face for being gone so long, then watches as she embraces and kisses him because she loves him so much. This goes on for several minutes, and the behavior alarms Audrey, who stands aghast at the aggressive, yet loving encounter. Her reserved English up-bringing had not prepared her for such a display. Quickly, she begins to understand that what she considers standards of normal behavior will, at times, mean nothing to the Yzaguirres, and accepting the differences she sees, is what will make her truly "one of the family."

On the second leg of their honeymoon, Raul and Audrey board a flight to Mexico City on a Mexican airlines and discover the plane has a flat tire. They wait for hours until the tire is repaired, and in the meantime are fed a sandwich made of three slices of bread—no meat or cheese, only bread. Once in Mexico City, they take a bus to the coastal city of Acapulco and pay for a room in a hotel with a heart-shaped pool, but no bathroom in their room. Later, they swim in the ocean, not paying attention to a sign that warns NO SWIMMING in that particular area. An undertow nearly sweeps a slim, willowy Audrey out to sea in a swirling, cascading wave, causing Raul to go into quick action, pulling her up in his arms just in time. "Audrey nearly drowned!" he says, reliving the panic of the moment.

Back at the hotel, still somewhat rattled by Audrey's near-drowning, the young couple falls into the hands of an itinerant organ grinder and his malicious pet monkey. "Later we saw a small pet monkey on a chain at the hotel," Audrey says. "The monkey entertained the guests, and it was cute. Suddenly, it jumped into my arms."

In a flash, the crazed monkey wraps its arms and tail tightly around Audrey's neck. No amount of demanding by its owner, nor attempting to pry it away from Audrey works. The monkey holds on tighter and tighter. "It was frightening," Audrey recalls. A crowd gathers, as people watch in horror, wondering what will happen as the obsessed monkey tightens its vice-like grip on Audrey's neck. Hotel personnel stand around anxiously hatching out a plan to rescue Audrey from the demented creature. Finally, Yzaguirre, in a moment of insane logic, grabs a compact mirror from Audrey's purse and shows the monkey its own reflection in the glass. Horrified upon seeing his own face, the monkey lets go and scampers away.

After a day of facing the near-drowning episode and the crazed monkey on the loose, the honeymooners welcome a relaxing time at dinner and after their meal walk serenely, hand-in-hand, along the beach, taking in the beauty of one of Acapulco's balmy, moonlit nights.

RETURNING TO D.C. with no further incident, the couple is strengthened by the trials they have already faced, not knowing that the hardest most exhilarating time of their lives is just around the corner. The birth of their first daughter, Regina Dolores, is to be followed by the births of Raul Humberto, Jr., Elisa Alma Linda, Roberto Hayse, Rebecca Morin, and Benjamin Ruben—six children who will witness love, success, hardship, and a close family, in spite of the numerous times their father will spend on the road away from them. Affectionately, they will be known as Gina, Hoagie, Lisa, Bobby, Becky and Ben.

Under scrutiny by the CIA in D.C. for leading a "radical student group," (NOMAS), Yzaguirre is to come into personal contact with President Lyndon B. Johnson and join his War on Poverty in spite of the fact that the president is often playing politics, on one hand building his Great Society, and on the other hand, wondering how to best keep a Democratic candidate in the White House—no matter what the price.

Hired as a program analyst in 1966 for the Office of Economic Opportunity, (OEO), Yzaguirre gains access to, as he describes, "some of the nation's best minds on education, employment and training." From this vantage point he quickly surmises that one way to challenge injustice is to work with federal programs that are set up to address discrimination and racism. Once on the pathway towards equality for Latinos and other struggling groups, there will be no turning back for him, or for Audrey.

The Yzaguirre's family portrait, Raul, Audrey and the children, is about to be painted on the canvas of the world, and soon the amazing scenes of their lives will appear.

12

MY DAD THE "PRESIDENT"

My dad was on the passenger side as I slammed into the fence. He pulled me back into the car as I tried to flee. 'You can go through this fence or house, but I cannot and will not let you be afraid,' he said.
—Raul "Hoagie" Yzaguirre, Jr.

LIVING THROUGH THE LEAN YEARS

MOVING TO MARYLAND and settling in Mt. Airy brings with it a new sense of adventure and ignites Raul Yzaguirre's national work as a civil rights leader, yet the move poses major challenges for the entire Yzaguirre family. "When we moved back to D.C. in 1973, I had already served in the Air Force Medical Corps, and had graduated from George Washington University. My organizing days had taken root in the D.C. area, and my work with NCLR was about to begin full-force. I had already tried moving my family back to South Texas, but that didn't work out for us, so I went back to D.C. We finally settled in Mt. Airy, Maryland. I knew the changes were hard on the kids, but the move had to be done. South Texas was a world away from D.C. and the cultures were entirely different. Audrey was from Maryland, and that helped us get our feet on the ground."

There are anxious times for the Yzaguirres, once the reality of making a living as a couple sets in. "When we were first married, I was still working at the lab in D.C. and Audrey was pregnant with our first baby. I left my job and was unemployed for a month and she never complained. I was hired by OEO in 1966, and once Nixon was elected as President, I decided to leave OEO to start my own firm, the Interstate Research Associates (IRA), and I told her this will be rough. We spent a year building up that entity. My income at the time was $3,000 a year and we had to go on food stamps. Our first two children were ten months apart, and after a year or so, we had a third baby on the way, and she never complained. Audrey never said why don't you get a real job. I knew I needed to get contracts to build up IRA as an institution that would serve as a consultant for community organizations. It was a rough time."

Raul, Jr. "Hoagie," vividly remembers days in the lean years when his parents had little money, constant car troubles and the responsibilities of a growing family. "Dad walked the walk," Raul, Jr., recalls. "He hitchhiked when he had to. We only had one car at the time, and there were four of us kids at that time. I remember Mom would get under the car's hood with a screw driver to fix a carburetor even when she was pregnant."

At times, searching under cushions of their couch for quarters to buy a Christmas tree, the Yzaguirres would wait until right before Christmas when the trees were cheap to make their yearly trek to an area designated for cutting down trees. The Yzaguirre's youngest child, Ben, remembers the Christmas tree tradition. "One of my favorite traditions was our yearly process of picking a Christmas tree. It was an endurance event. My parents made the rule that everyone had to agree on the tree before we would buy it. Hours would typically go by as each of us slowly formed alliances and were worn down by the others. And to add to the situation, we always went on a bad weather day."

Cultivating both Yzaguirre and Bristow holiday traditions, the family added Dia de los Tres Reyes (Three Kings) on January 6 to celebrate the holiday season. "After a while we stopped celebrating Los Tres Reyes," Yzaguirre says. "For our Thanksgiving meal, we added Mexican molé with tortillas, sauerkraut and German potato salad to our traditional turkey. We mixed our cultural traditions so the kids could appreciate both. On Christmas mornings all six kids would pile into our bed and get us up to demand that we go downstairs and open presents. On the kids' first day of school we had another tradition. Audrey would put on a disk or CD with music by Beryl Ives *My Funny Way of Laughing*. When he cried it was his funny way of laughing, and it made the kids laugh and their first day of school was less scary."

BABIES TURN TO BEAUTIES

Yzaguirre's first experience as a new dad reveals a deeper meaning to his understanding of fatherhood as modeled, for the most part, by his grandfather, Gavino Morin. Over the years young associates and mentees will describe him as a "father" who constantly cared for them and encouraged them through the hard times, but the birth of his first baby, Gina, brings him some surprising moments. "My wife thought she was beautiful and I thought she was ugly,"

Yzaguirre says. "I thought all the kids were ugly at birth, then they turned out to be beautiful. When they were first born they looked like little monkeys. I miss those days. I used to take my shirt off in the summer and put them on my chest and they'd peacefully go to sleep on my chest. I wish I had those days back."

Playing the role of Dad to his six children was in some ways similar to the role Yzaguirre played as a father figure to his younger siblings. "All my siblings, my brother and sisters lived with us at one time or another for a period of time. Alma lived with us for about a year. She loved to stay with us. I was a father figure to all of them."

Always the hardworking child apprentice growing up, Yzaguirre aligned himself with a life of hard work and expected the same from his children. He saw childhood as a learning experience, a way of establishing good work ethics and a time to build up a strong character. Riding beside his grandfather delivering ice all over San Juan taught him the value of what it meant to put in a hard day's work. As a young father, he wanted his own children to experience the same.

"My wife and I never had many fights, but we did fight about how to raise the kids. She was more lenient, and I wanted to instill the value of work. She's middle class, Anglo and believed that the kids should not be put to work. I'm the opposite. I was aggressive about making them work on weekends and it wasn't because I needed their work. I saw it as an important value I myself had learned early in life. She thought I was too tough on them, but they turned out well because they didn't expect anybody to give them anything. Instilling a work ethic was very important."

Yzaguirre's youngest child, Ben, a graduate of St. Mary's College of Maryland with a B.A. in History, and a Masters in Curriculum and Instruction from George Mason University, sees his parents' unique personalities as one of his most valuable assets. "My dad has taught me the virtue of hard work, which wasn't always appreciated growing up. But it has helped me tremendously as an adult. My mother's single best quality is her unconditional caring for others. I try to emulate both of them whenever possible."

Ben recalls a lesson about the value of hard work that his father taught him when he was a young boy; it remains one of the funniest moments in his life. "Dad expected a lot from us when we worked out in the yard. As a child, I didn't want to do any of it. One time he wanted me to dig the mud out of our family pond, and put it on the lawn because he was convinced it would help the grass grow. It kept me busy for hours. I don't know if it helped the grass grow, but we still laugh about it."

Raul, Jr., who earned a degree in education from Texas Pan American University, later completed a Masters in Business and studied Spanish in Jalisco, Mexico. He became the principal of one of the Yzaguirre Schools for Success located in Brownsville, Texas in 2008. The school offers students Dual Language Instruction (Spanish and English), and prepares them for higher education and civic leadership. "People used to tell me my dad was patient and insightful, but as a kid, I sometimes saw him as a grouch. He could be a bear when he wanted to, and of course, Mom was the kindest. He would yell at me, 'Get out here boy and cut some grass!' Then I remember once when we were driving from D.C. to Texas and he was patient with us all the way, and I told the other kids, 'I think he likes us.'"

"As a child, I was always Daddy's little girl," recalls Becky, Yzaguirre's youngest daughter. "I loved to be around Dad and sit on his lap whenever he was around. I always wanted to sip out of his glass and would pretend to like things I didn't really like just to please him. He would smile and act proud if I told him I liked chili sauce or sardines. Then later, as a teen, I rebelled and was never happy to hear Dad was coming home. My mom would make us stay home and spend time with him when he came back from a long trip. I resented that he was away so much and would always argue and get angry because I couldn't go out with my friends. At the time, I couldn't understand why his work was more important than being at home with his family."

In middle school, Becky experienced her dad's protective tendencies, the same type of strict fatherly care her aunt Alma witnessed as a teen when she tried to wear a two-piece bathing suit to Ocean City. "In sixth or seventh grade, a boy called. He was two years older than me, and had a deep voice. Dad answered the phone and told him, 'She's not home.' I think Dad would have liked it if I had become a nun, but he had a powerful presence and what he said was done. Mom would laugh about it, and even though she was conservative and used to set up curfews for us, she understood teen dating. My sister Gina got married when I was twelve years old, and Lisa got married when I was in college."

Between his wife's more lenient child-rearing philosophy and his own sense of duty to work, the Yzaguirre children played a balancing act and were able to find success in marriage and careers. "All of them went to the university and five of the six graduated with B.A. degrees," Yzaguirre says, proudly. "Two of the six hold graduate degrees. The one who didn't graduate, Bobby, actually makes more money in the medical computer programming business. All were financially able to buy their own homes and now live in different states."

Raul and Audrey's balancing act included accepting the things they could not change in their marriage, and moving forward in spite of differences. "Audrey's perfect the way she is," Yzaguirre says, "although sometimes I wish she was a little shorter. She's one and a half inches taller than me. Or, I wish I was taller. She's actually changed me in many ways and I've changed her in some ways. She used to believe in doctors completely. And I would say, that's not the way it is. Now she's gone to the other extreme, she's much more suspicious than I am. She believes in alternative medicine and appreciates whole foods and natural ways. Her desire for an orderly environment kicks in everyday and she wants to clean and make the beds as soon as we get up and that bothers the heck out of me. To get up and start cleaning is not my way of doing things. I want to lounge around and kick back. It drives her crazy when things aren't in order."

Impacted by her mother's love of nature, and her determination to provide organic foods for her family, Becky Yzaguirre has embraced a healthy life style by majoring in Exercise Science at ASU and becoming a Power Pilates certified instructor. "My mom has taught me to appreciate nature and to respect it. We have always had a garden and eaten organic foods. Even before there was a hype about eating naturally and staying close to nature, my mom was doing this and teaching this lifestyle to her children."

At times, Audrey also opened the family home to neighbors in need and treated them as lovingly as if they were family. "I remember some neighbors living with us when they fell on hard times," Becky says. "It was the family of two little boys my brother and I knew from school. Mom treated them like adopted family members."

Although the norm for most married women is to be more emotionally involved with their partners, it's different for the Yzaguirrres. Audrey's more reserved, English/German upbringing makes her cautious about sharing her feelings with her husband. "It's been the other way around for us," Yzaguirre explains. "I'm more interested in understanding her feelings and thoughts. She's a private person about her feelings and has always liked more intimate, personal meetings with friends, and likes to avoid big crowds. At first, I didn't like to take her to big social functions because then I would worry about her, and it was a bad evening for both of us. One thing she longed for was for me to stay home more and travel less, that was a big thing for her, and she worried about my health. She wanted me to take better care of my health."

Twice, the couple went back to Texas to live; once to recapture the cultural experience Yzaguirre thought his children needed, and the second time with plans to seek out a political career while establishing a non-profit organization that would impact community change. "I wanted to live in the barrio," Yzaguirre says, "which had decayed significantly by the time we went back in the early 70's. Audrey never complained. 'This is what you want, this is what we'll do,' she said. The older kids got to know the culture better, then we went to back to D.C. and eventually I became the CEO of NCLR. During the time when we didn't have money, Audrey didn't complain. I'm very grateful to her. We've had money and we haven't had money, but we've never fought about money. When we look back, those were some of the happiest times of our lives."

NCLR Conference Adventures

"I am the first-born son of a first-born son, and my Yzaguirre grandmother used to call me 'Your Royal Highness,'" Raul, Jr., says, describing what it meant for him to follow in his father's footsteps. Recalling the thousands of people who stood in line, waiting to shake his dad's hand at NCLR conferences, and seeing microphones set up and the news media in a frenzy to get a few lines from him, impressed young Raul, Jr., "I thought my dad was the president of a country. That's what I used to tell people."

The NCLR conferences provided a time for the whole family to see Yzaguirre in action. Raul, Jr., recalls a conference in 1978 at the Mayflower Hotel in Washington D.C. when he wore a baby blue suit, all polyester and got into the spirit of modeling his dad's friendly, open spirit. A few years later, on a fast run to get to one of the NCLR conferences, Raul, Jr., ends up meeting a couple of surprise celebrities. "I was working at a Pizza Hut in the late 80's and I was in a hurry to get to an NCLR Conference. I had to drive a good distance to get to the Hyatt Regency where the conference was being held, and decided not to go to the bathroom until I got to the hotel so I could stay awake while driving. When I got there everyone was shouting my dad's name 'Raul! Raul!' Then, I saw my dad dancing up to the stage with Selena as the music played. By this time I was jumping up and down to get to the bathroom, and when I got there, I saw Ricardo Montalbán. At another conference I got to meet President Obama when he was still Senator Obama. And at another conference, I experienced one of the proudest moments of my life, seeing my father shake hands with President Bill Clinton."

Ben relates that his experiences at NCLR conferences were different from his older siblings. "By the time I was coming of age, my father's time at NCLR was coming to a close, so I never had a lot of direct participation. It still has influenced me though in more ways than I can list. I was very young when he received the Aztec Eagle from Mexico, the biggest award given to a non-Mexican by the President of Mexico. And many years later, when he was sworn in as the ambassador for the Dominican Republic, I was so proud when I heard the remarks made by Secretary Hillary Clinton about my dad."

A history major in college, Ben was thrilled to read about his father in a class-assigned textbook. "Not only was my dad in one of the textbooks we were assigned, but my first internship at the Smithsonian Museum of American History was a partial result of the Latino initiative, which was a result of a study that my father had worked on at the Smithsonian. He had denounced Smithsonian officials for not hiring minority personnel."

As one of the youngest Yzaguirres, Becky wondered what her dad actually did for a living. "It was a mystery what he did, and at times very ambiguous for me. At conferences, we would meet all kinds of people and that's when I began to learn about the work he did. We liked to hear him make speeches. Now, as an adult, I am so proud of my dad and his accomplishments. Whenever I am afraid or nervous or do something challenging in my career, I think of all the public speaking my dad has done, regardless of the fact that he hates it. No one is ever aware that he is nervous because his speeches are so heartfelt that you believe him to be supremely confident and natural on stage. I try and remember this when I have to get in front of a new group of people and teach a Pilates class. I try not to evoke emotion, but try to teach them to move and use the right muscles, which can be a challenging task."

After NCLR conferences, the Yzaguirres would often take time to enjoy a vacation. "We would all go to whichever city the conference was in that year, and then travel somewhere else locally when the conference had concluded," recalls Ben. "I always laughed at the transformation my father made from the conference to the family trip. At the conference Dad was always so important, always the well-dressed executive, hounded by people for his time and input. He made important speeches, directed policy and so forth, but within twenty-four hours he would transform into a man trying to corral his children into family activities, negotiate rates with hotel staff and just generally manage the chaos that goes with being a parent."

Beginning to feel great stress over his numerous duties and commitments as President and CEO of NCLR, Yzaguirre one day confessed to Raul, Jr., "I'm burned out son. I'm thinking of quitting NCLR," at which point his son, always ready for a laugh answered, "If that's what you want Dad, do it. It's okay, but I thought you'd do this work until you retired. Now, you'll have to spend all your time with Mom. So he did another ten years," Raul, Jr., recalls.

FEAR NOTHING

Time and time again, Yzaguirre advocated for his son, Raul, Jr., as he made his way through school with learning disabilities and a diagnosis of Attention Deficit Disorder (ADD). Often characterized by excessive inattentiveness, impulsiveness and hyperactivity, children suffering ADD may squirm in their seats at school, and sense feelings of restlessness and agitation. ADD students procrastinate and are often disorganized in their thinking and planning, acting, for the most part, on impulse. Their behavior can cause problems in a classroom, and impede their ability to learn at the pace of non-ADD children. Patience and an understanding of ADD children is something parents and teachers must possess in order to work hand-in-hand for the successful integration of these students in a classroom setting.

"I struggled against an inferiority complex," Raul, Jr., relates. "I couldn't imagine filling Dad's shoes. It made me nervous. I was learning disabled and was diagnosed ADD. My test scores were low."

The move made by the family to San Juan, Texas and then back again to Mt. Airy in Maryland, added to Raul, Jr.'s struggles in school. Learning Spanish in San Juan as a youngster enabled him to communicate fluently in Spanish at home and in school. Back in Maryland, his Spanish wasn't appreciated. Family members living there were against him speaking Spanish, and instead of praising his fluency, ridiculed him and made negative remarks. With few Spanish speakers living in Maryland, English was the only language spoken in school. "I had a double-identity," Raul, Jr., says, relating his ambiguous feelings about his Mexican and Anglo ancestry. "In Maryland I was too Mexican, and in South Texas, I wasn't Mexican enough. My dad spoke to the principal and told him I should be praised for learning another language, not ridiculed and made to feel ashamed. Dad stuck up for me all the time. Not once, did he make me feel as if I was less than my other brothers and sisters. 'You're not a bad boy, son,' he would say to me. He always made me feel that I was a good person, and not any different than anyone else. Mom would encourage me with her words, 'I love you, Hoagie.'"

Raul, Jr.'s negative experiences with speaking Spanish at schools in Maryland ignited Yzaguirre's own memories of his segregation at Vida N. Clover school as a child, on the pretext that he had to learn English to satisfy PSJA District policies before being integrated with Anglo students. "I favor programs that allow for language growth, maintenance programs in particular," Yzaguirre explains. "Evidence shows that these programs not only help students maintain fluency in their native language, they also help them learn

English faster. Learning another language, in and of itself, can make you a smarter person, not only because you know a different language but because you have content that can be transferred to learn other languages and excel academically. Learning another language also increases the synapses (connections) in your brain that allow you to learn information faster, and that's a proven physiological fact. It mattered to me that my son had learned Spanish. I saw it as a big plus, rather than a minus and I always made that known to his teachers."

Raul's travels put a strain on his family. There were many times when his commitments kept him out of town for weeks at a time and Audrey had to play a double role. "I tried to attend school events, football games, PTA meetings, plays and conferences when I could. It was hard with all the traveling. And there were times when I had to do advocacy for my son, Raul, Jr. I got in a fight over my son and told the teacher, 'You're not fit to teach; you should be thrown out.' The school principal was there. He said, 'I take exception to that.' I told him he could take exception to it if he liked, but the teacher was putting down the kids who weren't learning, including my own son. He showed no intelligence about how to diagnose learning problems. My wife was taken aback with my action. Things did change. They put my son in a different school, and he did better. I believe a teacher's attitude results in grades that conform to their expectations, raising a student's ability."

Playing in the school band, as his father had done in school, helped Raul, Jr. discipline his mind, and learn to take things a step at a time, which helped him see information in smaller "bits." Learning in smaller steps helped him retain information and understand whole concepts. "Music helped me learn not to give up. I just practiced the same song over and over again until I learned it. And when I got a job at a Pizza Hut and was told to use the register for the first time, I took it a step at a time, like learning music. Then on to the next challenge, a twenty page research paper, and I said to myself 'wait a minute, I learned to play that song, I can do this.'" But as Raul, Jr. moves into his college years the academic requirements become greater. "I was more and more afraid of school and of not having academic success. I used to think—how will I compare to Dad?"

Raul, Jr.'s fears begin to cause more problems as he matures and takes on adult tasks. "I remember my dad teaching me how to drive when I was in high school, at age fifteen. We went out in a 1978 Hatchback Datsun F10. It was a stick shift. Dad kept telling me, 'Let out the clutch. Give it gas.' I tried that four or five times and gave it lots of gas. I headed towards a fence with the car out of control. I saw my dad step on the brake, and all I could think about was how mad he would be. My dad was on the passenger side as I slammed into the fence. He pulled me back into the car as I tried to flee. 'You can go through this fence or house, but I cannot and will not let you be afraid,' he said."

Taking the opportunity to teach his teen son that he was not to let fear control his life was one of the most poignant lessons Raul, Jr. would learn from his father. The lesson learned that day remained in Raul, Jr.'s mind, influencing him to reconfigure his actions, and opening the way for a new concept of self-acceptance and confidence to grow.

Plans to attend Texas Pan American University, and study Spanish in Mexico come into focus on the day Raul, Jr. has a heart-to-heart talk with his dad. "One day, my dad pulled me aside and said, 'All right boy, come outside.' We sat down together by the pond in our backyard. 'I'm worried about your future. You're at a point in your life where you're uncommitted. It's time for you to go out and find something you want to do.'"

Yzaguirre's words awaken something in his son that had lain dormant in his internal being, but soon surfaces to his conscious mind. Early on, Raul, Jr. had been forbidden to lean on his sister, Gina, for help with schoolwork as they made their way through school. "My dad would say, 'Remember son, you and your sister aren't going to school together.' He was worried she would do all the work for me, and wanted me to learn things on my own. Over the years, I learned to take things in smaller steps and not give up when I faced difficult tasks. I learned to be resilient."

Struggling with college classes, Raul, Jr. recalls that math was his worst subject, and try as he would, he would often have to drop a math class, only to retake it at a later time. "The painful things in my life, my dad made easy for me. In college I failed a math class and asked the professor to drop me. She made me feel bad and made a false assumption. She said my intelligence was inhibited by my smoking marijuana. I didn't tell her to go to hell, even though I wanted to. I didn't know how I would tell my dad that I wouldn't graduate on time. But later I found out that no matter how much I thought I had disappointed him, my dad never said anything negative to me. All he did was offer words of encouragement."

Playing in a little league football team, Ben recalls a time his father stepped in for him, even though his father's efforts caused him some embarrassment. "My dad couldn't always make the games, but when he did it was special. I was delighted that he came one afternoon, especially since I was doing particularly well that year and so was my fifth grade football team. We were undefeated. In this game, though, we weren't playing too well. Every time I came back to the sidelines, I heard whispers from the other players about a parent who was giving the coaches an earful for their decisions and techniques. In the back of my mind, I knew who it was, but kept it to myself. The following Monday, my team had their first ever parent-coach meeting about crowd behavior, which my poor mother had to attend in my father's absence."

Throughout his years of parenting, Yzaguirre was not spared episodes of accidents, unplanned childish mishaps and the general mayhem of being a father to six active children. As one of the older siblings, Raul, Jr. recalls two times in which his father, oblivious to red lights, and traveling at break-neck speed, came to the rescue of his precocious offspring. "We were in McAllen, Texas, when my little sister, Becky, did a swan dive to the concrete floor from a grocery cart at the supermarket. Dad and I drove like the Dukes of Hazard, with the car jumping over all kinds of things, to get to the hospital."

In another hair-raising ride, Raul, Jr., recalls his father racing to get to the hospital where his younger brother, Bobby, had been taken to after an accident. "Bobby fell out of a tree, and Mom immediately leaped on him to protect him from his moving, in case he had broken his neck. A neighbor helped Mom take my brother to the hospital. Mom called my Dad who was about two hours away. He picked me up to take me to Westminster Hospital. We were flying to get there and made the trip in one hour instead of two. When we got there, a nurse was trying to start an IV on Bobby, and couldn't find his vein. My dad said, 'Allow me.' His medical training kicked in."

Yzaguirre's lessons of confronting fear by facing difficult situations with courage, is something his children will remember throughout their lifetimes. Their father's indomitable courage is clearly witnessed by Raul, Jr. when he first notices signs of Parkinson's, the disease that will grip his energetic, hard-working dad, making his life a daily challenge. "The first time I saw signs of Parkinson's was at an NCLR Conference. Dad had his hand in his pocket. I later found out his hand was shaking. He wouldn't talk about it, and I didn't see him again until he was receiving an award. He told me, 'I'm not going to die,' but I worry about it all the time, and feel protective of him. I don't know if I've come to terms with it. He has to take medication, and he isn't able to sleep at night. I was working late once, at a McDonald's and remember Dad playing solitaire at 3 AM in the morning."

Serving as the principal to hundreds of children each year at the Yzaguirre School for Success, Raul, Jr. learned to emulate his father's courageous spirit as he dealt with students from a low-income, mostly Latino-based community in Brownsville. "I want to teach all children, and especially marginalized children to be like my dad. This is how you beat the status quo, this is how you change things by being active in the community, completing your education, voting and seeking equality. I want each student to be a productive member of society and realize the American Dream."

Echoing his brother's desire to realize goals important to his father, Ben commented on his own feelings of pride over his father's accomplishments. "I couldn't be prouder of my father. To do what he has done for so long and with so much passion amazes me. I've been able to experience so much because of him. I'm more appreciative of broader government policy and the role of advocacy and community-based organizations. I also have a better sense of people's points of view, something Dad has constantly worked with as he has dealt with countless different groups of people."

"My dad has taught me to be respectful to all people, and never be assuming," Becky says. "He has taught me to be grateful for the people I meet and for all of life's opportunities. I watch him interact with people he has never met before and watch how he makes a strong effort to help them just because it's the right thing to do. He uses his knowledge and connections to help lead people to the right places."

LEADING PEOPLE TO THE "RIGHT PLACES," shows up early in Yzaguirre's life, as he jumps into the ring of political fire in D.C. while still finishing his college degree. He will be among the first to set up a national student group, the National Organization of Mexican American Services (NOMAS), "No More," that both inspires young leaders, and intimidates the "powers-that-be"—those who view his ideas on equality for Latinos and leveling the playing field for all ethnic minorities as a radical call to action that will lead to more protests and demands for new legislation. President Lyndon Johnson will soon take special notice of NOMAS, and his unwavering gaze will spell the group's doom; although at the time, Yzaguirre found it hard to believe the president would lose any sleep over a small student group. With a little help from his friend and fellow activist, Roberto Reveles, the truth is soon revealed, and LBJ's plans for NOMAS surface quickly. As reality sets in, Yzaguirre, with his usual unflustered manner, shrugs it off—water off a duck's back—another lesson learned.

13

CIA INFILTRATION

Manuel Aragon and his brother Robert were trying to infiltrate NOMAS. I told Raul, 'I don't think these guys are who they say they are.' Raul couldn't believe the CIA would bother to infiltrate a struggling upstart group like ours.

—Roberto "Bob" Reveles

LBJ's Blacklist

MEXICAN AMERICAN VETERANS are coming home from the Vietnam War—but to what? Nothing has changed. They're still suffering discrimination, and their families are being treated like second-class citizens, going nowhere. Many Mexican Americans still labor in agricultural fields and live in poverty. The majority of farm laborers are *braceros* from Mexico, a term referring to the word *brazos* (arms) in Spanish—something America needed, "human arms" to help build the country after years of war. Other Mexican Americans find themselves segregated in barrios and are seen as a caste minority, used to serve the needs of Anglo Americans. Stereotypically, they're categorized as foreigners, gang members, trouble-makers and generally people who are not "real Americans." It will take a national protest effort—the Chicano Movement, El Movimiento—fueled by Latino civil rights leaders to begin to right the wrongs.

On fire as an organizer in D.C., Yzaguirre's frustrated by delays and political obstacles he must constantly face. President Johnson, often a friend of civil rights leaders and an advocate for fair and equal treatment for all Americans, proves to be an advocate for civil rights, but at the same time, orders CIA investigations of groups he identifies as "radical" and "left-wing." Yzaguirre is soon to find out that the group he chairs, NOMAS, is on LBJ's "black-list."

Born in 1908 in Stonewall, Texas, in a non-descript farmhouse built close to the Pedernales River, LBJ is quite familiar with Mexican Americans; he's seen them all his life in Texas. A descendant of a Baptist clergyman, George Washington Baines, on his mother's side, and her grandfather who became president of Baylor University during the American Civil War, he's brought up in a family rooted in Christian beliefs, and actively involved in social issues. Like Yzaguirre, LBJ excels in speech and debate in high school, and college and in 1930 graduates from Southwest Texas Teachers' College, (now Texas State University). Teaching Mexican American children at Welhausen School in a poor segregated community in Cotulla, close to San Antonio, provides him with much needed funds to complete his college degree and allows him to experience, first-hand, what it means for poor children to have limited educational opportunities. Later, he will reflect on his time at Welhausen and the sense of pain and loss he felt knowing that none of the children from the school would ever go to college—they were too poor. The memory of the children he taught led to his advocacy for educational rights and access to higher education as part of his vision for a Great Society.

As Yzaguirre's organizing efforts expand to attract civil rights leaders from across the nation, LBJ, now in office after the assassination of one of the most popular presidents in American history—John F. Kennedy, finds himself beset by a nation divided over the Vietnam War, and he watches as African American civil rights protests explode in the South, while his own Southern political backers hold his feet to the fire, many of them refusing to integrate even at gun-point. And now, he hears that the Mexican Americans are demanding their own liberation from long years of oppression, and he understands them, he's lived in poverty himself and has seen how Mexican Americans in Texas have suffered; but that doesn't make up for his suspicions that "radical" Mexican American groups are about to create new challenges and more problems. At the top of his list is a name he has heard only a few times, but one that will soon draw his full attention: Raul Yzaguirre.

THE LONGORIA AFFAIR

The intersection of Dr. Hector P. García and Raul Yzaguirre's lives began in 1953 when Yzaguirre ran away from home at age thirteen to search for adventure and independence in Corpus Christi. The strong connection between the two continued in D.C., as Yzaguirre took on the chairmanship of NOMAS in 1964, utilizing the skills he learned as a Junior GI Forum organizer.

"Dr. García had a great knowledge of history," Yzaguirre says. "He inspired me to think of civil rights and the Chicano Movement in historical terms because he was a great student of history. He knew the importance of organizing to get things done. He founded the GI Forum and practically funded it out of his own pocket for a long time. I was honored, as a teenager, to occasionally be his driver. On weekends, we would drive through the Valley in his Cadillac."

A passionate civil rights leader, and founder of the American GI Forum, Dr. García pressures the state of Texas, specifically then Texas Senator Lyndon B. Johnson, to right the discrimination suffered by the deceased World War II veteran, Felix Longoria, that finally resulted in Longoria's burial in Arlington Cemetery in 1949, the first Mexican American to be awarded this distinct honor. A decorated veteran of World War II, Dr. García battled against the state of Texas, positioning himself to defend the honor of Mexican American veterans killed in action, who came back to Texas in flag-draped coffins, only to be refused services in Anglo-owned funeral homes. Some Anglos had gone as far as refusing to bury the war heroes in their cemeteries, as if they would pollute the ground of their own beloved dead. García's rousing cry stirred activists nationwide. "¡Ya Basta! Enough is enough!"

"LBJ began working with the GI Forum in 1949 when a veteran, Felix Longoria, came home from the war to be buried, "Yzaguirre says, recalling the details of the racist behavior faced by Felix Longoria's family at the funeral home in Three Rivers, Texas. "The local mortuary wouldn't take his body because he was Mexican American, and Dr. García got incensed, that a war veteran couldn't be buried or treated in the same mortuary as Anglos. He made a big deal about it, and asked LBJ, who was then a U.S. Senator, for help. So Senator Johnson arranged for Longoria's body to be flown to Arlington Cemetery and he was buried there. After that, Dr. García and LBJ became close friends."

Dr. García's effective campaign in restoring dignity to Private Felix Longoria, ambushed by a Japanese sniper while on a volunteer mission in the Philippines during World War II, resulted in President Harry S. Truman instructing General Harry H. Vaughn to attend the funeral services at Arlington Cemetery and pay his last respects to "that Longoria boy from Texas."

The close ties between Dr. García and President Johnson forged a strong alliance, opening the doors of Johnson's Great Society and his War on Poverty campaign to Mexican Americans, creating fertile ground for Yzaguirre and other civil rights leaders to earn recognition in spite of bickering among ethnic groups, and heated discussions that went long into the night in which answers about equality and fair treatment for all Americans regardless of race, color or creed only seemed to raise more questions.

Active in the League of United Latin American Citizens (LULAC), founded in Corpus Christi in 1929, Dr. García, initially favors Lyndon Johnson for President, and switches his preference to John F. Kennedy only when he sees that Kennedy's nomination is imminent, and his running mate will most likely be Johnson. Joining in the Viva Kennedy campaign, he influences other Mexican American leaders to do the same. Their involvement in Kennedy's campaign is the first time Mexican Americans understand the power of uniting behind a presidential candidate, and exercising their voting rights to bring about a political victory. "Dr. García wanted the GI Forum to endorse LBJ over Kennedy for president," Yzaguirre recalls. "There was disagreement among GI Forum members over this. He was very loyal to LBJ, at times when he shouldn't have been. He said that when we had needed him, LBJ had come through for us." Later, Dr. García's loyalty to LBJ will ignite a volatile collision between himself and Yzaguirre—two strong-willed men who will eventually come to terms with their differences through sound reasoning and mutual respect.

Many years later, upon hearing of Dr. García's death on July 26, 1996, Yzaguirre would not hesitate to interrupt his attendance at the Olympic games in Atlanta, Georgia to travel to Corpus Christi and attend his funeral, joining dignitaries from all over the nation. "It was impossible for me to stay away," he recalls. "Dr. García was my inspiration and the reason I began my work in civil rights. His life gave meaning and purpose to my own existence, and I remain eternally grateful."

ROTATING HATS

Passionate about unifying groups that are working with the same goals in mind, Yzaguirre's style of finding the "common ground," a place where all can feel confident in sharing their views and plans, is something that often ignites rifts and divisions as organizations stand their ground, unwilling to relinquish what they consider valued goals. While a student at George Washington University in 1964, Yzaguirre organizes the student group, NOMAS, and with only a skeleton crew of ten activists, forges ahead.

"I was running the lab for my boss, Dr. Robinson, and decided to be up-front with him. I told him I wanted to leave the lab and work to lobby and organize for civil rights groups. He told me, 'I'm totally supportive of your decision, and will put in a separate phone line for you to use.' That made it possible for me to stay and be involved while I was still in school. Myself and eight or ten other guys from the Southwest who worked with the GI Forum, LULAC, the Huelga Committee and other organizations got together to form a group. We thought we needed something that would unite all organizations and could serve as a funnel of information. So, we formed this thing called NOMAS, and I was the chairman. It was the first leadership position I held at a national level. We used my office at the lab as a meeting place. We were a bunch of activists. One of them was Bob Reveles who attended Georgetown University. We were from all over the place. Some of us were students or part-time students, and some had just finished college."

"We organized the GI Forum, LULAC and our own *huelga* committee to support Cesar Chavez's boycotts, especially in front of grocery stores. We worked a lot with the Civil Service Commission to get Latinos hired. We approached the State Department to get twenty-five intern jobs opened for those working with us. One of the interns we hired was Willie Velasquez, and that's how I first met him. We did receptions, letters, and we informed the community back home on civil rights issues. We worked with Hubert Humphrey so LBJ would choose him as a running mate. We also worked together at times with the Urban League and the NAACP. Sterling Tucker was head of the Urban League at the time. There was competition between African Americans and Mexican Americans for funding, and we disagreed about how money should be allocated. It was a big deal. Altogether, NOMAS was working with about ten organizations, and there were only ten of us, so we would rotate hats. We formed the Wednesday Luncheon Club as a way to greet all Latinos who came into D.C. Every second Wednesday of the month, we would invite them to lunch but they had to pay their own way because we had no money for expenses. It was our way of networking with young Latinos coming into D.C. Some were college students, aides to congressmen and senators and others worked for the federal government. All of them were strong on civil rights and had high moral values and ideals."

Roberto "Bob" Reveles from Miami, Arizona attending Georgetown University in the School of Foreign Service, becomes one of Yzaguirre's core members in NOMAS. Having served four years in the Air Force during the Korean War, Reveles shares Yzaguirre's concerns over the discrimination suffered by returning Mexican American vets. "I saw this young kid, a student working at a medical lab in D.C. who was from Texas," Reveles says, describing his first impression of Yzaguirre. "I viewed him with caution, but he quickly demonstrated he was about a bigger mission. He became a good working colleague."

Years later, Reveles serves as the chief of staff for Arizona Congressman Morris K. "Mo" Udall, and earns a reputation as a formidable Congressional staffer. On a personal level, he serves an important role in Yzaguirre's life; he's chosen as his best man when Raul marries Audrey in 1965.

Yzaguirre's chairmanship of NOMAS leads him to the Ford Foundation, an organization crucial in affecting the creation of both the Southwest Council of La Raza (SWCLR), and NCLR. "Graciela Gil Olivarez opened the door to the Ford Foundation for us," Reveles says.

Born in 1928 in Barcelona, Arizona, a small copper mining town close to Reveles' home town of Miami, Graciela Gil Olivarez rises from poverty to become the first woman, and the first Mexican American woman, to graduate from the Notre Dame Law School in 1970. Over the years, she becomes affectionately known as "Amazing Grace," a name that reflects her ability to rise to positions of power, opening doors of opportunities for Latinos nationwide.

Dropping out of Ray High School when her family relocates to Phoenix, Olivarez enrolls at Lamson Business School and becomes a stenographer. Carving a place for herself in 1952 as a local disk jockey for KIFN, a popular Mexican radio station in Phoenix, Olivarez confronts opposition from the station's owners for her strong alliance with the impoverished barrios of South Phoenix. The owners of the radio station make it clear that they want her to pursue women's homemaking themes, and stay away from political issues, which she refuses to do. A determined civil rights activist, she serves as the director for the Arizona branch of the federal Office of Economic Opportunity (OEO) in 1965. Her natural intelligence and dedication to the community catches the eye of Robert B. Choate, member of the prominent Choate family from Massachusetts. Working in Choate's program "Careers for Youth," in Phoenix, Olivarez's work attracts the attention of the president of Notre Dame, Reverend Theodore Hesburgh, who encourages her to attend Notre Dame's Law School. Later, President Carter appoints her as the Director of the Community Services Administration, and she becomes the highest-ranking Mexican American "Chicana," as she referred to herself, to serve in the Carter administration.

"Graciela was with the Choate Foundation, and she was very generous with us. She paid for NOMAS members to go to the Southwest Conference on Poverty, and put us in contact with the Ford Foundation," Yzaguirre says, recalling the early days of the formation of NOMAS. At that time, representatives of NOMAS set up a meeting with Paul Ylvisaker of the Ford Foundation, but Yzaguirre did not join them, worried he looked too young to be believable. Unwilling to jeopardize the group's validity with Ylvisaker, he opted to take a back seat. Although expressing some interest, Ylvisaker admitted he knew nothing about the Mexican American community. "They considered us Mexican Indians," recalls Reveles, who, along with fellow activist, Manny

Velasquez and Yzaguirre, formulated the proposal that opened the door for funding from the Ford Foundation.

"Paul Ylvisaker was the vice president for national programs at the Ford Foundation," Yzaguirre says. "He was a person we talked to for funding for the Latino community and he was the guy who helped fund Southwest Council of La Raza and NCLR. He has since died, but he left a great legacy at the Ford Foundation."

Initially, Ylvisaker's decision to fund Mexican American organizations, does not directly benefit NOMAS, but sparks two major national studies of Mexican Americans that will uncover, for the first time, the challenges facing Mexican Americans described in the 1954 Supreme court landmark decision, *Hernández vs Texas* as a "class apart." The studies addressed distinct issues, such as Public Law 78, enacted by Congress in July 1951 which allowed recruitment of manual laborers from Mexico, *braceros*, for work in agricultural and railroad maintenance. The illegal use of undocumented workers by U.S. corporations, businesses and private individuals existed before implementation of the *bracero* program and after it was discontinued in 1965; the practice continues to fuel labor disputes to the present day.

Discussion of wetbacks, or *mojados*, in the reports fueled controversy between Mexican nationals and Mexican American citizens, as desperate families from Mexico sought employment in the U.S., competing directly with Mexican Americans living in the U.S. struggling with discrimination and racist treatment that resulted in low wages, poor living conditions and little-to-no provisions for their safety and welfare as employees. The studies, in the form of reports, were presented to the Ford Foundation and became pivotal points for understanding the social, economic, and political issues that fostered poverty, social dependency, unemployment, delinquency and educational and cultural deprivation that struck at the heart and soul of Mexican American communities.

McCARTHYISM ON THE RISE

Reflecting aspects of the McCarthy era, suspicions come to a head in President Johnson's administration concerning civil rights groups that are labeled as being radical and fostering a communist agenda. The Central Intelligence Agency (CIA) is under orders to keep these organizations under surveillance, which violates the law that prohibits the CIA from doing any operations domestically. One of the groups infiltrated by the CIA is NOMAS. Aware of LBJ's plan to weaken group leaders through divide and conquer tactics,

Yzaguirre seeks to create strength in numbers by formulating a plan in which all groups move as one, or not at all.

"We wanted NOMAS to look more like the Urban League, conservative and non-partisan. But there was lots of bickering among organizations, lots of ineffectiveness. Ninety percent of a group's energy went into organizational maintenance; planning the laws and bylaws and all procedures, logistics and group goals. The energy would run out by the end of the meeting and nothing new was accomplished. There was a severe lack of sophistication of management, resources and funding. We had to find something hard-hitting that measured progress and didn't create 'smoke and mirrors.' I wanted community involvement focused on solving problems. Clearly there was to be a political role, and I wanted that to be lobbying. If we were to use public money, it would be twenty percent of the group's income—which were IRS rules for lobbying. We tried to sell that vision to all organizations—to be under one umbrella, with negative results. Everyone appreciated their own sovereignty. There were lots of egos floating around."

Undaunted by the lack of response for unity from diverse groups, Yzaguirre reflects, "I wasn't disappointed, and knew it would take time and work. A national united Latino movement was hoped for at the time, but in all, I felt it was a very good experience for me. I had already worked with Dr. García in the GI Forum and in the congressional campaigns of Henry B. Gonzalez, and Kika de la Garza and had heard President Johnson speak in Texas when he was still a senator."

"Some leaders were obsessed with being White," Yzaguirre says, identifying a point of great contention within the Mexican American community. "Dr. García fought over the question of being White. He was obsessed with the idea that we had to be labeled Caucasian. He would get angry with me over the White issue because I believed we should keep our identity as Mexican Americans. Dr. García also sided with LBJ, no matter what. I thought LBJ had some blind spots, but Dr. García considered him his friend and always took his side."

Contending with an array of political leaders, and issues crucial to civil rights for Mexican Americans, Yzaguirre was to feel the full-force of President Johnson's unwavering decision to clip the wings of "radical" groups that might pose problems for his administration. "The CIA was investigating us all the time," Yzaguirre recalls. "LBJ put people on the road to discredit us because at one point, we tried to keep our leadership from meeting with him. Unknown to us, Manuel Aragon was one of the CIA agents. He was a student activist from California who called us up and said, 'I'm with the National Student

Association and I'd like to be helpful to you. Tell me what you're doing.' He was tall, well-educated and well-dressed. He had a brother who worked along with him, Robert Aragon. Manuel bought us lunch, joined in meetings and he would do little things for us, like gather information for meetings. Later, Manuel and his brother would attend meetings and suggest radical ideas as part of NOMAS activities, but I just thought they were being militant. Bob Reveles worked on the Hill and was acquainted with the House Un-American Activities Committee (HUAC). Bob said to me, 'There's something funny about Manuel Aragon. I'm going to check him out.' I told him he was being paranoid, but Bob insisted he might be CIA."

Using the cover of looking for prospective employees for his organization, Reveles's first contact with Manuel Aragon comes by way of a phone call in which Aragon identifies himself as a Chicano from California presently working with an import/export company in New York City, and interested in helping with what NOMAS is doing in support of the Chicano Movement. "He asked that we let him know when we would be meeting and that he'd come down to meet us and help," Reveles says. "From that time on he would make it a point to contact us and inquire about whom we were meeting with and what we were planning. His pattern of persistent and probing questions raised suspicions with me that he was not just the helpful 'import/export employee' that he claimed to be. Sometime later his cover as a CIA covert agent was blown as part of a major investigative exposure documenting U.S. spy activities being channeled through the National Student Association, an organization with which Aragon and his younger brother Robert had been active leaders. I was certain that Manuel Aragon and his brother Robert were trying to infiltrate NOMAS, and I told Raul, 'I don't think these guys are who they say they are.' Raul couldn't believe the CIA would bother to infiltrate a struggling upstart group like ours."

In another instance, also part of CIA investigations, Reveles remembers seeing a man eyeballing the crowd at a performance at Howard University of El Teatro Campesino, a theatre troupe directed by playwright, Luis Valdez, who in 1969 produced a short film of civil rights leader, Corky Gonzales's poem *Yo Soy Joaquin*. Valdez is the first Chicano director to have a play, *Zoot Suit*, performed on Broadway, and in 1981, the play was made into a movie. In 1987, his film, *La Bamba*, portraying the life of singing sensation, Ritchie Valens, brought him international fame.

"Let's have some fun," Reveles recalls telling Yzaguirre. "I went up to the guy I recognized as an investigator with HUAC and said. 'welcome to our event. It's good to have someone from HUAC here.'" The following day,

Reveles, working in the same building housing the HUAC, approaches the investigator and apologizes to him for exposing his cover the previous night at El Teatro Campesino's performance. The investigator then invites Reveles to the HUAC office and says, "Do you know who you're associating with?" Then he pulls out a file on Luis Valdez.

Unaware he had aroused the CIA's attention by his trip abroad, Valdez, a young activist from California recalls the reason why he may have been tagged a communist. "In 1964 I went to Cuba with other students from San Jose State and toured into Europe as well. I guess that's where the CIA may have gotten the idea that I was a communist," Valdez says. His evening performance at Howard University was one of the first times an east coast audience heard the cry of Mexican American *campesinos* who labored in the fields and were determined to seek justice against cruel racism. "The night we performed at Howard University was a powerful experience for all of us. We sang our own version of *We Shall Overcome*, called, *Nosotros Venceremos*."

Switching his major from math and physics to English at San Jose State University, Valdez pursued his love of theatre, earning a degree in English, with an emphasis on drama and playwriting. He established El Teatro Campesino and created a series of *actos*, similar to one-act plays depicting the life of the migrant farm worker and eventually broadening to other cultural themes. "I met Raul in 1967 on a tour across the country to boycott grapes as part of Cesar Chavez's protest against unfair treatment of farm workers by American growers," Valdez recalls. "We traveled in an old white van all the way to Washington D.C. Pete Seeger, Joan Baez and other popular singers joined us there. It was an opportunity to get national visibility. Robert and Edward Kennedy were involved in the event as well as Henry Ford's daughter. We performed our *actos* in the Senate Courtyard at noon to a packed crowd of senators and other legislators. Raul made it all happen. He helped create a national consciousness that extended from coast to coast. We were not only from one region, we belonged to a whole country. Raul established a national network and gave *la raza* a human face. We were now a part of the fabric of American life."

The fact that numerous Mexican American leaders and groups, including artists and reporters were on the CIA's list for investigation, becomes a fact of life during the highly charged years of Chicano protests, marches, sit-ins and walkouts. The practice of destroying "radical" organizations is to eventually mark the end of NOMAS and the beginning of Yzaguirre's work in President Johnson's War on Poverty.

CRUSHING NOMAS

"NOMAS was asked to function as the secretariat for the Albuquerque walkout participants," Yzaguirre says. "Specifically, the walkout members were concerned about divide and conquer tactics by the LBJ administration. We learned about these tactics and made a deal that nobody would talk to Johnson's administration unless authorized to do so. NOMAS was only a small group of students, yet LBJ felt threatened by us. Walkouts agitated the Latino community and brought to the forefront that here was the Great Society Program, still ignoring Latinos. Everything was about African Americans and nothing about Latinos. LBJ got into office due to Kennedy's assassination, so he was afraid of the 1964 election. That's why things were so sensitive. He was afraid of losing votes."

A political strategist at heart, LBJ seeks a way to gain access to political groups he identifies as subversive to his views. With this in mind, he turns his attention to Chicano leaders who are at the forefront of the Mexican American civil rights movement.

"LBJ called five of our leaders to the White House for dinner," Yzaguirre says. "We saw it as a dog and pony show. They were leaders from the GI Forum, PASSO (Political Association of Spanish-Speaking Organizations), MAPA (Mexican American Political Association), LULAC, and the Crusade for Justice. Subsequently, NOMAS tried to force them to get permission from the entire group on the position we would take. I was keeper of the promise, so to speak, and told them we would only negotiate with the president if we stuck together. LBJ was very crafty, and could pick us off. He was a towering figure, sure of himself and most perfunctory. The leaders first met at a hotel near the White House. I rounded up my guys and we descended upon them and I said, 'remember what we pledged to do.' It was very tense. Bert Corona of MAPA told me to go to hell. Dr. García, who had been like a father to me, was very angry with me. Judge Hernandez from LULAC held his ground, and said, 'We are here to keep this together.' We were able, through his leadership, to agree to have a conference call with all the other leaders. In Bert's case, I think he just wanted to go to the White House and wouldn't let a kid like me stop him. Dr. García was loyal to LBJ and wouldn't do anything against him. Judge Albert Peña and Corky Gonzales and all the other big names agreed on what we would do as a group. They had a late dinner with LBJ and it was very tense. LBJ found out how NOMAS had tried to keep him from dividing the leaders and he put maybe four people to go out and destroy NOMAS and they did so by tasking three individuals to work almost full time on discrediting us.

One of those three individuals, and perhaps the lead person, was David North, who worked with the Department of Labor (DOL) and later would become a friend and business associate."

David North, an advocate of a restrictive immigration policy, clashed with Yzaguirre, who firmly believed in opening citizenship and labor opportunities to immigrants. "I met Raul through Ruth Graves," North relates. "She and I came to D.C. in the spring of 1961 as very junior political appointees in the Kennedy Administration. Ruth and I worked in the Labor Department. Six years later, in 1967, we had advanced within LBJ's administration. She was director for part of the War on Poverty (OEO) that handled grants for farm workers programs and I had become the Staff Director of the Inter-Agency Committee on Mexican American Affairs, an arm of the LBJ White House."

Working in President Johnson's administration, North played a key role in moving against NOMAS. "They put out the word not to deal with us," Yzaguirre recalls. "We got a little money from AFL-CIO and we were doing some work with them, but once the word was out not to deal with us, they stopped giving us money. There were only ten or twelve of us and Manny Velasquez said, 'I don't need this. I need to go out and make money.' So, he went off to do his work as a lawyer. Manuel Aragon and David North were two of the key people in crushing NOMAS. North made us *persona non grata*. People who contributed to the AFL-CIO stopped talking to us, and organizations that felt they were part of the White House began to distance themselves from us. Some of the members who worked for the government had their jobs threatened. NOMAS never raised its head again. We later read an article on the front page of the *Washington Post* that related how the "radical" group NOMAS had been infiltrated by a chief military intelligence officer, Manuel Aragon. He was an organizer provocateur. Aragon later admitted his role as a CIA agent. A few years later, he went to work as a community action core director and ran for Congress against Esteban Torres."

In spite of carrying out his charge to destroy NOMAS, David North came to respect Yzaguirre's dedication to the Mexican American community. "Raul helped manage the Cabinet Committee Hearing on Mexican American Affairs in El Paso, North recalls. "This turned out to be a major gathering of Mexican American leaders with minor participation from Puerto Ricans and a major outreach by the LBJ administration to America's Hispanics. My impression of Raul at that time, and since, was that he was a somewhat rough-hewn force for good, sensible assertive and both a spokesman for, and a leader in the faction-ridden Mexican American community. He had a sense for how to obtain and use political power, and was never afraid to use those skills."

With NOMAS activities coming to a close, Yzaguirre now turned his attention to President Johnson's War on Poverty. It's not long before he's asked to join the president's efforts in creating greater opportunities for Mexican Americans, and bringing some closure to the rift prevalent between Mexican American and African American communities. "The Civil Rights Commission, was set up on or about 1957 to focus on civil rights issues. It had advisory bodies and state groups, and tended to focus almost exclusively on Black issues. NOMAS spent a lot of time and energy trying to get this entity to pay attention to Latinos," Yzaguirre says, describing the 'invisibility' of Mexican Americans during the early years of the Civil Rights Movement.

Later, Yzaguirre becomes the first Latino to be elected to the Leadership Conference on Civil Rights (LCCR) and is able to wade through contentious dialogue with Black leaders to create awareness of civil rights for Latinos nationwide. His personal contact with the president later earns him the LBJ Award, recognizing his dedication and leadership in the cause of civil rights.

"There were not many appointments of Latinos in the Kennedy administration," Yzaguirre states. "LBJ did better. He surrounded himself with more Latinos, and we got invited to more functions. At first it seemed incredible to be in the White House, like a movie, but later it became routine. LBJ opened the White House to Latinos."

One of the positive outcomes of the controversial White House dinner with President Johnson was the appointment of Vicente Ximenes of Floresville, Texas as the commissioner of the Equal Employment Opportunity Commission (EEOC). President Johnson had been Ximenes's second grade teacher when he served as an educator in the Texas public school system. Ximenes also attended the University of Texas at Austin where he became good friends with Dr. Hector P. García, who had a hand in recommending him for the cabinet position in Johnson's administration. Ximenes, the original chair of the Interagency Cabinet Committee on Mexican American Affairs, was appointed as the Assistant Inspector General for President Johnson's War on Poverty. Previously, he served in the Kennedy administration as program officer and economist for the U.S. Agency for International Development in Ecuador.

"Not many significant changes came about for Latinos," Yzaguirre admits, recalling, the early days of Johnson's administration. "Vicente Ximenes was a strong voice, but he was only one voice. We still had a long way to go."

THE "LONG WAY TO GO," had a beginning, once shrouded in mystery and myth. The history of thousands of years, the ancient world of the Mexicas was to emerge as a hot topic in the Chicano Movement, El Movimiento, and Chicano radicals, Yzaguirre among them, would soon experience the nebulous world of Aztlán, land of "whiteness," land of plenty, also known as Siapu, the place of origin. Theirs was a forgotten homeland somewhere north of present day Mexico City, built around seven caves, as surely as Rome had been built atop seven hills. Ancient time would catch up to real time in 1969 in one energizing moment and surprise the Chicano radicals—and young Chicano poets would lead the way.

14

AZTLÁN, THE MANIFESTO

I am the masses of my people
and I refuse to be absorbed. I am Joaquín.
—Rodolfo "Corky" Gonzales

Poets in Command

Young Chicanos gather in Denver, Colorado in March 1969 for the first National Chicano Liberation Youth Conference, unaware that they are about to make history. Some are college and university students. They come in cars, buses, and by hitching rides along the way when they have no transportation. They come from small towns, farmlands, barrios and major cities across America for one thing: to figure out who they are. They're open and ready to learn something new. Rodolfo "Corky" Gonzales, leader of the Crusade for Justice in Denver is their compelling leader, handsome, charming and filled with the conviction that tough times for Chicanos must come to an end. Musicians are there, and guitars accompany voices that declare that change is for everyone—and the time is NOW! Many students hear Corky's passionate, riveting words in his epic poem *Yo Soy Joaquín...I am Joaquín.* The poem is a powerful, heart-wrenching declaration of the terrible legacy of centuries of oppression of Chicanos and Mexicanos who have suffered under the lash of racism, and blatant hatred by White supremacists who aim destructive, demeaning pronouncements, like so many bullets into the heart of an ancient culture, settlers and civilizers of the American continent before there *was* an America.

I am Joaquín, lost in a world of confusion,
caught up in the whirl of a gringo society,

confused by the rules, scorned by attitudes,
suppressed by manipulation,
and destroyed by modern society...

Yo Soy Joaquin weaves the true history of Chicanos, one fraught with injuries and injustices—so many, they cannot be accurately measured. Corky delivers one of the most profound cries of defiance in the history of the Chicano nation. It is a charge against the lies believed about Mexican immigrants and those born in America, bent over their labor, a caste minority, never accepted by racists as their equals. It's an indictment of an America that cannot gauge the reality: Chicanos are here to stay.

I have survived the toils and slavery of the fields.
I have existed
In the barrios of the city
In the suburbs of bigotry
In the mines of social snobbery
In the prisons of dejection
In the muck of exploitation
And
In the fierce heat of racial hatred.
And now the trumpet sounds,
The music of the people stirs the
Revolution.

It's the word "revolution," that stirs White supremacists to indignation, and ushers in a sense of fear that maybe the Mexican Americans who have long been held in contempt by racist groups might forge a plan that would cause uprisings and protests like the battles already going on in the South with Black Americans. And their fears will, in fact, become reality in the years of the Chicano Movement, as Mexican Americans and other Latinos band together to wage war against discrimination and segregation in all its forms. Corky ends with a ringing conviction that *la raza* will endure.

La raza! Méjicano! Español! Latino! Chicano! Or whatever I call
myself, I look the same I feel the same I cry
And
Sing the same.
I am the masses of my people and I refuse to be absorbed.
I am Joaquín.

The odds are great
But my spirit is strong,
My faith unbreakable,
My blood is pure.
I am Aztec prince and Christian Christ.
I SHALL ENDURE! I WILL ENDURE!

Another young poet takes center stage at the conference. He seems lost in his thoughts as he approaches the microphone. Known by his *nom de plume*, Alurista, Alberto Urista recites a poem that is destined to awaken participants to a new consciousness of their homeland and their true identity.

In the spirit of a new people that is conscious not only of its proud historical heritage but also of the brutal "gringo" invasion of our territories, we, the Chicano inhabitants and civilizers of the northern land of Aztlán from whence came our forefathers, reclaiming the land of their birth and consecrating the determination of our people of the sun, declare that the call of our blood is our power, our responsibility and our inevitable destiny.

Born in Mexico City in 1947, but raised in San Diego, Alurista awes the crowd with his poem, *El Plan Espiritual de Aztlán*, which takes the form of a manifesto, outlining a new sense of self-hood for Mexican Americans. *El Plan* is a call to nationalism and an identity as Chicanos, a title reminiscent of the word, Mexicas, also referred to as Xicanos, an ancient name for the modern-day Aztecs, indigenous ancestors of the Mexican, *mestizo* nation. Aztlán refers to the mythical land of the Mexicas, the "land of whiteness," a land of plenty, shrouded in mystery since the beginning of time. Its location "to the north" gives little indication of its exact location, and some historians believe, the Mexicas may have originated from as far north as Colorado, or Utah. Migrating in 1325 to what is now the Valley of Mexico, they established their capital, Tenochitlán, now, modern-day Mexico City. The Mexicas (Aztec) thrived for over two hundred years, until the destruction of their culture at the hands of the Spanish conquistador, Hernán Cortés, who had mistakenly been identified as Quetzalcoatl, the Mexica god of peace who would return in a One Reed Year, on a 9 Wind Day, which happened to fall on April 22, 1519, Good Friday, the day the Christian conquistadores landed on the shores of Cozumel off the Mexican mainland. Mexica Emperor Moctezuma, ruling from their capital city, Tenochitlán, never faltered in his belief that the ancient prophecy had come true. Quetzalcoatl was back to reclaim his throne from Smoking Mirror, another manifestation of the war god, Huitzilopochtli. Fair-skinned, bearded, dressed in black and wearing a helmet, similar to the headpiece of Quetzalcoatl, Cortés had no intention of reclaiming an ancient throne. Instead, the Spanish conquistador lusted for power and gold, and signaled the destruction of the Mexica culture and the beginning of the nation of *los mestizos*. He renamed the land New Spain, placing it under the authority of the king of Spain. And so it remained for 300 years until the rising of *los mestizos* and the Mexican Revolution, which ended Spain's domination in 1821.

"Aztlán was a mythical place of the Aztecs, perhaps, somewhere as far north as Utah," Yzaguirre reflects. "No one knows how vast the land was, but it is clear the Aztecs journeyed south to find a new home. It was something like manifest destiny—a God-given right to own land, freely. If you see Aztlán as a myth, yet one grounded in historical legends, then it is a point of pride and identity, but if used politically as a way to conquer the Southwest, then it becomes impractical."

Yzaguirre draws a parallel between Aztlán, and the possession of new lands claimed by the ancient Mexicas. The indigenous peoples once possessed an inherent right to settle on land, freely, revering and protecting it as keepers of the land. Buying and selling of land was unknown to native peoples until the arrival of Europeans. Land ownership, sealed by U.S. government policies, became the prominent custom, displacing indigenous populations from their native lands. It signaled conflicts between Indians, Mexicans, French and Anglos that lasted for centuries, even to the present day. It fanned the fires of young Chicano radicals gathered at the Denver Conference in 1969, who, for the first time in their collective memory, had come to realize their own history—one conveniently omitted from the history books in American schools.

THE RADICALS

"I met Corky when I was in the American GI Forum in my early days," Yzaguirre recalls. "He was also an activist in the GI Forum and a boxer. I liked Corky a lot. He was a leader in Denver, Colorado and we had lots of conversations. I found him very exciting and very committed. Later on he became head of OEO's Community Action Program (CAP) in Denver and I got to work with him there when I was with OEO. Then he went on to found the Crusade for Justice. I think Corky's biggest legacy was *Yo Soy Joaquin*, the poem which was turned into a movie. He was a handsome, charismatic figure, an icon who motivated many. Corky was inspirational, but not someone who could move agendas. Personally, I did not attend the Denver Conference, but funded others who attended. Over the years, Corky and I lost touch, and I heard he got pretty militant. Unfortunately, he had a car accident on his way to one of the conferences and lost a lot of his memory."

Growing up in one of Denver's tough eastside barrios, Rodolfo "Corky" Gonzales's fiery nature causes his uncle to nickname him "Corky," which refers to a cork, ready to pop. Experiencing poverty and the loss of his mother at the age of two, Gonzales is destined to lead the first National Chicano Liberation Youth Conference and later joins in efforts to establish a Mexican American political party, La Raza Unida Party (LRUP) in 1970.

Alurista's manifesto on Aztlán, read at Gonzales's Denver Conference, prompts studies by Chicano leaders of the ancient homeland, and brings to the forefront a fiery, militant Chicano who identifies himself as "Indohispano," Reies Lopez Tijerina. Born in 1926 near Falls City, Texas, Tijerina's determination to restore New Mexico land grants to their Spanish colonial and Mexican owners opens up old wounds and ignites a spark of hope for securing ancient tracts of land. Drafting a plan for securing "stolen land," Tijerina, with his five brothers and a group of followers, organizes the Alianza Federal de Mercedes (Federal Alliance of Grants), on February 2, 1963, the 115th anniversary of the signing of the Treaty of Guadalupe Hidalgo. The group sets out to organize and acquaint Spanish land grant heirs of their rights.

In 1966 Tijerina leads a march from Albuquerque, New Mexico to the state capital in Santa Fe where he petitions the governor, Jack Campbell, to investigate Spanish and Mexican land grants, accusing the U.S. of stealing land from original settlers and not abiding by the articles of the Treaty of Guadalupe Hidalgo, through which the U.S. secured the greater portion of the American Southwest after the Mexican-American War (1846-48).

"A friend of mine, Alex Mercure, was one of the ones who talked me into running as CEO of NCLR," Yzaguirre says, in describing his introduction to Reies Tijerina. "He became president of a university in northern New Mexico, and later he became undersecretary of the Department of Agriculture under Jimmy Carter. After Carter's defeat, I offered Alex a job with NCLR, and he became one of our V.P.'s. But before all that, he was executive director of Health, Education and Land Programs (HELP) that specialized in rural communities. Alex and I were very good friends, and he was also a member of my consulting firm, Interstate Research Associates. Through him I got to know Reies Tijerina. When Reies revolted in 1967 and attacked a courthouse in Tierra Amarilla, New Mexico, he attacked with armed men. Two men, a prison guard and a sheriff's deputy were shot during the confrontation, but no one was killed. Reies fled, and the National Guard went after him. We were concerned because of the relationship between him and HELP. Alex and others persuaded Reies to give himself up. Reies was also anti-semitic [as expressed] in many of his talks. He tied into a vein of thought and emotion for people in New Mexico who wanted not only the history of their land, but they wanted to be recognized as people who developed New Mexico. In Arizona, Latinos founded the state, but in New Mexico, they were able to keep it in the history books. Reies was able to plug into the emotion of history and land ownership. He went to jail and supposedly they gave him shock treatments. They thought he was unbalanced, so they used shock treatments."

SU VOTO ES SU VOZ

While Yzaguirre is still a young organizer with the GI Forum, Willie Velasquez rises as a leader in the Chicano Movement. Working with the Bishop's Committee on the Spanish Speaking of Texas, Velasquez, is someone whom Yzaguirre describes as "more like my way of doing business." Determined to end unfair voting practices, Velasquez turns his full attention to fighting for equality in voting rights. "Willie formed the Mexican American Youth Organization (MAYO) and it morphed with La Raza Unida Party, but Willie stayed away from it." Yzaguirre explains. "He didn't believe in an ethnic [political] party and neither did I, but we both believed very strongly about registration for voters and political power."

Born on May 9, 1944 in Orlando Florida, Willie Velasquez was the son of William Velasquez, Sr., a union organizer, stationed in Orlando during World War II. Originally from Texas, the Velasquez family returned to their home state, and Willie graduated from Central Catholic High School in San Antonio, then went on to receive a B.A. in Economics in 1966 from St. Mary's University. While doing graduate work in economics at St. Mary's, he helped Cesar Chavez by organizing farm workers in the Rio Grande Valley. A prominent leader of the Chicano Movement, Velasquez concentrated his efforts on voter registration, and his words *su voto es su voz*, (your vote is your voice) became a battle cry, uniting grassroots efforts to register millions of Latino voters who had never realized the power of the vote. Velasquez founded the Southwest Voter Research Institute, currently the William C. Velasquez Institute (WCVI) in 1984, to hold accountable the Latino electorate, keeping voters informed of important policy issues.

Working along with NCLR, Velasquez also founded the Southwest Voter Registration Education Project (SVREP) in 1974, the oldest and largest non-partisan Latino voter registration organization in the nation. Transitioning from NCLR as Yzaguirre became CEO, Velasquez, with Yzaguirre's backing, created SVREP as a separate entity. "Voter registration was Willie's passion, and he dedicated his life to creating a powerful organization. Through his efforts, thousands, perhaps millions, of voters now have a voice in how our government works, and that is a powerful legacy to leave behind."

Willie Velasquez died unexpectedly on June 15, 1988, at age forty-four. In 1995, President Bill Clinton posthumously awarded Velasquez the Presidential Medal of Freedom, honoring him for his distinct role in advancing civil rights.

EL MOVIMIENTO

Often overlooked on the civil rights scene when compared to the much-publicized struggle for civil rights by African Americans, Mexican Americans have a long history of standing up for their rights. They were among the first to initiate law suits against segregation and unequal treatment of their children in Texas and California schools as early as the 1930's. By the 1960's, the Chicano Movement, El Movimiento, emerges as a formidable force, illuminated by *El Plan Espiritual de Aztlán*. Latinos, nationwide, join in the struggle to become "visible" to a society that has looked the other way for too long. Identified as a "class apart" on May 3, 1954 after the team of Texas attorneys, led by Gus Garcia, successfully plead *Texas v Hernández* before the Supreme Court, Mexican Americans are no longer considered Caucasian, and are assured protection under the Equal Protection Clause of the Fourteenth Amendment. But even with the Supreme Court's decision, things take their time.

On the east coast, Yzaguirre's chairmanship of NOMAS brings national attention to Mexican Americans from the Southwest that many east coast Americans didn't even know existed. El Movimiento gains strength in the 60's, as Mexicans and those who identify themselves as Chicanos, put their lives on the line in the struggle for civil rights for Mexican Americans who had, for the most part, been invisible to mainstream America. Among the numerous organizations created nationally were: the Mexican American trade union, Asociación Nacional México-Americana (ANWA) supported by the Mine, Mill and Smelter Workers (Mine-Mill), and the Mexican American Political Association (MAPA), launched in 1959 in Fresno, California, whose leaders, Humberto "Bert" Corona, Herman Gallegos, and Ed Roybal were destined to become prominent leaders in the Chicano Movement.

In Los Angeles, the Community Service Organization (CSO) carries out voter registration campaigns and brings to national attention one of the most formidable Chicano union leaders, Cesar Chavez. Working hand-in-hand with Saul Alinsky's Industrial Areas Foundation (IAF) a "how-to" for community organizing, Chavez, along with Dolores Huerta, forms the United Farm Workers Organizing Committee, which evolves into the United Farm Workers (UFW) labor union.

In 1960, Mexican Americans from Texas, expanding on the Viva Kennedy campaign, form the Political Association of Spanish-Speaking Organizations, (PASSO), a coalition of Mexican American civil rights organizations. The coalition becomes active with the Teamsters and La Raza Unida Party (LRUP), and regroups in 1963 under an aggressive, liberal advocate, county commissioner, Albert Peña Jr. The Mexican American Youth Organization (MAYO) is formed in 1967 in San Antonio, Texas, by Los Cinco, five student activists from St. Mary's College (now St. Mary's University), who will become fellow civil rights associates with Yzaguirre: José Ángel Gutiérrez, William "Willie" Velasquez, Mario Compean, Ignacio Pérez, and Juan Patlán. The following year, 1968, activists initiate the formation of the Mexican American Legal Defense and Educational Fund (MALDEF) in San Antonio, Texas. Created to pursue litigation in civil rights cases affecting Mexican American communities, MALDEF is backed by LULAC, and the NAACP Legal Defense Fund (LDF).

Amid the rise of activism in the Mexican American community, and his own commitment to the struggle for civil rights, Yzaguirre completes his studies at George Washington University, and receives an honorable discharge from the Air Force in 1963. "I had just gotten out of the Air Force and was working in a medical laboratory in Washington D.C. when I heard that President Kennedy had been assassinated. I had seen him give his inauguration speech on a cold day in January. His speech made me believe in him and his vision for this country. I used to see him come in Air Force One and land at Andrews Air Force Base. He was a symbol of what was possible and what was good in America."

Only five years later, Yzaguirre, along with Rick Bela, a fellow activist and attorney who would become his business partner at IRA, are confronted with the violent aftermath of yet another assassination. "When Martin Luther King, Jr. died, I was also in Washington and there were riots everywhere. My friend Rick Bela, and I decided to walk down and see if we could do anything to help stop the rioting. Two Black guys came up to us and said, 'You guys better get out of here.' I asked him why, what's happening? 'They're going to kill anybody who's White.' We said, we're not White. And he said 'You are to us.' So we had to walk back the other way. Many parts of the city were up in flames."

The assassination of two of America's most enigmatic leaders creates in Yzaguirre an even greater desire to continue to work in the hard grind of grassroots civil rights organizing. His leadership as the chairman of NOMAS brings into focus one of the most important goals of his career: real power for Latinos must come through unification.

FIST FIGHT IN CONGRESS

A fight breaks out on the floor of Congress. Shouting is heard, fists fly. There's a scuffle going on. The word "communist" is shouted and curses follow. Legislators stop to watch, and it doesn't surprise them that Congressman Henry B. Gonzalez of Texas is the one hurling the punches. He's known to have a short fuse, and will stop at nothing when he is challenged. Another legislator has accused him of being a communist, and Gonzalez is on the attack. The House Un-American Activities Committee (HUAC), the same agency that destroyed NOMAS, is the entity that scrutinizes legislators and "radicals," under the direction of Edgar J. Hoover. The FBI not only infiltrates groups, but also looks into the private lives of citizens for communist leanings. "It was a difficult time for everyone, "Yzaguirre says. "McCarthyism was something we all had to contend with, well into the 60's."

Beginning as early as 1917, the anti-communist surge is re-ignited by Republican Senator Joseph McCarthy of Wisconsin in 1950, with the goal of ending the Communist Party of the United States (CPUSA), and anyone not considered a "true" American falls suspect. Activists, celebrities, civil rights leaders, legislators and ordinary citizens turn up on McCarthy's blacklist, and often suffer the loss of their careers, or worse.

That's why sparks fly on the day Henry B. Gonzalez takes on a fellow colleague on the floor of Congress, over one word: *communist*. Later, the congressman will accuse fellow Mexican Americans of working in league with communists led by Fidel Castro. It will take years for the terrible sting of his accusations to finally be put to rest.

I WON'T FORGET WHO I AM

Born in San Antonio, Texas in 1916, Congressman Henry B. Gonzalez was known to stir political controversy among Mexican Americans and in the halls of Congress during his long term, thirty-eight years (1961-1999), representing Texas' 20th Congressional District. Suspicious of groups like NOMAS, Gonzalez often found himself at odds with protestors and what he considered the "radicals" who, in his mind, put more distance between themselves and mainstream America. He didn't accept the word *Chicano*, and saw it as a way to advance radical issues. When illness struck Henry B. in 1997, he decided not to run for a 19th full term, and was succeeded by his son, Charlie, who served in Congress from 1998 through January 2013. Between father and son, they served fifty-two years in Congress.

Keenly aware of the long history of discrimination and racism in Texas, and the descendant of two Mexican-born parents, Gonzalez willingly put his life on the line for *la raza*, even though he often took issue with members of Mexican American groups he thought were too radical, accusing them of being Castro-trained activists. He went as far as investigating groups he found too anti-establishment, often standing his ground against well-established Chicano leaders, as he did during the 1969 March in Del Rio, Texas that attracted 3,000 participants. Demanding better education and equality with Anglos, key leaders, Dr. Hector P. García; José Ángel Gutiérrez; Texas state senator, Joe Bernal, and Bexar County Commissioner, Albert Peña, Jr., spoke boldly against the blatant injustices suffered by Mexican Americans in Texas. "Are you with us Henry B?" shouted Commissioner Peña, during the rally, only to find Henry B.'s answer the next day, in the newspaper: "Not only no, but, hell no, Albert P."

"Henry B. Gonzalez was the hero of the American GI Forum, and my hero too when I was growing up," Yzaguirre says. "He was a pioneer, and as a Texas congressman he stood up against the segregationists, and filibustered segregationist bills. He was a good speaker, fiery and not afraid to challenge injustice. He ran for governor, and I worked hard on his campaign during my junior year in high school. I put together a conference of youth groups in the Valley and asked him to speak after he lost the governorship. He came in second, beating out a former governor, who placed third. He did reasonably well considering the odds against him. He accepted my invitation and spoke to our youth in the Valley."

"Henry B. was very honest, with lots of integrity during his service in Congress, but he didn't like the word 'Chicano' and he didn't stand up for liberalism at times when we needed him. He ended up opposing the Chicano groups that were trying to bring about change. Before his death, he extended a gesture of peace towards those he had alienated."

Eligio "Kika" De la Garza, a fellow colleague of Henry B., represented Texas's 15th congressional district for thirty-two years, (1965-1997) and concerned himself with education and the environment. Born in 1927 in Mercedes, Texas, De la Garza took the lead in pressing for better relations between the U.S. and Mexico, backing up legislation that brought about the North American Free Trade Agreement (NAFTA). "Kika was a friend of my uncle Pete. I remember as a kid going with my uncle into the community to set up posters for De la Garza, and joining in De la Garza's political rallies. He didn't believe in being aggressive for Mexican American issues, and his main emphasis was agriculture."

Both Henry B. Gonzalez, and Kika De la Garza were veterans, and both emphasized Mexican Americans' dedication to military service, at times using their status as veterans to identify themselves as real Americans. "We are Americans, we want to be accepted was the message," Yzaguirre recalls, "even though at times they were anti-immigrant and supported Operation Wetback. That's where we were at the time. We wanted to show we were Americans and patriotic. We're not like those Mexicans in Mexico; we're like you. We fight like you do. We're White like you. Later, generations of Chicanos would say, I am an American. I will fight for this country and work here, but I won't forget who I am."

THE NEW AWAKENING IGNITED BY THE CHICANO MOVEMENT, El Movimiento, of the 60's, both gathers and scatters Mexican American civil rights groups, challenging them to identify themselves in the panoramic history of America. The ancient homeland, Aztlán is the jumpstart they needed—a swift kick in the backside that takes many by surprise. Like a kaleidoscope spinning new colors, Mexican American civil rights groups revive and survive or suddenly disappear into the distance. Controversies rage, right and left as leaders, of all ethnic groups, stand up for their beliefs. Political in-fighting is the most volatile, and in the midst of all the private and public wars going on across the nation, President Lyndon B. Johnson, as Yzaguirre describes him, "a southerner with a conscience," stands at the helm.

15

IS THIS FOR REAL?

The president [LBJ] positioned himself at the door of the East Room, and shook hands with every invitee who walked in. He seemed like he was seven feet tall, and his presence was very much felt by all. What I remember most is the way he grabbed my hand, and gave me a strong handshake, then he looked intently into my eyes. For a brief moment, I had the president's entire attention.

—Raul Yzaguirre

THE INTERNATIONAL HIT

THE "VOLUNTEER" IS SITTING IN THE OVAL OFFICE. President Lyndon Johnson, called the "volunteer," among other names by the Kennedys, is now the President of the United States. After the assassination of JFK, new battlegrounds begin to form across the country. The cry for equality for all Americans is now a rousing shout coming from Black Americans who have had more than they can bear of Jim Crow's oppressive, demeaning policies. It's time to act. Mexican Americans, Native Americans, and Latinos of all ethnic groups now join in the cry for justice. It's up to LBJ, who has spent much of his time as Vice-President doing nothing worthwhile, as President Kennedy didn't assign him much to do, except represent America abroad.

During his time as Vice-President, LBJ shows class and political know-how as he travels to foreign countries and enraptures thousands with his down-home, Texas antics. His Stetson hat draws attention, as does his height, size and gracious demeanor. He delights crowds, some of them poor people living by the skin of their teeth, with his easy-going, friendly manner and the small gifts he presses into their hands—cigarette lighters, pens, and other small mementos engraved with his initials, *LBJ*. People from all over the world find him easy to approach, a jovial American who even conducted an interview once while taking a bath! Later, his global friends will serve him well as president, but back home it's quite another story. There, he suffers affronts and ridicule by President Kennedy and his brother Robert, as well as by the entire Kennedy staff—but as an international figure, LBJ is a hit.

A born politician, both knowledgeable and cunning, LBJ uses face-to-face meetings and endless hours of cajoling and convincing to get his rivals to come over to his side. Once he's President, he takes a good look around him and notices there's not only one civil rights movement going on, there are several, as Mexican Americans, led by community activists like Raul Yzaguirre and many others, mean business. Then, there's the poverty—millions of Americans are living in the richest country in the world barely making enough to keep their families off welfare. Then, there's Vietnam—Southeast Asia—striking at the very heart of America. North Vietnamese soldiers are causing havoc for American troops—and our boys are fighting hard, as they always have, unafraid to make the ultimate sacrifice; but political games tie their hands and make it hard for them to understand exactly how hard they should fight.

LBJ is now the most important man in the world—something he has longed for, but never suspected would happen. A Navy man himself with a distinctive service record, he now finds himself at the center of several major battles that will challenge everything he's ever believed in or trusted. Shadows will pursue him, private wars within, holding him captive as he faces major battles both on the American home front and abroad.

On Shriver's Team

Following President John F. Kennedy's lead in pursuing civil rights legislation, Johnson faces multiple divisions in the House and Senate that threaten his own political career. Southern Democrats filibuster against the Civil Rights Act of 1964 that outlawed discrimination based on race, color, religion, sex or national origin. The act ended unfair voter registration practices, and racial segregation in schools, at the workplace and in facilities that serve the general public. Signed by Johnson on August 20, 1964, the Civil Rights Act becomes law shortly after the President signs the Economic Opportunity Act on July 2, 1964.

With the successful passage of landmark civil rights legislation, President Johnson's vision of a "Great Society" becomes an established fact, and his determination to address programs for economically disadvantaged populations shifts into high gear, ignited by his War on Poverty campaign. Yzaguirre quickly realizes that linking social reform with the federal government is the most effective way to bring about change at a national level, and address the needs of millions. Working alongside Tom Karter, director of the Migrant Division of the Office of Economic Opportunity (OEO), he and fellow OEO employee, Rick Bela, soon learn what it means to deal with federal funds, grantees and the logistics of coordinating programs nationwide.

"I was still volunteering for NOMAS in 1966 when I was invited to attend a meeting at the State Department where they were going to explain to us what the War on Poverty was all about," Yzaguirre says, describing his initial introduction to the President's campaign. "I went there, and I was kind of bored at first, then it started to sink into me that the government of the United States was planning to organize people and help form organizations that would help them solve their own problems and they had the money to do it. Wow! It would be magnificent. As I listened to the presentations I got more and more excited. The legislation had the promise of real change. What I was hearing from the presenters was that the federal government would provide funding to help people out of poverty, and that farm workers were specifically targeted. Not only was there specific language targeting farm workers, but grants made under Title III-B did not require the approval of a state governor, nor a local matching requirement. I immediately saw the opportunities and I desperately wanted to be part of the agency."

During the meeting, Tom Karter described in detail aspects of the program that would specifically target seasonal and migrant farm workers, most of whom were Chicanos. Born and raised in South Texas amid one of the biggest populations of migrant farm workers, and having worked as a day laborer in the fields as a youth, Yzaguirre understood the importance of implementing the program.

"I said to Tom Karter, I can't believe what you're telling me. Is this for real? And he said, 'Yes it's for real.' I said, 'I want to be part of this.' Tom asked me a couple of questions about what I did and then he asked, 'Have you worked with Dr. García?' I told him that he had been my mentor. Then, he said, 'Well, I'm going to have a job for you.'"

"So I went back to my lab and told my boss, Dr. Robinson, I thank you very much you've been great to me, but I'm gone. I gave him two weeks' notice and worked into getting into the Office of Equal Opportunity. Dr. Robinson thought I was crazy. I had just gotten married, just bought a new house, did not have a job offer, and I was resigning a well-paid job for an uncertain future."

Yzaguirre soon finds that securing a job with OEO is not an easy thing to do. He remains unemployed for several months and is forced to take a night job, so as to reserve time during the day to seek employment at OEO. "I used every angle I could imagine, not knowing that I was one of some twenty-five or so program officers who had actually worked with migrant farm workers and indeed was born and reared in an area with the largest concentration of farm workers. I was finally hired as a consultant and subsequently as a program officer."

Backed up by his mentor, Dr. Hector P. García's letter of support in 1966, Yzaguirre is offered a position in President Johnson's administration as a program analyst for the Migrant Division of OEO. This position also identifies him as a special advisor to then director of the OEO, Sargent Shriver. In that capacity, Yzaguirre helps oversee national programs, opening doors for migrant farm workers, as well as working to help establish Job Corps; Volunteers in Service to America (VISTA); Community Action Programs; Legal Services for the Poor; Foster Grandparents and, lastly, the Head Start Program, a structure similar to what Yzaguirre had envisioned as a youth, which created much needed preschool education for underprivileged children.

"At OEO I began to organize the few Latinos who were in the agency," Yzaguirre recalls. "My colleagues and I managed to bring up the fact that the agency was, for the most part, ignoring Latino concerns. The result was an internal advisory committee on Latinos. I was appointed to the committee that never formerly met, however, through my involvement in raising concerns about Latinos, I had several conversations with Sargent Shriver, and had the opportunity to also visit at his home. Years later, I was privileged to receive an award from the Sargent Shriver Center on Poverty."

Born in Westminster, Maryland in 1915, Robert Sargent Shriver, Jr., President Kennedy's brother-in-law, and husband of Eunice Kennedy, was instrumental in the creation of the Peace Corps as a way to initially foster peace and understanding between the U.S., and the Soviet Union during the Cold War. The Peace Corps grew into one of the nation's premier foundations for encouraging youth to serve in foreign countries, spreading abroad concepts of democracy and bridging differences in social and cultural perspectives.

A dedicated and compassionate leader, Shriver earned many prestigious awards, and was honored with the Presidential Medal of Freedom by President Bill Clinton on August 8, 1994 for his life-long service to the nation. Working under Shriver's 'open door' policy in response to the needs of America's struggling minorities, Yzaguirre caught the spirit of excitement and the vision of a nation focused on leveling the playing field for minority groups disenfranchised from mainstream America.

Tom Karter, described by Yzaguirre as "energetic and a risk-taker," led the Migrant Division of OEO with confidence and a sense of mission. "Tom was the one who hired me. He lived just north of where I lived, so he would often pick me up in the mornings so we could 'talk shop' for an extra hour. He was a thorn on the side of his boss, Noel Klores, who had the unenviable job of trying to control a wild bunch of folks, including Tom Karter. He did this by staying on top of the formal communications between OEO and the field grantees. Noel mandated that all correspondence, including letters from Tom, were to go out under his [Noel's] signature, which gave OEO the option of denying or disavowing any verbal communication."

Launching a new program required long hours of work, yet the hours were not problematic for Tom Karter's staff, Yzaguirre recalls the opposite. "In the next three years I learned a great deal about policy, programs, the role of the federal government, and about politics in Washington D.C. and across the nation. In terms of programs, I learned about housing, education, immigration, labor, and many other federally funded programs. We had the best in the country working as consultants in our office, so I learned from the very best. It was an exciting time. Five o'clock would come and Washington, D.C. bureaucrats would vacate the city, but not at OEO. The enthusiasm and excitement at the agency spilled over long past quitting time."

Southerner With a Conscience

Working as part of Johnson's War on Poverty serves to enlarge Yzaguirre's understanding of the lack of support for America's Latinos, who refer to themselves by numerous titles, including Mexican Americans, Chicanos, Mexicanos, Cubans, Puerto Ricans, Central Americans, South Americans—the list is extensive. "We realized that we were still getting the short end of the stick, so we began to create a broader vision of what we could have. All of a sudden, the War on Poverty brought prominent leaders of the Chicano Movement together. We began to frame our issues. There was a growing number of Puerto Ricans and Cubans in D.C. and New York who began to assert themselves. There was no competition or animosity between us at the time—we just didn't know each other. Dialogues between us sometimes occurred in the evenings with five to eight people sitting around drinking beer. It was a time in which we got to know each other. Our gatherings were a part of daily life and were important in realizing who we were and where we were going."

Gaining in strength and numbers, and forging new ground in the struggle for Latino civil rights, Yzaguirre looks to President Johnson for realization of goals outlined by the War on Poverty. "I first met LBJ when he was a Texas senator, and I was in the GI Forum Juniors. Years later as part of OEO, I saw the president at meetings, and heard him reminisce about teaching Mexican American students in Texas. He had Latino friends, like Dr. García and other Latinos leaders from several organizations around him. He was a Southerner at the core, but he was redeemable. He had a conscience and had developed a passion for activating government to solve social problems. He invested in human beings, not just in ideas. At times, I think he was overwhelmed by the tasks at hand. He would have done more for Mexican Americans and Latinos in general, but the focus then was on African Americans in the South and the war in Vietnam."

Civil rights groups get a new charge of energy with the signing of the Civil Rights Act, but there's often in-house fighting between various groups and leaders that erupt at times in shouting matches, and disagreements that are difficult to reconcile. A nod from President Johnson and federal funding becomes a dividing line, of sorts, for getting a seat at the table, and establishing real goals for national programs. "It became clear to me, at the time, that if we are not at the table where decisions are made, we get the scraps," Yzaguirre reflects when recalling the scramble for federal funds.

One leader who resists taking federal funds is Cesar Chavez. Working for the Migrant Division at OEO, Yzaguirre comes into direct contact with Chavez, whose goal was to organize the great majority of Mexican American migrant farm workers into a powerful union, the United Farm Workers (UFW) established in 1962. The UFW initiated collective bargaining with growers for fair wages and humane working conditions. Born in Arizona in a poor migrant community near Yuma, Chavez spends his years as a child and young adult working in migrant labor camps in Arizona, California and throughout the U.S. as his family follows the crops.

Throughout their childhood, Chavez and his brother, Richard, attend as many as thirty-seven schools, and often suffer corporal punishment and humiliation for speaking Spanish. In one incident, Chavez is made to wear a dunce cap and a sign around his neck that declares: *I am a clown, I speak Spanish*. In 1939 the Chavez family settles in a barrio of San Jose, called Sal Si Puedes (Get Out if You Can). The name may have been a catalyst for Chavez's famous words, "*Sí se puede*," (Yes, we can.) which becomes a battle cry for his work among migrant farm workers.

Enlisting in the Navy, Chavez serves two years, and returns to California determined to right the injustices migrant farm workers suffered in the pesticide-infested fields and dangerous, sub-human living conditions of the migrant labor camps. His pledge becomes a cause, La Causa, which he leads through non-violent tactics: protests, marches, boycotts, strikes, prayers and fasting. Uniting farmworkers into a union and thus securing their civil rights is the cornerstone of Chavez's dynamic work as a national leader.

On April 23, 1993, Cesar Chavez died peacefully in his sleep, not far from his childhood home in the Gila River Valley, near Yuma, Arizona. Helen Fabela Chavez accepted the Medal of Freedom awarded posthumously to her husband by President Bill Clinton on August 8, 1994.

"I first met Cesar Chavez in the fields when I worked for the Migrant Division of OEO. He didn't make a big impression on me at the time, but I had a lot of respect for what he was doing," Yzaguirre recalls. "Throughout the years, we got to know each other better. There was a bit of tension between us because we were in the same business, but working in different ways. I was in the business of helping farm workers better their lives by providing them with education and services. He was in the business of organizing them to form a union. So he would accuse us of bringing *piñatas* (breakable candy displays) as he called them, and we couldn't understand why he would do that. He was trained by Fred Ross, a community activist, who adhered to Saul Alinsky's Industrial Areas Foundation (IAF) on organizing, by destroying everything, then starting from the ground-up to create something new. One of the principles of IAF was, you reorganize to serve what you want. Cesar was striking against our nonprofit organizations, so there was some tension, but we remained supportive of the union. The UFW changed their tactics over the years because Cesar couldn't organize immigrants. It was easy to cross the border and get a job as a farm worker, and at first, he was anti-immigrant. His focus was on Mexican American farm workers."

"I tried to get Cesar some money when I was in OEO and he refused to take any government money. So we supported his cause in other ways. Cesar had a bit of a problem because like most unions, the philosophy was anything you gain should come to the union. And our position was we'll help farm workers no matter where the resources come from, whether union or government or private philanthropy. When Cesar and Dolores Huerta left the Community Service Organization, they began to organize the UFW and the philosophy was to try to devalue everything that existed and start something new. I had a problem with that because we had formed a lot of good farm worker organizations that provided services and support for farm workers. I didn't think one side was totally right and the other totally wrong. It was just a different approach, but there was competition on how much organizations were doing in the community."

Initially, Yzaguirre meets Chavez's co-founder, Dolores Huerta, through a mutual friend while working at his consulting firm IRA, and describes her as a "fireball," often adding her strong opinions to migrant farm policies. Over the years, Huerta becomes a voice to be reckoned with and leads assertively and with a deep sense of passion and a non-flinching attitude towards those working in government programs and anyone else who would dare cast a shadow of doubt on Chavez's ideals. "Dolores and I didn't always agree on issues, but I was conscious of her value to La Causa, and her tireless work among migrant farm workers," Yzaguirre says.

On May 29, 2012, Dolores Huerta received the Presidential Medal of Freedom from President Barack Obama for her activism in pursuit of a better life for millions of migrant farm workers, and for her achievement as a respected role model for other women in the labor movement.

BOXED IN

Yzaguirre's relationship with President Johnson gives him a close-up view of a leader who reflects the values of President Franklin D. Roosevelt. Roosevelt's twelve-year term as President was challenged by the bitter economic turmoil of the Great Depression and the bombing of Pearl Harbor in 1941, signaling America's entrance into World War II. His "New Deal" concept ignited new programs of reform, establishing current social security benefits for seniors under the Social Security Act, signed on August 14, 1935. Roosevelt showed compassion for the poor, setting severe controls over banks and utilities, while levying heavier taxes on the wealthy and creating work relief programs for the unemployed. "LBJ brought us the Great Society programs that were centered on poor struggling families, and focused on jobs and education, similar to Franklin D. Roosevelt's New Deal," Yzaguirre says, reflecting on Johnson's identification with Roosevelt. "Roosevelt was his hero. As a U.S. senator, Johnson had to go to the right because of the conservative state he served, but his instincts were always what to do for the people. He had a genuine concern for the poor and for civil rights. His Great Society and War on Poverty campaign began to get a bad name in conservative circles, but the core of what they were, remains to this day."

Working as a program analyst for OEO, Yzaguirre is able to delve into LBJ's War on Poverty and witness the highs and lows of a master political strategist, facing a nation still reeling from the horror of the Kennedy assassination. "LBJ was the first president I had a personal relationship with. While I served on the Cabinet Committee on Mexican American Affairs, we met in the East Room of the White House. The president positioned himself at the door of the East Room and shook hands with every invitee who walked in. He seemed like he was seven feet tall, and his presence was very much felt by all. What I remember most is the way he grabbed my hand, and gave me a strong handshake, then he looked intently into my eyes. For a brief moment, I had the president's entire attention."

Defeating Goldwater in the 1964 presidential election by a landslide, President Johnson powerfully secures the reigns of government during the turbulent years of pressing civil rights legislation, and a war that was fast becoming the most unpopular war in American history. "LBJ had two thirds control of Congress. No president has ever had so much power and so much to gain," Yzaguirre, recalls reflecting on the reach of Johnson's power and ability to advance legislation through Congress. Yet, the Vietnam War took its toll on the president, creating havoc globally. "Latinos were late in being anti-war," Yzaguirre says," but proportionally, we had more Latinos in Vietnam because we weren't getting any deferments. Lots of our guys didn't attend college or dropped out and made themselves a target for the draft."

Yzaguirre experiences a personal crisis, as he struggles with issues of patriotism on one hand, and ending the war on the other. Worried about his brother Ruben, in active combat on the front lines in Vietnam, he begins to question the validity of the war. "The way my mind worked was that we couldn't lose this war. I wanted to be part of a country that never lost a war. We had to find the right formula for winning; it was a matter of implementation, tactics and competency. But, I wasn't sure if our national security was at stake. There were complexities in Southeast Asia that didn't fall neatly into place. If we lost Vietnam we were told we would lose the entire region, and slowly the realization came to me that too many poor people in Vietnam were being killed, and it was the same in the U.S. I saw the connection between poor Latinos, Blacks, Native Americans, and others who were victims of the war, and poor Vietnamese being killed in Vietnam. I began listening to Dr. Martin Luther King, Jr., as he argued that Vietnam was a moral issue. I read all I could get my hands on about the war. Atrocities were being committed, as it was hard to distinguish friend from foe, and the command was usually, 'shoot before you ask.' There was no way to fix that."

In spite of victories won through Congress and implementation of ground-breaking programs, Yzaguirre observes, first-hand the negative effect the Vietnam War had on the president. "Even though he knew how to get things through Congress, and was one of the most skilled legislators this country has ever seen, there was a sense of tragedy around LBJ as the Vietnam War progressed. He didn't want to be blamed for losing Vietnam. I saw LBJ physically change his demeanor. He became morose and his weight fluctuated. Here was a man who had been enormously successful in so many ways, who had barefoot soldiers in Vietnam pushing our troops around. He didn't realize it was a different kind of war. He got boxed in and couldn't get out. He had a lot of pride, and his pride got the best of him."

GARDNER'S VITAL COALITIONS

Voicing a strong opinion against the Vietnam War was a man who played a crucial role as one of Yzaguirre's most powerful mentors. John Gardner, Secretary of Health, Education and Welfare (HEW) served as a captain in the United States Marine Corps during World War II. As part of LBJ's cabinet, he took on the task of helping to launch Medicare, and expand the reach of the Secondary Education Act of 1965, (ESEA) which redefined the federal government's role in education, and targeted funding for poor students. Gardner also became President of the Carnegie Corporation and the Carnegie Foundation for the Advancement of Teaching. The goal of his extensive political career, was to reform government through organizing citizen initiatives, creating new leaders, and helping ordinary people solve the problems of their own communities.

Gardner's signature role was that of creating coalitions, and discovering the common ground between diverse groups, bringing unity and greater effectiveness for accomplishing goals. Awarded the Presidential Medal of Freedom in 1964, during Johnson's administration, he nonetheless resigned his post as Secretary of HEW in 1968, unable to align his anti-Vietnam stance with the president's ongoing policies in Southeast Asia.

"I met John Gardner when he was secretary of HEW, which is now broken up into two entities, Education and Health and Human Services," Yzaguirre says. "He was a nominal Republican and a liberal thinker. John had a Ph.D. in Psychology, and was a very creative thinker. He used to joke around and say that he could catch his own forward pass. Over the years he was one of my greatest advisors and mentors. He was chairman of the National Urban Coalition, and founded Common Cause, the White House Fellowship Program and the Independent Sector—pretty big organizations, and I was part of all of them. I succeeded him as chairman of the board of the Independent Sector. The Independent Sector gathered information on the functioning of about 800 private foundations, including NCLR, Salvation Army, Red Cross, and many others. I had frequent meetings with John Gardner and he opened many doors for me. He is an unsung hero of the American landscape. I was enormously proud to receive the John Gardner Award for Leadership in 2004."

It was John Gardner's ability to form coalitions that becomes a foundational framework for Yzaguirre in his determination to open communications with African American groups, establishing lasting relationships that serve to unify Latinos with Black leaders.

"In the early days of my tenure with the NCLR, I spent a great deal of my time trying to form viable coalitions with African American leaders," Yzaguirre recalls. "I sought and got some very useful advice and tangible assistance from John Gardner. John suggested that I work with M. Carl Holman, the African American President of the National Urban Coalition. I approached Carl with the idea of organizing a Black/Brown coalition. Together, we formed the National Committee on Concerns of Hispanics and Blacks. To his credit, Carl insisted that the term 'Hispanics' come before Blacks. We invited all of the major African American and Latino organizations for an early morning meeting. All or nearly all of the Hispanic groups including Congressman Roybal, at that time the Chair of the Hispanic Congressional Caucus, were at the meeting. Only three of the Black groups showed up. Vernon Jordan, then the Executive Director of the Urban League, showed up but promptly excused himself. Despite this setback, we moved on and had some success working with specific task forces on issues related to the media and on farm workers."

Participating in the Leadership Conference on Civil Rights (LCCR), Yzaguirre clashes with Black leaders who are focused on advancing their own agendas, and ignoring all other ethnic groups. "The major forum for all civil rights policy formulation was, and still is, the Leadership Conference on Civil Rights. Most, and arguably, all of the important civil rights legislation and/or executive orders had been initiated and/or modified at the Leadership Conference. I had been the first, and at that time, the only Latino on the Board of the LCCR. The chair of the Conference, at the time, was the Washington lobbyist for the NAACP, Clarence Mitchell. Clarence was so well respected that he was known as the '101st United States Senator.'"

"Unfortunately, Clarence was short sighted when it came to inclusiveness. Simply put, he wanted legislation that would cover only Blacks, although he stated that he would be willing to support separate legislation that would protect Hispanics and other groups. We had some difficult meetings and we both said some harsh words. The LCCR hid some of the negative wording before reporting on civil rights issues discussed at the conference. Rabbi David Saperstein, active in the Bishops Council of Civil Rights, often served as a mediator and helped us resolve some of our differences."

The Voting Rights Act, signed into law by President Johnson in August, 1965, becomes one of the most contentious pieces of legislation between

Black and Latino leaders at the LCCR conferences. "Henry B. and other congressmen were supportive of Spanish-speakers being included in the language of the Voting Rights Act, but the African American community said they didn't want to jeopardize the bill by adding more specific language. Later the Voting Rights Act went up for reauthorization and Clarence Mitchell said 'We'll support you on another bill.' But the chances of getting another bill were negligible. I participated in this discussion in D.C. in offices on Massachusetts Avenue, and other locations. We'd yell at each other and arguments would get heated. Black leaders figured that once the bill was authorized, they could come back and get another bill or amendment to include Latinos and they would be supportive. The Civil Rights Act provided for all minorities, but I don't think the first Voting Rights Act covered Latinos. One of the Black leaders at the conference said, 'You were never prohibited by law from marrying a White person, we were.' And that was significant for them, even though in some places interracial marriages with Latinos were frowned upon, but we had also been segregated and lynched as they had. Occasionally, they would mention slavery. I argued that it didn't matter who had suffered the most, wasn't the ideal equal opportunity regardless of ethnicity or race? Couldn't we see that we could achieve more together and not apart?"

"I tried very hard to bring about a coalition with Latinos and African Americans. In my estimation, the people you are coalescing with can help or hurt you, and at that time we could not help African Americans. Some Black leaders had a broader vision, but others like Vernon Jordan of NAACP were not interested. They saw Latinos as having no power to hurt or help them. We went to Congress proposing a very modest budget increase for underserved populations, and the reaction from representatives of African American colleges was racist in nature. They wanted the increase in funding to be designated for historically Black colleges. It was plain greed."

Over the years the relationship with the African American community, takes a positive turn, and Yzaguirre is able to forge ahead with plans for achieving lasting coalitions. "Hugh Price, the subsequent President of the Urban League was a great ally, and later we both served on the board of directors at Sears. Benjamin Jealous who served as president of NAACP, as well as other high profile Black leaders, became regular speakers at NCLR events. Coretta Scott King also became a great friend and was invited to speak at NCLR Conferences. Likewise, I received invitations to speak several times at the Ebenezer Baptist Church in Atlanta, Georgia, Dr. Martin Luther King, Jr.'s own congregation."

On February 2, 2003, continuing his efforts to form strong coalitions between African Americans and Latinos, Yzaguirre delivered a keynote address at the National Association of Minority Auto Dealers, entitled: "Building Bridges Between Brethren." In it he relates, "I submit to you that the real obstacles to a unified civil rights community are not our inherent characteristics, but rather our lack of understanding of each other and a lack of leadership, both of which we can—and must remedy." Citing common goals among Blacks, Latinos, Native Americans and Asians, he zeroed in on shared beliefs. "We want a justice system where the outcome is based on the facts of the case, and not on the fact that the case involves people of color." Underlying several principles for forming strong coalitions he observed, "There can be no unity without trust. There can be no trust without understanding. And there cannot be understanding without frankness. So let us commit ourselves to that unity by being respectfully frank with each other. You see, I do not remember Dr. King or any of those brave men and women who fought for justice in the sixties saying, 'We want civil rights just for us.'" In Yzaguirre's view, Latinos have also undergone a "very real and bloody civil rights struggle," beginning in America's early history, before Anglo colonization was a reality. Yet he remains hopeful that, "We can move forward only by creating the will to come together. That is the all-important first step."

Myrlie Evers became another powerful African American ally and supporter of Yzaguirre's efforts for unification with the Black community. As the outgoing board chair of NAACP, Evers supported NCLR's goals through her role as director of community affairs for the Atlantic Richfield Company (ARCO). The widow of slain civil rights activist Medgar Evers, assassinated on June 12, 1963 in Jackson, Mississippi by a racist-driven member of the White Citizen's Council, she led a decades-long fight seeking justice for her husband's murder. A distinguished veteran of World War II, Medgar Evers was buried with full military honors at Arlington Cemetery, and is remembered for his stance against Jim Crow laws and his courage in facing the brunt of Mississippi's militant racists.

In the midst of President Johnson's determination to create his Great Society in a nation plagued by bitter controversy over civil rights, and a war in Vietnam that was becoming increasingly unpopular, Richard Nixon began strategizing to capture the Republican nomination for the 1968 presidential election and approached John Gardner with a request. "Nixon wanted John to run on the ticket with him," Yzaguirre recalls. "Unknown to us at the time, John Gardner might have become President of the United States, once Nixon resigned, but he declined Nixon's offer."

BAD GUYS TAKE OVER

The structure of OEO and its programs began to change towards the end of Johnson's term as President. Under Kennedy's administration the Mobile Youth Fund had been organized to coordinate neighborhood councils composed of local officials, service providers and community members who were focused on ending juvenile delinquency. The Economic Opportunity Act expanded on this, requiring that community action agencies be involved in all OEO programs. Involvement of the federal government at the state level did not set well with many local state officials, and attacks began on OEO. Political lobbying in Congress resulted in a curtailing of funds allocated to OEO, and programs went through restructuring.

"When it was first created, the War on Poverty emphasized getting poor people to participate in making decisions on how federal money was to be spent in community action programs," Yzaguirre explains. "Originally, the OEO was given the power to override any governor's veto against funding allocated for a community agency. By the end of LBJ's term the battle over control of community action programs had shifted to local state government. With passage of the Green Amendment, governors could veto federal grants, and community agencies once funded through OEO, now had to report to local state officials and ceased to exist as independent entities."

With the election of Richard M. Nixon in 1969, Yzaguirre witnesses sweeping changes in overall policies and programs, and specific to the OEO, the changes are drastic. As Nixon's administration begins in 1969, Yzaguirre, along with the director of OEO, Sargent Shriver, Tom Karter, and many others, turn in their resignations. President Nixon's plan is to transfer most of OEO's successful programs to other federal departments. Under his administration, the OEO becomes a ground zero for new programs. Once proven successful, the programs are turned over to an appropriate federal department. This process adds pressure to programs, withholding funding until time restraints are satisfied.

Resistant to OEO programs, Nixon does not seek funds for OEO's Community Action Program (CAP) division; however, Congress decides to allocate funds for its functioning anyway. Appointing Howard Philips as the new director of OEO, Nixon orders him to dismantle the agency, keeping back funds allocated by Congress for community agencies. A series of lawsuits arise across the nation, led by the Federal District Court in D.C., to rule that the president cannot refuse to spend funds appropriated by Congress. As part of the ruling, Philips is ordered to resign because his nomination had not been confirmed by the Senate.

"Nixon then appointed Donald Rumsfeld, who had voted against the War on Poverty, to head OEO," Yzaguirre recalls. "Years later, Rumsfeld would become the Chair of the Corporate Board of Advisors to NCLR before he was appointed as Secretary of Defense by President George W. Bush. We became friends, and even though he was a conservative Republican, he had an open mind. I believe that Don genuinely cared about poor people. But he once asked whether NCLR wanted to create wealth among Latinos or did we want to eliminate poverty. He correctly understood that how we answered that question determined the policies we would support. I answered that we were interested in both, but eliminating poverty was the most important priority."

Executing the closure of the OEO on January 4, 1975, President Gerald Ford faced a backlash from supporters of the agency who rallied behind the programs, and reached a compromise with the president, replacing the OEO with the Community Services Administration (CSA). The bulk of OEO programs were incorporated under CSA, and others such as the Head Start Program were transferred to the Department of Health, Education and Welfare (HEW), which meant that the majority of OEO employees were now hired by CSA.

"LBJ was eligible for reelection, but he clearly told the American public, 'I will not run, nor accept the nomination of the Democratic party for President of the United States,' Yzaguirre says. "His health had deteriorated and the frustrations he had faced had torn him apart. I saw trouble coming when Nixon was elected. It was as if the 'bad guys' had taken over the White House. I began to make plans to leave my work as program officer for OEO as soon as Nixon was elected."

"In retrospect, Nixon surprised me by accomplishing important gains for Hispanics. He was the first president to appoint Latinos to sub-Cabinet posts and as heads of important independent agencies such as the Small Business Administration. On the other hand, Ford was from Michigan and had little exposure to Latinos, which meant that even though we had access to his administration, we had little influence."

By 1968, Yzaguirre receives his college degree (B.S.) in the mail from George Washington University. He decides not to go into a masters program and instead completes a fellowship at Harvard in the Institute of Politics, full-time for four months. He returns to Harvard in 1989 to teach, as one of the first Hispanic Fellows of the Institute of Politics at the John F. Kennedy School of Government.

"In the summer of 1968, I got a call from a friend of mine, a Mexican American Republican from San Antonio who had converted to Judaism. He was a hairdresser when I first met him, and had been politically involved. He said, 'I want you to meet someone from the Committee to Re-Elect the President. I asked, 'Why would I want to do that, I'm a Democrat.' He said, 'You need to educate Nixon's administration on the issues in our community. This guy's a lawyer and you can come and meet him in his office,' so I did. He was a little guy with glasses and a low voice. We were supposed to meet for a half hour or so and we met for almost two hours. At the end of those two hours he said, 'I work for Richard Nixon. This is my first campaign with him and he's going to be reelected as President and I'm going to be in the White House and want you to come and work for me.' I said, 'It's not going to happen because I'm a Democrat and I don't want to get involved in Nixon's administration.' Over the years I forgot all about my conversation with the attorney. When I returned to D.C. from Texas in 1974 to run NCLR, I met the same friend, and he was now a filmmaker. He invited me to lunch and he brought up the attorney who had offered me a position in Nixon's administration. He said, 'That was John Dean. You could have both been in jail over the Watergate scandal if you had accepted his offer.'"

Yzaguirre recalls this incident as a lesson learned in living out his life's philosophy: *stand up for what you think is right.*

UPON RESIGNING HIS POST AT OEO, Yzaguirre meets with like-minded individuals who will help chart a course with him that will draw the nation's top Latino leaders into the world of high-level consulting, research, management, financial planning, technical training and leadership. Unbeknownst to him at the time, are the challenges he will face living on the other side of the War on Poverty. He faces a bleak year with no money and a dark financial future. "I went from fighting poverty to living it. Our savings was gone, and we lived on food stamps, but Audrey never complained. She carried me emotionally and supported me in so many other ways."

When Raul and Audrey look back on their long marriage, they agree that the year they were "starving" was one of the best years of their lives.

16

THE IRE OF GOD

We wanted the significance of the organization to be conveyed through its works and not through a fancy name. We wanted our deeds to be greater than what the name indicated, not vice versa.

—Rick Bela

THREE MEN AND A PLAN

Raul Yzaguirre, Rick Bela and Juan Gutierrez sit together one afternoon in 1967 in Austin, Texas, along with several other Chicano activists. They're on a new quest, an ideal they've been thinking about for some time. Raul and Rick's work at OEO has opened their eyes to what it means to lead organizations at the national level, and Juan's work as a community organizer in Texas adds further credibility to their potential for forming a non-profit, technical consulting firm for, and by Spanish speaking Americans. The three have some bright ideas for forming a consulting firm that will specifically address the needs of fledging Latino-based organizations, and assure their success in a world of complex programs and policies that at times don't make sense. It's time to do something—take the bull by the horns, and help guide Latinos in the right direction.

The trio starts by voicing plans for their consulting firm to other young activists who feel drawn to them like moths to a lighted bulb. They can see that these guys have it together—their ideas at least, and that a new way of doing business is looming ahead. And business it will be, unknown to any of them, big business that will form a pathway for them to directly access federal funds to help combat poverty and open up unheard of opportunities for struggling minorities. Finally, their consulting firm will be one of the reasons corporate America will open its eyes to the buying power of Latinos. Thus far, corporate America had not seen Latinos as important enough to address through their publicity and marketing campaigns. But all that's about to change, as Yzaguirre leads the charge to a unified front and the first step-up for Latinos in realizing their own worth in a high-stakes, competitive world of financial betrayals, missed opportunities, volatile racial explosions and Yzaguirre's nemesis—chaos.

A New Cosmos

"One of the first things we had to do was come up with a name," Yzaguirre says. "We went round and round, throwing out names that often sounded too biased or too bland. We wanted something strong, but also something that would be inclusive and inspire confidence. You can imagine how that went. Everybody thought they had the best name for our consulting firm. Finally, we settled on Interstate Research Associates. The acronym turned out to be IRA, which some said sounded like the Irish Republican Army, and others said the term would get mixed up with an IRA, Individual Retirement Account. The word 'research' was important because it meant we had to come up with statistics and other important information for organizations that would help them establish their goals and structure their programs. Then we went back and forth about how much technical advice we should offer. That was a big deal because technical skills were vital for the success of the non-profits we hoped to help."

There were disagreements among members of the tight-knit group. Some didn't want to stray too far away from the historical perspectives of their Mexica ancestry important in the Chicano Movement—words like Aztlán, *raza,* barrio, and Chicanismo mattered. Could an Anglo-sounding name effectively reach out to millions of Latinos? Would the name carry weight when working with local leaders in helping them understand the intricate, technical and multiple facets of structuring and designing effective programs for Latino communities? Would it adequately target the group's major goal: helping Latinos understand their own needs and solve their own problems?

Rick Bela, Corporate Counsel of IRA, and a native of New Mexico, was raised in the mining communities of his home state and of El Paso, Texas. Earning a law degree from the University of Texas at Austin before he began working with Yzaguirre at OEO, Bela became the top marketing specialist at IRA and was an obvious fit as the leader of the group's managers. Describing himself as an "artist caught up in *el movimiento*," he probed the significance of the organization's name. "We wanted the significance of the organization to be conveyed through its works and not through a fancy name. We wanted our deeds to be greater than what the name indicated, not vice versa."

Cautioning against over-reacting to the choice of the name, Yzaguirre moved forward with confidence. "We used to be defensive about our name because we were accused of not wanting to use 'Mexican,' 'Hispanic' or 'Chicano,' but we're not defensive anymore. It's no longer important, we've given substance to the name."

Hired from a variety of host communities, IRA technicians came on board ready to start building job opportunities for local agencies, while tapping government funding and developing community resources. They found that local programs were as varied as the communities themselves: day care services for pre-school children; community centers for the elderly; services for migrants; vocational training; family health care; training of advisory councils and boards of directors, and opening the way for young interns to join the organization, were but a few examples of the expansive opportunities that opened up for IRA technicians.

The Spanish term, *ira de Dios*, or the "ire of God," refers to the ire, or feelings of anger prevalent in Latino communities as they realized that established government programs often did not provide for their most pressing needs, nor did the programs address the real problems of a complex and changing population. Realizing the influence consulting and research firms had on decisions made by the government in allocating federal funds, Yzaguirre concluded that, "If the problem could not be seen in America, it did not exist."

One of the first tasks facing IRA was how to positively use the energy of the *ira de Dios*, the "angry energy" to help agencies gather research, statistics and information that would help identify their needs and problems, while assisting in constructing innovative programs that directly addressed a community's unique needs. "Latinos lacked institutions," Bela explains. "Our goal became to build the first national Latino institution in the country patterned after the Brookings Institution. We thought IRA would serve that purpose. Through Raul's leadership, the institution turned out to be NCLR."

IRA Senior Associate, Juan Gutierrez worked as a teacher and social worker before being elected as Justice of the Peace in Mercedes, Texas. A political science graduate of Pan American College in Edinburg, he was raised by immigrant parents from Mexico in a small farming community in Mercedes, and was considered the field general or "George S. Patton" of IRA. Gutierrez came to realize that descriptions of IRA varied. Some viewed it as a technical assistance firm, others as a foundation, research institution, educational organization, or a minority corporate arm of the Chicano Movement. "They were all correct," he says. "We wanted to be all these things and more. It's hard to describe IRA in ten words or less or even in a two-volume dissertation. You have to live it to understand it."

Linking the old with the new, IRA members worked to develop an image for their logo that best portrayed the significance and meaning of their target goals. They chose the Aztec Sun Stone, for its depiction of a universal cosmos, a mysterious circle of gods, goddesses, prophetic visions, the passage of time and the sun god, Tonatiuh, in the center with the image of the Western Hemisphere superimposed on its surface. Uncovered in 1790 by workers excavating beneath the Zócalo, the Central Plaza of Mexico City, the Sun Stone miraculously survived the destruction of indigenous artifacts by the Spaniards and over the centuries became one of Mexico's most coveted historical treasures.

More than a calendar marking the passage of time, the Aztec Sun Stone depicts deep-held beliefs of Mexica mythology and the cosmos. Twelve feet in diameter, the original Sun Stone weighs twenty-four metric tons. Totaling the days in a year at 360, with five days added for good and bad luck, the Mexicas had correctly identified the earth's annual rotation around the sun—360 days, plus five days for good and bad luck. Tonatiuh, the Fifth Sun in Mexica mythology, is the last and present era of life on earth. The god's protruding "tongue" is actually the symbol of an obsidian knife, a horrific reminder of the victims sacrificed to honor the war god, Huitzilopochtli.

Destruction of the previous suns is shown on the Sun Stone in the first circle: destruction by jaguars, wind, fire, and a flood. The Mexicas believed that the Fifth Sun, our present age, would end by *ollin*, which is movement of the earth, or earthquakes. Magically, the Sun Stone can also be used as an instrument of divination, as the circles are spun around and aligned like a huge cartouche to discover personal characteristics and prophetic messages.

The Mexica nation's link to the modern world becomes a stunning reality in the choice of this dynamic logo by IRA, emerging as a way to recapture the ancient world of dreams, chants, and mystical seers hidden in the reality of hard facts, rigid rules, and "business as usual" in America's everyday life. *Da Le Gas* becomes IRA's motto: "Give it Gas." This was the way business would be accomplished, full throttle, holding nothing back, taking on new territory as if it was already won. IRA, with all its trials, errors, and daunting challenges was on its way to becoming one of the most successful consulting firms in the nation. It would become a modern day rendition of a new cosmos.

THE TINDER BOX

It's early 1968. America's battling the aftermath of the McCarthy era. The Civil Rights Movement, passionately led by Dr. Martin Luther King, Jr., is front and center in news reports. Vietnam is looming in Southeast Asia, and American soldiers are suffering the brunt of the North Vietnamese military invasion of South Vietnam...and still America hangs on, hoping to be victorious. Elements of rage and despair snap at the heels of the young IRA activists, most of them Mexican Americans, now known as Chicanos, as they cling to the day when they will see equality rise for their own battered communities located all over the U.S. They've developed the structure of IRA, set up their goals, come up with a symbol and a motto, now it's time to dig their heels in and start working.

Questions and debates arise among them and everyone's ready to take risks they would have thought impossible a few years ago. They grapple with several important questions. How do we make ourselves visible? How do we learn to solve our own problems? How do we live up to who we really are: an intelligent and powerful people ready to lay down our lives for America? Their enthusiasm catches fire, from one to another, a tinder box, ready to be set off by a single match.

By choosing Raul Yzaguirre to head their organization, they feel they've done the best they can to stay focused and get on the fast track. Yzaguirre is unstoppable—plugged into an energy source that radiates to all of them. Getting his feet back on solid ground after the election of Nixon, Yzaguirre's poised to begin something new; he has no financial backing, but things like that haven't bothered him in the past...chaos is part of who he is. Soon he'll lead the group of IRA enthusiasts through good times and bad times, meeting men and women who will shape his own destiny. A filing cabinet, turned into a baby crib, will be part of the office décor and a Sephardic Jew will step up to the plate, and become a guiding light for all of them.

STUBBORN MOTIVATION CREATES IRA

"The IRA idea evolved from conversations I had with others active in community service." Yzaguirre recalls. "Here's what happened. There were a bunch of us who were in OEO and in other government agencies who began to understand the power of consulting firms as routes or ladders to government and public office, and more important as a source of influence in policy making and gathering information for national studies. This was a new world for us. We were beginning to understand the power of entities such as the Brookings

Institution and the Heritage Foundation and how they influenced Congressional funding. We needed our own institutions, so we evolved the idea of a non-profit consulting firm and I had a hand in shaping it. My supervisor from OEO, Tom Karter, was also leaving OEO at the time to form his own firm. He said, 'It's time for you guys to get on the ball if you're serious about this. I'll help you get started.' Tom was very generous and offered us office space. So everybody got together and asked me to take over as director."

Yzaguirre's skill at bringing in competent Chicano and Chicana leaders to serve in IRA was noted by Rick Bela, who was already working with him in D.C. "Raul would find someone whom he considered exceptional in experience and commitment to *la causa*, and ask me to help him strategize on how to recruit that individual to work with us. That's how he found Juan Gutierrez. He told me 'I've met this unusual and talented Justice of the Peace in San Juan. He's the youngest person ever elected as JP in Texas. Help me figure out how to offer him a job.' And, of course later Juan came on board with us, opening an IRA office in San Antonio."

Newly married at the time, the Yzaguirres were yet to understand that Raul's decision to take over as director of IRA would result in a year of hardships that would challenge them at multiple levels; however, once his decision was made, there was no turning back. "It was the same as when I ran away from home at age thirteen," Yzaguirre says. "I had to complete the quest I was on, and would not return home until it was done. My stubbornness is part of my motivation. I don't like to fail at anything. I knew deep in my bones that this thing would turn around, but what finally clinched it for me was that I was fed up with talking about doing things and never seeing them come to reality. I talked to Audrey and explained that we could expect some hard times ahead, but that IRA was something that needed to be done and apparently, I was the only one available. The talking was over, now it was time to put up or shut up. Audrey agreed, and I went into the thing with everything I had."

Testing time started dramatically for the Yzaguirres, and the first year of IRA was fraught with financial woes. "Our second daughter, Elisa, was born in the charity ward of a local hospital, and we had to go on food stamps. There were times when we were glad for bones and cabbage to make soup, and quarters we found between the cushions of our couch. But in spite of the fact that my annual income that year was only $3,000, Audrey and I felt it was the best year we ever had. The struggle brought us closer together."

The ball starts rolling for IRA when Raul and Rick decide to vacate their positions at the Migrant Division of OEO after Nixon's election as president. Attracting activists from all corners of the U.S. is not as hard as they thought it would be. Soon they have a group of dynamic students, social workers, educators, attorneys, politically minded, passionate leaders intent on one thing: serving *la raza*.

"Most of us were volunteers, or part-time. We were all in our twenties then, and times were financially hard for all of us. There was no money to pay anybody when we first got started," Yzaguirre recalls. "Dr. Sylvia Gonzales who had worked with me on the Commission on Civil Rights in D.C., later joined us at IRA, but she had to get a part time job to support herself. She had left to work in Brazil for a time, but knew we had been making plans to get IRA off the ground. She told me, 'If you ever get a grant for IRA, I want to work with you.' So when we got a grant and started IRA I asked her to come work with us and she did. Along with Bettie Baca, another committed activist, both women helped us get started, and made significant contributions to the organization."

Bettie Baca's younger sister, Pauline 'Polly' Baca, another dedicated activist working alongside Yzaguirre during his IRA days, earned a BA in Political Science in 1962 from Colorado State University, and put her political know-how to good use as a volunteer in the Viva Kennedy Clubs. Hired as an information officer for President Johnson's administration, she later joined Robert Kennedy's campaign in his bid for the presidency. Polly Baca was destined to be elected to the Colorado House of Representatives from the 34th District in 1974, and would later be the first Latina to serve in the Colorado State Senate. She chaired the House Democratic Caucus, and in 1985 was elected to chair the Senate Democratic Caucus, making her the first Latina woman in a leadership position in any state Senate in the U.S.

"I met Polly when she was working for the Young Democrats in the 60's in D.C.," Yzaguirre says. "She was attractive, sophisticated and very smart. Gradually, she became more involved in Chicano issues, and was one of the first persons hired as a public information officer by the Southwest Council of La Raza in Phoenix. She married one of the staff members, Michael Barragan, a Chicano activist and former priest. Over the years, she stayed in touch with the NOMAS group and the IRA bunch. When she left the Council, she came to work for me at IRA. I remember she would bring her newborn baby to the office. We used a filing cabinet as a baby crib."

"It took a year to get IRA going. Then, we got some major contracts and within three or four years we were up to one hundred or more staff and had a decent budget, and were doing very well. In that capacity we did lots of things; one of them was a big event for Cesar Chavez. We asked Anthony Quinn, Ricardo Montalbán, and other artists to join us, and it was a very successful fund-raiser for Cesar."

Initial growth for IRA begins fast and furious, yet too much too soon actually becomes a problem. Success follows success and the initial excitement turns into twelve to fourteen-hour workdays, seven days a week for Raul and most of his managers, specialists, office personnel and board members. Hundreds more hours are spent in traveling to meet with community activists, training IRA technicians, and visiting sites where new field offices will be established. And to add to the mix, grant applications have to be written that will bring in a steady supply of funding for new programs, and on top of this, evaluations have to be designed from beginning to end. Events, conferences, and the struggle for civil rights take up another great part of the already packed lives of IRA technicians. Brewing just ahead are highs, lows, starts and stops, and sometimes they find themselves going back to the drawing board readjusting and reconfiguring as needs change and new opportunities open up.

PITY FOR THE SOB WHO WILL TAKE OVER

Often identified as a "think tank," because of its ability to innovate new programs and bring to the table current Latino issues, IRA is soon able to successfully access government contracts. "We wanted to have a real presence in local communities by creating our own models and selling them to community-based organizations," Yzaguirre explains. "Our goal was to develop organizations from the ground-up, and some of those we worked with over the years eventually became multi-million dollar organizations. Almost every well-known Latino activist worked for us as consultants. We wanted them to know there was a role they were to play as experts in their fields, something many had not realized. We would fly them in, hoping to give them the same experience we had; mobility, understanding of the community and getting paid for services. We competed for government contracts, and that's how we paid our consultants at one time or another. By the time I left in 1973, we had forty contracts going and more coming."

The avalanche of contracts creates obstacles that have to be dealt with one-on-one, and plans are often changed or rearranged as experience and knowledge of what it means to create successful programs grows. "The economic peaks and valleys of the consulting business and the keen competition for such work made us sometimes feel that we were on a never ending tread mill," recalls Rick Bela, describing the sense of constant motion and service at all costs.

In the midst of matching organizations with appropriate IRA consultants, training and infrastructure plans, IRA gets a lucky break. Emily Gantz McKay, a community activist, who developed a deep love for civil rights, and worked in Pittsburgh's anti-poverty program is invited to join the IRA staff. A descendant of Sephardic Jews on her father's side, McKay becomes Yzaguirre's special assistant for Planning and Evaluation and continues her alliance with him years later, serving as the Executive Vice President of NCLR. An excellent writer, McKay uses her skills to describe IRA's program goals, taking into account the how's and why's of doing business as the first-ever Hispanic consulting firm. "I worked for Raul for a good part of my professional life, sometimes in the number two position at NCLR," McKay says. "He was enormously important in my life, as my boss and as the outstanding Latino nonprofit leader for many years. I come from a civil rights family, beginning with my grandmother who went around the country in the 1940's speaking about interracial justice for the national YWCA, accompanied at times by the poet, Langston Hughes. My mother's family was active in Ohio on the Underground Railroad. I knew as a college student that I wanted to do civil rights work with people of color, but I also knew that as an Anglo I had to come with skills, rather than expect the organization to help me develop them."

"In 1970, I wrote a proposal as a consultant for an African American consulting firm in DC, the BLK Group, for a project called PEBSI—Program Evaluation for Summer Interns," McKay recalls. "The idea was to use college and graduate student interns to help staff a consumer-focused evaluation of Health Education and Welfare, (HEW) which was a precursor of Health and Human Services (HHS) programs in ten sites, with three of them being the three major migrant streams, California, Texas and Florida. BLK won the one million dollar contract, and when they ran into challenges getting the evaluation tools approved by the Office of Management and Budget, they asked me to help write them. The subcontractor to BLK for following the three migrant streams was Interstate Research Associates, which Raul ran. It was the nonprofit component of a group that included Inter-American Research Associates, which is a for-profit extension of IRA. I met Raul as we worked on the tools, and I ended up becoming staff at BLK, so myself and others at BLK, worked on the project with him."

Taking on the migrant streams involved visiting service recipients in the fields as they labored over the crops. "We were subcontracting with BLK in a very innovative program, using students and community folks to evaluate the effectiveness of migrant programs at the grassroots level," Yzaguirre relates. "We had to train the workers and supervise them to do interviews and questionnaires with laborers and their families who were receiving migrant services. Out in the fields and labor camps we were met at times with shot guns, and hostile growers who didn't want us investigating."

"I met Emily when we got our first big contract at IRA, a joint venture with an African American consulting firm, BLK. I was so impressed with her that I asked her to do some work for IRA, and she did and when I went to NCLR I needed someone who knew my language and understood what I wanted to do, so I asked her to come volunteer for a while until we got enough money to pay her. She was terrific—dedicated and very smart. The only problem was you had to get her to slow down, because otherwise she would work too hard, she was very committed."

Linking with IRA had positive results for numerous organizations, but Olga Aros, who served as Executive Director of the Migrant Opportunity Program (MOP) of Arizona in 1969, had a different experience. A longtime activist in the farming community of Tolleson, Arizona, she was born to a family of hard working farmers who spoke little English. She remembers the discrimination against speaking Spanish in school, and the humiliation she suffered, similar to Yzaguirre's own experience at PSJA in San Juan. "If we were caught speaking Spanish in school, we were made to stand by the fence at recess," Aros recalls. "I was one of the ones punished one day, and I stayed by the fence, the entire day. It was a hot day, and we had no water. The teacher had forgotten all about us. It was a time when we were taught to obey our teachers with no questions asked. My mother came to the school looking for me, and she was livid when she saw what had been done. She went on a campaign to get signatures from other parents to end this practice of punishment."

Influenced by her parents' sense of responsibility in defending her against discrimination, Aros became active in the struggle for justice and has spent a lifetime seeking an end to discrimination against Latinos. The founder of eLatina Voices, a non-profit women's organization designed to bring to light the needs of Arizona children, she challenges government officials, demanding answers for mismanaged programs.

"I met Raul in Denver when I was the director of MOP," Aros says. "IRA got the Department of Labor contract, and Raul's technicians were to do training for board members of all migrant programs. They sent trainers to work with my board, but I didn't like the training they offered. I spoke to Raul and complained about it. He said 'I guess you're one of the ducks that's not lined up. I understand you're not happy with the training. Do you know how damaging this is to an organization?' He sent me new trainers, and things worked out. Later, I met him in D.C. when he was transitioning to the Southwest Council of La Raza and then to NCLR. Raul was a listener. He'd listen quietly, then he would say maybe fifteen words and settle everything. He was the voice of reason."

Later, Yzaguirre joined Aros and other brilliant Latina women leaders, among them, Linda Mazón Gutiérrez, Angie Lopez, Erlinda Tórres, and Nancy Jordan to help develop the Hispanic Women's Conference in Phoenix in 1981. "Raul backed up the Hispanic Women's Conference, and NCLR became the fiscal agent," Aros recalls. "Graciela Olivarez, who had also been on the NCLR Board, was our first keynote speaker. We had no money at the time, but once Raul made the commitment to support us, he kept his word."

Aros and Yzaguirre worked together as part of the Hispanic Association of Corporate Responsibility (HACR) and both were committed to educating corporate executives on the value of the Hispanic market and how to invest in it. Olga witnessed Raul moving ahead into corporate America, and felt he was leaving her own expertise behind. "We had our differences at times, and I used to call him an elitist. He would ask me if it was going to be the tail wagging the dog or the other way around? He wanted to be the one to deal directly with corporate executives from Fortune 500 companies, and they were the big ones—Coca-Cola, McDonald's, Miller Brewer, Phillip Morris, PepsiCo, AT&T, and so forth. Raul opened dialogue with corporate America and led Latinos to an unheard of level of influence. He put us at the decision-making table. There are times when we don't understand the importance of history as it is being made, and in Raul's case, I believe that's what happened. We can look back now, and see what he has done to make us visible to corporate America."

IRA's ability to serve the Latino community at the grassroots level has been the reason for its success. Yzaguirre considered IRA part of El Movimiento, and a way to empower Spanish speakers to take on their own problems, resolve them, and build new avenues for change and lasting institutions. It was because of initial involvement with organizations such as the GI Forum; LULAC; the Southwest Council of La Raza (SWCLR); Mexican American Legal Defense and Education Fund (MALDEF); the Crusade for Justice; the Mexican American Unity Council of San Antonio (MAUC); Chicanos Por La Cause of Phoenix (CPLC), and other Latino-based organizations that gave IRA the edge as a Latino consulting firm. In 1970, IRA completed over $500,000 in contract work, and in the next year it doubled its business enterprises, tripling its business by 1971. Today, the firm remains a multi-million dollar research and consulting agency.

InterAmerica (InAm), became the for-profit arm of IRA and allowed for funds to be secured for lobbying in Congress. Led by Juan Gutierrez, InAm contracted with private sectors such as the Los Alamos Scientific Laboratory in New Mexico, the City of San Juan, Texas, the Center for Community

Change in Washington D.C. and the Urban Coalition. Creating a new agency for lobbying became a reality once a new source of funding was found.

"Paul Montemayor was a saint. We knew each other from the GI Forum days," Yzaguirre says. "He helped me when I wanted to do something in the way of lobbying in Congress. In those days we couldn't do lobbying because IRA was a non-profit. We had to have a different source of funding. So we created this entity called El Congreso. I took some money out of the for-profit InterAmerica and gave it to El Congreso to start lobbying operations. Then, I needed more money so I went to my friend, Paul Montemayor, who was at AFL/CIO, which was labor money. Later, we worked very close together because he was on the board at NCLR. He was just a wonderful human being. Unfortunately, he became ill with cancer. I went to visit him a few times. He talked very calmly about his impending death; it was a pretty sad situation."

Montemayor's help in getting El Congreso active in lobbying in Congress brought an increase in visibility of Latinos, who at the time, constituted only about five percent of the total population; however, things were about to change. Having worked with Hubert Humphrey's campaign, Yzaguirre felt a "kinship" to him. "I was surprised when Hubert Humphrey did not win. I worked closely with him, and he stood for all I stood for. It made it more painful for me when he lost. When Nixon took over, most of the programs benefiting Latinos were cut or restricted. We were only five percent of the population at that time, and did not pose a threat. Now, of course, things are different, and our population has increased to the point that no President would dare ignore us. I worked with a Japanese, Marimoto, who handled Hispanic Affairs under Nixon, and some progress was made. Some of the programs developed were Minority Enterprises, the Minority Business Development Agency, and the Affirmative Action Program. Even though we weren't strong in numbers, El Congreso became an institution and apparently a threat to Nixon's administration. At election time, they made efforts to neutralize El Congreso. Alex Almendariz, a Chicago Republican activist, told us his goal was to neutralize us. He was reporting to the Committee for the Re-Election of President Nixon that Democrats nicknamed 'CREEP.' I never met Nixon face to face, but had lots of interaction with his administration. I never shook hands with him, and had no desire to do so."

By 1973, Yzaguirre felt that the consulting business had changed; fewer opportunities were available, and it was straight business through the Nixon era. "There was a contract out to do family planning in Latin America through an international development group. IRA was in the best position to win the contract. I just didn't want to do it anymore. The climate had changed. There was less exploration and community outreach. When we had been a small group, I had never worried about payroll, but now I had 120 people to feed. If contracts were not renewed I had to lay off people, and that was a worry. Things began to level off, and a new infrastructure had to be developed."

Receiving an invitation to return to South Texas to work in the Center for Community Change (CCC) which would encompass several services—Head Start, Housing, Health, and others, Yzaguirre concluded that, "It was very tempting. This was home, and it was time to go home, so I resigned from IRA and gave the business over to Juan Gutierrez and Rick Bela, and they made a lot of money and are still running it."

With plans to go into politics and possibly run for Congress, against his uncle Pete's old friend, Kika de La Garza, Yzaguirre packs up his family and heads to the Rio Grande Valley. He's offered a position as part-time Vice President for Technical Assistance at CCC, which will allow him to work from his home. "The agency served a run-down neighborhood that had fallen into disrepair, but it was home for me—the place where I was born. Audrey and the kids spoke no Spanish, and they were thrown into the barrio. I worked there for a year, and had plans to organize politically in the Valley. As part of CCC, I worked with an organization called, Colonias Del Valle in South Texas that had offices in Austin. They were an affiliate of NCLR, and NCLR had been one of my clients when I ran IRA. Chicanos Por La Causa was another big affiliate, and many others, so I knew all the players. In Austin, I attended a meeting and my host told me there was chaos on the NCLR board. I knew Henry Santiestevan from working with him at IRA. He was the Executive Director of NCLR at the time. The guy told me they were planning to fire Henry. And I said, "I pity the poor SOB who will take over that organization, and of course that turned out to be me."

Yzaguirre's disparaging comment about the problems facing NCLR, previously the Southwest Council of La Raza (SWCLR), was reflective of the fire already raging among the leadership of the organization. Amid the fiery actions, political maneuvers, and passionate speeches made by members of NCLR, for and against changing its structure to "hard programs," Yzaguirre would rise to gather the burning embers and forge a new fire that would remain a permanent part of America's dynamic, diverse landscape. He was destined to light the fire that would set ablaze one of the most powerful, nonprofit, advocacy based Latino organizations in American history: the National Council of La Raza.

17

CHICANOS AT THE LUHRS

At his core, Raul Yzaguirre is this kid who suffered, yet learned to take his strength from his family and community. He wanted to make the world a better place for others. His sufferings over the years caused him to be who he is. He never lost the kid who dreamed of doing big things.

—Tommy Espinoza

THE SKY'S THE LIMIT

THE FLOW OF IMMIGRANTS, like the trickle of a dry wash, come and go throughout Arizona's history, depending on the economic weather that brings them to the desert in the first place. One such immigrant was George Nicholas Luhrs who escaped being drafted into the Prussian Army in Germany in 1867 by immigrating to the United States. An ambitious young man, Luhrs learns the trade of building and repairing wagons for gold miners in California. He secures his U.S. citizenship, then makes his way to Phoenix where he and a partner, Nowell Herrick, start a wagon-making business and stable on the corner of Central and Jefferson in the heart of the dusty, desert city.

By 1887, Luhrs had built a comfortable home for his wife and four children, an unusual and extravagant place—a twenty-room hotel on the southeast corner of Central Avenue and Jefferson, named the Commercial Hotel. Within a few years, Luhrs buys out his partner's interest in the hotel and renames it Hotel Luhrs, then proceeds to found the Luhrs City Center, which encompasses land across the street from the hotel on Central all the way to First Avenue and Jefferson. Borrowing $553,000 for his new enterprise, Luhrs builds Phoenix's first skyscraper. The Luhrs Building officially opens on April 1, 1924 with top-notch office space for potential businesses.

The ten-floor building is followed by the Luhrs Tower within the same city block, a fourteen-story skyscraper completed in 1929 that showed up briefly in the 1960 film, *Psycho*.

The skyline over Phoenix begins to change, and with it come taller skyscrapers, industry, businesses, merchants, tourists, and thousands of immigrants, the majority from Mexico. Mexican Americans living in Arizona mining towns and cities along the U.S. border who had lived in the region as U.S. citizens for centuries, joined immigrants like George Luhrs and his family, and pioneer Jack Swilling, the founder of modern-day Phoenix (1867), and his Mexican wife, seventeen year-old Trinidad Mejia Escalante.

A new generation of Mexican Americans, now calling themselves Chicanos, a term reflective of their ancestors, the Mexicas—who referred to themselves as Xicanos, secure a safe haven at the Luhrs, and Raul Yzaguirre soon finds himself visiting them from D.C., as his consulting firm is destined to chart a new course for fledging nonprofits that will set the pace for growth, and defy the "caste minority" that's kept so many organizations gridlocked in self-defeating attitudes. The old saying, "the sky's the limit," is soon to become a reality for emerging Latino non-profits.

ROOSTING WITH THE ELITE

Opening their headquarters in the Luhrs Building, the Southwest Council of La Raza (SWCLR) sets up residence in one of its posh, historic offices, claiming a modern roost among the mostly Anglo, affluent clients who enjoyed pleasant surroundings amid marble floors, plush carpeting, chandeliers and suites overlooking downtown Phoenix.

"We met in the Luhrs Building," Danny Ortega, Jr., says, recalling the days when NCLR was still the Southwest Council of La Raza. Ortega was in his twenties then, a student at Arizona State University and a leader in the Mexican American Student Organization (MASO) which evolved into MECha, Movimiento Estudiantil Chican@ de Aztlán, a dynamic youth organization seeking Chicano unity and empowerment through political action.

Struggling to make a living between Ciudad Juárez and El Paso, Texas, Danny Ortega's parents worked in clothing factories in Juárez, and eventually his father gained employment as a stone mason in El Paso. Born in El Paso, Texas, Danny is one of eight children. While Danny was still a child, the family relocated to Arizona to be close to his maternal grandparents, Jose and Rosa Avila, and Ortega recalls telling his parents, "I'm going to that school someday," as his father drove the family car past Arizona State University.

Experiencing a life of poverty in a one-room house in Guadalupe, Arizona and working in the fields with his father and uncles picking onions and other crops, made the possibility of his ever attending ASU seem like a far-fetched idea to his parents. Yet, Ortega, an exceptionally bright and ambitious student, took on jobs as a youth to make his way through high school and college. Graduating with honors from Phoenix Union High School, he exhibited strong leadership skills and was unafraid to take on new challenges, always seeking a better life for his local community. At his side, his wife, Barbara, financially helped support their young family with her teaching job, as Danny made his way through his studies at ASU. Graduating with honors from Arizona State University with a B.A. in Political Science in 1974, and a Juris Doctor degree from Arizona State University College of Law in 1977, Ortega put his skills to good use as a powerful advocate for Latino civil rights, and soon became one of the most prominent attorneys in Phoenix.

Destined to cross paths with Yzaguirre through his work with SWCLR, Ortega, mentored by Yzaguirre, would later be elected to serve one of the longest-running terms as Chairman of the Board at NCLR.

"The idea for the Southwest Council of La Raza came about because I had proposed through NOMAS that such an entity be created by the Ford Foundation," Yzaguirre recalls. "The Ford Foundation didn't want to give us money directly, but instead responded to us in two ways. They gave one million dollars to UCLA to fund a research project, and hired three distinguished men, Dr. Julian Samora, Dr. Ernesto Galarza, and Herman Gallegos to do the writing for the project. They were asked to travel around the country to analyze and assess the problems facing Mexican Americans. The research resulted in the formation of the Southwest Council of La Raza, which later changed its name to the National Council of La Raza, and became my client. I also helped Chicanos Por La Causa get started and other affiliates of NCLR. This was important because I played a small role in founding NCLR and knew it well because it had been one of my clients at IRA."

A direct outcome of Yzaguirre's proposal for funding from the Ford Foundation, the SWCLR was formally established in February, 1968 in Phoenix. By April 1968, the organization acquired its 501(c)(3) tax exempt status. Yzaguirre's proposal outlined the need to bring to light social and economic problems facing Mexican Americans. The initial study in 1968 produced a report, *The Mexican American People: The Nation's Second Largest Minority*, that lay the groundwork for further exploration of the Mexican American experience.

LOS TRES MAGOS: THREE CHICANO WISE MEN

In 1966, the Rosenberg Foundation hosted a conference of scholars and community activists to review a new book by Notre Dame Sociology Professor, Dr. Julian Samora, *La Raza: Forgotten Americans* (1966). Among those in attendance was Ford Foundation Vice President for Programs, Paul Ylvisaker. Noting the passion of those presenting and the intellectual depth of their discussions, Ylvisaker made up his mind to fund another study, this time with an emphasis on creating greater understanding of cultural, social, economic, environmental and psychological perspectives which played a part in the day-to-day living conditions of Mexican Americans.

Herman Gallegos, recalls Paul Ylvisaker's words, "Go out and dream your dreams," as they set out on the two-year study that proved crucial to understanding the reality of the Mexican American experience in relation to the history of the United States. "The three men [Samora, Galarza and Gallegos] were the best choices for this endeavor," Yzaguirre relates. "Not only were they scholars and community activists, they had also experienced years of discrimination against Mexican Americans, including insults, violence and attacks on their communities, while facing questions about their legitimacy as U.S. citizens."

The lives of all three men replicated, in many ways, what Yzaguirre experienced in the Rio Grande Valley. Always an uphill battle, the three struggled to attain degrees in higher education while facing the brunt of discrimination with few opportunities for growth offered to Mexican Americans.

Born on March 1, 1920 in Pagosa Springs, Colorado, the first of Dr. Samora's many struggles began in first grade, when he was forced to repeat the school year on the assumption that he did not speak proficient English. In high school he ran for student body president, only to be defeated by one vote, cast by his own roommate who had no intention of voting for a Mexican. Determined to succeed at all costs, Samora attended Adams State Teacher's College in Alamosa, Colorado, and earned a degree in history and political science in 1942. Traveling to Fort Collins to interview for graduate school, he was turned away from lodging by signs that read: NO DOGS, INDIANS OR MEXICANS ALLOWED. Finally, he found a dilapidated hotel and was allowed to take a room because the owner mistook him for a traveler from India.

Attending Washington University in St. Louis, Samora became the first Mexican American to receive a Ph.D. in Sociology and Anthropology. In 1959 he took a tenured position in his field of study at Notre Dame University, and served as the Director of the Graduate Studies Program until he retired in

1985. Recognizing his high scholastic success, the Ford Foundation generously funded him for what he considered his greatest accomplishment, the Mexican American Graduate Studies program at Notre Dame. A prolific writer and researcher, Dr. Samora's contributions to Sociology, History, Law, Psychology and Political Science are highly valued by generations of Latinos and many others seeking clarity in understanding diverse perspectives in America.

"Dr. Samora invited me to one of his classrooms at Notre Dame. I was very impressed by his knowledge and rapport with his students," Yzaguirre says, describing Samora's expertise as a university professor. "He was a founder of the Southwest Council of La Raza and was one of the original people on their Board. His leadership led to research into the life of Mexican Americans in the U.S. and for the first time, we showed up in a detailed study that made sense to mainstream America."

Struggling to win over poverty and blatant forms of discrimination leveled against Mexican Americans, Dr. Ernesto Galarza's life experiences duplicated, in many ways, the lives of Yzaguirre, Samora and Gallegos. Born in Jalcocotan in the state of Nayarit, Mexico, in 1905, Dr. Ernesto Galarza made his way to Sacramento, California in 1910, pursuing work in fields and canneries. Losing his mother at an early age, he was raised by an uncle and quickly learned English. Awarded a scholarship in 1923, he was able to attend Occidental College in Los Angeles, and like Yzaguirre, he became a member of the debate team and was commended for his oratory skills. Upon graduation from college, Galarza received a fellowship to study Latin American history and political science at Stanford University. Receiving an MA in 1929, he then attended Columbia University in a doctoral program focused on Latin American history. Obtaining his Ph.D. in 1944, he spent almost eleven years in Washington, D.C., working as a research assistant and Chief of the Division of Labor and Social Information at the Pan-American Union. His interest in the movement of *braceros*, across the U.S. border for use as laborers in agriculture, mining and the railroad industry led him to begin a life-long study of unfair labor practices, and how the movement of *braceros* negatively impacted employment for Mexican Americans who could not make a living on wages paid to desperate Mexican nationals who sent American money back to families in Mexico where it reaped a higher value. His goal was to hold both sides of the border accountable for unjust labor practices.

Helping to set the groundwork for Cesar Chavez's farm labor movement, Galarza became the director of the National Farm Labor Union in 1947. His book *Merchants of Labor: The Mexican Bracero Story* (1964), shed light on the plight of poor Mexican workers who suffered indignities and death—the price they paid for their hard labor. Galarza's passionate love for his community earned him the title "Dean of Chicano Activism."

Herman Gallegos, the third member of the illustrious team, was born in Aguilar, Colorado in what he describes a "harsh, small mining town—bleak and poor." Not far from Aguilar, the mining town of Ludlow, a *colonia* of Mexican miners and their families, lay nestled at the entrance of a canyon along the foothills of the Sangre de Cristo Mountains. In 1914, Mexican laborers revolted in a strike against the Anglo coal mining company at Ludlow, and the militia were called in. "They machine-gunned men and women," Gallegos relates, describing the historical event known as the Ludlow Massacre. "Children suffocated in the dirt cellars where they lived underground protected from the cold. I grew up with that history."

Suffering the loss of his left leg above the knee at the age of nine, a young Gallegos was forced to confront the rift between mainstream America and Mexican American communities. "It was then that I realized that as minorities we suffered great disparities, not just the loss of my leg as I had experienced." As his family struggled to make a living, Gallegos recalls that it was big government that came to their rescue with distributions of food, and the opportunity for his father to attend night school to train for a vocation away from mining and the dangers of black lung disease. "Easter Seals helped my family get a wooden leg for me for one hundred twenty-five dollars, and now the prosthetic one I wear is worth thirty thousand."

The words said to him by one of his high school counselors, "Don't think of going to college, your family is too poor," did nothing to dissuade Gallegos from pursuing a degree in social work from San Jose State University. Putting his degree into practice, Gallegos worked with Saul Alinsky, Fred Ross, Cesar Chavez, Ernesto Galarza, Henry Santiestevan and other local and national activists on a myriad of social issues facing Mexican Americans.

Meeting face-to-face with Latino activists and acquainting themselves with policies and programs that directly affected Mexican Americans, Samora, Galarza and Gallegos traveled throughout the Southwest. Their publication, *Mexican Americans in the Southwest*, (1969-70) is a comprehensive study of history, culture, psychological perspectives, housing, labor, voting rights, health and education as they affected millions of Mexican Americans in the late 60's, causing disparities in power, distribution of goods and a marked difference in the standard of living. The breadth of the research is poetically framed in the first two passages of the study, as reference is made to the Spanish conquest of Mexico in 1521, and the later establishment of Jamestown in Virginia in 1607. Ancient ancestors of modern-day Mexican Americans had their beginnings in the western hemisphere long before the English reached their destiny on America's eastern coast.

The study served to uncover the identity of Mexican Americans, rooted in ancient indigenous history, yet moving forward in a cosmic display of many cultures and ethnicities creating what we now know as the Southwest region of the U.S. Poverty, afflicting urban and rural Mexican Americans and the lack of resources to enable them to attain advocacy for civil rights issues, are noted as major social conflicts. The Ford Foundation responded to the study by funding MALDEF, which would serve as the counterpart of the NAACP Legal Defense Fund. The research team's goal was to energize entire communities, joining forces with Anglos, Blacks and other ethnicities to secure programs and services for barrio communities.

"The research conducted by the Chicano team of scholars was one of the main reasons the Ford Foundation decided to fund the Southwest Council of La Raza, which later became the National Council of La Raza. They also got money from the National Council of Churches, and the United Auto Workers Union," Yzaguirre recalls.

Herman Gallegos assumed leadership of SWCLR after its formation, and Samora became a founding member of the Board, while Galarza served as a consultant for the organization. Henry Santiestevan succeeded Gallegos as Executive Director in 1970. Beginning his career as an activist in Washington D.C. Santiestevan worked for the "Viva Kennedy," campaign during JFK's run for president and later campaigned for Senator Robert Kennedy. He was present at the Ambassador Hotel in 1968 when the senator was assassinated.

Attending Occidental College in Los Angeles, Santiestevan honed his skills as a journalist, writing for the AFL-CIO and other watchdog agents of social change. "I met Henry when he was a staffer for the United Auto Workers. He was writing for their publication," Yzaguirre says. "Henry was the sweetest man you could ever meet—kind and with goodwill towards everybody. He was a wonderful human being, and took me to meet all the influential leaders he knew."

Maclovio Barraza, a passionate union leader from Tucson who had worked extensively in the copper mining industry, became the first Chairman of the Board for SWCLR. As a union leader, he worked for the Mine-Mill and Smelter Workers and the United Steelworkers of America. A vocal advocate for Latino rights, Barraza worked with MALDEF, Southwest Voter Registration project, (SVRP) and helped found Chicanos Por La Causa (CPLC). Taking on the position as Board Chair, Barraza served for nine years. An investigation by the federal government's Subversive Activities Control Board falsely identified him as a member of the Communist Party. A zealous spokesman for labor rights, Barraza died in 1980 at age 53 during contract negotiations with the Magma Copper Mining Company in Phoenix.

"Maclovio Barraza and I had an interesting relationship," Yzaguirre recalls. "My predecessor, Henry Santiestevan asked my consulting firm to do some work for NCLR and we did. Henry introduced me to Maclovio Barraza and Maclovio was a little bit cool towards us. He was Chairman of the Board at the time and did a great job. He was a strong personality, but things deteriorated and the Board wanted to get rid of him and Henry Santiestevan."

It would be Henry Santiestevan as Executive Director who would face a 'changing of the guard,' as the focus of NCLR changed directions and the Council took on a new role, one of innovating hard programs, advocating for social change, and embarking on systematic research and policy analysis. "The Ford Foundation told NCLR to start doing hard programs or they would stop their funding." Yzaguirre recalls. "They wanted programs for employment training, economic development, housing and so forth, and Henry had no experience in those arenas. He saw the organization change around him and he couldn't match it. He was too kind hearted and couldn't fire the people that needed to be fired."

Ford Foundation's expectations for NCLR were quickly challenged by Yzaguirre, who found their micro-management of the organization insulting. "We could not make a decision without their approval. They didn't trust our ability to lead our own organization." His tenacity pays off, and he's able to convince the Board that diversifying and not depending on one funding source is the way to go.

Trying to keep afloat the "frail craft" that represented NCLR in the midst of contention among its Board members and affiliates, Santiestevan made a decision to step down and allow new leadership to take over the reigns of power. Unbeknownst to Yzaguirre, the task of strengthening the "frail craft," would fall upon him, and his leadership skills would be challenged, as NCLR emerged as a giant in the highly competitive world of non-profit, constituency-based, advocacy organizations.

Yzaguirre's proposal to the Ford Foundation had traversed the United States, opening up the doors of hotels, like the Luhrs, to Chicanos who were ready to do big business on behalf of Latino communities. "We had all these tall buildings all over the nation," recalls Chicano activist, Ronnie Lopez, "and we weren't on the board of directors in any of them, until people like Raul Yzaguirre, Maclovio Barraza and Herman Gallegos put us at the table."

READY TO RUMBLE IN PHOENIX

Yzaguirre's vision for community organizing and his concept of "community first," inspired young Danny Ortega, Jr., stirring in him a deepening love for *la raza*. Recalling his first meeting with Yzaguirre, he says, "I was impressed with Raul's deep sense of commitment at higher levels of decision making. His agenda was always the community, not his own self-interest. I really trusted that he was speaking on behalf of our community and would gain nothing on a personal level. Raul is an intellect, but if you put him on the streets, he's one of us. He has this humility that says, I'm a servant of the people."

Riding on the crest of the Chicano Movement, MeCHa students and local activists from Arizona began to prepare themselves to take on the rigid, racist policies of state politicians, and calloused educators who turned the other way when protests erupted from the Mexican American communities demanding a better education for their children and fair wages for Mexican American laborers. Prominent as Arizona leaders during the 60's were Maclovio Barraza, Chairman of the Board for SWCLR, and Polly Baca, public information officer, along with MeCHa students—among them, Danny Ortega, Jr., Mary Rose Wilcox, Dr. Belen Servin, Pepe Martinez, Bob Pastor, and ASU professors, Dr. Miguel Montiel and Dr. F. Arturo Rosales, both prolific writers and Chicano scholars who, through their leadership, began to shape the focus of the Chicano Movement in Arizona.

Joining MeCha students in charting out the structure of CPLC, were Joe Eddie Lopez, who was later elected as an Arizona State Senator; his wife, Rosie Lopez, destined to found the Arizona Hispanic Forum; at the time County Supervisor, Ed Pastor, who later became the first Latino from Arizona to serve in Congress; activist and future State Senator, Alfredo Gutierrez, and general counsel for the group, Armando de León; along with activists Sonny Nájera, Bill Soltero, Gus Gutierrez, Agustin Cardona, Tommy Espinoza, Pete Garcia, Ronnie Lopez and his wife Angie, who served as secretary of SWCLR, and committed women activists, Graciela Gil Olivarez, Terri Cruz, Carolyn Rosales, and Elisa De La Vara, the first woman to rise to become Executive Vice President of CPLC.

"We were determined to have our own organization," recalls Joe Eddie Lopez. "Southwest Council of La Raza invited us to be a participant. They had plans for staffing five organizations throughout the Southwest. There was active competition for funding, but we had an upper-hand because we knew Maclovio Barraza and Polly Baca. The Council gave us funding and Olga Aros of MOP helped us get started with desks and office supplies."

Assuming leadership of the group, Joe Eddie Lopez became the first Chairman of the Board of CPLC in 1967, and Juan Alvarez served as the first Executive Director, followed by Ronnie Lopez who, in 1974, faced-off with Yzaguirre for the position as CEO and President of NCLR. Tommy Espinoza, an enterprising young businessman at the time, and Pete Garcia were both destined to become CEO's for CPLC. Pete would affectionately be known as "Big Dog," and would serve twenty-three years, developing CPLC's reputation as one of the most successful and prestigious nonprofits in the entire country. Following in his footsteps, Edmundo Hidalgo, CPLC's Chief Financial Officer, was hired to take over as CEO, and after twenty years of service, turned the reins of power over to the newest CEO, David Adame.

Amid conflicting views on whether CPLC should focus only on migrant farmworkers, founding members decided to become more inclusive. "Our focus had to be on urban issues, education, housing, family services, immigration, employment and empowering Latino voters," relates Joe Eddie Lopez.

"The push for emphasis on rural or urban services was a dividing line for many nonprofits," Yzaguirre recalls. "The decision to go with urban needs was the right choice for Chicanos Por La Causa. This set the pace for new funding and for programs that would directly help families out of poverty."

Initially defining their structure and parameters, CPLC members moved to the next structural level for their organization—choosing an official name.

What's a Chicano?

The word "Chicano," draws bitter contention among several members of the fledging group as they passionately oppose the use of the term, which to many implies a radical group that's dubbed as an outcast by conservative Mexican Americans. "Agustin Cardona named the group, Chicanos Por La Causa," recalls Rosie Lopez. "No other organization had the word 'Chicano' in its name, and some of the members thought it would be a handicap, but the name is still the same today."

Analyzing the dissension around the word 'Chicano,' Ronnie Lopez linked the term to a generational disconnect. "Our parents and grandparents didn't like the word, 'Chicano.' They never got used to it. There were so many ways to be American for us. We were farmworkers, students, veterans, ordinary working people, and those who protested the Vietnam War. We won so many medals in the war; we were heroes, but suspicious Anglos still called us communists. We dreamed up a word that told of our past, as children of the emperors of the Mexica Nation; we called ourselves, Chicanos."

Experiencing the segregation of Mexican Americans in the small copper mining community of Miami, Arizona, Ronnie Lopez witnessed first-hand the determination of his hardworking parents to secure a better future for their children. "We lived in the canyons, and the Anglos lived in the hills. We weren't invited to their parties, and couldn't speak Spanish at school. I remember seeing signs on some businesses that said: *We don't serve Mexicans or dogs*," Lopez recalls.

One thing that worked in favor of Mexican American students living in copper mining communities, was that taxes imposed on the mines supported their schools, providing a better education than that experienced by inner city Mexican American students. Low property taxes in barrio neighborhoods meant less educational services and lower teacher wages. In many ways the mining communities were a God-send for young leaders like Ronnie Lopez, Ed Pastor, Alfredo Gutierrez and many others, creating a new generation of educated community leaders who would call themselves—Chicanos.

Early in his involvement with the Chicano Movement, Yzaguirre confronted the on-going controversy surrounding the use of the term, 'Chicano,' viewing hostile reactions as a reflection of the pain lingering in Mexican Americans who had been called disparaging remarks since the days when his own land grant family, headed by Juan Pantaleón Yzaguirre, had settled in Texas.

"We're *mestizos*, a fusion of cultures and bloodlines, which makes us *la raza cósmica*, as José Vasconcelos describes," Yzaguirre says. "My position is, you have the right to call yourself whatever you want to, Chicano, Mexicano, Indio or whatever. What's important is we're part of the same family. I like the word 'Chicano.' It was born and bred on this side of the border. A real Chicano is someone who has had a certain experience. Growing up in a school system at odds with American society, a Chicano understands certain American behaviors and identifies a difference in cultural perspectives from his Anglo counterparts. When I was growing up there was tension between the native-born and foreign-born Mexicans, but I don't have those issues anymore. I have used both words, Chicano and Mexicano to describe myself."

Disputes over names and identities linger to this day among Latinos of diverse ethnicities; yet there's a strong urge to step over the land mines left over from years of contentious back biting and realize one of Yzaguirre's rock-solid beliefs: unity is power.

THE TRANSFORMATION

Raised for the greater part of his childhood in the Marcos de Niza Projects in Phoenix, Pete Garcia, one of the longest serving CEO's of CPLC, and now CEO of the Victoria Foundation, named in memory of his beloved mother, shares much of Yzaguirre's story—both were born in close-knit barrio communities clinging to the outskirts of mainstream America. "My mother told us never to go past Van Buren Street," Garcia recalls. "In those days the rich lived on the north side of Van Buren, and the poor on the south, so as my aunt used to say 'curiosity killed the cat,' we didn't go too far north."

"Mom used to say, 'we're poor, but we don't have to be dirty,'" Garcia says, describing his mother Victoria's reflection on living a good life. "She kept a clean house, and stood up to my dad. He was an alcoholic and a couple of times tried to burn our house down with us in it!"

A hard working woman—packing lettuce in the marketas, cleaning houses and ironing in spite of arthritis, Garcia credits his mother for, "Keeping us out of the joint. Most of my friends ended up in juvenile or prison, but mom would make us come home by eight every night. Our friends were afraid of her. She didn't hold back in giving them a scolding and chasing them off."

Living on welfare in the projects prepares Garcia for his future role: helping people turn their lives around. Making his way through Lowell, his elementary school and Phoenix Union High, he exhibits negative behaviors and recalls one counselor telling him, 'You have the worst attitude. You'll never get anywhere.'"

Determined to beat the odds, Garcia worked at odd jobs as a teen, did a stint in the Army from '63 to '65 stationed in Germany in the Armored Cavalry Division, and eventually returned to complete studies at Arizona State University, working for a time as a teacher and counselor for the Phoenix Elementary School District. Later, he earned a Masters Degree in Public Administration from the University of Southern California (USC). In California he tracked down his father, nicknamed "Caballo," (Horse) someone he barely remembered, and had to pay an old Black man five dollars to find him along the produce warehouses that made up the marketa in Watts. Dressed in black slacks and a white shirt, Garcia relates, "I felt overdressed when I met this ragged man who was my father."

Garcia could not have imagined, that like Raul Yzaguirre, his struggles as a youth would give birth to a determination to succeed at all costs. He would one day become a mentor for thousands of youth seeking the way out of a life of poverty, domestic violence and prison walls. Transforming the lives of others would prove Pete Garcia's dedication to *la raza*. Like Yzaguirre, once he took the plunge into community service, there was no turning back.

"I first met Raul in Del Rio, Texas with a bunch of other activists who were forming community development centers throughout the nation," Garcia recalls. "We were partying in the evening with members of NCLR, and Raul had just been appointed CEO. We were by a lake and Raul asked Tommy Espinoza and me what we thought of the lake. You call this a lake? I asked, joking around. We flush more water in the toilet in Arizona than you have in this lake. We were sitting on a boat at the time, and Tommy says to me, 'Row to the middle of the lake, what are you thinking, he's from Texas!'"

Catching a glimpse of D.C. as an intern during his time at USC, Garcia comes to realize that unless Chicanos can confidently access higher levels of government, they will go nowhere. Years later, when he returns to D.C., traveling with then head of CPLC, Tommy Espinoza, they seek out Raul Yzaguirre, whom they had met in the river mishap in Del Rio, Texas and through working with his consulting firm, IRA.

In D.C., Pete and Tommy are immersed in the ups and downs of doing business in the nation's capital. An invitation from Graciela Gil Olivarez helps open doors for them. She tells Espinoza she's willing to help him locate funding for the expansion of CPLC. "Graciela was so gracious to me. She said, 'Ven, mijo, come to D.C.,' recalls Espinoza. "She had this big office on Massachusettes Avenue. She assured me I'd get funded, and called in her Japanese assistant, Jerry Mukai, who sat down and smoked one cigarette after another. She gave me a big hug, and said to Jerry, 'This is Tommy Espinoza from Arizona. I want you to make sure he is well taken care of.' Jerry was responsible for signing multi-million dollar projects. After that meeting I got on a list to go to state dinners at the White House."

Realizing Yzaguirre was one of D.C.'s movers and shakers, Espinoza and Garcia approached him with a funding problem tied to Title VII grant money. "I needed approval to get a planning grant, so I called Raul and asked if he could help me because I knew he knew all the players," Espinoza says. "Raul quickly agreed to help me and was able to bridge the divide between Republicans and Democrats. He helped me get in touch with Congressman John Rhodes, who was the minority leader of the House at the time. Rhodes didn't want CPLC to get funded because he said we were involved in politics, which was against the rules when running a non-profit. Pete Garcia was with me in D.C. and we both met with the congressman and were able to convince him we were not interested in getting involved in politics. We wanted to build up our community. I knew Raul had already put in a good word for us—that's why things worked out."

Espinoza's initial impression of Raul centered on a sense that there was a child harbored somewhere at the heart of who he was, that was very much alive, possibly the same youth who had run away from home at age thirteen to venture out on a quest, seeking meaning in his life. "At his core, Raul Yzaguirre is this kid who suffered, yet learned to take his strength from his family and community. He wanted to make the world a better place for others. His sufferings over the years caused him to be who he is. He never lost the kid who dreamed of doing big things."

Meeting Yzaguirre in Phoenix and following the workings of NCLR over the years, Joe Eddie Lopez credits Yzaguirre for building institutions for Latinos where none had existed before. "I don't think people can measure what Raul has done. He came from very humble beginnings and grew up knowing the problems in our community, and was willing to do something about them. He's like a Cesar Chavez or Corky Gonzales, and deserves that type of stature. NCLR became a parent to a lot of organizations like CPLC that have done a lot of good throughout the nation."

By 1972, SWCLR, now the National Council of La Raza, also known as "La Raza," relocates its headquarters from the Luhrs Building in Phoenix to D.C., reflecting an expansive, national direction. Major funding from the Ford Foundation, totaling over 40 million in grants over a span of several decades serves, initially, as the organization's most important funding source. This will later change under Yzaguirre's leadership, as diversification is sought.

The chess pieces are set, and the game is about to begin. NCLR is destined to test Yzaguirre's stamina and willpower, stirring up his old nemesis—chaos. It will fill the empty spaces inside the kid from the Rio Grande Valley whom Tommy Espinoza so eloquently described as "the kid who dreamed of doing big things."

A WILD RIDE

It's 1973, one short year before Yzaguirre is hired as the CEO of NCLR. There's a rodeo going on in Cheyenne, Wyoming and locals have crowded the state fairgrounds. One of two Chicanos visiting the town while attending a GI Forum conference is about to take a dare. He's not dressed as a cowboy, doesn't even have a hat on, but that's of no consequence. He's been challenged by a fellow GI Forum member, and pride won't let him turn down the dare. Watching the ferocious bulls spring out of their stalls while real cowboys ride them, clinging with one hand for dear life, then flying off the bull's backs in seconds, doesn't bother him. He's determined to ride a wild bull—a dare is a dare, and he'll take his chances.

"My friend and co-worker, who became an Associate Director at NCLR, was Ed Terrones, from Colorado. He had been a GI Forum member, and Vice-President of the Forum. We had also worked together at OEO. He was my roommate for a while before he brought his family to live with him. We were together at the American GI Forum in Cheyenne, Wyoming in '73, and part of the agenda called for us to go to the rodeo. There was a professional and amateur bull-riding event that afternoon, so Ed challenged me to ride a bull, and I said, I'd do it, not knowing what I was getting into. I was wearing a dress shirt, brown jeans and a pair of ordinary dress shoes. I got on this gigantic bull and I rode him until they sounded the horn. Then, I got off and the crowd was very appreciative. I was tied for first place, with a professional who went ahead of me but only lasted about four seconds. He got thrown almost immediately, and he was riding a smaller bull, which I think was a disadvantage for him. I think it's easier to ride the bigger bulls. From the crowd's stand point here was this smaller, younger man on a bigger bull, an amateur against a professional. I rode the big bull all the way to the other side of the enclosure. He didn't throw me, I just slid off of him, and the crowd just went wild! They stood up and yelled and screamed, and I got a trophy and brought it home, and my children proceeded to destroy it. It was the first and last time I ever rode a wild bull."

YZAGUIRRE'S WILD BULL RIDE was an ominous sign, a foreshadowing of things to come. The times would become even wilder for him, the ride would last longer, and he would not be thrown off, until he, himself, would call it quits. NCLR's ride would last for thirty years, and yes, the crowd would applaud again and again in 2004 in an electrifying NCLR farewell conference in Phoenix, Arizona, the birthplace of the Council. It was fitting that the ride ended in the city that had birthed its beginnings, in the old Luhrs Building, now a historical relic tucked away in the midst of a bustling metropolis, yet still a part of the story of Chicano unity.

PART THREE
UNLESS WE UNITE

—

18

SNOW IN JUNE

In some ways the media treated NCLR like we were radicals and the real radicals thought we were establishment. We must be doing something right if the far left thinks we're establishment and the establishment thinks we're radicals. We have to be doing something right.

—Raul Yzaguirre

MYTHS REVEAL THE TRUTH

A LEGEND AS A PRIEST for the Presbyterian Church, Dr. David Rammage, is destined to become one of Yzaguirre's favorite friends and mentors. Dr. Rammage is good at challenging Yzaguirre to use his skills as a debater and analyze a difficult situation from multiple angles. The black and white of a question is fraught with gray areas of debate that can move outcomes in a whole new direction. It's the gray between the black and white that's identified as the "common ground," and it's here that Yzaguirre will learn to excel. His ability to reason out things in a logical manner and find the common ground, even in volatile situations, will seal his success as a leader who's willing to listen carefully before he acts.

Arriving in South Texas in 1973, after leaving IRA in the hands of his close associates, Juan Gutierrez and Rick Bela, Yzaguirre faces an uncertain future. He's decided to run for Congress in his home state of Texas.

"I decided I wanted to go back into politics, so I took a job with an organization called the Center for Community Change in South Texas where I could have more freedom to do what I wanted to do. For the most part, I would be working out of my home in Texas. The organization was very much like NCLR in terms of its function, but it worked with all ethnicities. I was hired as the national Vice-President for Technical Assistance, a part-time job, which would give me time to organize politically in the Rio Grande Valley. The president of the organization, Dr. David Rammage, had been trained as a community organizer through the principles of Saul Alinsky. The Center had been one of my clients at IRA so I was acquainted with their purpose and goals. Dr. Rammage tried to help me understand things from his perspective. At times, we would drive through Texas and visit community programs, evaluating them and giving feedback. Some of our discussions would center on religion and philosophy. One day he said to me, 'Raul, do not underestimate the power of myth as a carrier of truth.'"

Dr. Rammage's words inspire Yzaguirre as he struggles with the myths of his own life. Nothing is certain for him, and his desire to run for Congress and live in South Texas appears to be an idealized concept, an illusionary goal that will never materialize, yet it will lead him to the truth.

Helen Cavazos, Yzaguirre's high school friend, recalls that Raul was often referred to as the "Ice Man," because he worked with his grandfather hauling ice for customers throughout the San Juan community. His ability to do hard labor and function for long hours as a youth nurtured his ability to work steadily through strenuous situations, a quality he would sorely need as he encountered the chaotic dynamics of serving the community as a civil rights leader. Spending only one year working at the Center for Community Change (CCC), Yzaguirre faces a 'kidnapping of sorts' by friends who see in him the leader they need. A trip back to D.C. leads the way for the next big decision of his life. The myths of his life, both real and illusionary, are about to unravel.

You're It

Snow's falling in Denver, not an uncommon sight, unless it's June and the beginning of the summer season. In the mornings, grey skies loom overhead, harboring clouds of snowflakes, tiny white embers that sparkle in the sunlight as they fall on the city, dreamily—hushing Denver's bustling city streets. Softly, the snow falls, lightly—an iridescent, cover of powdery flakes. The distant mountain peaks wear white caps that all but disappear by noon as the sun's rays melt the ice away.

Raul Yzaguirre makes his way from the airport to a hotel in the center of town wondering why there's snow falling so late in the year. It's unexpected, the locals tell him, snow is rare in June, but they've seen it before. Yzaguirre's trip has been one of many he's taken in the last few months. He's weary from all the traveling and the enormous decisions he's facing, and wants nothing more than to sit in front of a fireplace, a warm drink in hand and watch the snow fall. He imagines himself ending the day—after doing what his friends have asked him to do. He hopes the Board won't take long in voting for the right candidate, but most of all he's hoping the trip will end quickly and he can get back to Texas.

"Three or four people asked me to apply for the CEO position at NCLR in 1974 and I would not do it because it was a fraction, economically, of what I had made at my consulting firm. They were asking me to come back to Washington D.C. for less than what I had left for. Besides, I had already relocated to Texas and had plans to run for political office, so the answer was no. The Council had a five million dollar lawsuit against them, they had no funding sources, and they were on a terminal grant with the Ford Foundation. The staff was demoralized and most of the members put in only twenty hours of work a week. It was a mess so I thought it was better to start something new than try to revitalize the organization."

"Besides all that, people told me Maclovio Barraza thought he could save his position as Board Chair by reaching out to me and making me president of NCLR. He did this through an intermediary, Paul Montemayor, a good friend of mine. But when I thought about it, it was too messy. I told Maclovio I wasn't interested in doing it. Then one of the most important affiliates at the time, Juan Patlán, director for the Mexican American Unity Council of San Antonio asked me to apply. And I said no. Paul Montemayor then invited me to come to Washington D.C. He locked me up in a room with a few of my best friends, Alex Mercure, Rick Bela, Polly Baca, Juan Gutierrez, Manny Fierro, and Juan Patlán. Paul was head of the Latin American Council for organized labor, part of the AFL/CIO. They said to me, 'You're not leaving this room until you agree to apply for CEO of NCLR. You're it. You're the only one who can take over the Council.' I told them I was sorry. but I had made other plans. They said, 'You're true to the Chicano Movement, you have to be true to do this.' I told them I'd put in my application but wouldn't guarantee I would accept the job if it was offered to me. We all decided to do some things that day. Polly decided to go back to Denver and run for political office. She became the first Latina Colorado State Senator. Juan Gutierrez made a commitment to run IRA. Rick Bela agreed to go to Texas and become a community developer. Paul agreed to become the Executive Director of the Labor Council for Latin American Advancement at the AFL-CIO, and chairman of the board of the lobbying organization, El Congreso. Manny Fierro would continue as Executive Director of El Congreso, and IRA and the AFL-CIO would continue to fund El Congreso. Amazingly, all the plans came to fruition. There was good interaction between all of us."

"I submitted my name and interviewed with the Council in early June 1974, in Denver, Colorado, and it snowed on that day. When I got to the board meeting, there was an organized effort to put in somebody else. Later the other man, Ronnie Lopez, became a very successful leader. He wanted the job badly. I went into the interview room and I said, look guys, I'm not interested in the job. Let me tell you why, your Board is screwed up and you don't have your act together, and I walked out of the room. By this time, Maclovio Barraza had changed his mind about me, and decided that Ronnie Lopez was his candidate, so he brought in Tommy Espinoza and all the Arizona gang to Denver to influence the Board and back up Ronnie. That was fine with me, it didn't make any difference to me if I won or not, so I went upstairs to my hotel room to watch television while they debated. I came back down after the process was over and they asked both me and Ronnie to stand up and they said, 'Unanimously, we have agreed on Raul Yzaguirre as the CEO.' I was shocked. Maclovio Barraza stormed out of the building in anger, so we didn't start out very well. In my mind, they had no money, and they were dysfunctional. Why would anyone want to take the job? I told them, you are going to have to convince me that we're able to work together. At the time, I was sure that was the end of my conversation with them, but they asked me to come back and said, 'You're it.' They didn't talk salary, or terms they just said you're now the new Executive Director and President of NCLR. There was no job description. The meeting was over and I was in charge. I had to move back to D.C. It was a very difficult situation because there was a lot of inner fighting. It took me two to three years, just to clean things up before I could really get moving. I can't stand chaos."

Recalling Yzaguirre's election and style of leadership, Ronnie Lopez, former director of CPLC relates. "We were hungry and thirsty for knowledge and Raul had the vision, passion and a road map that would navigate for change. The stars were aligned for him. He was the right man for the right season, well-read and a great leader. He was a real asset, a renaissance man, articulate in the White House and with the poor in Texas. He knew how to sustain and translate his vision into one national voice. His greatest strength was building bridges of communication between different groups. His way of articulating change was to find areas of common ground. Over the decades, he served NCLR and our nation very well, guiding us to the unity we needed to achieve our future goals."

Meeting Yzaguirre initially in D.C. in the '60's, Lopez described Raul's inspiration as contagious. "He was one of the visionaries who fired up young Mexican American leaders to begin dreaming of an America that would acknowledge their worth as true Americans and not exclude them as foreigners or consider them less because they spoke Spanish or lived out their Latino cultural traditions. After traveling to D.C. and meeting with Raul I didn't feel as tired. I was re-energized and re-motivated. The desire for change got stronger. The cause was right and just. We'd share ideas then come back to Phoenix and build on those ideas making people's lives better in Phoenix. Raul motivated and touched others to carry on the good fight. Our community has been far better for knowing him."

Eventually, fences were mended with Maclovio Barraza in the early days of Yzaguirre assuming leadership of NCLR. Reconciliation came through an unlikely source: UFW workers. "We had a couple of Board meetings, and Maclovio got a littler warmer to me. And then an incident occurred. My secretary's boyfriend at NCLR worked for the United Farmworkers, and one day he and his colleagues came into the office and started taking supplies. I stepped into the office and asked what was going on and they said, 'We've always had this policy where we can walk in and take whatever we need,' and I said, the policy just changed. I'm very supportive of the union, if you need something come and ask me and if I can, I will help you, but you just don't come in and take what you want. And they said, 'What are you going to do about it?' and I said I would do what I had to. They asked, 'Will you call the police?' I said, I don't want to, but if I need to I will. You're not going to steal from me. So they said, 'Cesar will get back to you.' Well I didn't have to deal with Cesar. I got a very nasty letter from Joe Padilla which I showed to Maclovio Barraza my Board Chair at the time. Before long Maclovio called me up and said, 'I need to meet with you, it's urgent.' I knew what it was about. We met and Maclovio said, 'This letter from the UFW says you blocked union workers from taking office supplies. Did you do this?' I told him yes, it was exactly what had happened. He said, 'I want to congratulate you, you have balls the size of basketballs. Those characters, you give them ninety-five percent of what they want and they get another five percent and turn on you, and I'm tired of it. I'm glad you stood up to them. I love the farm workers, but this is not the right behavior. You're the first one to stand up to the UFW and I'm going to back you up all the way.' Maclovio and I got along fine after that, and we became very good friends."

"As NCLR got stronger, Cesar Chavez and I got to know each other better. Years later, there was an event in Washington D.C. where I was to present him with an award, and it was covered by Univision. I gave him the award, and later we had a good conversation. I told him that together we had solved a number of problems, and I hoped to bring our work under the umbrella of NCLR. He said NCLR was the most powerful Latino organization in the country and to my surprise he told me, 'I want to be affiliated with you.' Unfortunately, a few months later he passed away."

Later, critics would say the Ford Foundation, first funders of the Southwest Council of La Raza, set it up for Yzaguirre to become CEO of NCLR, as he was someone who was not described as a radical and would not risk challenging the establishment. Others would go even further to describe him as a 'sell out,' *vendido*, to corporate America, although over the years Yzaguirre proved again and again that no amount of money could woo him away from his one focus: the betterment of the Latino community.

The snow in Denver on the day Yzaguirre accepted the leadership of NCLR signaled more than an aberration in the weather, an anomaly for Denver in June. With his election as CEO, a new era began for NCLR, one that would deviate from the usual way the Council did business. Denver's unpredictable weather set the stage for the storms ahead, and the capacity for something impossible to appear in a world of harsh realities.

THE WHITE HOUSE HAMMER BLOW

Yzaguirre begins his role as CEO of NCLR by facing his colleagues in D.C. and acknowledging that there are major problems going on in the Council. Transferring their headquarters from Phoenix to D.C. and changing their name from the Southwest Council of La Raza, to the National Council of La Raza, signals the organization's willingness to take on national issues, yet internal contentions strike at the core of the organization, ending in disagreements among members. Having spent only two years in their D.C. office, the Council now finds itself struggling with two major issues that tear at the fabric of their structure: the 1969 Tax Reform Act, and pressure from the White House to endorse Nixon's re-election.

The 1969 Tax Reform Act set up "expenditure responsibility" for non-profits, making organizations accountable to their funding sources, and discouraging advocacy that might lead to inappropriate use of funds by grantees. The Act also limited voter registration, seeking to eradicate politically partisan activities. It required that voter registration projects work in conjunction with overall registration efforts in various states, thus restricting organizations from receiving more than 20% of funding from a single source. A voter registration component also meant an organization would function under a special tax-exempt status. This stipulation led Willie Velasquez, an employee of the Council at the time, to create his own non-profit, a spinoff of NCLR, the Southwest Voter Registration Project (SVRP) that opened the way for voter registration to communities, who due to racist policies and gerry-mandering, had been disenfranchised from equal representation in the voting process.

With Henry Santiestevan as Executive Director (1970-74) at the helm, several of the Council's early affiliates were redefined as community development corporations (CDCs) able to build housing, develop for-profit enterprises, and provide social services to their local communities. The three major affiliates formed during this time were: Chicanos Por La Causa in Phoenix, the Mexican American Unity Council in San Antonio, and the Spanish Speaking Unity Council in Oakland.

Active in the development of the CDCs, Siobban Nicolau, the Council's Program Officer at the Ford Foundation, became an active partner in establishing CDC's. Later, he relates, "The single accomplishment of my career in philanthropy of which I am most proud, is the fact that I had the opportunity to support the development of the National Council of La Raza."

Facing new government regulations set up by the Tax Reform Act of 1969, the Ford Foundation informs the Council that they will not provide any more funding for community organizing and advocacy. The Council will have to establish "hard programs" that must be pre-approved by Ford, and measurable by stated goals and objectives. Their feet held to the fire, the Board votes to change its focus to the required "hard programs," beginning with housing, economic development, and education.

"NCLR took itself very seriously," Yzaguirre recalls. "Some of the members were very pompous. They were making pronouncements for the future of NCLR, and considered themselves leaders of the Mexican American and Latino community but there was no substance behind it. There was no real constituency, there were no real resources, nor ability to get things done, which made it an incredibly demeaning situation. Because of how NCLR and other non-profits had operated, Congress had found it necessary to pass the 1969 Tax Reform Law, which held foundations responsible for the actions of non-profit organizations they funded. It was called expenditure responsibility. That was when the Ford Foundation assigned a monitor to check up on NCLR to see that we weren't doing anything wrong. We were treated like children. In fact, as our sole funder, the Ford Foundation had to sign off on everything we did. The way you got out of that position was to get public funding or diversify. You went from being a private foundation, which was covered by the Tax Reform Law, to one receiving public funding which did not have expenditure responsibility. It was important for me to achieve that status, so for that reason and because I wanted to get over the humiliating situation with the Ford Foundation, I made plans to diversify. The one thing I knew how to do was to access government programs. I didn't want to be dependent on only one federal program, so I set in motion a plan to get money from lots of different government agencies. I knew how to do that well, so we went from a $300,000 budget to a ten to twenty million dollar budget within three or four years. By 1980 we were a sizable organization, we had extended our national outreach and had an office in D.C and offices all over the country."

As the media takes notice of NCLR's rise in power, local and national news reporters identify the Council as 'radical,' while the real radicals resent the label, and treat the organization as if it were part of the establishment. Between a rock and a hard place, Yzaguirre sees both labels as lacking in the description of the Council's fundamental goal—which is to advance civil rights for millions of Latinos nationwide. "In some ways the media treated NCLR like we were radicals and the real radicals thought we were establishment," Yzaguirre says in analyzing the extremes of both labels. "We must be doing something right if the far left thinks we're establishment and the establishment thinks we're radicals. We have to be doing something right."

Believing that there was a time to be radical, and a time to find common ground with the establishment, Yzaguirre confronts both the left and the right with equal candor. His priority in working for the good of the Council at any given point in time, regardless of the shifts in public opinion, leads him up a steep incline. The "radical" label attracts the attention of politicians, federal program developers, community organizers, and eventually comes to the attention of President Nixon himself.

Openly contending with NCLR, the Committee to Re-Elect the President (CREP) labels the Council as radical, and threatens to cut federal funding, unless the Council endorses Nixon as president and aligns itself with the administration's goals. Federal policy changes come rushing in like an avalanche as the Council struggles with internal leadership issues and the process of redefining its structure. The War on Poverty becomes a thing of the past, and the gap between mainstream America and struggling communities of color take on a new urgency.

The response from the White House comes like a hammer blow: all federal funding stops abruptly. President Nixon has no intention of putting up with anything or anyone that he suspects is a threat to his presidency. NCLR becomes one of the obstacles his administration is determined to defeat. Yzaguirre realizes it's time to re-evaluate NCLR's overall structure, long-term goals and its ability to gather a Latino constituency that will not be defeated by presidential whims, nor bend under the threat of loss of federal funding.

Misjudging his original plan for clearing up some of NCLR's critical issues, the "two years," Yzaguirre had predicted he needed to clean things up turned into twenty-three years of ambitious changes and forging forward with an expansive national agenda.

Finally, it falls on Armando de León, a retired Arizona Superior Court Judge, who was then NCLR's legal counsel, to lead the charge against President Nixon's uncompromising stance on non-funding of "radical" organizations. De León doesn't hold back in building a firewall that insures the Council's survival through the battles ahead.

PART OF EVERYTHING

Making their way from the León region in Spain to Mexico, Armando de León's ancestors settle in Tepic, the capital city of Nayarit, Mexico founded in 1542 by the Spanish. His parents, Maria Socorro, and Bernardo de León, a former Congressman of Nayarit, meet in Nogales, Arizona. Later, they marry and cross the border taking up residence in the Tucson community. For a while, the couple moves to Los Angeles, only to return again to Tucson after World War II where de León's mother gains employment at Raytheon Missile Systems. In Los Angeles, de León recalls listening to international news on the radio with his mother and aunt, Lola Rivera. "Even as a child, I was interested in politics and government. I would talk to my mother and aunt about the things being discussed and developed an interest in international affairs."

De León comes face-to-face, for the first time with illogical racism, one day after school, and in the scuffle, discovers his own identity.

"I was seven years old and we were living in Los Angeles, some kids, two African Americans, were chasing me after school one day and they caught up to me and asked me, 'Do you want to fight?' And I said no, I'm a Catholic, I don't fight. 'What does that matter?' They asked, and I told them that Catholics only fight in self-defense. 'You're nothing but a Mexican,' they said. No, I'm not, I'm a Catholic, I said. But they kept saying I was a Mexican, and chased me and roughed me up. I ran home and asked my mother if I was Mexican. And she said, '*Sí, eres Mejicano.*' (You are Mexican) Until that time, I thought I was part of everything. I had friends from all nationalities, I knew no difference."

Learning that he was someone others didn't approve of came as a shock to a young de León. He had not yet been indoctrinated into the world of racism and name-calling that he would confront all his life as an activist in the Chicano Movement. Born in Nogales, Arizona, only a stone's throw away from the other Nogales, across the border, he was raised in a loving family and immersed in both the Mexican and American cultures, seeing, as a child, little difference between tacos and hotdogs, Mexican soccer, and American football. In his mind he was part of everything. It all belonged to him, until he came toe-to-toe with the dark side of human nature: the mistaken idea that skin color matters and that someone can be judged as less because they are of a different racial group.

Strong supporters of education, de León's parents shared their values with their son, and it wasn't long before he was noticed by members of the Optimist Club at his high school in Tucson. "They were very good supporters who liked me and helped me get my education. They saw me as a leader and funded me to go to different conferences and gatherings and speak to others about the Optimist Club and the importance of education." Financially supporting de León with scholarships, the Optimists opened the way for him to pursue a college education. "Later, I became president of the Optimists, to pay back for the all the good they had done for me and many other students."

Earning a law degree from the University of Arizona in 1959, de León set up a private law practice in Phoenix in 1965, his wife Sylvia Soto at his side. Specializing in international law, he offered his services as general counsel and volunteer pro bono attorney for as many as twenty nonprofits, including NCLR, MALDEF, SVREP, Los Abogados Hispanic Bar Association, the Phoenix Hispanic-Jewish Coalition, and LULAC.

Destined to become the first Hispanic to reach the status of One Star General Brigadier in the U.S. Air Force, de León served 32 years in the Air Force Reserve as a Judge Advocate General (JAG), and was honored numerous times with prestigious medals. His service abroad as a JAG for the American Embassy in Spain inspired his son Louis de León, a Phoenix attorney, to follow in his footsteps, and he committed to service as a JAG for the American Embassy in Bogota, Columbia.

Meeting Yzaguirre during the tumultuous years of the Council's early history, de León recalls seeing a poised and determined young leader who was ready to move NCLR forward. "Raul was very well prepared for everything. He was bright, receptive, well-spoken and very hospitable. I admired him for his leadership skills. He's one of the sharpest leaders I have ever known and I'm glad our lives crossed paths."

"Armando was there for us when we needed him the most," Yzaguirre recalls. "We could count on him for expert counsel. He was open-hearted, kind and generous to all in our community. He was more than an attorney to us, working long hours, pro bono. We could count on him to get things done. He advised us that the Council would violate tax-exempt regulations that restricted non-profits from engaging in partisan activities. He counseled us to refuse Nixon's endorsement, and remain non-partisan. The Council could then freely pursue equality for Mexican Americans."

Over the years, both Yzaguirre and de León become experts at dodging political bullets, and setting the record straight: fairness and equality belong to all Americans.

THOSE WORDS AGAIN

Born in Oaxaca, Mexico in 1882 to parents of European ancestry, José Vasconcelos lived in Piedras Negras, Coahuila, and spent some of his time along the U.S. border, attending school in Eagle Pass, Texas. Active in politics, he earned a law degree from the Escuela de Jurisprudencía in Mexico City in 1905, and lived in Washington D.C. for a time as a representative of the Anti-Reelection Club. He supported the Mexican Revolution of 1910, backing up President Francisco I. Madero. Constantly embroiled in one dispute or another with Mexico's parade of presidential candidates, he was forced into exile in Paris, and became actively involved with a growing number of intellectuals and artists. His experiences along the U.S. border in a region well-known to the Yzaguirres, were critical in establishing a deeper understanding of what it meant to share in the cultural traditions of Latin American *mestizos*, whom he believed constituted, *la raza cósmica*, the 'cosmic race' through a shared ancestry with Indians, Europeans, Asians and Africans. He firmly believed this would be the race of the future, and boldly attacked Anglo expansionism and the focus on materialistic values that he felt bred greed and violence. He would later write about his philosophical views in an essay entitled: *La Raza Cósmica*, (1925) setting White supremacists on edge and cornering himself into his own brand of racism by embracing fascism and anti-Semitism during World War II. Vasconcelos's belief in, *la raza cósmica*, became a philosophical view embraced by a growing number of *mestizos* searching for their true identity, and unwilling to be defined by White supremacists who viewed Mexican Americans as second-class citizens. Vasconcelos inspired a cosmic view, embracing a pan-Hispanic panorama of ethnicities best described as a 'world culture.'

The term *la raza*, used by Vasconcelos, and echoed in rhetoric by leaders of the Chicano Movement, takes on new meaning as Yzaguirre begins his term at NCLR. "One of the first things I had to face once I took over as CEO was the organization's name. This became a sore spot for many and another excuse for contention and debate."

The National Council of La Raza, often referred to as 'La Raza,' for short, goes through its own 'naming game' process before settling on its title. Disagreements border on several points: (1) the name is too Latino; (2) the name excludes other ethnic groups; (3) the name is reflective of a 'superior' attitude about Latino identity. Yet, the name hangs on, and becomes the one distinguishing feature that will carry the organization to new heights.

"I had reservations about the term 'La Raza.' My concerns had to do with several issues. First of all the term has been used as a Chicano term, and my vision was for a Latino organization. The term also combined a Spanish language phrase with an English language phrase, and the meaning of 'La Raza,' can have several connotations. La Raza can mean 'the race' or 'the people,' and specifically, '*la raza cósmica*,' or the 'race of all the people,' the term used by José Vasconcelos."

"The way I understand Vasconcelos's term is that we're *la raza* meaning 'race,' which could include Europeans, Caucasians, Jews, Arabs, Blacks and Native tribes, so we represent the cosmos, the whole world. Yet, I struggled with the name because I knew it would be a problem for those who would see it as exclusive to Latinos. I knew the time to change it was when I first got there, but I couldn't get myself to do it. That was who we were, that's how we defined ourselves. I talked to Puerto Ricans, and Cubans and explained what *la raza* meant to me and they were comfortable with it. One of the real accomplishments for NCLR was that it saw itself as a pan-Hispanic organization, yet it took a lot of work and effort over the years to bring in non-Mexicans under the umbrella. At first everybody said, you can't do it we're tribes, and the tribes are never going to work together. But we accomplished it. We built an organization where Puerto Ricans, Cubans, Dominicans, Salvadorians, and others formed a working coalition. The only thing I couldn't change was the logo for NCLR, the Aztec god of war, Huitzilopochtli, also known as the Hummingbird. I tried to get the board to change it, but they wouldn't. The non-Mexicans objected to it. We don't use it as prominently as we used to, but it's the official logo of the organization. I gradually came to the conclusion that the organization would be known for what it did, and not for its symbols. The most important symbol was the name, 'La Raza,' the cosmic race, the race of all the people."

Backing up Yzaguirre's decision, NCLR stood its ground, taking the position that *la raza* means 'the people,' indicating the Hispanic people of the New World, and not one specific race. It encompasses Mexicans, Mexican Americans, Chicanos, Hispanics and Native American tribes, ancestors of modern-day *mestizos*. The term becomes inclusive as defined by NCLR, embracing Black, White, and Native American cultures from around the world. Thus, Latinos share a common heritage and destiny with many other ethnicities.

Uniting an immense group of Spanish speakers and their descendants, who might be speakers of other languages and members of other cultures, continues to fuel controversy, but without this major decision, Yzaguirre's hope of creating a pan-Hispanic organization would have been crushed from the onset. "Mexican Americans couldn't win the battles alone," he reflects, "nor could Puerto Ricans, Cubans and many others think they could do it by themselves. Separately, our numbers are not that big. The only way to achieve power was for us to be united."

Women Rising

Amid internal controversy and the forfeiture of federal funds during the Nixon administration, the Council experiences animosity among women members who demand seats on the Board. Initially, Audrey Rojas Kaslow of California becomes the first woman on the SWCLR Board, followed in 1970 by two more women of the Board's 26 member seats. "I inherited lots of problems," Yzaguirre says. "My dear friend, Graciela Gil Olivarez hated NCLR. She had been thrown off the Board because she was trying to promote women. When I took over, I had to spend a lot of time mending fences with affiliates and funding sources and cleaning up the culture. It was a difficult task."

In reflecting on Olivarez's efforts to establish equality for women on the Board, Danny Ortega felt that her proposal to have an equal number of women and men on the Board actually protected men. His belief is that strong women leaders would have represented at least 75% of the Board, rather than the 50/50 proposed, which was eventually adopted as a bylaw.

Emily Gantz McKay one of Yzaguirre's close associates, describes her long-time boss, el jefe, as "extremely intelligent, passionate about social justice for Latinos, and someone driven to do as much as possible as quickly as possible." Working with him when he was still president of IRA, she began a life-long relationship with Yzaguirre whom she would later describe as "THE non-profit model for Latinos for decades," and as one of the most important non-family members of her adult life.

McKay became one of the first women to join Yzaguirre in his vision of establishing a pan-Hispanic institution that would address critical issues affecting the lives of Latinos throughout the U.S., while advocating for social justice and an end to segregation and discrimination for communities of color. "When Raul took over the National Council of La Raza in 1974, I became a volunteer consultant, helping to write several proposals to expand funding to foundations other than Ford, especially Carnegie for work with Migrant Head Start Centers in Florida, and the federal government for technical assistance

grants and contracts," McKay says, describing her sixteen year-long association with Yzaguirre and NCLR.

"I had the privilege of working closely with Raul, assisting with a variety
of programs and tasks. I learned huge amounts from him about the Latino community and about negotiation and advocacy and thousands of other things.
Those of us in management positions at NCLR worked very long hours, and
often the after-hours periods were when we worked most closely together on
developing program ideas and positions, and addressing challenges. It takes
a long time to really get to know Raul and to gain his full trust, and the evening work provided that opportunity. Because of Raul, I was able to feel I was
making a difference regarding social justice and anti-discrimination work in
this country, as I worked with literally hundreds of Latino community-based
organizations that provided services at a local or state level. I learned how to
help run a large organization, became an expert on a whole range of complex
issues, honed my public speaking skills, and learned to write and to teach others how to write a wide range of policy documents. I was a supporting player
in the Latino Civil Rights Movement from 1978 to 1994."

Yzaguirre's casual attitude in addressing meetings, his manner of silent
listening, and at times humorous escapades, established a warm working environment, and in time, some members saw him as a father figure, not unlike
the role he played as the oldest of his four siblings. "Raul used to joke around
and say NCLR had a 'height limit' for staff, meaning no one should be taller
than he was," McKay recalls. "Of course, he admitted this would be difficult to
enforce, since he's not a tall man. He always used to wear Mexican half-boots,
which he found very comfortable and which made him a bit taller. They were
also one of those characteristics *la migra* used to target people to be stopped
for questioning. They would stereotype Latinos by what they wore or how
they looked and assume they were undocumented. We always rather hoped
Raul would get stopped and we could have a lovely public outcry since ethnic
profiling was such a civil rights issue."

California activist, Arabella Martinez, stepped up to the plate as an early
leader of women's demands for greater influence on the NCLR Board. "Arabella was a true pioneer," Yzaguirre says, recalling Martinez's dedication to
the goals of NCLR. "She headed one of the original NCLR affiliates, the Spanish Speaking Unity Council out of Oakland, California. Shortly after I became
President of NCLR, Arabella was appointed as an Assistant Secretary at HEW
in the Carter administration. It was a major coup and she did well. After Carter
got defeated, Arabella went back to Oakland and took over the SSUC that had
declined considerably during her absence. I consequently encouraged her to

join our Board where she served for a total of twelve years. NCLR bylaws permit two consecutive terms of three years after which you must vacate your seat, but you can, on rare occasions, be brought back to the Board after you have vacated for at least one year. Arabella has shown a commitment and a devotion to her community that is truly outstanding. Years later, Arabella was on the search committee to select my replacement."

Dr. Cordelia Candelaria, former ASU professor and Chair of ASU's Department of Transborder Chicano/a and Latino/a Studies and a graduate of Harvard University, met Yzaguirre in 1976 shortly after he had become head of NCLR. She recalls arriving in D.C. as a research officer for the National Endowment of the Humanities on a mission to integrate the goals of NEH with multicultural organizations and forge alliances that would strengthen the humanities in communities across the nation. Outnumbered as a minority *and* a woman, Dr. Candelaria recalls that no one would take her seriously, her calls went unanswered as she was not considered important enough to invite to meetings with targeted leaders.

"The only one to answer my call was Raul Yzaguirre. He set up an appointment with me but told me he didn't think NCLR worked with the humanities." Dr. Candelaria went on to explain to him the importance of philosophy and culture in evolving identity and history for all ethnic groups. "He told me, 'I think what you are doing is great, but I don't think the Council does Humanities.'"

Yzaguirre's answer eventually shakes up NCLR's position on the arts, and becomes a critical marker for the Council's involvement in arts media. Yzaguirre's commitment to honor Latino artists is realized through his creation of the ALMA Awards. Established in 1995, the ALMA Awards has honored artistic achievements in television, film, and music, building a network of national media and garnering publicity for Latino artists on par with the Academy Awards.

"He gave me a savvy and connectedness on how to leverage my own sense of mission," Candelaria recalls, "He had a low-key intensity, quiet strength, and very clear and logical thinking. He also had an amazing international network of contacts and good executive sense that would make any project work."

Eventually, Dr. Candelaria attained three million dollars from NEH for NCLR's sponsorship of *The Ballad of Gregorio Cortez* (1982) based on Américo Paredes's historical novel on the life of Gregorio Cortez. Moctesuma Esparza's film, scripted by author Victor Villaseñor, introduced Edward James Olmos to a national audience. "Victor Villaseñor was arguing in a loud voice with fellow writers one day about the script," Candelaria recalls, "and Raul heard the noise from outside his office. He came in and said to Victor, 'Why don't you ask Américo Paredes about it.' Raul handled it well, he told them to go with what the author said and, of course, that was the best solution."

As women pressed for seats on the Board, Yzaguirre set up goals that would guarantee transparency for Council elections, terms of service, and gender equality. Dr. Candelaria became the third woman to serve on the NCLR Board, fulfilling Yzaguirre's "vision of rightness and inclusion in every dimension," as he joined forces with like-minded men on the Council who sought to integrate women into an all-male board. "I was very impressed with Cordelia. She was very bright," Yzaguirre says. "As the officer for the Endowment for the Arts and Endowment for the Humanities, she was very helpful in getting us funding for *The Ballad of Gregorio Cortez*. She has been a wonderful person to be aligned with over the years."

Dr. Marta Sotomayor became the first woman elected Board Chair in a 1978 conference held in Mexico City. Not too far into her term, a dispute arose about her leadership of the Council and a decision she had made to establish her own organization, patterned after NCLR. "Dr. Marta Sotomayor was the Chair of my Board in the early days," Yzaguirre says. "She was very bright and very ambitious. Long story, short, she sought to become head of NCLR and failing to do so, set up her own organization modeled after NCLR. Later her management of the organization was investigated due to missing funds. Nothing was clarified, and she subsequently disappeared from our radar screen. It was an unfortunate situation."

EXPERIENCE ON THE HIGH SEAS PAYS OFF

Yzaguirre's once ambitious role as a fourteen year-old sailor aboard the *Barbee Nell* enabled him, in many ways, to methodically navigate the 'frail craft' that represented NCLR as he assumed the office as President and CEO. His ability to steer Captain J.L. Murrell's prized schooner, the *Barbee Nell*, safely in and out of the harbor at Corpus Christi takes on new significance as Yzaguirre steers NCLR into uncharted waters, determined to weather out storms amid the perils of an unpredictable journey, that only through patient perseverance will eventually create a 'seaworthy craft.'

The first leg of the journey begins with a Board that will be open to Yzaguirre's ideas, yet unafraid to challenge him when they feel he's off course. Serving as Board Chair during the early years of Yzaguirre's long term as CEO, Ed Pastor, Arizona's first Latino to serve in Congress, (1991-2013) often negotiated between Yzaguirre and women's demands for more seats on the

Board. Born in Claypool, Arizona, a small mining town adjacent to Miami, Arizona, Pastor, the oldest of three children, grew up in the same environment as Roberto Reveles, Ronnie Lopez and Alfredo Gutierrez, all part of an extensive Mexican American community that labored in Arizona's copper mines. In spite of humble beginnings, Pastor went on to graduate from Arizona State University, and after teaching chemistry at North High School in Phoenix for several years, returned to ASU to earn his law degree. Along with his wife, Verma Mendez, Pastor charted out a course of civic service that would one day lead him to Capitol Hill. By 1976 he was elected to the Maricopa County Board of Supervisors, and served three terms. Pastor's active leadership in the Latino community marked him as a strong civil rights advocate, and his unwavering stance for equality for all groups irrespective of race, sexual orientation, or religious beliefs has earned him the trust of Arizonans for decades.

"I first met Ed Pastor when he was Deputy Director of the Guadalupe Center in Arizona," Yzaguirre says. "IRA consultants worked for him, and continued working with Ed and Executive Director, Lauro Garcia at the Guadalupe Center even after I went to the Center for Community Change in Texas. I got to know Ed better when he spent some time in Washington. He eventually became Chairman of the Board at NCLR at a very critical time when we were going through a difficult financial crisis, and worked very well responding to women's demands for more seats on the Board. He was a supportive and stabilizing influence."

Of his initial meeting with Yzaguirre in the late sixties, Pastor recalls that IRA was a gathering place for Chicano activists from across the nation. "We would meet informally, guys like José Ángel Gutiérrez, the Chavez workers, Willie Velasquez, people from NCLR affiliates, Esteban Torres of California, and many others. We slept on couches and ate potato chips and sandwiches. As IRA consultants we were able to monitor Mexican American activities throughout the U.S. We knew who was getting money from OEO or the Center for Community Change. We kept track of where federal funds were going and worked to reach out to community based organizations."

Upon assuming the position of Chairman of NCLR's Board, Pastor became aware of the many issues facing Yzaguirre. "I liked Raul," Pastor says. "He was bright and worked hard. He always treated me with lots of respect. However, there were several women who didn't like him. They felt he displayed the Napoleon Complex, and wanted to fire him. He had support from women involved in various organizations nationwide, but had issues with women who felt they were being nixed from the Board. After discussing the issues with Armando de León, our legal counsel, I found no grounds for firing him."

"I was very supportive of women," Yzaguirre relates. "The problem was that we couldn›t get enough candidates to pass through the Board committees. So we had to recommend a more extensive effort to make that happen, and as a result of that I agreed to have a women's task force on the Board. They were my biggest supporters and made positive changes and we were able to resolve several issues. Ed had a hand in the negotiations. He was very cordial with me, very gracious."

Pastor served as Board Chair for eight years, and resigned his position when he was elected to Congress in 1991. Active as Pastor's campaign manager, Danny Ortega served the remaining three years of Pastor's term, assuming his own position as Chair for six more years. Ortega later returned to serve another term, accumulating twelve years of service as Chair.

"Danny was someone Ed Pastor fought hard to get on the Board of Directors to succeed him in his place. Danny was very good on the Board, and served his six-year limit and then, what we like to do occasionally, is once off the Board for a year you can serve again. Several years went by, and Danny came back and once again became Chairman of the Board. I have been very proud of him and greatly esteem his service."

From his vantage point as Board Chair, Ortega observed, first-hand, Yzaguirre's unique leadership skills and his focus on creating an efficient and well-run organization. "We spent a great deal of time and effort on governance and accountability," Yzaguirre recalls. "We had four interlocking governing bodies: the Board, the Executive Committee of the Board, the Affiliate Council, and the Corporate Board of Advisors. We paid for room and travel for all but the Corporate Board. This investment in governance was costly and time consuming, but the investment paid off in the long run. We were well governed and we audited every penny that we spent. We received several community commendations for excellence in management and accountability."

"I learned a lot about the dynamics of Board politics from Raul," Ortega recalls. "He always had an agenda and most of the time the necessary votes to carry out his plans. You could not be on the Board if Raul didn't want you there. He offered lots of opportunity, but also needed to be in control, but in spite of this, I never felt he was making a deal to enhance his own career. Everything he did, he did for our community. When I became Chairman of the Board for NCLR, I was elevated in Raul's eyes to a person of importance and influence. I had never felt that way before. He treated me with such high regard, when it was I who revered him. I felt I didn't deserve such recognition, yet the importance he put on me made me more effective. This was part of how Raul passed the torch to build up others."

Passing the torch to young leaders, and focusing on transparency in his dealings with the Board will become key issues for Yzaguirre as he struggles with a Board often at odds with his passion for public policy, and his decision to increase the Council's affiliate relationships, rather than concentrate on individual memberships. Running the Council with an eye to achieving unification for Latinos throughout the U.S., while focusing on building institutions and reining in corporate America, will become the cornerstones of Yzaguirre's legacy, propelling him, dramatically, into the national spotlight.

19

LIFE ON THE HILL

Raul provided a very high ethical standard that I know affected all of us. Staff felt they needed to hold themselves to a higher standard because they were at NCLR, and people chose to stay for many years. They made NCLR their life's work because of Raul.

—Emily Gantz McKay

LONGITUDE 0:0

Apitol Hill, once referred to as 'Jenkins Hill,' becomes for Yzaguirre a symbol of what it means for Latinos to have "arrived in America." Without recognition from Congress, there can be little future for NCLR as a first-class institution that can effectively influence policymakers and create new pathways for social reform. With headquarters in D.C., not far from Capitol Hill, NCLR moves closer to the nation's source of power, and Yzaguirre, never missing an opportunity to enhance the organization's national voice, is ready to take on the challenges posed by Congress and presidents who exert their power, engaging in political intrigues that ebb and flow like tidal waves along the Atlantic seashore.

The Hill has its own story to tell. The story begins with a twenty-three year-old French immigrant, Pierre Charles L'Enfant, who arrives on the eastern coast of the United States in 1777, and takes up residence for a time in New York. He's determined to join the American Revolution and fight for independence from Britain in the name of the American Continental Army. He's passionate, quick-tempered, and unafraid to voice his opinions, arguing vehemently when he has to, to get his point across. His one prevailing talent shows up almost immediately: he's an architect and can design cities and buildings on a grand scale. Embedded in his memory are the visions of Paris

241

and its magnificent buildings, palaces and museums. Grandeur to him is simply the next plan he'll draw up—it's as easy as taking a stroll down a city street and seeing the map of a new city come alive in his imagination. It won't be long before the services of Pierre Charles L'Enfant will be needed by General George Washington, once he's elected as the first American President. A prince among architects in D.C., L'Enfant's meteorite rise to fame will be undone by his own stubborn will—his fall from prince to pauper takes only a few short years.

L'Enfant first serves as a military engineer under the direction of Major General Lafayette, and soon adopts the American name, 'Peter.' He rises quickly to the rank of Major and serves under the command of General George Washington during the battle of Valley Forge. It doesn't take Washington long to recognize L'Enfant's unique talents as an architect, and when plans are to be drawn up for the design of the nation's capital in 1791, he appoints L'Enfant as the architect who will head the project. A location with the longitude of 0:0 is chosen for the Congress house to emphasize the importance of the structure and symbolically capture the beginnings of a nation that will last for all time. L'Enfant's plan, designed in an elaborate, baroque-style, envisions the President's House, now the White House, connected to the Congress by way of Pennsylvania Avenue, and a broader 'grand avenue,' which eventually became the National Mall.

Within a year, L'Enfant's insistence on engaging in power struggles with the Commissioners assigned to oversee the project, costs him his post, and President Washington fires him. American architect, Andrew Ellicott, takes up the project in spite of L'Enfant's refusal to hand over most of the original designs. Relying solely on memory, Ellicott does his best to recapture L'Enfant's designs. Unpaid for his services, L'Enfant spends the greater part of his life, trying to get Congress to pay him the tens of thousands he says they owe him. What's finally paid is only enough to satisfy his debtors, and a report after his death, marks his only valuables as three compasses, three watches, and an assortment of maps, books and surveying equipment totaling about forty-five dollars. It will take eighty-four years before L'Enfant receives recognition for his contribution in designing what is now Capitol Hill. In 1909, his remains are re-interred with honors in the Arlington National Cemetery in Virginia on the crest of a small hill overlooking the famous city he helped to design.

Sixty-five years after L'Enfant's re-interment at Arlington National Cemetery, Yzaguirre assumes leadership of NCLR, setting his sights on the same hill that once fascinated L'Enfant. He begins the most important phase of his life's work with NCLR—the establishment of governing policies, positions on advocacy, gathering research and statistics, and setting priorities for the most crucial issues for lobbying Congress on behalf of the nation's Latinos. Forming the foundation for his plans will be powerful affiliates scattered throughout the nation—NCLR'S constituency, the backbone of the Council and his ticket to the City on the Hill as originally envisioned by L'Enfant; the grand city, longitude 0:0, reflecting liberty and freedom from oppression.

THE REINS OF POWER

"In 1974 when I took over leadership of NCLR, I felt empowered and emboldened to speak on behalf of Latinos," Yzaguirre says, explaining the metamorphosis he experienced as he realized the organization's future potential. "We were lagging in our presence on the Hill. We had yet to understand our ability to influence Congress and didn't have enough self-confidence, but as time went by, we became more aggressive. I felt anointed to pursue advocacy, research, public policy and a strong affiliate constituency."

His old friend from Texas, Representative Henry B. Gonzalez, initially blocked Yzaguirre's efforts in Congress. "Henry B. started attacking NCLR before I came on board and attacking the Ford Foundation because they were funding what he thought were melting groups in San Antonio. He put so much pressure on the Ford Foundation that MALDEF, which had once been headquartered in San Antonio, had to move out because he had made life so miserable for the organization's members. So when I came to the Council, there was still that animosity towards NCLR from Henry B. Eventually, he ran into a couple of problems and one in particular in which he actually had a fist fight with a member of Congress who dared to call him a Communist. We supported him through this, and after a while I called him up and told him, look you had a problem with NCLR before I came into office, let's put that behind us. We've been supportive of you, but I'm not going to be supportive anymore unless we have peace. And he said, yes we would have peace and we were allies after that. He was head of the Housing Committee and we did good work together. He was interesting because he stood up for civil rights, but was against ethnic civil rights. He was against anything that seemed too radical and felt we should share the same philosophy as White America, which is good in some ways, but in practical terms it doesn't work. You can't be the same if you're treated unequally."

A fearless lobbyist on behalf of Latino issues, Manny Fierro, Executive Director of El Congreso, took over as the lobbying arm of IRA, freeing Yzaguirre to build up NCLR's constituency. "Subsidized with labor money,

Fierro's work was critical in attracting the attention of legislators and senators. I was the power behind the NCLR Board Chair, but Manny was the public voice. Running a non-profit, I could do no lobbying, but worked instead to strengthen our constituency so we could get things done in Congress."

Emily Gantz McKay, working with Yzaguirre since his work began with NCLR, recalls Dr. Michael Cortés as another powerful lobbyist. Cortés spent long hours along with Manny Fierro, researching, gathering statistics and formulating reports to present to Congress. "Raul brought in Mike as a lobbyist to link our affiliates with a national public policy," McKay says. "African Americans had Black churches and Black colleges to help them create national policy, but we had neither, so nonprofit organizations were a hugely important training ground for Latino civil rights activists and leaders. Raul would explain this to corporations and foundations and public officials constantly. Congressman Esteban Torres was one of many Congress members who came out of the nonprofit world. Led by Raul, NCLR became a critical source of visibility, sub-grants, training and capacity-building for its member nonprofits, and gave them input to national policy making."

Attorney Ramon Murguia, former Board Chair, and brother of Janet Murguia, current President and CEO of NCLR, credits Yzaguirre for sharing his knowledge of nonprofits with him and giving him the skills to serve in board positions with philanthropic institutions. "I first met Raul at the NCLR national conference in 1989 in Albuquerque," Ramon Murguia recalls. "At the time, I had been asked to participate in a workshop at the conference on philanthropy because I was chairing a Latino fund for philanthropy in Kansas City. Aside from the inspiration Raul has been over the years, and the example he set for servant leadership, he also generously opened his network of connections to me and encouraged me to take on leadership roles. He taught me never to shy away from speaking the truth about our Latino community to the decision makers."

Reflecting on Yzaguirre's ability to unite diverse groups and bring them together to implement social reform on Capitol Hill, Ramon Murguia comments, "Raul was the first person to credibly build a pan-Latino civil rights organization. No one thought it was possible, but through perseverance, honesty and force of character he was able to put it together. Raul effectively connected policy work in D.C. directly to the lives of Latino families. The NCLR affiliates serving those families, informed the work and issues NCLR focused on in D.C. While other organizations like the G.I. Forum and LULAC were founded years before NCLR, they never reached the level of sophistication or talent that NCLR was able to establish in Washington, D.C."

Tommy Espinoza describes Yzaguirre, as "our Tip O'Neil," in his ability to influence Congress and refine his position on multiple issues in his numerous testimonies before Congressional subcommittees. Wielding his power in Congress, O'Neil inspired respect from Irish compatriots, as well as from those who disliked him, and Yzaguirre exhibited the same style of leadership. "Raul had lots of power on the Hill," Espinoza says. "He faced multiple issues, immigration, housing, labor, education—all the big ones and often crossed over the aisle to do so. He impacted more than Latinos, befriending even his enemies. His number one goal was to get things done for our community,"

Working in D.C. in the early days of Yzaguirre's term as NCLR's CEO, Mark Van Brunt, one of the longest serving members of NCLR, began working with farmworkers in Casa Grande, Arizona and was later transferred to one of NCLR's offices in Phoenix in 1976. "I'm glad Raul was an equal opportunity employer. I was one of the non-Latinos he hired," Van Brunt explains. "Raul was a man on a mission. He was commanding and engaging. There were not many like him at that time. He laid the groundwork for expanding community development and stayed away from partisan politics in D.C. He didn't align himself with one political party, but questioned both sides, putting them to the test on Latino issues. He was not afraid of opposition, and often used his influence to bring Latinos into national board rooms where they began to make inroads in American society and culture, coming into their own as leaders."

Remembering NCLR's early days of financial struggles in D.C., Van Brunt relates, "We were trying to raise money to promote our programs, and many of us were going without to help the organization. I remember my paycheck bounced at one point and I got on the phone to find out what had happened, and the phone was dead! Those were the days when meeting with NCLR staff was sharing a bag of chips and drinking a 6-pack of beer. We had a saying, 'Don't let them eat your lunch.' Those were meager years, when we might skip a pay period, but I always knew Raul could pull it off—and he did. He felt responsible for all of us and felt he had to do the work, or it wouldn't get done."

Unbeknownst to Mark Van Brunt at the time, he and Tommy Espinoza were destined to share in the leadership of one of the most powerful nonprofits in NCLR history: The Raza Development Fund (RDF) initiated by Yzaguirre in 1998. "Raul challenged all of us," Van Brunt recalls, "especially the young leaders. He would tell them, 'You can change your neighborhood. You can organize, you can be leaders.' He was always encouraging and challenging his staff. In that way he has been a role model of self-determination.

Raul's name may not be a household word, but the visibility of a leader is not as important as positively impacting the next generation. The test of time is how a life well-lived has changed the generations. Raul's DNA is all over this generation—his influence will stand the test of time."

UNBRIDLING THE POWER

Young Raul, Jr. "Hoagie" sits in the audience at the Mayflower Hotel in D.C. in 1978, watching as his father steps up to the podium. It is NCLR's first national conference. Hoagie's wearing his favorite baby blue, polyester suit, and senses the thrill of seeing his dad approach the microphone. "I sat there and listened to my dad, and I looked around and saw all the respect everyone had for him. Everything he said made so much sense. He was talking about equality and fairness for everyone, and about making changes for the sake of those who were struggling in America. It was a very proud moment for me."

Taking a leap onto the national stage, NCLR emerges as one of America's leading non-profits as forces align to bring about the first annual NCLR Conference in 1978. Viewing NCLR, in many ways, as an extended family, Yzaguirre, always a family man, rallies the Board and staff to begin plans for what will eventually become a tradition: the NCLR Annual Conference, one of the biggest events for non-profits in U.S. history.

Using the annual conference as a way to draw attention to issues NCLR will address, Yzaguirre joins forces with the National Spanish-Speaking Housing Development Corporation in 1974 and NCLR becomes the first national Latino organization to identify housing as one of its primary concerns. Establishing itself as a major player in founding the Forum of National Hispanic Organizations consisting of a broad range of Hispanic groups nationwide, NCLR serves as the organization's secretariat and first Chair. Conscious of the need for collaboration among various community groups, Yzaguirre leads the way in establishing a working relationship with organizations such as IMAGE, which focused on Hispanic government employees; LULAC, the oldest Hispanic civil rights organization in US history; the American GI Forum, founded by Dr. Hector P. García to fight for Hispanic veteran's rights; MALDEF, a leading Latino civil rights organization; SER, securing jobs for low-income minorities, and the National Economic Development Administration (NEDA) which was set up to assist Spanish-speaking business personnel. Eventually, Yzaguirre's outreach draws in the National Urban League and the NAACP, organizations working for equality for Black Americans, joining them in projects as varied as energy conservation, welfare reform, minorities in higher education, and voting rights.

Federal grant money once closed to NCLR by the Nixon administration, becomes available once again as Vice-President Gerald Ford takes over the White House at the beginning of Yzaguirre's term as CEO. The Council begins to receive federal grants, initially for housing, community development training and technical assistance, and then for employment and training capacity-building. Through funding from the Community Services Administration (CSA), which had replaced the War on Poverty's OEO program, and the Office of Minority Business Enterprise (OMBE), NCLR is able to bring together the Western Association of Spanish-Speaking Community Development Centers (CDC's) in a conference in Scottsdale, Arizona in August 1975. Over seventy organizations were present, joining in networking and capacity-building. Among them were forty CDC's and other groups interested in creating hard programs that would impact community leaders willing to step up to the plate and become resources for struggling communities. The success of the conference increases federal funding allowing NCLR to establish field offices in Albuquerque, and Yzaguirre's stomping ground, the Lower Rio Grande Valley. Emphasis is placed on expanding services to low-income barrios and rural communities that lack infrastructure and community developers.

Yzaguirre's vision of establishing diversified funding sources slowly becomes a reality as more than two-thirds of NCLR'S funding shifts to corporations and foundations, while the rest comes from government sources. By 1975, a new funding proposal is introduced to the Ford Foundation outlining NCLR's determination to reduce its dependency on Ford, and seek federal funding and support from corporations and other foundations. By 1976, Yzaguirre's leadership decreases funding from the Ford Foundation to below half of the organization's total budget, and by 1980, Ford provides only 6% of NCLR's funding. Although Ford's core monetary support is indispensable, funding is now balanced by an increase in monies from other sources. By the end of the decade, NCLR had helped generate more than $100 million in funding to Latino organizations throughout the Southwest.

Identifying NCLR as an institution dedicated to improving the social and economic status of Hispanic Americans, Yzaguirre describes the Council as serving its constituency in two fundamental ways: (1) providing research and advocacy to impact public policy; and (2) providing technical assistance, loans and sub-grants to enable affiliates to meet their goals and objectives. The Council's strategy of collaboration and cooperation sets the standard for forming working relationships with affiliates, government agencies and a host of organizations nationwide.

Seeking to diversify the Council's Board membership, Yzaguirre presses for the inclusion of multiple Latino ethnicities representing various geographical locations both urban and rural, and including members from nonprofits, and corporations, as well as government and private industry. Major NCLR field offices in Chicago, Los Angeles, Phoenix, San Antonio, and San Juan, Puerto Rico link affiliates with the NCLR headquarters in D.C. establishing a network of closely aligned organizations that move powerfully as one voice.

Increasing NCLR's visibility becomes a critical issue for Yzaguirre as he works to establish the Council's leadership in pursuing social reform and creating a reputation for being accountable to its constituency. "Although our first conference in 1978 was small in comparison to the tens of thousands that would attend future conferences, it was a start. Initially we thought the conference would be a good way to formulate policy but we found that because there were so many different people in workshops and so much going on, the annual conference was not a good time to formulate policy, so we redefined the role of the conference. It became a way to connect with our affiliates, it was a way of gaining attention to our movement, it was a way of generating funds, and it was a way of educating the public about who we were as a community. The conferences improved communications between affiliates and Board members and an extended network of community groups, private and public funders, and policy makers. It was a place for networking and forming strong alliances with NCLR's national network."

"I was impressed by Raul's energy and leadership skills, "Ramon Murguia says, describing Yzaguirre in action at one of the annual conferences. "He commanded the room's attention. I had never seen anyone speak with such eloquence and sense on the issues of Latinos in the United States. I agreed with everything he said. In those days there were few people speaking on our issues."

Fellow Texan, Hilario Diaz, active in Campesinos Unidos one of NCLR's affiliates, met Yzaguirre in 1974 in D.C. and later served five years as a member of the NCLR staff. He recalls one of the early conferences that took place in Milwaukee. "It seemed Raul never prepared his speeches before the conference, but he knew exactly what he wanted to say. He was relaxed and had a lot of confidence. At the Milwaukee conference me and Emily gave him some points to discuss, and I was so surprised at the end of his speech when he told the audience, 'By the way if you want copies of my speech, just ask Hilario Diaz.'"

Reflecting on the NCLR conferences, Alma Yzaguirre relates, "They were exciting. It was a time to really get to know one another, and to hear my brother speak on a variety of national issues. I was so proud of how he addressed the public and how knowledgeable he was on everything to do with Latinos."

ALL OR NOTHING

Tense meetings, long nights, disagreements among Council members, more long nights, and Yzaguirre's old pal, chaos, following like a shadow as he moves headlong into the mix of Council problems, politics and pressing national questions, take their toll on Yzaguirre's life, making him wonder why he didn't stay in Texas like he had planned to do in the first place. His initial surprise at becoming CEO of NCLR, begins to wear thin as reality hits. The confusion about the direction the Council should take and in-house disputes among members work against his vision and design of creating an inclusive institution that moves forward in collaboration with African Americans, mainstream America, and hundreds of Latino ethnic groups struggling to find their place in America's increasingly diverse landscape.

The controversy over who will be the spokesperson for NCLR comes to a volatile climax at a meeting in San Diego in February 1979. The Board Chair, restricted by bylaws that limit the number of years of service on the Board, is not considered a reasonable choice, yet there's intense debate among members about giving the position of primary spokesperson to the CEO.

"I guess at the beginning when I took over the Council we had staff who had been left unguided and wanted to keep the same patterns going, while I was trying to bring order out of chaos," Yzaguirre recalls. "Before I took over I had a conversation with the Board asking them if it was clear that I had the power to make changes, and they said, 'Do what you have to do.' I was over-confidant that I could motivate anybody and it turned out that was a huge mistake on my part. One of my employees was living with a controller of NCLR and had a close friend, a German guy, and they started to organize against me. Later, I found out some of the Board members were in cahoots with them and wanted to take my job. I thought I didn't want this in the first place so why am I involved with somebody who wants my job? Why should I care? I was ready to quit. It would have been easier for me to quit and start another organization than to take over something as screwed up as NCLR was. I kept asking myself why I was doing this? I had left an organization I had created out of nothing. I had named my own Board and had total control, and now I was back to this."

"One of the first big issues I had to deal with was who would be the spokesperson for the Council. The question was, am I your leader or not?

Once I won that battle things began to turn around. At times, the Chairman of the Board would speak for the organization, and I had to go back and clean things up because something wasn't said right. It was undermining my ability to lead, so I put it to them this way: If you folks want your elected part-time Chairman of the Board to be your spokesperson that's fine, but understand that he's not accountable to you. He's a volunteer. I'm accountable to you and I'm your President and CEO. If you want your Chairman to be your spokesperson that's fine, but I'm not going to be your clerk, either I'm your leader or I'm out of here. This was in San Diego and when we walked into the Board meeting I thought for sure that was the end of my tenure. When I walked out of there, I found out every Board member had voted for me except for one, and the other one who didn't vote, abstained. They supported the CEO as the primary spokesperson for the organization with the understanding that I could delegate. And my delegation was pretty broad. I wanted everybody to feel they could talk to the press if they knew what they were talking about. If they didn't, then kick it upstairs. This was not about me being the leader, this was about the organization and I wanted it to have many different faces, but I also felt I had to be accountable to the Board as the primary spokesperson. The buck stopped with me."

At the same meeting, amid much debate, NCLR affirms one of Yzaguirre's most important goals: the expansion of NCLR as an advocate for all Hispanics, serving all Latino subgroups and becoming one unified voice for all. Addressing the meeting Yzaguirre's reflections reach quarreling members, bringing order to a long-standing dispute. "If you want to remain a Mexican American organization, you have to understand that we're always going to be a fractured community. We will not only have to compete with African Americans, we'll have to compete with Puerto Ricans, Cubans, Salvadorans and many other Hispanic ethnicities. We need to emphasize our Latino roots and to treasure our differences. Our goal is to define ourselves as a broader coalition."

Unbeknownst to him at the time, Yzaguirre had just sealed his own legacy. By redefining NCLR as a pan-Latino institution, he opened its doors to limitless power by uniting America's Latinos, once and for all, into a network of millions, with one voice, and one direction.

COUNCIL ON STEROIDS

NCLR's growth under Yzaguirre's leadership increases from two federally funded projects to fifteen by 1978. Its first corporate grant comes from the Equitable Life Assurance Society of the United States, followed by funding from the Carnegie Corporation. Unwilling to trust the up's and down's of federal funding, Yzaguirre leads the way for NCLR to make private-sector funding a priority. By this time the Council's involved with the Immigration and Naturalization Service (INS) Advisory Committee on Hispanic Affairs with Yzaguirre as a member, and later acting as the Chair.

Meeting at another NCLR conference, the Forum of National Hispanic Organizations, a non-partisan group, begins to make plans for influencing the 1976 presidential elections, signaling the power Latinos would unleash as America's largest minority. No presidential election would ever be the same again, once NCLR and other non-profits began the process of educating Latinos on the power of the vote as a way to effectively change public policy in America.

Stepping down in 1977, Maclovio Barraza, founding Chair for the Council, is replaced by Juan Patlán, Executive Director of the Mexican American Unity Council. As Patlán takes over as Chair, the Board decides it's necessary to further empower its constituency, and votes to have half its members elected from among representatives nominated by its affiliates, thus giving the nearly one hundred affiliates who had thus far joined NCLR, a stronger voice on the Board.

Taking a closer look at the Council's management structure, Yzaguirre, along with the Board, decides that the current structure of Executive Director, Associate Director, and several component directors needs to be replaced by a corporate structure. In early 1978 at a Board meeting in Mexico City, the NCLR Board adopts a corporate structure, officially making Yzaguirre President and CEO, and a voting member of the Board. Five major offices are identified, each headed by a vice president, nominated by the President and approved by the Board. At the same meeting, the first woman Chair, Dr. Marta Sotomayor, then serving as a member of the Alcohol Drug Abuse and Mental Health Administration (ADAMHA), is elected as Board Chair.

Establishing a tier of vice-presidents, is crucial to Yzaguirre's overall plan for delegating important tasks and eliminating an influx of reports from several directors. The structure allows him more time for creating new programs, attending national conferences, testifying before Congress and establishing himself in the role as NCLR's spokesperson. Emily Gantz McKay is named NCLR's Executive Vice President, becoming second in command and assisting Yzaguirre in seeking highly qualified staff. "I hired Charles Kamasaki from NCLR's Texas office in Edinburgh to come up to D.C. in 1982 when we got funding for the policy center," McKay says.

Kamasaki served as NCLR's Senior Vice President for over twenty years, and became one of many long-term VP's who made NCLR their life's work.

Mark Van Brunt, served as Deputy Vice President of Community Development beginning in 1981, then went on to help establish the Raza Development Fund (RDF) in 1999. Also serving long tenures were Cecilia Muñoz, vice president of the office of Research, Advocacy and Legislation who served eighteen years then continued her service as an advocate for Latinos by accepting President Obama's appointment in 2011 as director of the U.S. Domestic Policy Council. Sonia Pérez, Deputy Vice President has also served a life-long term at NCLR, and Lisa Navarrete, a fellow Texan of Cuban descent, has clocked over twenty-seven years at NCLR working on civil rights issues, and serving as Vice President of Public Information and Communications. "Raul provided a very high ethical standard that I know affected all of us," McKay reflects. "Staff felt they needed to hold themselves to a higher standard because they were at NCLR, and people chose to stay for many years. They made NCLR their life's work because of Raul."

"We had an understanding of how we managed the organization," Yzaguirre says. "I had an open door policy but I didn't want to undermine the positions of supervisors. Anybody could come and talk to me, but once they did they had the responsibility to go talk to the supervisor and tell them what we had talked about so that access to me did not undermine any of the vice-presidents or managers. Our internal organization was made up of a number of vice presidents who took on roles as leaders. They oversaw policy advocacy, affiliates, management, technical assistance, funding and many other areas. We had a hierarchy, but it was important that the hierarchy did not prevent ideas from going to the top. The open door policy was in effect, but if an agreement was made with me, the employee needed to tell the supervisor about the agreement. Some new principles and old principles for management were used, and some we created specifically for NCLR. We found that the policies we adopted had to have a firewall between funders and policy makers, so the policy folks never talked to the funders. For instance if Walmart funded us, the policy people would be protected from any pressure from Walmart or any other agency to act on its behalf. We dealt with issues of integrity, and wanted to keep everything transparent."

Yzaguirre's tactics as a leader opened pathways for his staff to evolve their own thoughts, insights and plans. Some staff felt he was too casual at times, giving too much leeway, leading by suggestion and the sharing of ideas, rather than by introducing a preset plan. Writing thorough reports and relying on policy analysis to understand issues and problems facing Latinos, became Yzaguirre's tool for providing staff with the knowledge they needed to understand the dimensions of a multi-faceted issue. Laura Pollard, Yzaguirre's debate teacher in high school would have been proud of the way her former student was able to take an issue and view it from every angle. His strongest point as a debater had always been spontaneous debate, and it was about to be put to the test. Those around him became adept at reading between the lines and anticipating what he was referring to, and how their own thoughts would complement, or challenge his views. Yzguirre accepted both positive and negative feedback as a way to see through the issues facing NCLR and figure out what they were really all about.

"We developed rapidly, but there were certain quirks that needed to be clarified. I wanted to treat people the way I wanted to be treated. Sometimes that got a little confusing and sometimes I'd go up to somebody and say, 'Hey what do you think about doing such and such?' And he'd say, 'Maybe that's a good idea.' And I'd say, 'Yeah I think that's a good idea,' and I'd walk away. And they'd think it was just an idea, but it wasn't just an idea it was something I wanted to see happen. Just because I didn't say I wanted a staff member to do x, y, or z by such and such a time, which is typical, didn't indicate that I didn't mean it. I wanted people to have a chance to challenge me. If I said, 'I have an idea.' or 'What about this?' That was inviting a staff member to challenge me and convince me not to do it, or tell me why it could, or couldn't be done. I wanted my employees to feel empowered to take action with some clarity as to what they could and couldn't do. I wanted them to have the power to try to convince me of whatever they felt was important. I wanted them to have opinions. I valued those opinions. I wanted people who could think for themselves who could lead and go on and do better and greater things. I didn't want 'yes people' around me. I wanted people who were smarter than I was and who were more energetic and more committed than me. And when I found those people, I hired them."

Yzaguirre's choice of employees, for the most part, were hand-picked by himself as he searched for those who exhibited all the strengths he valued, beginning with the complex give and take that was part of the trained mind of an effective debater. Joining Emily Gantz McKay, would be staff members like Charles Kamasaki, who played "devil's advocate," when it mattered the most; Cecilia Muñoz who would be honored with a McArthur Fellowship for her work on immigration issues at NCLR; and Alex Perilla, a young intern who would become as close to Yzaguirre as if he were his own son. These and many more would sit at Board meetings, and conferences, and Congressional subcommittees, and share long nights in Raul's office working on an extensive list of projects. They would become acquainted with his wife Audrey, his children Gina, Raul, Jr., Lisa, Bobby, Becky and Ben, and although Yzaguirre was guarded about his private life, the Yzaguirre family members found open arms everywhere, and through all the tumultuous years, when things got rough for Raul, they would find time to laugh with him when he 'cut loose' and told his humorous stories or played a surprise prank on some unsuspecting soul.

"I was most closely acquainted with Lisa and Bobby, Raul's two middle children," recalls McKay. "They used to spend a lot of time at the office during vacations and holidays, and they spent a good deal of it in my office. I was known for having cashews and other snacks. They are delightful people and we had lots of interesting discussions. Lisa was always very committed to helping others and worked for quite a while in residential settings for either mentally ill or developmentally disabled people. Bobby ended up in the non-profit world, doing youth development. I like to think they were significantly affected as children by being around their father and the staff at NCLR."

Yzaguirre's long-time friend, and former Mayor of San Antonio, Henry Cisneros, along with NCLR staff and their families enthusiastically participated in the Encuentros, gatherings away from the frantic pace of business-as-usual, at the beginning of each New Year in January, when they would lounge in a relaxed, family atmosphere at a sunny location to become for a whole week what Yzaguirre valued above all else—a family. His grandparents, Gavino and Licha Morin's love of family had inspired their grandson to build not only a lasting institution, but one that boasted a staff that would become— the NCLR Family.

The beginning of Yzaguirre's thirty-year tenure as NCLR President and CEO, started amidst great controversy, on-going debates, and highly charged meetings that often seemed to spell the end of his tenure before he had a chance to get it off the ground. Yet, the beginning was only a taste of what was to come. There would be unification among NCLR members, in spite of opposition voiced from all corners of the U.S., as Yzaguirre formulated public policy that ignited controversy nationwide. Immigration, fair housing practices, better education for Latinos, tax reform, voting rights, and the North American Free Trade Agreement (NAFTA), were only a few of the issues he would face. Always ready to roll with the punches, his tenure would shake up Congress, call U.S. Presidents to greater accountability, and forever change the way America viewed Latinos.

Yzaguirre's long-time associate, Tony Salazar, clearly identified what happened as a result of Yzaguirre's willingness to stay the course. "Raul was the glue that brought Latinos, including Mexicans, Puerto Ricans, Cubans,

Central Americans and many others together under one canopy. It was Raul who took a fledgling nonprofit and transformed it into a national institution. It was Raul who served as the spokesperson for Latinos in national public policy debates. It was Raul who used NCLR to fight for inclusion opportunities in federal programs, business franchises and foundation grants. It was Raul who became legendary for helping Latinos find their place in American society."

Pierre Charles L'Enfant's vision of the City on the Hill, longitude 0:0, was about to take on new dimensions, as Raul Yzaguirre took his place on Capitol Hill among the nation's movers and shakers, unafraid to face personal defeat, if it meant victory for America's Latinos.

20

PUBLIC POLICY OR PERISH

The building of the Policy Center would not have had a big footprint without programs. Raul wanted it all, both public policy and programs. He built NCLR into a strong nonprofit that ended up with both arenas; it was not only a trade association of affiliates, but a strong voice for the community.

—Charles Kamasaki

WHO ARE YOU DOING IT FOR?

IT'S LATE, AND IT'S BEEN A TOUGH DAY at NCLR headquarters. Discussions have run long, and tempers have flared. Yzaguirre is now facing a handful of his staff members. It's past 10 PM and there are still things to discuss. Some members are on board with Yzaguirre's plans to build a policy analysis arm of NCLR, others are totally convinced that the work of NCLR should be concentrated on its affiliates and the programs they offer. They fear that by not addressing the community with "hard" programs, they'll be criticized by their funders for not substantiating their efforts with concrete results. How did you spend our money? That's the question funders want answered. Other staff members fear they'll suffer the loss of confidence from their affiliates and the public in general if they focus on influencing public policy. They want to send out the message that NCLR is ready to assist affiliates with planning, programming, technical advice and a variety of other services. Yzaguirre's tired of the debates and asks a question that sets them all in the right direction. "Who are you doing it for?" Weary staff members stare at him. They know how much work a policy center will be, but they know Raul. They know that service to the community is his one enduring goal. We're doing it for the community is the only logical answer any staff member can give, and it never changes.

"We can't move forward, unless we do public policy," he tells them. "It's that simple. We've got to advocate in Congress *and* work the programs for our affiliates. We'll do it all."

New Horizons Rising

Yzaguirre's words, "If you can't document a problem in this country, it doesn't exist," becomes a focal point for creation of the Office of Research and Policy Analysis in 1975, replacing NCLR's National Services component. Dedicated to helping Yzaguirre create NCLR into an institution that will give Latinos a national voice, Emily Gantz McKay becomes Vice President for Research Advocacy and Legislation in 1980 and assists in creating reports and analyzing statistics and research that will make visible, millions of Latinos, who through Yzaguirre's efforts are beginning to unite under one banner, no longer exclusive to Mexican Americans, Hispanics, or Chicanos; advocacy has to encompass a global perspective.

"Raul always did a good job of being non-partisan," McKay says, describing Yzaguirre's work with legislators. "Clearly, most of NCLR was closer to the philosophy of the Democrats than the Republicans, given the latter's traditional views on some of our key issues. Raul always said we had to play a 'gadfly' role, getting our friends to do more and keeping the pressure on both friends and foes alike until our goals were accomplished."

Determined to build NCLR into an institution that would gain respect as America's Latino 'think tank,' Yzaguirre steps boldly into the Congressional arena, ready to take on public policy. "The board fought me very hard but I got through another function, policy advocacy. At first, they didn't want to work on public policy, but I pushed them in that direction. I wrote one paper, then another and outlined how we were going to do it. We needed to build institutions. I shared it with the Board and with the staff, and they read it and understood where we were going."

"Our breakthrough came when we asked the Rockefeller Foundation for a large fund to do public policy. We had been doing this with our own money and they assigned a consultant to determine if we were capable of doing a certain amount of public policy advocacy. The person they assigned did a very thorough job of investigating us and came out with a report that said NCLR, by any standards, was the most effective and outstanding Latino organization in our country and could do the job. So we got a significant grant by the standards of those days from the Rockefeller Foundation. From then on we were leaders on advocacy for Latinos in Congress. We were active at both state legislatures and in Congress. Our team of lobbyists would go out and effectively advocate for the most important issues facing Latinos nationwide."

Noting the effectiveness of NCLR's ability to tackle public policy, Yzaguirre was honored in 1979 by the Rockefeller Foundation, and became the first Latino to receive the Rockefeller Award for Outstanding Public Service, endowed by John D. Rockefeller, Jr. from the trustees of Princeton University. The Rockefeller Foundation described Yzaguirre as "brave and angry," yet "wise and exhibiting a statesmanlike quality that converted emotion into constructive energy." The foundation credited him for orchestrating the fragmented energies of many local groups into a unified and powerful movement that addressed the concerns of the nation's Hispanic Americans. "The award carried a $10,000 prize, and at the time I sorely needed the money to stabilize my family's income," Yzaguirre says. "Due to economic pressures suffered by NCLR, my salary was one of the lowest paid to a CEO, and the prize money was a God-send."

IGNITING IMMIGRATION

Born on June 9, 1939 in Victoria, Texas, Leonel J. Castillo grows up in the coastal city of Galveston. His life reveals a familiar path well-known to the Yzaguirres who settled in the Rio Grande Valley in early frontier days. Meeting in Victoria, Texas Castillo's parents eventually move to Galveston where there are plenty of jobs in the shipping industry. His father becomes a labor leader for the Docking Gang, a crew of mostly Mexican American laborers who take on the most dangerous jobs on the docks for very little pay. Eventually, his mother becomes a school teacher, and Castillo is raised by two socially conscience parents who develop in him a yearning for justice and fairness for Mexican Americans at a time when segregation and Jim Crow laws hold sway over communities of color.

Graduating from St. Mary's University in San Antonio with a B.A. in English in 1961, Castillo later earns a Masters in Social Work from the University of Pittsburgh in 1967. Sharing Yzaguirre's 'itch' to see the world, Castillo joins the Peace Corps and settles in a small village in the Philippines, where he becomes a supervisor and works as director in various community projects. There he meets his wife, Evelyn and the couple eventually moves to Houston, Texas. In Houston, Castillo becomes a community activist, rising quickly to leadership positions for nonprofits, the AFL-CIO and the Teamsters. He is the first Latino elected as City Controller of Houston in 1971. His election as controller, and his run for mayor, catches the attention of President Jimmy Carter's administration as they scout around for a candidate who is knowledgeable of immigration issues and acquainted with the two thousand mile border between the U.S. and Mexico. In 1977 President Carter appoints Castillo as the Commissioner of Immigration and Naturalization Service (INS), making him the first Latino to occupy the controversial office.

Identifying immigration as one of the top concerns of his administration, Carter advances plans for militarization of the border. The militarization plan is expected to be carried out by the El Paso Intelligence Center (EPIC). The plan calls for deployment of U.S. armed forces to protect the border, and for direct sanctions against employers who hire 'illegal aliens,' a term that will later be disputed by Yzaguirre as an inflammatory, racially-biased label, best replaced by the term 'undocumented workers.' Carter's plan opens the door for amnesty for undocumented workers who had been employed in the U.S. on a long-term basis. Castillo felt that militarization of the border was only the tip of the iceberg and would further aggravate the already strained relations with then President of Mexico, López Portillo.

"One of my Board members, Leonel Castillo, from Houston, was a bright upcoming figure in the Mexican American community," Yzaguirre recalls. "He was a very nice guy, and was vice-chairman on my Board at NCLR when we started to deal with immigration issues during the Ford Administration. We started to put pressure on Ford's INS Commissioner because of the conduct of the Border Patrol and other issues. The commissioner appointed a committee, the INS Commissioner's Hispanic Advisory Committee, and asked me to be the Chair. Leonel was one of the members of the committee. At the end of the Ford Administration, Carter came in and appointed Leonel as Commissioner of INS. So, now my own Board member was the Commissioner of INS. News of his appointment got on the front pages of magazines. Leonel Castillo was like the Henry Cisneros or Bill Richardson of his time. We worked hand in glove because we were close, then I made allegations concerning reports that the Border Patrol were routinely raping women who came across the border without documents. I asked for an investigation by the Justice Department, and accountability for the crimes, and the Border Patrol Union complained to the White House about my actions, and so my good friend Leonel fired me as the Chair of the Hispanic Advisory Committee. Years later, he sent me a letter of apology."

After his dismissal from the Hispanic Advisory Committee, Yzaguirre continued a bitter debate over immigration, charging Carter with failure to appoint enough Latinos to important staff positions, and for advocating for employer sanctions. Antonia Hernandez, President and General Counsel of MALDEF, at the time, joined Yzaguirre in his efforts to win fair labor rights for undocumented workers. An expert in philanthropy, civil rights and immigration issues, she served as an attorney with the Los Angeles Center for Law and Justice and worked as counsel for the United States Senate Committee on the Judiciary before joining MALDEF.

"Immigration was the first big issue I faced at the beginning of my tenure," Yzaguirre says. "I picketed the Carter White House when I was a member of the Board for the Leadership Conference on Civil Rights which included a lot of labor folks and NAACP members and others. Many battles were fought in the LCCR with lots of debates, yelling and egos. The LCCR held their annual dinner in D.C. and were going to honor me, and Antonia Hernandez of MALDEF because they wanted to make peace with us. The AFL/CIO was a problem because they supported employer sanctions and the whole thing turned into an interesting situation. We wanted the LCCR to come against employer sanctions, but they wouldn't because labor vetoed them for taking that position. So we picketed that dinner and the labor folks had to cross the picket line, which they hated to do. Then Antonia and I went in and received our awards, and I blasted them, and made a plea for support to oppose employer sanctions. I wasn't going to let them off the hook. It was my understanding that immigrants saved American jobs because they paid more in taxes than they received in services, and took on jobs most Americans didn't want."

Yzaguirre's signature role as spokesman for NCLR, empowered him to fiercely challenge Republicans and Democrats on both sides of the immigration debate. His determination to take on policy issues in Congress began a steep uphill climb as he battled for immigration reform. Yzaguirre offered his insights into the unfair use of employer sanctions in the bi-partisan work of Representative Romano L. Mazzoli, a Democrat from Kentucky and Alan K. Simpson, a Republican senator from Wyoming, who worked on passage of the Immigration Reform and Control Act (IRCA), also referred to as the Simpson-Mazzoli Act, which, after much debate, finally passed both chambers of Congress in 1986. It was set up to stop illegal immigration to the U.S., and included legalization for undocumented aliens who had been employed in the U.S. since 1982, as well as for certain groups of agricultural workers. It also included sanctions for employers who knowingly hired undocumented workers and mandated increased military enforcement along the U.S. borders. In spite of bitter controversy over the legalization of undocumented workers by aggressive, anti-immigrant groups, approximately three million illegal immigrants were granted legal status through the IRCA.

"Immigration was a big issue then and a big issue now," Yzaguirre says. "There was a lot of testimony before Congress. I debated many times with

Senator Alan Simpson, chairman of the Senate Immigration Subcommittee. We had differences of opinions, but we were able to find common ground. We got invited to universities to discuss immigration and other issues. I would get invited to be on panels, and I would ask for him and when he was invited he would ask for me. At that time immigration was the most difficult issue. We struggled with the same people, like John Tanton and his organizations. He was the opthamologist from Minnesota who funded and started groups like the Federation for Americans for Immigration Reform, the same group that enacted the Arizona SB 1070 Law (April 2010), and the English Only propositions in several states. John Tanton was working with Senator Simpson at the time, and that put me and the senator on opposite sides, but we still learned to respect each other. By 1986 we did get some things changed. We agreed that some of Tanton's actions would cause massive discrimination against Latinos. We inserted a provision in the 1986 Immigration Reform and Control Act, that the Government Accounting Office (GAO) an independent agency reporting to Congress, would conduct a study to see if IRCA would cause employment discrimination solely as a result of the legislation, a very high standard, but that was the best we could do. To our surprise, the study concluded that there was massive employment discrimination caused by the law. There was an understanding that if the study was conclusive, Congress would repeal the law, but Congress reneged on that promise. Clearly, the discrimination of Hispanics was implied by the law."

Yzaguirre's complaints about the Border Patrol that had resulted in his dismissal as Chair of the Hispanic Advisory Committee, ignites retaliation from the Carter White House. Serving as Carter's Under Secretary of Agriculture for Small Community and Rural Development, Alex Mercure, long-time associate of Yzaguirre, and one of the Council's original Board members, witnesses, first-hand, the antagonism held against NCLR when the president's policies were challenged. Emily Gantz McKay recalls Mercure's unwavering loyalty to Yzaguirre's stance on immigration and other crucial issues, even when standing up for NCLR meant defying Carter's administration. "The White House used to hold briefings for Latino leaders," McKay recalls. "When NCLR had been particularly vociferous about a policy issue, Raul would not be invited. Then Alex would tell the White House that he was sorry but he couldn't participate in the briefing if such an important leader was excluded. So maybe thirty-six hours before the briefing, Raul would suddenly get an invitation. Alex personified Raul's view that we should be pushing from the outside and Latino elected and appointed officials should be pushing from the inside. Because Raul was always gracious to Democrats and Republicans both when they were in appointive office and when they were out of power, he had a very good reputation for being fair and open-minded even when there were disagreements on issues."

"Alex Mercure made sure my name got on the list of invitees for important briefings. He was effective in his position, not only for Latinos, but for the good of the whole nation. The immigration issue was especially difficult and opened controversy with the White House, but we were able to meet issues head-on because of leaders like Alex."

BRIDGING THE DATA GAP

NCLR takes up its role as a non-partisan, Latino advocacy network seriously, and Yzaguirre, at the center of national policy issues, soon finds himself defying legislators, corporate leaders, and U.S. presidents as well as a broad range of critics nationwide, including Latinos with differing views on how nonprofits should function and what constitutes sound policy.

Standing firm with the Latino community and Yzaguirre's stance on immigration and the need to compile statistics and data on Latinos was Congressman Edward Ross "Ed" Roybal of California. Roybal's long service in the House of Representatives began in 1963. Elected as the first Latino Congressperson from California since the 1879 election of Romualdo Pacheco, he was dedicated to the education of Latinos, and initiated the first bill in 1967, giving federal support to bilingual education and designating the creation of specialized language instruction for immigrant populations. Active in the Chicano Movement, Roybal became one of the founding members in 1976 of the Congressional Hispanic Caucus (CHC), and later co-founded the National Association of Latino Elected and Appointed Officials (NALEO). Along with Yzaguirre and other national Latino leaders, he ardently opposed the Simpson-Mazzoli Act that imposed unfair sanctions on employers of undocumented workers.

Roybal led the way for the enactment of Public Law 94-311 in June 1976, a Joint Resolution before Congress relating to the publication of economic and social statistics for Americans of Spanish origin or descent. "Ed wanted to make federal agencies accountable for collecting, tabulating and reporting data on Latinos. He even went so far as to demand that Census materials be written in Spanish and that Spanish-speaking Census workers be hired through an affirmative action program," Yzaguirre says. "Statistics on how Latinos were served by federal programs were inconsistently collected, and there was no way NCLR could advocate for fair policies in Congress without the 'hard facts'"

Determined to bridge the 'data gap,' Yzaguirre begins by first gathering reliable information and statistics on the socioeconomic status of Latinos and the services received from federal programs and state agencies for immigration, labor, education, health, criminal victimization, and a host of other vital social services. Under Yzaguirre's direction, the Council seeks to create a reputation as an organization that is knowledgeable of the Latino community, and has hard facts to back up its advocacy. NCLR's growth as the nation's premier 'think tank' leads to its signature role as a leader in policy analysis. The Rockefeller Foundation's multi-year commitment, granted in the Fall of 1980 serves to establish NCLR's Policy Analysis Center under the direction of Emily Gantz McKay, Vice-President of the Office of Research, Advocacy and Legislation (ORAL). "The Rockefeller Foundation grant did more than give us resources," Yzaguirre recalls, "it gave us a great deal of legitimacy."

Meeting Raul in the summer of 1970 at a training conference in McAllen, Texas, Dr. Michael Cortés is unaware that his connection with Yzaguirre will forever change his life. A descendant of Mexican, Scottish/Irish parents, Michael Cortés was born in 1956 in Berkeley, California. "My father, Eduardo A. Cortés, was born in Mexico," Cortés says, "but he refused to teach us Spanish at home. I grew to love his collection of Spanish records, and remember my grandmother, also from Mexico, teaching me to count to ten in Spanish." Suffering the discrimination and class segregation of the early 1900's, Cortés's grandfather, Carlos Eliseo Cortés y Ortigosa, managed to get the paperwork needed to come to the U.S. Politically active in the Mexican Revolution, his grandfather aligned himself with Mexican President, Francisco Madero. "Madero asked my grandfather to become his 'Jefe Politico de Jalisco,' which was considered the position of mayor in the city," Cortés relates. "Once Madero was assassinated, there was a price on my grandfather's head."

Immigrating to the U.S., the family arrives in the bay area when Cortés's father is only three years old. His grandfather attends Stanford, studying engineering, at a time when higher education for Mexican citizens in the U.S was relatively unknown. The oldest of three siblings, Cortés grows up, as Yzaguirre did, with a sense of responsibility for his younger brother and sister. As a teenager, he becomes active in the Civil Rights Movement, and the struggle of Chicanos to find their place in a society that, for the most part, considers them foreigners.

The first inkling that Cortés will live a life as an advocate for civil rights, begins in high school, when he joins the American Friends Service Committee, a social justice arm of the Quakers. "I started going to their meetings," Cortés recalls, "and started organizing students at my high school for the

'Fast for Freedom,' campaign, encouraging them to give up their lunch money for minority voter registration projects in southern states that were denying Black citizens the right to vote. I was called into the principal's office and he told me, 'You don't have permission to collect money from students, and plus you're wearing sandals to class.' I argued with him that girls were wearing sandals to school too, but he went on to say that sandals were causing a distraction from classroom studies. I asked him if boy's toes were more distracting than girl's toes, and he had no reasonable answer for me. I agreed to wear socks with my sandals, and in return the principal allowed me to continue collecting lunch money, although in a more discreet manner. It was the first time I began to appreciate political compromise and it influenced a lot of what I did later."

Cortés earns a B.A. in Psychology in 1968 from Berkeley, a Masters in Social Work from the University of Michigan in 1971, a second Masters in Public Policy from Berkeley in 1984, and finally completes studies for his Ph.D. in Public Policy, also at Berkeley in 1992. While studying at the University of Michigan, he learns of the summer intern project PEBSI in South Texas that was working under contract with Yzaguirre's consulting firm, IRA. His participation in the Program Evaluation for Summer Interns (PEBSI) under contract to the U.S. Department of Health, Education, and Welfare, becomes a stepping stone for Cortés's appointment years later as the first director of the NCLR Policy Center. "My first impression of Raul was that he was clearly the guy in charge, firm but friendly and committed to what he was doing," recalls Cortés. "I started working for him as a summer intern at IRA while I was a graduate student. After I graduated, I joined the IRA staff and later I joined NCLR."

"As part of the PEBSI summer program, I joined one of the teams to do interviews of migrant farmworkers. There were three major streams, Florida, Texas, and the Imperial Valley. The growers were violent, and used baseball bats to smash windshields. One night at 2 AM, Rick Bela called to tell me I was now one of the supervisors. One of the doctoral students had quit and there was no one to take his place. Later Raul offered me a job in Washington D.C. and I started working with IRA in 1971 after completing my MSW at Michigan. At IRA I helped with research on anti-poverty programs for U.S migrant farmworkers."

"Dr. Michael Cortés came to work with me at IRA. He was a very interesting guy," Yzaguirre says. "He's half Mexican and half Anglo, and at the time he was a little unsure about his identity. I found him to be an extremely competent person. Mike was my first director for our Policy Analysis Center and he did a great job. Subsequently he divorced and married one of our staff, got his Ph.D. and went back to Colorado. He's been a friend ever since. Mike set the standards for how we did business in public policy at NCLR."

Inspired by Yzaguirre's determination to form a strong public policy team, Cortés returns to school to complete studies at Berkeley. "Raul changed my life again. I was recruited by one of the first five schools of public policy in the nation. I headed back to Berkeley to complete studies on public policy." By 1976 Cortés is employed by NCLR as the director of the Policy Analysis Center. "We testified at hearings, lobbied Congress and Federal agencies and prompted public policy for Latinos throughout the U.S." In 1980 Cortés opts to leave NCLR and joins Levi Strauss & Company to do community work for the foundation, eventually creating the Hispanics in Philanthropy (HIP) organization. "It was time to leave the shop," Cortés recalls, "Everything was going well, and Emily McKay took over running the Policy Center."

Reflecting on Yzaguirre's ability to mentor others, Cortés remarks, "Apart from my father, Raul is probably the single most influential male in my life. His values, commitment to activism in the cause of social justice, style of leadership, and sense of strategy have all shaped my own career. I suspect that Raul will be remembered primarily by people whose lives he helped shape, and whose careers he did much to launch. His greatest legacy is the continuing work for social change he has inspired in others."

THE MAN FROM EDINBURG

"Charles Kamasaki started as an intern in our NCLR Edinburg office while he was still in college," Yzaguirre says, describing one of his right hand VP's at NCLR. "He just kept coming up and taking on more responsibility, and he became the third longest serving individual besides me at NCLR. He became Executive Vice-President and his talent was to find and train people. He trained Cecilia Muñoz who is now Director of the Domestic Policy Council for the Obama White House, and a whole bunch of other folks who are in administration. He has a knack for choosing good people and training them and bringing them up. He played a role that was very important. Charles didn't work for me; Charles Kamasaki worked against me. And what I mean by that, is that Charles took on the role of being the Devil's advocate. So every idea that I had he would try to shoot it down. And that was a good role for him to play because it kept me from doing things that were foolish and the things that he opposed that were good ideas, he made better."

Raised in Hawaii, Kamasaki's parents and grandparents were witnesses to the aftermath of World War II, and the patrolling of Japanese neighborhoods by U.S. troops. "Hawaii had a population of over one third Japanese," Kamasaki says. "After the bombing of Pearl Harbor, the authorities rounded up Japanese leaders of the community and took them to camps in another island. My mom was the youngest sibling of her family and was not intimidated by the soldiers. She said she would run up to them and bargain for rations and war coupons. Sometimes they gave the kids candy."

"My father was very smart and could have finished work for a Ph.D., but he struggled with hemophilia back in the day when treatment consisted of whole blood transfusions. He was ill frequently, and bedridden for weeks at a time, but he never took vacation time from his job as a scientist for the U.S. Department of Agriculture. He saved all his vacation and sick days for times when he needed them. He was a specialist in the study of fruit flies, which are the plague of citrus trees. My parents would send us to live with my grandparents when my dad would get sick. My grandfather was a mango grower on the island, and he also owned beehives. He grew or fished for most of what we ate. At my grandparents' farm, my brother and I were free to climb trees and enjoy our time together."

It's his father's area of expertise in the control of fruit flies that leads the Kamasakis from Hawaii to Mexico City, Miami, Indiana, and finally to the Lower Rio Grande Valley where Kamasaki's mother joins the workforce by taking on a job as a school teacher. Once in the Valley, the family lives temporarily in the home of his father's boss. "The Valley was segregated," Kamasaki recalls. "There was a disagreement between the real estate lady who was looking for a house for us, and the boss's wife about where we should live. The north was for Mexicans, and the south for Anglos but we were Asian. At the time the Valley was a hotbed of activism, and the Anglo community was afraid of a 'Mexican takeover.' The boss's wife thought we would be more comfortable on the north side with the Mexicans, and the Anglo real estate lady said we were as American as the Anglos. So we ended up two blocks south of the railroad tracks, somewhat on the Anglo side, in a more integrated neighborhood. It was the first time I realized that Latinos in South Texas, even after centuries of living in the region, were still not fully accepted as Americans but were considered foreigners."

Sharp and politically minded, Charles Kamasaki quickly rises as a leader of socio-economic change, community development and civil rights legislation in Yzaguirre's own backyard, the Lower Rio Grande Valley. His education at Baylor University in Waco, Texas and the University of Texas Pan American in Edinburg, give him the back-ground he needs to pursue a life-long career in community service. "I worked in Edcouch, Texas in 1979 as an intern in urban planning. I was heavily involved in community development and helped prepare applications for Community Development Block Grants and Urban Development Action Grants. One year later, I was employed in one of the field offices of NCLR in Edinburg as Programs Office Director. NCLR was paying my salary as part of their internship program. I remember we needed a speaker for one of our events and were planning to invite Kika de la Garza, but he couldn't make it, and someone suggested Raul because they said he was a major player and everyone agreed. I picked Raul up at the airport and, of course, he didn't know me from Adam. He was not very talkative and seemed to be very introspective. At the event he gave a great speech, and won lots of fans. Raul was gracious and spoke with the mayor and anyone who approached him. I was very impressed with him. He was quiet, but aggressive in asserting the need for housing and parks, and he said good things could come to a community when Latinos got active. He sounded different from militant Chicano activists. Raul was aggressive on the civil rights agenda, but not especially threatening. He was not one to force or coerce. Raul persuaded people to change. He was skilled in persuasion."

Kamasaki was not the only one impressed at their first meeting. Yzaguirre took an instant liking for the young intellect who had a knack for community development and even spoke some Spanish. Kamasaki seemed at home with the multicultural community in South Texas, and was well acquainted with the struggles Latinos faced in the Valley. "I told Emily about him," Yzaguirre recalls, "and asked her to invite him to D.C. to apply for one of our positions. He was a bit hesitant at first, but Emily told him he would be working with the Housing Bill that was going before Congress. Housing was one of Charles's areas of expertise. She told him it would only be a couple of years, but the couple of years, turned into a lifetime."

By 1990, Kamasaki becomes vice president of NCLR's Policy Analysis Center. His communication skills, and ability to write and formulate complex policy issues are seen as vital to the Council and the development of the Policy Analysis Center. Disappointed at one point with the obligations of staff meetings, and formulating budgets and timesheets, he makes plans to leave NCLR. "I had a talk with Charles," Yzaguirre recalls, "and convinced him that the organization side of NCLR was just as important as lobbying and analyzing public policy. They were two sides of the same coin, so he decided to stay."

"Testimonies before Congress were normally held at legislative hearings," Kamasaki says. "The fact that NCLR was invited was significant. Our staff was taken seriously as researchers with statistics and hard facts, and the Congressional staff basically knew what we would say. The most important thing we had to do was research the breadth of the subject at hand. We had files on everything, from immigration to energy, education, taxes, and more. Raul's signal achievement at testimonies before Congress was the fact that he advocated for a pan-ethnicity approach to policies and programs. Lots of issues were interconnected, and Raul knew we couldn't have tunnel vision. We had to have the breadth of vision needed to understand the bigger picture."

HOT TOPICS

One of the first major battles facing NCLR after establishment of the Policy Analysis Center was immigration. Instrumental in crafting NCLR's position on the Immigration Reform and Control Act (IRCA) of 1986, Kamasaki successfully advocated for fair policies in a broad range of civil rights legislation, including, education, labor, housing, health and many other pressing issues faced by the Council.

Major provisions of the 1986 IRCA, were consequently revised upon the signing of the Immigration Act of 1990 by President George H.W. Bush. The new immigration policy increased legal immigration opening quotas and supplying needed labor to the U.S. It also increased the number of visas allotted on the basis of family ties. The Act also addressed politically-driven exclusions that restricted immigrants on a variety of predetermined conditions, and enforced the arrest and deportation of illegal aliens involved in drugs and violent crimes. Most importantly, it sought to deter discrimination based on employer sanctions that Yzaguirre and his staff at the Policy Analysis Center had been determined to curb.

Yzaguirre viewed the provisions of the Immigration Act of 1990 as having an impact on what happened many years later, in 2014, as unaccompanied minors sought refuge in the U.S. along the Southwest border. "The Immigration Act of 1990 provided protection for families fleeing from civil conflict. Many Americans were opposed to the U.S. intervention in Central America during the Reagan administration, and blamed our own policies for the subsequent unrest. U.S. protection was extended to Central Americans and created a path for legal immigration, but that didn't sit well with many Americans, including some Mexican Americans. NCLR took the position of embracing the Central American community."

In 1997, NCLR took a firm stand for the Nicaraguan Adjustment and Central American Relief Act (NACARA) that provided tens of thousands of Central Americans with immediate adjustment to permanent status in the U.S., defying the harsh immigration acts that had severely limited legal immigration from that region.

Pledging to support fair immigration policies for minors, NCLR strongly advocated for fair treatment of minor immigrants by supporting Representative Luis Gutiérrez (D-IL) in his proposal of the "Immigrant Children's Educational Advancement and Dropout Prevention Act 2001," introduced on April 25, 2001 during the 107th Congressional Session. Expanding on Gutiérrez's bill, Senators Dick Durbin (D-IL), and Orin Hatch (R-UT) introduced the "Development, Relief and Education for Alien Minors" (DREAM) Act, to the Senate on August 1, 2001 as a bipartisan effort. If enacted, the bill would provide permanent residency for immigrants who had arrived in the United States as minors and had lived continuously in the U.S. for at least five years prior to the bill's enactment. The bill included stipulations for permanent residency for minors of good character who had completed a high school education, and pursued a four-year college degree, and those who had served in the military for at least two years. Controversy over the DREAM Act has incited protests and marches nationwide, by young Latino leaders who dare to declare their undocumented status and risk arrest or deportation. In the thick of the debate, NCLR has challenged one presidential administration after another, facing sharp criticism by racist groups that consider the DREAM Act another form of amnesty.

Although taking on the role as a major advocate for fair immigration and other critical legislative proposals, NCLR continued to struggle with the unification of Latinos, and questions were raised by Council members. Who were they advocating for? Should NCLR become a pan-Latino institution? Should NCLR concentrate on expanding its Policy Analysis Center and phasing out programs? These questions fueled internal debate at NCLR headquarters. Favoritism of one Latino group over another became suspect, but Yzaguirre was determined to establish an organization that united Latinos from all corners of the globe. "Raul was most forceful and persistent about a pan-Latino identity at a time when that was not popular," Kamasaki recalls, reflecting on Yzaguirre's insistence on unification. "Uniting Latinos was controversial, and many were against uniting, but Raul's idea of a pan-Latino identity was very important to him. He envisioned a Latino community that would build up critical mass purchasing. Some wanted to do only public policy because field offices were expensive to run, but Raul said no. The building of the Policy Analysis Center would not have had a big footprint without programs. Raul wanted it all, both public policy and programs. He built NCLR into a strong nonprofit that ended up with both arenas; it was not only a trade association of affiliates, but a strong voice for the community."

Uniting Latinos under one banner meant calling on the carpet, corporations that were unresponsive to the Latino community and advocating for goals that would steer NCLR and its sister nonprofits in the right direction. "At first it was easy to hold meetings together." Yzaguirre says, "We were not a threat to anybody, we were so weak in the beginning. Then, as we got stronger and we made efforts to form coalitions with our sister organizations. I told them, here's the vision, we're only going to make it if we stick together and we're not competing with each other, but instead are reinforcing one another. So I took it upon myself to raise money for my sister organizations. They began to feel more at ease with me, and didn't see me as a competitor but as an ally."

"One of the things that made our unity stronger was the Coors boycott of 1984. NCLR supported the boycott and even though we had not started it, we were supportive of it. Then later, all my sister organizations signed a petition to stop the boycott, but we didn't. The Coors Company called me and said, they wanted to advertise at our annual conference, and I said no because we supported the boycott. So Peter Coors, who headed the company at the time, said 'Why don't you bring all the organizations together to see if we can work out an agreement?' So I put all the major organizations together. We had an agreement that was worth a billion dollars, but before we signed it, I called the American GI Forum members in Colorado to get their buy-in. They were the ones who had initiated the boycott. They were ecstatic when they found out their efforts had resulted in tangible results for our community. We signed the agreement and it worked out very well, and brought lots of advantages for the entire Latino community."

"Unfortunately there were detractors, people who didn't like Coors no matter what they did. There was one part of the process that allowed us to write in benchmarks for every part of the agreement. If in the area they recruited for employment, we were ten percent of the workforce then we should represent ten percent of Coors' workforce. If we were ten percent of Coors' consumers, then we should be ten percent of their charitable giving which sounded logical to me, but the detractors said we were encouraging consumers to drink more beer. The more beer they drank, the more charity we would get. But they didn't stop to think that the money wasn't going to come to us, it would go to the Latino community, but some folks criticized us anyway. I personally called everyone who had been involved with the Coors negotiations, and made sure we were all in agreement. They felt good that something positive had come out of us holding Coors accountable to the Latino community."

Building on the success of the Coors Boycott, NCLR assumes a leading role in establishing the Hispanic Association on Corporate Responsibility (HACR), with Yzaguirre taking the position as Chair. HACR is destined to become a strong link for negotiating Hispanic agreements tied in with investments by corporate America. The ability to discuss issues with America's corporate leaders who directly impact the lives of Latinos nationwide, marks a big step forward for NCLR.

Unbeknownst at the time to Yzaguirre, things are about to change dramatically for NCLR, and other nonprofits throughout the nation as "Reaganomics," takes a foothold in Congress, drastically curbing federal funds for nonprofits. Yzaguirre's inclusion of corporate America in his recovery plan is about to take on new proportions as his vision of a Corporate Board of Advisors begins to take shape.

REAGANOMICS

"Before Reagan came into office in 1981, I thought I knew how the federal government worked," Yzaguirre recalls. "I had gotten money from several government agencies by diversifying and I thought I'd be protected, so if one funding source failed, funding wouldn't stop all at once, but I was wrong. Ronald Reagan, came into office just as a report prepared by the Heritage Foundation came out which was a very detailed study of what they called 'leftist organizations.' They recommended defunding the left, which included organizations like school PTA's, the Urban League and NCLR. Immediately after Reagan took office the federal government moved quickly to take advantage of a clause that allowed the federal government to cancel contracts because of a catastrophic situation or due to war."

"So, I said okay, never again will we be dependent on federal funds. We made a commitment that only twenty percent of our funds would come from the federal government, and the rest from private sources. We stuck to that from then on, but that meant that we had to go out and find the private resources. That's what I did—knocked on doors, and walked the streets to build a different kind of funding base."

Massive budget cuts, approved during Reagan's administration, eliminate almost all direct funding for community-based nonprofit organizations and the technical support needed to keep them running. Specifically targeted are organizations, such as NCLR that have been identified as 'leaning to the left.' Yzaguirre's efforts to undo NCLR's dependency on federal funding, turns the funding base upside down, and over the years draws an extensive array of foundations, corporations and private industry willing to invest in NCLR's national programs.

Before 'Reaganomics' hit full force, NCLR's funding had reached a new high of about $5 million and it employed almost 100 staff and operated 24 different projects, 21 of them publically funded. Less than a year later, the Council had lost all but 32 staff and was operating on a budget of $1.7 million, mostly money secured from foundations and corporations. The number of affiliates fell from 124 to 74, and about a dozen of these had no staff. NCLR cut costs where it could, consolidated positions and relied heavily on Yzaguirre's "knocking on doors," as he sought reliable funding from the private sector. "It was one of the most difficult times of my life," Yzaguirre says. "There were moments when I felt we would never get to the end of it, but we survived, and were empowered to find new ways to diversify our funding."

Tony Salazar, a Board member during the Reagan years clearly remembers the "knocking on doors," Yzaguirre had to do. "During the 1980's when NCLR was still a fledging organization, I, as a Board member traveled the country with Raul," recalls Salazar. "We met people throughout the U.S and Raul broadened the view of the national issues confronting Latinos. As a young man from the mid-west, it was the first time I had ever met with Puerto Ricans in New York, and in their homeland. I met with Cubans in Miami and with hundreds of community leaders working in their respective communities. Raul was fearless and was willing to go anywhere and speak to anyone about Latino issues. He showed me how to find the common ground that united us all."

Adamant about securing the common denominator between Latino ethnicities, Yzaguirre welcomed Cuban-born Dr. Amhilda Gonzalez-Quevedo in 1982 as the first non-Mexican American to join NCLR's Board. "We finally broke the ice, and began to open our doors, something I had wanted for so long."

Bringing in the Big Guns

Yzaguirre's long-time Administrative Assistant, Helen Coronado, recalls the state of affairs when she joined NCLR during Reagan's administration. "Raul affected and helped change countless lives in both their personal and professional arenas. It got harder for him when Reagan got elected president. During President Reagan's administration, government funding was severely curtailed and communities everywhere were hurting. Raul approached corporate America and asked them to join NCLR, thus forming the Corporate Board of Advisors. Because of this initiative, our affiliates and other organizations were able to receive funding which enabled them to continue to provide services to Latino communities."

Inspired by his mentor John Gardner, a master in creating coalitions and finding the common ground among disparate groups, Yzaguirre held the position of Chairperson of the Independent Sector, a nonprofit coalition of over 850 corporations, foundations and voluntary organizations. His experience with the Independent Sector and service on the Boards of organizations such as Sears Roebuck & Co., the Enterprise Foundation, the National Democratic Institute (NDI), the Salvation Army, and 4-H Club, provided him with a comprehensive look into the world of nonprofits, ushering him into the arena of the nation's most charismatic business leaders.

"Initially, our Corporate Board was made up of only six corporations, but it was significant that they were willing to join and assist us in developing new strategies and plan for new programs." Coming on board in 1982 to become the first charter members of the Corporate Board of Advisors, (CBA) were: Gulf Oil Corporation, G.D. Searle & Company, Equitable Life Assurance Society, Time, Inc., General Motors Corporation, and Coca-Cola USA. Donald Rumsfeld, CEO of G.D. Searle helped in recruiting the original members, and James "Jimmy" Lee, Chairman and CEO of Gulf Oil became the first Board Chair. Each corporation identified a member and a liaison staff member for the Board. The corporations were not only funders, but were valued as advisors, and assisted NCLR in advocacy work.

Eventually the CBA grows to 25 major corporations and their liaison staff. Giants such as: A T & T, Bank of America, Chevron, Citi, Ford Motor Company, McDonalds, PepsiCo, UPS, and Walmart are among the corporations now linking their fortunes and expertise to NCLR. "Corporations traditionally see Latinos as consumers," Yzaguirre reflects, "but we wanted to be seen as managers and stockholders, and be identified as folks who had good ideas to bring to the table. Latinos spend billions of dollars on products and services annually, so that meant we were responding to corporate marketing, but we wanted more. We wanted respect and to be included in corporate decisions that benefited our community."

In spite of criticism from a number of community leaders who felt Yzaguirre was selling out to corporate America, the need to stabilize NCLR affiliates struggling to meet their growing budgets, becomes one of Yzaguirre's major concerns. Working closely with the private sector, and in keeping with NCLR's focus on collaboration and cooperation, he forms lasting alliances with America's most prestigious corporations, raising awareness of Latinos nationwide and eventually making corporations accountable to Latinos whose growing buying power signals the need to invest in their communities. Information provided by the CBA becomes invaluable in assessing the effectiveness of public policies on education, health, business, public relations, and fund raising.

Hilario Diaz recalls the impact Yzaguirre had on corporate America as he worked with others in the Rio Grande Valley to establish the first Raul Yzaguirre School for Success. "Knowing Raul had connections with corporations, I asked him to the Valley for a golf tournament in 2006 to raise money for the Raul Yzaguirre School for Success to be founded in Brownsville. We needed at least $10,000 to start the project. The vice-president of Walmart asked me if I could bring Raul to the Valley for the tournament. Without any hesitation, Raul asked the vice president to make the award $15,000, so Walmart gave him the money in cash for the school. The corporation people knew, there was nothing phony about him. Once Raul committed to something, he did it. He never sought the spotlight, everything he did, he did for *la raza*."

THROUGH ESTABLISHMENT OF THE POLICY ANALYSIS CENTER, Yzaguirre began NCLR's long history of advocacy in shaping legislation that would positively impact Latinos for decades to come. Yzaguirre's efforts helped expand the Earned Income Tax Credit for working families in the 1990's, which created a partially refundable tax credit for low-income workers impacted by the 2001 Bush tax cuts. NCLR fought for the restoration of benefits to legal immigrants that had been eliminated in the 1996 Welfare Reform Law, and expanded access to federally funded early childhood, elementary, and secondary education programs. The Council's stance on affirmative action, and equality in higher education has never wavered.

Yzaguirre's opinions related to the North American Free Trade Agreement (NAFTA), would play a vital role in shaping commerce throughout the western hemisphere, and as NAFTA became a reality, Yzaguirre led the way for reevaluating the most controversial issues resulting from its implementation. "I am aware of the negative impact NAFTA had, especially on the poor subsistence Mexican farmers of corn. They could not compete with the agribusiness mass corn producers in the American mid-west. That phenomenon was in progress and would have accelerated with or without NAFTA. Our hope was that through a more rational negotiated process, the negative effects would be mitigated. We wanted to open dialogue focusing on the side agreements that addressed some of the negative impacts. The positive impact including the economic integration of North America was the prime motive of NCLR's support. I was very disappointed in the way NAFTA was implemented including the lack of funding for the North American Economic Development Bank."

Yzaguirre's determination to embrace affiliates that would innovate new community programs, while pressing for diversification in funding, led the way for NCLR to become one of the most prestigious advocacy groups in the nation. "I had watched the Washington scene for years,"Yzaguirre says, "and came to the conclusion that we could not do policy advocacy successfully without a constituency; nor could we do successful advocacy without the hard facts. Having both made us credible. We did well at the national level, but the larger goal of stimulating our affiliates to do the same thing at the local and state level was more challenging. We did a number of things to stimulate that work, which still remains a challenge."

Slowly, NCLR was creating a new image of what it meant to be Latino in America.

21

POLARIS AND ITS AFFILIATES

There are those shooting stars that flash across the sky and when they're gone it's not even clear that they were there. They leave no trace. Then there is the North Star that's in the same spot in the sky every single night and provides a guide for travelers. It's reliable. The North Star in our community is Raul Yzaguirre.

—Henry G. Cisneros

TUNED TO THE "A"

BY THE MID-1980's, Yzaguirre finds himself at the center of forces that pull on all sides as the demands for legislation and policy analysis take on a new urgency, while the expansion of affiliates along with the multiple programs and community services they offer increases at a phenomenal rate. The shifting sands of political administrations bring to the forefront an infinite number of pressing issues that need to be addressed by NCLR, each one colored by its own set of lobbyists, right and left wingers, Congressional sub-committees and the ups and downs of public opinion. Rising on the horizon is the administration of George H.W. Bush, then the Clinton years, George W. Bush and finally Obama's administration. Side-stepping his old nemesis, chaos, Yzaguirre reflects, "Each administration brought on new problems and enormous challenges. It seemed every time I thought there was smooth sailing for us, there was one more critical issue to cover. We were busy, it seemed, 24/7 at NCLR. If it weren't for Audrey, my kids and close friends, I have to admit I don't know how I would have survived."

Fueling the fires of on-going controversy is Yzaguirre's unwavering stance on establishing NCLR as a pan-Latino institution. On one hand, his vision inspires NCLR staff and Board members to view the organization through a global lens, one that includes all Latino ethnicities. On the other hand, the push for inclusivity grates on the nerves of those who complain that NCLR's goals will disintegrate and the organization will be weakened by opening its doors to multiple agendas. It will be a young NCLR intern, Alex Perilla, who immigrated to the U.S. from Columbia, that in one memorable moment, will make sense of it all, effectively capturing Yzaguirre's comprehensive vision for the future of NCLR.

"One of the first speeches I heard from Raul, was in Houston in 1985. He used the orchestra that was at the conference to point out that all the instruments had been tuned to the 'A' on the first violin. As they were tuning, the music seemed discordant, but once the performance started it was all about harmony. We were like instruments Raul said, made up of different ethnicities, but together we could speak as one." Alex Perilla's reflection of Yzaguirre's ability to find harmony in the most discordant and chaotic situations is a quality he attributes to Yzaguirre's "pan-Latino sensibility." In the end, it's Yzaguirre's insistence on uncovering a singular purpose among hundreds of voices speaking that gives NCLR the clout it needs to realize an inclusive vision for Latinos.

Yzaguirre's leadership tactics would be described as 'wishy-washy,' by critics and his determination to find the common ground was often considered a ploy to achieve his own personal gains. "I think Raul understood his positions quite well," Perilla says. "The positions he took tended to be complex. We prefer a black and white response, but Raul was good at finding the center point." It would be the center point, the instruments tuned to the 'A,' that would finally find an audience. After years of tedious efforts to unite the nations' Latinos, Yzaguirre would finally reap the rewards of a unified coalescence of diverse ethnicities. "Raul's priority wasn't NCLR per se, it was us, the community," Perilla recalls. "He would always say, 'If it's good for the community, then we'll do it.'"

Moving from Columbia with his mother in the 1970's to the suburbs of D.C. proved to be a radical change for young Alex Perilla. Born in South America, he found unique perspectives in the experiences of Mexican Americans and Chicanos who had lived in the U.S. all their lives. "They were part of America, and yet they weren't. They had been through so many struggles and had their own history that I didn't know existed. I could not identify with the Chicano Movement, or the protests and marches that Raul and others had been through. It was all new to me."

"Alex Perilla was an intern from a high school program, "Yzaguirre recalls. "He has been a very committed NCLR staff member for many years. He took over the special events of NCLR, and I found that even though he was young, he could do more complicated tasks and take on greater responsibilities. We got him to go to Harvard when he was still at NCLR. Later, he came to work with me at ASU."

Placed in an intern program in 1983 at NCLR through Mt. Vernon High School in Fairfax, Virginia, seventeen year-old Alex Perilla had no idea that the internship would turn into a lifetime of service to the Council. "At that time, Reagan was President," Perilla recalls, "and there were very few staff members at NCLR because of all the funding cuts done by Congress. I knew nothing about NCLR, only that I was to work there as part of a high school program. Raul was busy keeping the organization alive. To me, he seemed larger than life, but still down-to-earth. Occasionally, he joined us copying or collating paper work. He was never too big to help. He invited me to join in important tasks at NCLR and I got to see him testify before Congress several times. His intellect was impressive. He'd find something in each person's point of view that connected. He could align viewpoints and make sense of them, and he could do this with incredible speed. This is an extraordinary quality for a leader."

Working his way through college as a member of NCLR's staff, Perilla says he "fell in love with the organization." After college, he made a decision to stay on permanently at NCLR. On the heels of his decision to remain at NCLR, a doctoral dissertation on the Council was released by Christine Sierra, alleging that Yzaguirre had abused his power when taking over as CEO by terminating current staff members and replacing them with his staff from IRA. "Christine was an interesting person," Yzaguirre relates. "She wrote a dissertation on us when I first took over, not understanding that I had inherited a staff that was still working only four days a week, and I was used to my staff at IRA working every week day until late. The Council was facing a huge financial deficit, and funding was all but gone. I thought I could bring the staff around, but I couldn't. They started to conspire against me, and so I decided to fire them. Christine was doing an evaluation while this was going on, and I was bringing in IRA Board people I could trust. I needed some support quickly, so I took staff from where I could find them. Together, we started to work ourselves out of the financial and management hole the Council was in. She finally got over it, but she never asked, 'Why did you do it?' She just went on to publish her dissertation and never gave me a chance to respond to her judgments."

Officiating as Chairman of the Board, Gilbert "Gil" R. Vásquez, a Los Angeles certified public accountant and member of the Los Angeles Olympics Organizing Committee, faced the new budget direction initiated by Yzaguirre at NCLR—increased funding from private sources, a sharp decrease in dependency on federal funds, and only 6% of the total budget coming from the Ford Foundation. By 1980 NCLR's affiliates increased to 125, all served through the headquarters in Washington, D.C. Field offices located in Albuquerque, Chicago, Dallas, Phoenix, San Francisco and South Texas, although operating under strained budgets, were holding fast to their goals for implementing community programs. "It wasn't policy advocacy versus programs," Yzaguirre recalls. "It was essential that we have both."

"Raul looked to a time when there would be equality for all," Perilla notes. "He's a big picture person and focused on a mission. His mission was to change the world for the better, and part of that included making NCLR's affiliates stronger."

Focusing on the structure of affiliates and how they deal with specific community needs, becomes part of Yzaguirre's mission to strengthen NCLR's affiliates. Because federal funds had been drastically cut, he began negotiations with the Charles Stewart Mott Foundation to secure a seed grant program to help in developing community-based programs.

In spite of gains in private sector funding, NCLR's struggles with its funding base continued. And to add more pressure to an already strained budget was the formation in 1981 of a for-profit subsidiary, La Raza Production Center (LRPC) established to expand NCLR's influence via public and network television. Bringing awareness of Latino issues, the production company's primary goal, in the end, proves too expensive to maintain. "The TV show we produced was called 'Latin Tempo,'" Yzaguirre recalls. "The purpose of the show was to reach younger English dominant Latinos and Americans in general. It usually had four segments, one of which was a serious public policy issue, and another was a 'feel good' story about Latinos. We featured news as well as better-known Hispanic political and media personalities. The show helped the careers of many of our current celebrities as well as media entrepreneurs. Financially, the show was vulnerable. We had to syndicate the show station by station. That meant that we could not have a set time of the day or week that would allow us to promote the show. The stations got the show for free in return for half the ad time. We in turn, had to sell that 'bartered' time. In the early eighties, we did not have the clout to lean more heavily on corporate sponsors. We lost money and had to close the show after two years, but the experience made us more knowledgeable about media and laid the ground work for the ALMA Awards."

Yzaguirre's determination to end dependency on federal funding, in the long run, reaps many benefits for NCLR affiliates. Advocacy and lobbying at the state level become focal points for developing resources and programs, and for bringing awareness to Latino issues and a buy-in for needed services. NCLR's shift to state-level advocacy leads the home office in D.C. to create program models that either provide funding and support to existing community-based organizations, or send NCLR staff directly to the states to do advocacy work. Yzaguirre's pan-Latino sensibility, as described by Alex Perilla, and his ability to create harmony from discordant and chaotic situations, now found new challenges as affiliates 'tuned' their efforts to the Council's national directives, sharing in making decisions that affected NCLR's work both at the state and national level.

NCLR's Backbone in Jeopardy

"The second most important issue faced by NCLR, after finances was how to build up our constituency and strengthen our affiliates," Yzaguirre reflects. "The Council's relationship with its affiliates was weak in the beginning and with the Reagan cuts, things got worse. We determined that our affiliates needed resources and technical assistance. So we built up our capacity to make our relationships more meaningful."

"One way to empower our affiliates and Board was to form committees. Strong committees developed on the Board and on policy and affiliate relations. These committees grew in influence and people will tell you they served on a committee and did a lot of work. Committees were highly regarded and gave us the ability to debate issues and come up with strong alliances. The Board was taken very seriously and members would go through several Board meetings before they would crystallize a policy. We would then inform our affiliates and find out what they were thinking. Committees would form, and the issues would be discussed. A good example of this process was dealing with tobacco companies. We accepted money from tobacco companies, but there were concerns. Some said it didn't matter if we smoked or not, just take all the money we could get. The Board took that information and said they would allow that to happen if that's what the majority wanted. As the evidence became clearer on the dangers of smoking, committees reported back to Board members asking them to reconsider the position. Our health affiliates brought up the fact that if we accepted tobacco money, it might or might not promote more smoking, but it would send a message to our constituency and to the nation that smoking was acceptable. NCLR would be legitimizing companies that should not be legitimized, so our Board and affiliates agreed not to accept any money from tobacco companies, and that cost us a lot of money, but it was the right thing to do, and I'm glad we did it. To this day, that is still the Council's policy."

Party loyalty and public opinion mattered little to Yzaguirre when the pressure was on to do the right thing for the community. Throughout the Nixon years, when NCLR refused to endorse Nixon's reelection and lost considerable funding, and during the Reagan years when Congress allowed for massive cuts of federal funds for programs vital to communities of color, he held his ground. Toward the end of Reagan's administration, Congress began loosening its grip on federal funds and new monies became available, but with strings attached.

During this time, two technical assistant grants slated for use by NCLR affiliates become available and negotiations begin with the Reagan administration until the president nominates Edwin Meese III to be his Attorney General (1985-88). Meese's actions in two financial dealings are questionable and allegations are made that he violated ethical standards and, in three more instances unethical behavior is suspected in his dealings with people who later receive government appointments. "We had not planned to testify at the Senate hearings for Edwin Meese," Yzaguirre recalls, "but we knew that he was not someone we could support. We were warned not to testify if we wanted our funding grants to go through. Ed Pastor was my Board Chair at the time and we both agreed that even if we lost the money, we had to stand up for our principles. We had to put our constituency before our need for money, so we testified against Meese, and our funding was lost. This was not unusual for us, challenging the right and left, both Democrats and Republicans when they violated what we thought was right for our affiliates. This was a no-brainer, we knew what we had to do."

In the late 1980's, NCLR receives federal funding to help with capacity-building efforts for nonprofits involved in combating the AIDS epidemic. NCLR is successful in obtaining a five-year grant from Human Health Service Centers for Disease Control and works closely with the organization as one of the nation's top 'think tanks' taking on the challenges of AIDS both in the U.S. and abroad. Positioning itself as an organization that takes on critical health issues affecting Latinos was part of Yzaguirre's plan to expand NCLR's reach as an advocate, armed with hard facts, and ready to do business on behalf of all Latinos.

Reflecting on the tough decisions Yzaguirre had to make during his tenure as CEO, Alex Perilla remarks, "Raul managed to navigate NCLR through sensitive issues. He put the community first, and his personal self-interest behind him. I asked him once why he didn't accept the money from this one corporation that was offering us a considerable sum of money, and he said, 'No, if I take the money people will think that's why I did it.' When Raul got involved in something, he was always fair. His vision of community first, put us on the map."

NCLR's commitment to provide capacity-building assistance to its affiliates, while adopting new guidelines with clearer application procedures and an outline of expectations, leads to the development of three categories of affiliates: (1) Charter affiliates which NCLR would directly help establish and which would be identified by the Council's name; (2) Regular affiliates which were Latino controlled community organizations; and (3) Associate affiliates which would have Latino goals but might be operating in an organization that was not necessarily Latino controlled.

"There were several kinds of affiliates," Yzaguirre says. "There were nonprofit organizations like Friendly House and Chicanos Por La Causa in Phoenix that have been long-time community based organizations which we started and funded. All of these organizations paid dues, so they all had the right to get grants and loans from NCLR. We advocated on their behalf and pushed legislation that would benefit them, but more than anything else we pushed legislation that would impact the larger community not just our constituency. We would put together an initiative for employment and training and we would look for organizations that were addressing those issues and we would help develop programs. We would secure funds for the organizations and keep some for the national office so we could continue running the shop, paying salaries and meeting our overhead. One example was the development of housing programs. NCLR gets a good chunk of money from Housing and Urban Development and finds local organizations to do housing counseling from that pot of money and someone at the national level does technical assistance and monitors collection of data and best practices, while advocating for fair housing for low-income families at a national level. There are lots of federal programs and our efforts at times cross racial lines. African Americans, Anglos and others may get ten percent of the benefits, but the rest we try to use for Latino organizations."

Meeting Yzaguirre in the 1980's, Mari Carmen Aponte recalls seeing him for the first time at a Hispanic event in Washington D.C. "He struck me as being very intelligent, dedicated, a risk-taker and aggressive." Earning a B.A. in Political Science from Rosemont College, a Masters of Arts in Theatre from Villanova University and a law degree from Temple University, Aponte's life's path would intersect again with Yzaguirre in 2010 when they would both serve abroad as ambassadors—she in El Salvador, and he in the Dominican Republic.

Born in Puerto Rico, Aponte's knowledge of world affairs embraces an inclusive view of Latinos, as does Yzaguirre's. Reaching out to Yzaguirre when she was elected to the Board of Directors of the United Way of America in the late 1980's, she was not disappointed. Although funding was tight for NCLR, Yzaguirre presented Aponte with ideas on how they could work together. The United Way became another vital link established over time with a national nonprofit, part of Yzaguirre's plan to connect more organizations with the NCLR network. "Raul talked to me about the relationship of the United Way and the Hispanic community. Comparatively few Hispanic organizations at the time had relationships with the United Way. We developed strategies on how we could work together to remedy the situation. Years later, Raul served on the Board for the United Way."

Seeking to acquaint its affiliates with Washington movers and shakers, NCLR created more direct access to elected officials in Washington, D.C. by initiating a National Advocacy Day. The event convenes affiliate members from a number of states who are briefed on the most important issues facing Latinos at the national level, including education, labor, health, and immigration. They meet with members of Congress to educate them about the needs of the Latino community and ways in which state-wide Latino issues overlap with national goals and objectives.

Perhaps the most successful NCLR venture created to empower affiliates is the Raza Development Fund. RDF offers financing solutions that increase opportunities for the Latino community in the areas of affordable housing, education and health care. "The Raza Development Fund was a major accomplishment," Yzaguirre says, "but I had a hard time getting my Board to guarantee the loan that created the fund. The Fund has made it possible to channel hundreds of millions of dollars to housing and other development projects sponsored by affiliates. These loans have in turn leveraged over a billion dollars of investment. The two leaders who brought all this together are Mark Van Brunt who started with NCLR in 1981 as a housing specialist. He's been a steady influence, a good technician and the second longest serving staff member at NCLR. He became the Deputy Vice President of Community Development and second in command of the Raza Development Fund. Tommy Espinoza, who worked with the Southwest Council of La Raza in Phoenix before we became NCLR, became CEO of the Fund. Both men are experts in banking and finance."

With the development of three major objectives, RDF leads the way for financial security for a variety of nonprofits nationwide. First, is a strong conviction that the stewardship of dollars loaned, or the technical support given to organizations will have a direct impact on Latino families. Secondly, it is hoped that the relationship with borrowers will become a business partnership and lead organizations to become bankable on their own merits. And lastly, technical support is offered with help in underwriting projects to bring about measurable results, management leadership and long-term sustainability.

Tommy Espinoza, President and CEO of the Fund, along with Mark Van Brunt, Chief Operating Officer (COO), are responsible for RDF's success as the largest Latino Community Development Financial Institution (CDFI) loan fund in the U.S with total assets in excess of $100 million. Over 125 organizations have received over $135 million in community development loans, leveraging $681 million in private capital for projects directly impacting low-income individuals and families. The fund's Charter School Development Initiative has helped create more than 40 new schools and strengthened more than 45 others, including the Yzaguirre Schools for Success. An extension of its health care objectives has led to the creation of the Institute for Hispanic Health which is set up to develop and implement health education and prevention programs and conduct health advocacy activities in partnership with its nationwide network of affiliates. Realizing that Yzaguirre was criticized as being a 'sell out,' *vendido*, because of his business interests, Espinoza remarks, "If building opportunities for housing, education and health care, and if creating employment programs and offering business loans to struggling non-profits is selling out, then I guess I sold out too."

"Raul was our biggest advocate and our biggest critique," Van Brunt recalls. "The Raza Development Fund was created as a financial institution for community development. Initially, there was discussion about whether we were competing or complimenting NCLR. Raul had confidence in Tommy and me, and aligned us with NCLR's goals. RDF offered access to capital that banks were not offering to the Latino community. Raul took a seat on the Board of RDF as the Chair and his direction was that we act with scrutiny and great transparency. Raul's role was to keep RDF disciplined, and even during the 2008 recession, we had lower percentage rates than banks. Raul encouraged us to be creative with our financial investments, offering funds to the Latino community that other lenders would not have funded. RDF was good for our affiliates and set many on the road to success."

The lasting effects of Yzaguirre's influence in dealing with NCLR's affiliates, is told in a poignant story by former Board Chair, Ramon Murguia. "It was sometime in the Fall of 1998, and we were having an Executive Committee Board meeting of the NCLR in Seattle, Washington. As part of the meeting, we visited El Centro de La Raza and met with then Executive Director of the organization, Roberto Maestras, a veteran of the Chicano Movement. The staff of El Centro gave our group of NCLR Board members a tour of their facilities—a recovered old school building. We all marveled at the work being done in the community by this affiliate. Finally, we were led to a makeshift auditorium where families served by El Centro had gathered and awaited us to give a hearty welcome. We walked in led by Raul, who finally got to greet Roberto. When the two embraced, everyone could feel the energy in the room unleashed by Raul and an old lion like Roberto Maestras. Families were near tears applauding the two. It was very apparent that Raul had been there for the community when they needed his help the most. As with many affiliates, Raul always delivered with financial aid, technical assistance and encouragement to keep *el movimiento* going. Those folks in *la lucha* never forgot Raul's willingness to help and work on their behalf. It struck me that night that much of the Latino Civil Rights Movement was not so much about court cases or political advocacy in Washington, D.C., but rather about fulfilling the desires of Latino families for a just society with equal access to education, employment and full participation in the U.S. democracy. I believe it was for those reasons that the families at El Centro were unafraid to bare their emotions with Raul and Roberto. Affiliate partnerships across the country were a credit to the years of contact and investment of time Raul had made with such leaders as Roberto Maestras and the families of El Centro de la Raza."

Los Padrinos

Ensuring that the NCLR family of staff and affiliates would have a place to meet in a casual, family oriented environment, Yzaguirre came up with the idea of Encuentros, informal gatherings after the Christmas holidays that provided time to enjoy one another's company away from Board rooms and the halls of Congress. Well-known film producer, Moctesuma Esparza, who worked with NCLR to produce *The Ballad of Gregorio Cortez* (1982) and *The Milagro Beanfield War* (1988), met Yzaguirre in 1967 when Esparza was still in high school and a member of the Young Chicanos for Community Action, a civil rights group in East Los Angeles. Invited to participate in the Encuentros, Esparza recalls Yzaguirre's composure and sense of purpose in everything he did. "Raul was among that rarefied small group of role models committed to the community," Esparza says. "I was impressed by his demeanor, quiet and calm. The 60's were tumultuous years, but I remember a feeling of power from Raul. He was educated and intelligent. I met him at a conference at UCLA in '67, part of the Chicano movement along with Corky Gonzales, Reies Tijerina, Luis Valdez and others. Raul was at the meetings, strategizing for the community. When goals and plans were blurred or confused, Raul's words kept everyone focused on community: 'Who are you doing it for?' He would ask."

Born in Los Angeles in 1949, Esparza was to experience the dynamic history of the Chicano Movement, and capture the struggles and victories of Latino communities through his documentaries and films. Graduating with a B.A. and Masters from the UCLA School of Theatre, Film and Television, he became a partner in the Esparza-Katz Productions with Robert Katz, and over the years has been the recipient of numerous awards, including an Emmy, a Clio and Alma Award, and nominations for an Academy Award and the Golden Globe Award. His work led to collaborations with stars such as Robert Redford, Jennifer Lopez, Andy Garcia, Robert Duvall and Martin Sheen. A dedicated community activist, Esparza went on to found Maya Entertainment, a company that produces and distributes films based on multicultural and Latino themes. "Moctesuma is a creative genius," Yzaguirre says. "He impressed me as an artist with great creative energy and knowledge of his craft. He's able to capture in film what would take many hours or a whole year of history to grasp. His reach is worldwide."

Participating in the Encuentros, Esparza identified Yzaguirre and Henry Cisneros as spiritual fathers, or *padrinos* at the gatherings. In the ten years of meeting as entire families at the Encuentros, new ideas were discussed, numerous visions for community programs were set in motion, and national Latino issues were tackled in a relaxed family atmosphere. "Sixty to eighty people were present," Esparza recalls, "including children, and everyone reaped the benefits of being together, sightseeing, golfing, swimming, and sitting together at meals with plenty of time for conversation. Raul and Henry invited me to be a part of the Encuentros and every year I would look forward to meeting with people from across the country, including clergy, Puerto Ricans, Cubans and many others. I don't remember frustration in Raul, even when we had to make difficult choices; he was there to heal things. He and Henry took roles as *padrinos*, and set the tone for leadership. Everyone was involved in the betterment of our community and Raul was behind it all."

Cisneros's love for community was nurtured by his parents, George Cisneros and Elvira (née Mungia), who highly valued education and the arts. Cisneros was named after his mother's younger brother who, at age fourteen, was afflicted with Hodgkin's disease and upon his death bed asked his sister to name her first son after him. A descendant of early Spanish settlers in New Mexico on his father's side, and a Mexican journalist who opposed the regime of Porfirio Díaz on his mother's side, Cisneros was encouraged to seek a higher education and use his knowledge to change the lives of others for the good.

Working with Henry Cisneros to create gatherings that were fruitful for all involved was not something Yzaguirre thought would ever happen. He had heard of Cisneros, a fellow Texan, and was aware of Henry's commitment to the Latino community, yet initially the two did not see eye to eye on how to best communicate their concerns to the nation. A native of San Antonio, Cisneros was the second Mexican American elected as mayor of the city, since the harried escape across the U.S. border of Juan Seguin, a captain in Sam Houston's army in 1842.

Over a century later, in 1981, Henry G. Cisneros became the youngest elected city councilman at age 27, in San Antonio history. His political career in motion, he was then elected mayor of San Antonio running as an independent. Cisneros served three terms as mayor, and established a 'hands-on' approach as he engaged with the city's residents, pressing for improvements in the daily lives of Latinos segregated in his own west side community from middle to upper-class Anglos.

Beginning his education in Catholic schools, Cisneros went on to earn a B.A. from Texas A&M University in 1968, specializing in city management. Completing an M.A. in Urban and Regional Planning in 1970 also from A&M, he then pursued studies in 1973 for a second M.A. in Public Administration from the John F. Kennedy School of Government at Harvard University. Expanding his interest in city planning, he turned his attention to urban economics and completed doctoral research at the Massachusetts Institute of Technology in 1974. In 1976, he was awarded a Doctor of Public Administration from George Washington University. Cisneros served as an infantry officer in the United States Army, and in 1969 he married his high school sweetheart, Mary Alice Perez.

Firmly grounded in urban planning, housing and city management, and an active member of the Democratic Party, Cisneros caught the attention of President Bill Clinton's administration. Clinton appointed him as the 10th Secretary of Housing and Urban Development (HUD), and Cisneros served from 1993 to 1997. Like Yzaguirre, he was determined to make a difference in the lives of Latinos by using his expertise in fair housing practices to provide pathways for home ownership. He is credited with achieving the nation's highest rate of home ownership and opening opportunities for low-income families to buy their own homes, something they had never dreamed possible.

Yzaguirre recalls his first encounter with Henry Cisneros as negative and confrontational. "We started by clashing," Yzaguirre recalls. "I didn't know him before he became mayor, and after he became mayor we sort of took shots at each other without giving each other's names. He understood what was going on and had the decency to ask to meet with me. We met and he asked me, 'What's the problem?' I told him, the problem is that you go around preaching feel good generalities and saying how things are wonderful for our community, and while I don't disagree with some of what you have to say, it forces me to be the bad guy and tell how bad things really are. I don't mind saying things are good, and positive, but we can't ignore the problems we have in our community. So you're Pollyanna and I'm the bad guy. And I don't appreciate that. You are now a national figure and I think you're pushing the wrong message, because if everything's wonderful there's no reason to get involved and be active and that's the logical conclusion of your message. He agreed with me, and he began to change his rhetoric and we became friends and allies and have done a number of things together over the years. He was seeking political gain at the time, but it wasn't inappropriate. It may have been why he wanted to bypass negative issues. Over the years, Henry has proven himself to be an excellent advocate for the Latino community, and I doubt any of us really know the extent of all the good he has done."

In reflecting on Yzaguirre's life and influence on American society, Cisneros likens him to the North Star, Polaris, that does not rise or set, but remains in nearly the same spot over the northern horizon year-round. The Earth's axis points almost directly at it, and the other stars circle around it. "There are those shooting stars that flash across the sky and when they're gone it's not even clear that they were there. They leave no trace. Then there is the North Star that's in the same spot in the sky every single night and provides a guide for travelers. It's reliable. The North Star in our community is Raul Yzaguirre."

THE SYMPHONY THAT PLAYS THE SAME NOTE, or the North Star that brightens the night sky, are symbols easily identified with NCLR's steadfast leadership in creating avenues of social reform for millions of Latinos. Its affiliates, born and bred from issues arising in communities as diverse as the members of an orchestra, or as unique as bodies of stars in the night sky, reflect NCLR's true mission, for without its affiliates the Policy Analysis Center and all the advocacy done in Congress would only be a gong sounding on deaf ears. With a solid foundation of affiliates, NCLR has been able to weather the storms of changing presidential administrations, Congressional ups and downs and the fickle uprising of conservatives who still think they live in a country that is governed by White, Protestant principles with no regard for others who have been a part of the culture, history and legacy of the Western Hemisphere before there *was* an America.

"Over time we developed a solid relationship with our constituency," Yzaguirre says. "We went from having fifteen affiliates to three hundred affiliates with a combined budget of four billion dollars and serving close to four million people. We became by any standard the largest Latino nonprofit, constituency-based organization in the nation."

NCLR's extensive affiliate network works in the daily grind of life, politics, and unique state by state needs as it addresses services as diverse as: charter schools, job training, English-language preparation, home ownership counseling, health centers, civil rights, juvenile justice, substance abuse services, parent engagement, and a host of other services that enhance the lives of millions of Latinos yearly. Yzaguirre's vision of a pan-Latino identity has been met in its affiliates as NCLR extends its invitation to diverse ethnics groups within the Latino world: Cubans, Puerto Ricans, Salvadorans, South Americans and many others. No one is left out, and the criterion for all is that they are Latino led, and Latino serving 501 (c)(3) nonprofits. Every year, a select group of affiliates are honored at the NCLR Conference in July with the "Affiliate of the Year Award," and their service to the Latino community becomes national news.

Janet Murguia, current President and CEO of NCLR expresses her belief in NCLR's integrity as a one-of-a-kind institution that leaves no stone unturned in providing assistance, and passionately advocating on behalf of its expansive network of affiliates. "I believe that through a great American institution like NCLR, which has a long history of fighting for our community, we can advance an agenda that will benefit our community and society as a whole."

In spite of progress made during the first years of his service to NCLR, more trials awaited Yzaguirre. Standing on the sidelines, ready to spring, his old nemesis, chaos, looked for an opportunity to set up roadblocks—direct confrontations with presidents and legislators, and a host of racist agitators that would test his stamina and endurance over one of NCLR'S most endearing issues: EDUCATION.

22

COLD DAY IN HELL

This administration does not believe in legislating by executive order. It'll be a cold day in hell before this president signs an executive order.

—John Sununu

MacArthur Fellow

L EAVING BEHIND THEIR HOME in La Paz, Bolivia, originally known as Nuestra Señora de la Paz, Cecilia Muñoz's parents immigrated to Detroit, Michigan with high hopes for securing the American Dream. Cradled for centuries in its own bowl-shaped indentation on the earth's surface, La Paz, founded in 1548 by Spanish conquistadores, is a distinct opposite of Detroit's bustling automobile factories, commerce and skyscrapers rising miles high in the heart of the city. La Paz's shifting weather, from misty cold mornings to tropical temperatures, are unlike Detroit's freezing winters and hot, humid summers. Set in the midst of Spanish colonial churches with buildings and homes climbing like stepping stones along the surrounding mountains, the ancient city of La Paz didn't offer opportunities for work and advancement as did an American city like Detroit. Muñoz's father, an automotive engineer, made a decision to move his family permanently to Detroit where he had been accepted as a student at the University of Michigan.

Nurturing close family ties, Muñoz's parents encouraged their four children to seek a post-secondary education. The youngest of four siblings, Cecilia followed in her father's footsteps and attended the University of Michigan, graduating with degrees in English and Latin Studies. She then headed for California to complete work on a Masters Degree also in Latin Studies from the University of California at Berkeley.

291

"One of my first jobs was in the Archdiocese of Chicago, running a legalization program that followed the Immigration Reform and Control Act of 1986," Muñoz says "I came to know NCLR and its work through Charles Kamasaki who was managing the immigration portfolio at the time. Through working with Charles, I knew that NCLR was a high-quality organization. There was no Internet back then to allow for quick research, so I knew very little about Raul, until I started to work for him. I first met him in May 1988 when I interviewed for a job at NCLR. I was interviewing for a newly-created middle management position and he did the interview himself along with NCLR Vice President, Charles Kamasaki. He was pretty terrifying because he said pretty much nothing throughout the entire interview. He started with, 'So tell me a little about yourself,' and said very little else. I had no idea, at the time, that I was meeting a man who had done so much to shape the country and Latino community, and would do so much to shape my own life."

Gaining momentum as an advocate for immigration, Cecilia Muñoz was entrusted with the responsibility of running twelve field offices in the metropolitan Chicago area for the Catholic Archdiocese and helped more than 5,000 immigrants obtain U.S. citizenship. In 1988, her work with the immigrant community led her to seek employment with NCLR, and she was subsequently hired to serve as the senior immigration policy analyst.

"I worked for Raul for 16 years, and his influence on my life and career is impossible to overstate," Muñoz relates. "From him, I learned what it means to work on the basis of a deep lifelong commitment to a cause greater than yourself. I also learned the value of doing your work with integrity, no matter the cost. I watched him make many difficult decisions about public policy, funding and the direction of the institution, and he never once lost sight of the mission, the core of the work. In the long run, his reputation for integrity was an extraordinary asset to NCLR and the movement. I find myself doing my best to apply those lessons almost daily in my work."

At one point, Cecilia Muñoz's career seemed as if it would stall as she contemplated her role as a new Mom and was uncertain what that might mean in the intense, demanding role she played at NCLR. "Raul is directly responsible for the fact that I have been able to have a successful career in public service while also being true to my values as a Latina and as a Mom. I was the first relatively senior woman at NCLR to have a baby and the news of my pregnancy inspired a small parade of colleagues to show up in my office to wonder about my future, as if my pregnancy likely meant that I had to leave the organization because nobody had ever done this before, and the culture of the organization would surely not allow for it."

"So, I went to Raul directly, never an easy thing to do as he is not a talkative person and for years whenever I met with him I felt like I was babbling to fill the space occupied by his thoughtful silence. I told him that others seemed to think that there was no room for a working mother on the policy team, and asked him if this was his assumption as well. I will never forget this—he softened visibly, and told me what nobody else at the organization yet knew, that his daughter was expecting his first grandchild. He said, 'We talk a lot about how our community's values are family values. It's time to put our money where our mouth is.'"

"Raul was as good as his word. I had a generous family leave and while I kept a demanding schedule when I returned, nobody ever looked at me sideways when I had to stay home with a sick child or walk out of a meeting because it was pickup time at daycare. His expectations remained high, but he provided me with flexibility to serve my community and serve my family both with the same high standards. Not only did my family benefit immeasurably from Raul's commitment, but we blazed a trail for other parents at NCLR as well as our sister organizations. I can say without hesitation that my husband and I were able to raise terrific children, and I was able to do the work of my heart—because Raul made it possible. He guided friends and associates through personal crisis, and approached his own illness when he was diagnosed with Parkinson's disease with uncommon grace and courage. I am one of many, many inspired by his example."

Always a trail blazer, Muñoz opened the door for other staff who saw in Yzaguirre, not only their boss, *el jefe*, as he was referred to at times, but a cordial father figure who would listen to their personal plans and share in helping them make decisions. The first-born of five children, the role of father figure came naturally for Yzaguirre. Tony Salazar recalls his own need to have a private consultation with him on a sensitive issue that arose for him at NCLR.

"While serving as Chair of NCLR I fell in love with Denise de la Rosa, a staff member of the organization," Salazar relates. "Denise had been working for the organization for five years and Raul had very much become her father figure. As the relationship got more serious I was forced to visit privately with Raul and disclose the affair, (neither one of us was married at the time). The discussion was not between friends, not between the Chair and the President of the organization, but more like a suitor asking a father for his daughter's hand. It was very awkward, but in the end Raul gave his blessing and he even served as the best man at our wedding."

Yzaguirre's determination to empower those around him, led him to form strong mentorship bonds as he worked to build confidence in staff members, encouraging them to take on difficult tasks. "Raul's willingness to challenge assumptions, to empower others and to take risks for the sake of what was important, led to my very first Congressional hearing," recalls Cecilia Muñoz. "We were working on a bill that was to become the 1999 Immigration Reform Bill, an early version sponsored by Senators Edward Kennedy and Alan Simpson. We felt the bill had overreached in its cuts to family-sponsored immigration. The Senators asked Raul to testify, but he was traveling and he designated me to represent the organization. At the time I was only twenty-seven years old. Senator Kennedy's staffer politely requested that I ask Raul to reconsider, which I dutifully did. Raul looked at me and said, 'Go, and rise to the occasion.' I worked harder on that testimony than on anything I had ever done because I wanted to honor his confidence in me."

"Cecilia's intelligence and ability to articulate NCLR's position on complicated issues was something I could count on," Yzaguirre recalls. "She never shrank back from anything new or controversial. When she was named a MacArthur Fellow, I knew she suffered over it because she felt the award should have been mine. On the other hand, I felt it belonged to her for the exceptional work she had done on immigration. Later, her appointment to head President Obama's Domestic Policy Council was the correct choice, and I never doubted she could perform the job and move the Latino agenda forward."

One of the most prestigious awards granted in the U.S., the MacArthur Fellowship is often referred to as the "Genius Grant," and honors an individual working in any field of work who shows exceptional merit and promise for continued service and extraordinary contributions in their area of expertise. The prize carries with it a considerable stipend, given to the recipient over a five-year period. Nominations and selection are anonymous and recipients often know nothing about it, until they receive a phone call advising them they have been granted the award.

In 2000, Charles Kamasaki remembers getting a call from someone on the fellowship committee concerning Muñoz's work at NCLR. "Some of us at the Council knew this was happening. I had been asked for a reference, and others were also providing references. Cecilia got the call at home advising her that she had been selected for the MacArthur Award for her work in civil rights and immigration. In the morning she went in to tell Raul, and could not get the words out. She burst into tears because she felt he should have gotten the award. She told him he had been so generous to her by allowing her to be quoted extensively in the media, and had allowed her to testify before Congress and advocate for policy issues related to immigration. It was almost embarrassing to her because Raul had built the movement. Yet, Raul stood by her, and congratulated her for her work and told her how proud he was of her."

Serving in the presidential campaign of Barack Obama in 2008 as a top immigration adviser, specializing on issues related to the vast growing numbers of Latinos, Muñoz was destined to influence important policies affecting millions of Latinos nationwide from her position at NCLR. In 2009, President Obama appointed her as the White House Director of Intergovernmental Affairs, and in 2012 she became Obama's appointee as Director of the White House Domestic Policy Council.

Instrumental in helping shape Senate Bill 744, a bipartisan bill, introduced in the spring of 2013 by the 'Gang of Eight,' Senators Charles Schumer (D-NY), John McCain (R-AZ), Dick Durbin (D-IL), Lindsey Graham (R-SC), Robert Menendez (D-NJ), Marco Rubio (R-FL), Michael Bennet (D-CO), and Jeff Flake (R-AZ), Muñoz advocated for the most extensive expression of the bill, which would address all aspects of immigration, including providing citizenship for 11 million undocumented immigrants living within the U.S. The bill ignited controversy nationwide, and left-wing immigrant rights groups like NCLR, and MALDEF were charged with not doing enough to protect the nation's borders. Further angered by funding for left-wing groups, conservatives formed a coalition of hostile opponents of the DREAM Act, stirred into action by the Tea Party movement—radical conservatives within the Republican Party.

Introduced in the Senate in 2001 by Dick Durbin (D-IL) and Orrin Hatch (R-UT), The DREAM Act, perhaps the most important legislation to date addressing education for undocumented immigrants, if enacted, will provide citizenship for millions of immigrants who were brought to the U.S. as minors and attained their education in the U.S. The DREAM Act was something Cecilia Muñoz, Charles Kamasaki, Emily Gantz McKay, and others at NCLR's Policy Center spent numerous hours writing preliminary drafts, framing important features and expanding on the underlying principles of the Act. "The DREAM Act was drafted at NCLR headquarters," Kamasaki recalls, "and it led to what would become an important piece of legislation that offered opportunities for millions of immigrants who had been brought to the U.S. as minors and would finally find a place in American society."

PANDORA'S BOX

Addressing students of all ages, from pre-school to post-secondary education, NCLR, along with its affiliates, takes, very seriously, the national educational crisis plaguing Latino students, namely, high drop out rates. To further capture the urgency of the educational gap among Latinos, NCLR released *Hispanic Education: Selected Statistics* in 1983, the first in a series of informational documents identifying federal and statewide practices that impede Latino educational success. And, by 1984, under the leadership of Board Chair, Ed Pastor, who had served as a member of the Maricopa County Board of Supervisors, and by 1991 would become the first Latino to represent Arizona in Congress, NCLR began a systematic approach in dealing with the educational needs of Hispanic Americans.

Collaborating with its affiliates, and other nonprofits throughout the nation, NCLR's focus is on shaping policy and strengthening educational programs that address the needs of millions of Latino students, and others whose language base might be other than English. Yzaguirre's work with President Johnson's War on Poverty had brought him face to face with civil rights issues that addressed discrimination, segregation, lack of role models in schools, and the labeling of Latino students solely on their ability to speak English.

The Bilingual Education Act (1968), introduced by Senator Ralph Yarborough (D-TX) became the cornerstone for addressing the needs of Limited English Speaking Ability Students (LESA), which were later referred to as English as a Second Language Students (ESL). The BEA, also referred to as Title VII, then became part of the Elementary and Secondary Education Act of 1968. The Act provided for federal funds to be distributed to school districts for the creation of innovative language programs that addressed the needs of ESL students. Working in collaboration with other organizations, in particular with one of its affiliates, the National Association of Bilingual Education (NABE), NCLR was instrumental in pushing for the reauthorization of the BEA in 1994 with support from Senators Edward Kennedy (D-MA), John McCain (R-AZ), and Congressman Esteban Torres (D-CA).

As the BEA evolved, stipulations were added for district-wide programs that would meet the needs of all language diverse students, stressing the learning of English. The bill's reauthorization in 1994 leads to something Yzaguirre had worked for years to bring to reality—the development of bilingualism and bilingual programs that foster learning in two languages. His own experience in the Rio Grande Valley, and the segregation he had experienced there had convinced him that language was more than learning phonics, reading and writing. It was a part of self-identity, pride and developing a good self-concept. "Raul worked hard with NCLR and NABE to help draft the Bilingual Education Reauthorization Act," Charles Kamasaki says. "Raul spent a lot of time on this, and it was worth it in the end, as the Reauthorization went through."

Teaching a class on immigration and language at the Institute of Politics at Harvard in 1989, part of the Kennedy School of Government, Yzaguirre used his skills as a debater to engage in discussions with his students that often continued after class at Grendel's, a nearby tavern. "Spontaneous conversations with my students reminded me of the extemporaneous debates in Ms. Pollard's class. We often debated tough issues, and were able to come up with new ways of looking at things we had taken for granted. My students experienced the give and take of listening to opposing views without flying off the handle."

Yzaguirre's essay, "The Perils of Pandora: An Examination of the English-Only Movement," written in 1986, discloses issues related to the loss of language due to the pressure to become mainstream Americans. His own stance remains that of cultivating a student's own language base and linking knowledge in one language to knowledge in another. Ideally, the Maintenance Model of ESL Instruction, best describes Yzaguirre's belief that a student's first language should be nurtured and validated, rather than rejected, or worse still, held in contempt. His own son, Raul, Jr.'s plight in facing ridicule because he spoke Spanish in Maryland schools, further served to convince him that two languages were better than one for expanding students' knowledge.

Under Yzaguirre's leadership, NCLR's Policy Analysis Center began a bold stance against the National Interest Act of 1995 which unfairly separated U.S. citizens from their family members, and the passage of legislation such as Proposition 187 (1994) in California which denied social services to undocumented immigrants, and SB 1070 (2010) in Arizona, one of the strictest anti-immigrant laws in the nation that created a 'police state' in viewing undocumented immigrants as criminals and forcing them to carry identification papers at all times.

Adding support to the ideals of equality for America's immigrants, and advancing educational opportunities for Latinos nationwide, the Congressional Hispanic Caucus (CHC) formed in 1976, created a platform for members of Congress that promoted discussion of issues directly affecting the lives of the nation's Latinos. Although non-partisan in structure, Congressional Democrats dominated the leadership of CHC. Backing up NCLR's Policy Center as another 'think tank,' and advocacy network, the CHC went into action with congressional leaders such as: Ed Roybal, Esteban Torres, Kika de la Garza, Ed Pastor, Joe Baca, Nydia Velásquez, Charles Gonzalez, Xavier Becerra, and Rubén Hinojosa. Cuban-born Senator Bob Menendez of New Jersey, the only senator active in the CHC, was later appointed as Chair of the United States Senate Committee on Foreign Relations in 2013.

Wielding power and influence in Congress, NCLR and the CHC stand solidly behind progressive education for Latinos; however, Yzaguirre's own personal relationship to education tends to be a bit more complicated, and embraces his own conviction that education is a tool, that in the hands of qualified educators will give meaning and purpose to life.

"I tended to have a schizophrenic view of education," Yzaguirre says, reflecting on his personal connection to education. "It was important for everyone except me. College courses seemed meaningless to me. I met my wife because I wouldn't attend class and started tutoring lab students to make up for class credit. Personally, education was not a priority for me. High school was exciting, the subjects were new to me, but college was repetitive and not as exciting. My mother was all about education and expected us all to go to college. Half of my college credits came from tests I took. I found out I could get up to 60 college credits by testing out of subjects. I've always been good at taking tests, so it was easy to earn the credits. There were some classes I loved, and others I found dull and repetitive. I felt as if I was going through the paces, through rituals. I needed to memorize dates, places and facts, but was missing relationships and connections. We need to change the way we teach, or we will continue to have the same high rate of high school and college drop-outs. Education has to have meaning in the real world. The closest I came to that type of education as a child, was the little house on San Juan's main street rented by the two ladies from Mexico. They taught culture, traditions and the meaning of what it meant to be Mexican on both sides of the border. Students in their school learned pride in their own identity and heritage."

Recalling the little house on main street, Yzaguirre's efforts to establish schools that fostered pride in history and heritage, led him to take a closer look at how a community dealt with education outside of the formal walls of public and private schools. "Raul supported community based schools," Kamasaki says. "He maintained that community based schools provided elements of culture and native language instruction that facilitated learning in the classroom. Raul was ahead of his time. He conceived the notion of Academias del Pueblo, Saturday and after school community based programs that morphed into charter and alternative schools."

Yzaguirre's experiences working as a program analyst during Johnson's War on Poverty gave him insights into the value of education as the foundation for expanding opportunities for Latinos, and opening doors for employment that remained shut to non-graduates. In higher education, he favors a Liberal Arts curriculum that includes not only the core subjects, but also the humanities. "The broader the perspectives of knowledge introduced to students, the greater will be the connections they make in the real world, and the purpose for learning will have that much greater significance."

EXECUTIVE ORDER VS. COLD DAY IN HELL

"NCLR was on an 'education boom' in the 90's," Yzaguirre says. "By then, we had helped establish 100 charter schools throughout the nation. Bilingual education was under attack, and that made us work harder to help affiliates that were running educational programs. We used a whole spectrum of tools, seed money for programs to get going, and we offered technical assistance, parent training and Head Start programs for underserved communities. We secured half a million dollars by advocating in Congress."

Working with a variety of Hispanic-led organizations and advocacy groups, NCLR's support of federal and state educational programs, such as the Federal TRIO Programs consisting of organizations like Upward Bound, that helped low-income students achieve a college degree, would become a major part of the Council's plan to eliminate high drop-out rates of Latino students. Gaining Early Awareness and Readiness for Undergraduate Programs (GEAR UP), a post-secondary educational program, was established to fund education for high-poverty students identified in middle school, then following them through high school and their first year of college. Working in collaboration with the Hispanic Education Action Plan (HEAP), NCLR has continued to support efforts by the Hispanic Association of Colleges and Universities (HACU) to increase Latino students' success in college and in their chosen careers. To continue their commitment to secure 'hard facts,' NCLR's Policy Analysis Center identified points in the educational pipeline at which Latinos were most vulnerable, and Yzaguirre, along with other Latino leaders, pressed forward for a national initiative.

Excellence in Community Educational Leadership (EXCEL), created to address elementary to post-secondary education, places emphasis on a liberal arts approach encompassing science, math, philosophy, religion, economics, global issues and the behavioral sciences. Among a variety of services, students are offered tutoring, technological assistance, accelerated language learning, and direct instruction in reading, writing, and test-taking skills. The needs of students afflicted with Attention Deficit Disorder (ADD) are also addressed through these specific programs. Slowly, NCLR's educational affiliates began to adopt EXCEL objectives as part of their curriculum and structured programs. Over the years, they documented successful programs and offered ways to improve failing or weak programs while zeroing in on tactics for improving service delivery. Hard facts and statistics gave the EXCEL objectives validity and increased NCLR's visibility as a knowledgeable Congressional advocate.

The pan-Latino view for delivering services nationwide led to more changes on the NCLR Board. By 1984, the Council amends its bylaws to require numerical representation of major Latino subgroups as well as regional representation of the ever-growing Latino community, at that time, based on the 1980 Census. In 1987, the Board elects its first Puerto Rican Chairperson, Rita DiMartino of AT&T who, during the 1980's, served as U.S. Ambassador to UNICEF. It's DiMartino who expands NCLR's contact with Presidents Reagan and George H.W. Bush, and offers her own brand of expertise in dealing with the private sector. With DiMartino's election as Board Chair, Latino representatives of subgroups who had been waiting on the sidelines to see if NCLR would adhere to its pledge for global inclusion, now felt confident that NCLR would advocate for their needs. "We went from being the fly on the bull's rump, to taking the bull by the horns and leading it to where we wanted it to go," Yzaguirre, says, reflecting on the growing reach of NCLR's influence throughout the nation.

During the administration of George H.W. Bush, (1989-1993) NCLR moves forward with its educational agenda, and demands answers from the president about how his administration will address the growing needs of Latino students. Increasingly aware of the educational needs of Latinos through NCLR's advocacy, the president is invited to attend an annual conference and in 1990 becomes the first sitting president to address the Council at its annual conference. "I had a conversation with the president, and discussed my concerns about education for the nation's Latinos. He listened and attended our conference, but there was not much else done at the time," Yzaguirre recalls.

Then, Dr. Lauro Cavazos comes on the scene as a newly elected member of G. H.W.'s cabinet. A fellow Texan, Cavazos had earned a B.A. and M.A. in zoology from Texas Tech University, and a Ph.D. in physiology from Iowa State University. The first Hispanic to serve in the United States Cabinet, Cavazos is directed by G.H.W. to initiate a series of hearings that will serve as platforms for the discussion of educational needs being brought to the attention of Congress through the efforts of NCLR. "We floated the idea around of getting the president to sign an executive order to address the needs of Latinos," Yzaguirre says, "and did a variety of things to try to get some traction, like sending letters to the president's administration. The executive order would require an assessment from every federal agency that had an educational component, including the Department of Labor and others. They would be required to report the participation of Hispanics, and if numbers were not sufficient, to develop a plan to recruit Hispanics to their programs. The executive order also called for the creation of a commission and a staff to provide technical support."

Meeting at the White House with George H.W. Bush's Chief of Staff, John Sununu, who had no interest in hearing about NCLR's plan for an executive order, Yzaguirre soon finds himself facing a stubborn opponent. "We were sitting around in a room at the White House," Yzaguirre recalls, "and I was discussing the plan to get the president to sign the executive order. Going on the defensive, John Sununu suddenly shouted, 'This administration does not believe in legislating by executive order. It'll be a cold day in hell before this president signs an executive order!' In frustration, a woman, sitting close by who had worked closely with my Republican mentor, John Gardner, threw a pillow at me to punctuate Sununu's obvious hostility. It took weeks of negotiations by members of NCLR's Policy Center, to convince the president that Latinos would stand together to get answers for the growing demands of parents for a better education for their children, and for funding and programs through affirmative action for Latinos at colleges and universities."

"The president used Lauro Cavazos as a way to show that his administration was not anti-Latino. He thought he could get rid of us that way. Lauro called for hearings on education throughout the nation, and we packed the hearing rooms and the administration took notice. We wanted to send a message that we were serious and organized, and our voices were one. The Republican Party was shown that they had to do better with Latinos. We got Latino newspapers and other media to put pressure on the president, and in September 1990, President George H.W. Bush signed the Educational Excellence for Hispanic Americans. We now officially had our executive order."

Criticizing G. H. W. Bush's weak stance on affirmative action, Yzaguirre strengthened NCLR's position in making universities accountable for recruiting Latinos and other minorities, and by packing the hearing rooms with enthusiastic supporters, he sent the president the message that Latinos would not be satisfied with half-way measures. On September 24, 1990, President George H.W. Bush signed the Educational Excellence for Hispanic Americans, Executive Order 12729, *to strengthen the capacity to provide quality education and to increase opportunities for Hispanic Americans to participate in and benefit from Federal programs.*

Establishing a commission, headed by a Republican, to oversee the implementation of the Order, Sununu appointed Yzaguirre as vice-Chair. "The

Executive Order first signed by President Bush was then signed by President Clinton, and every president since then," Yzaguirre says. "The order is a force of law, but it is only effective while that president is in power and when not in power, it no longer has any effect. Each president has to sign it all over again. And they all have signed, since Bush the first."

To Yzaguirre's disappointment, implementation of the Executive Order would be an entirely different matter. "Not a single federal agency had fully complied with the law after years of trying hard to get the agencies to respond and abide by the order's mandates, so I had to embarrass the administration by resigning my position as vice-Chair of the Commission. I was not necessarily blaming the president, I was blaming the bureaucracy that would not allow the process to move forward. We made some progress over the years and the Commission still exists today, but only in theory."

Taking office in 1993, Clinton appointed Yzaguirre as Chair of the Commission on Education. "The Bush Commission had both Republicans and Democrats, and I had a voice in the selection of members, but when Clinton took over, I had no input into the membership and the Commission was all Democrats, it seemed more politically based than anything else."

With NCLR seeking to be non-partisan, it didn't take long before Yzaguirre faced even more challenges. "We've criticized Democrats as well as Republicans. Clinton didn't like criticism but got over it. After six years nobody had acted on the findings of the Commission. The president wasn't pushing it. So what was the use of having something that wasn't working? NCLR is non-partisan. We've taken some Republican ideas, like charter schools, improved assessments and the merit system for educational reform. We've fought for legislation that's created earned income credit, and have stood up for Democratic ideals of civil rights, but we don't want to be a member of any party. We've had both parties speaking at our conferences. John McCain got a respectful audience with us, as did other Republicans. We only had one situation where we booed somebody. It was in Houston, over the census. The Secretary of Commerce, Robert Mosbacher, was sending signals that he would certify and mathematically adjust the 1990 census that would miss a lot of Latinos. He didn't speak at our annual conference but he did send an assistant, and the man got booed. I stood up and said we weren't going to boo him. So I left the place and ended up picketing our own conference. Mosbacher's census would lessen the resources for Latinos and congressional districts would suffer. So they needed to use a reliable formula for counting Latinos. The Secretary of Commerce later served with me on a commission, and we sat next to each other and I told him the story, and he said, 'I remember,' and said 'I got some bad advice. I should have gone to your conference, but I'll send you a letter of apology.' A year later he wrote a letter of apology."

The battleground for securing civil rights for Latinos, was something Yzaguirre was determined to ride into, full gallop. At the ready was NCLR's Policy Analysis Center, with brilliant minds that would stop at nothing to follow his lead. Clashes, conflicts and huge chasms would rise between NCLR, Congress, presidential administrations, and an ever-growing number of radical conservatives. The 'right' would move so far 'right' that liberals would begin to wonder if the Constitution of the United States still held any significance. One by one, presidents would come on-board with partisan agendas, critical markers for change, and legislative issues that spanned the globe. Panicked, at times, by the growing numbers of Latinos, some presidents wondered what the changing demographics would mean for future elections. The browning of America was becoming a reality and was ahead of its time. Researchers had predicted that one out of every four Americans would be a person of color by 2045, but their predictions had fallen short of the reality—things were changing faster than anyone could have ever predicted.

Yzaguirre had made up his mind years ago not to count the cost. He would forge ahead through volatile meetings, long nights at headquarters, desperate decisions, criticism by fellow Latinos, and guilt over time spent away from his family, and get up every morning ready to take on his old war-bitten adversary—chaos. His name would become synonymous with the word 'Latino,' 'Hispanic,' 'Chicano,' and everything else in-between

CAREER PHOTOGRAPHS

Raul and Lyndon B. Johnson, Washington, D.C., 1965.

Best wishes to Raul Yzaguirre

Jimmy Carter

Raul and Jimmy Carter. Washington, D.C. circa, 1978.

Raul and Jesse Jackson. NCLR Conference, Chicago, circa 1980.

Raul and Dr. Hector P. García at NCLR Headquarters
in Washington D.C., circa 1980.

Raul at a press conference in Washington D.C., discussing NAFTA, circa, 1982.

Raul and Ronald Reagan, Washington D.C., circa 1983.

To Raul Yzaguirre
With best wishes, Ronald Reagan

Raul at dinner with Ronald Reagan during Hispanic
Heritage month in Washington D.C., circa 1983.

To Raul Yzaguirre
With best wishes,

George Bush

Raul and George H.W. Bush in Washington D.C., circa 1990.

Raul receiving the Order of the Aztec Eagle from Mexican
President Carlos Salinas de Gortari. Mexico City, 1993.

Raul with Former NCLR Board Chairs Gilbert Vazquez, Rita DiMartino,
Irma Flores Gonzalez, Audrey Alvarado, Ramon Murguia.

Raul and Bob Dole in Washington, D.C., circa, 1995.

Raul witnessing President Clinton sign the Educational Excellence for
Hispanic Americans Executive Order in Washington D.C., 1997.

Raul and Newt Ginrich discussing legislation to study Mexican
land grants in the public domain which had been "stolen"
from original grantees. Washington, D.C., circa, 1996.

Raul and George W. Bush, Washington D.C., circa 2002.

Raul and Vicente Fox at NCLR conference, circa, 2002.

Raul and Iconic Alma Award.

NCLR Board Meeting. December 7, 2003.
Seating left to right: Danny Ortega, Jose Villarreal, RY, Janet Murguia, Horace
Deets, Monica Lozano. Standing left to right: W. Roger Haughton, Robin Read,
Patricia Fennell, Ricardo Urbina, Andrea Bazan, Isabel Valdés, Irma Flores
Gonzalez, Raymond Lozano, Arturo Rodriguez, Salvador Balcorta, Ken Trujillo.

Raul at NCLR Farewell Conference in Phoenix, Arizona, 2004.

Raul and Janet Murguia, his successor, at NCLR Farewell
Conference, Phoenix, Arizona, 2004.

Raul and Edward James Olmos at NCLR Alma Awards, May 2006.

Raul with Hillary Clinton and Dolores Huerta, NCLR
Conference, Miami, FLorida, 2007.

Raul with Janet Murguia and Hillary Clinton at NCLR Conference.

Raul with Herman Gallegos and Janet Murguia NCLR's 40th
Anniversary NCLR Conference San Diego 2008.

Raul and Emily Gantz McKay at Yzaguirre Building
Dedication, Washington, D.C., March 2008.

Raul and Janet Murguia at Yzaguirre Building
Dedication, Washington D.C., March 2008.

Raul and his family at Yzaguirre Building Dedication, March 2008.
In the front, from left to right: Alma, Teresa,(Raul's sisters) Raul,
Regina,(oldest daughter) Elisa (second daughter) and Ben, (youngest
son).. In the back, left to right: Roberto (second son), Audrey O'Cana
(Alma's daughter) and Michael Campanile (Regina's husband).

Official Grand Opening of the Raul Yzaguirre Building and Dedication of the Plaza de los Afiliados. Washington, DC, March 3, 2008. Left to right: Ron Estrada, Gerald Borenstein, Eric Rodriguez, Charles Kamasaki, Jose Velazquez, Delia Pompa, Raul, Delia de la Vara, Janet Murguía, Sonia Perez, and Lot Diaz.

Raul with Janet Murguia and Monica Lozano at Yzaguirre Building Dedication, March 2008.

Photo of Raul at ASU, CDCR Center, 2009.

Official U.S. State Department photo of Ambassador Raul H. Yzaguirre, 2010.

Raul, Tommy Espinoza and Janet Murguia at NCLR Conference, 2013.

Raul and Manny Mota at NCLR Conference in Los Angeles, 2014.

Raul and Barack Obama, Washington, D.C., 2015.

PART FOUR
If We Build Them...

23

INSTITUTION BUILDER

*Because of his {Raul's} work, we have strong institutions that provide
opportunity and assistance to those in need, and strong leaders in
communities all across the country who are linked in a common purpose
on critical issues that affect us all, like immigration reform, education,
health care, and economic issues. His contributions are extraordinary.*

—Cecilia Muñoz

BUILDING ON ROCK

SUBSTANCE. THAT'S THE WORD Yzaguirre grabbles with as he pushes
NCLR's agenda forward. He's disappointed with President George
H.W. Bush's Educational Executive Order for Hispanic Americans,
which does little to positively affect changes in the education of America's
Latinos. The Executive Order encounters enormous challenges and has no
real power to force compliance under Bush's administration, and subsequent
administrations that follow. The struggle for equality in education will be an
uphill battle, all the way.

Convinced that there has to be substance to what NCLR does as a budding American institution, Yzaguirre guides NCLR's structure, programs,
affiliates and tiers of power to achieve one goal: real change. There has to be
substance in the policies NCLR engages in—which includes gathering hard
facts and statistics. Substance, in real commitment to its growing affiliates and
the work they do in the trenches of America's Latino communities. In short,
what he's building at NCLR has to take root and become an institution with a
lasting part of America's history and heritage.

As early as 1977, only three years after assuming his role as CEO,
Yzaguirre wrote a paper, "Criteria for Building an Institution," in which he

identified several factors for the success of NCLR as a viable institution. "We needed a constituency, and a good reputation for being factually based. We needed accountability and the need to have independence in our finances so we wouldn't be held hostage by any one funding source, and for this reason, it was important to diversify. We had to have a way of making our Board governance transparent, and using best practices. We had to have terms for our Board members so they would rotate in an orderly fashion. Principles I had learned over time about what made an institution viable helped me formulate concrete plans. We instituted weekly staff meetings, led by good management staff, so everyone would know what their responsibilities were. We articulated what our governing policies were and the positions we would take so there was a clear understanding of where we stood on important issues. We decided which issues would be priority and which would take more time to develop."

In *Forces for Good: The Six Practices of High-Impact Nonprofits* (2008), NCLR was named one of the top nonprofits in the U.S., and a pioneer in building rapport not only with its members and affiliates, but with the public at large. Yzaguirre's focus on creating an institution that would reach out to all U.S. populations, prompted the development of an "issues network," which NCLR implemented to keep the public informed on an array of topics including HIV/AIDS, health, immigration, education and housing. *Agenda*, NCLR's quarterly newsletter also became a showcase for informing the public with up-to-date reports and data on issues affecting the nation's 50 million Latinos. Skilled at writing since childhood, and challenged to excel in English, using correct grammar, tone and style by the infamous Mrs. Brooks at PSJA High, Yzaguirre honed his writing skills, often contributing articles to the newsletter as well as preparing numerous reports for Congress and testimonials for Senate subcommittees.

Viewing institutions as a way to gain a reputation as a formidable source of knowledge and resources, Yzaguirre moved in a methodical and strategic manner to set up the building blocks of institutions that would permeate American thought and culture. Realizing that people listen to information they believe is revealing the truth, he didn't want to miss the opportunity to join in the high stakes game of awakening Congress and the American public to the lives of generations of Latinos who had lived in the shadows of segregation, discrimination and in many cases, outright distrust and distain.

"We changed the nomenclature," Yzaguirre reflects in discussing NCLR's determination to lead the way in establishing institutions. "We framed the issues and were proud of developing arguments against opponents of bilingual education, and politicians who used those terms and arguments to advance their political agendas. We created the replies and retorts on those arguments. We changed the terminology by making sure we were Latinos, and not separated into groups: Mexican Americans, Chicanos, Puerto Ricans, Cubans and so forth. We continued to emphasize that we were united. We created lots of institutions for Latinos that had not been there before, an infrastructure of defense and advocacy. We sought a development bank, formerly known as the Community Development Financial Institution, which is licensed by the U.S. Treasury Department and accumulated 300 million dollars in assets. So, we now had the capacity to talk something serious. We thought of ways to implement that money for civil rights in the U.S. in things such as the Raza Development Fund which created an array of grassroots community development agencies, civil rights organizations, charter schools, housing development, loans to affiliates for office buildings, and extending more technical and professional guidance. That was a big deal. Overnight we became the largest Latino service organization in the country. Since then, we have leveraged more than a billion, yes that is a 'b', dollars in loans to affiliates. We are now operating in the big leagues. As a result, local Latino groups own their own schools, office buildings, their own clinics, and thousands of Hispanic families now own their own homes."

NCLR's commitment to wealth building inspired the creation of not only the Raza Development Fund, but also the New America Alliance (NAA). In June 1999, Yzaguirre and Henry Cisneros organized a meeting attended by over thirty prominent Latino leaders who were focused on founding an organization that tapped economic advancement, wealth building and philanthropy for and by Latinos. The New America Alliance, a 501(c)6 and a 501(c)3 organization is dedicated to advancing the economic development of the American Latino community. Latino business leaders, now over one hundred strong in NAA, lead the way for building a solid foundation of economic success at all levels in the high stakes world of corporate America. Investment in local communities and coordinating philanthropy through public and private sectors, empowers the Latino community and establishes a place for the mentoring of new leaders and the "meeting of minds," that brings about new ideas and further challenges growth.

"I said to Henry Cisneros, we have enough people in our community who are successful, who are wealthy and want to do something creative with their wealth. And that's where the idea for the New America Alliance was formed."

Currently a Board Member Emeritus of NAA, Yzaguirre says, "Our emphasis was on economic empowerment and philanthropy, and building up our Latino communities. Years later, I was invited to speak at one of NAA's conferences, and was astounded at their growth, commitment and enormous success. It felt good to know that they had become so strong over the years."

Building NCLR into a multi-faceted institution turned into a search for inclusion, not only of ethnic groups, but of an expanding openness to America's business leaders. "Raul built a two-sided relationship with corporate America," Charles Kamasaki relates. "He didn't believe corporate America could be bought. He felt it was important for corporate America to understand Latinos. The Corporate Board of Advisors, made up of America's top corporations, helped sponsor the NCLR annual conference."

Objections by some NCLR members about how much corporate America should be involved, continued to spin a negative debate and some members insisted on accepting money only from NCLR's constituency. "Some people had limited vision during Raul's tenure," Kamasaki explains. "Raul's view was that if you limit your resource level, you limit your sphere of influence. He felt that no one tactic would transform best practices. We had to work in sync with our constituency and corporate America using many strategies."

One of the first corporate executives to begin a relationship with NCLR was Steve Reinemund, now retired Chairman and CEO of PepsiCo. He relates his own introduction to Yzaguirre and finding in him someone he could trust. "In 1990, I was in search of a national Hispanic leader to help me solve a very sensitive business challenge that was becoming a racially-charged national issue for our company.

"A mutual friend introduced me to Raul Yzaguirre. I remember at the end of a very long first meeting, Raul looked at me squarely in the eyes and said, 'I don't know why I am going to agree to help you because I really don't know you, but I will.' This began an amazing friendship with a man for whom I have the deepest respect, trust, and admiration. After weeks of long and often heated discussions, we resolved the problem which resulted in Pizza Hut buying out our franchisee. During this entire time, Raul never once asked for anything until it was all over. At that time, he had only one request, stating, 'You have taken out the largest Hispanic franchise from the Pizza Hut system—my request is that you do right by the Hispanic community.' I got Raul's message loud and clear and I was committed like never before."

Reinemund worked closely with NCLR, and after a couple of years, at Raul's invitation, joined the Corporate Board of Advisors. "In the years that followed, we did a lot together as I tried hard to make good on my commitment to do right by the Hispanic community. Over the years, I began to understand more and more what that really meant. When I became President of PepsiCo in 1999, I asked Raul to help me develop a Hispanic Advisory Board for our company and asked him to chair that Board. He agreed and we began another journey to blaze new ground in our company. Over a decade and a half, we developed a deep and meaningful relationship that changed my life. I learned from Raul's principled and caring style how to look at social, racial, and political issues in a very different way. Raul is firm in his unwavering commitment to be an advocate for the Hispanic community and to do that with integrity and thoughtful and logical persuasiveness. He always seems to find a way to make an argument that will result in a win-win rather than a win-lose situation. I have had the privilege during my professional life of learning from several wise leaders. Raul is one of those people who has changed my life."

A witness of Yzaguirre's pioneer work in developing institutions, Rick Bela comments, "Raul affected social political change through the formation of institutions. That was very important to him. He was committed to learning how American institutions worked and how they affected change in America's public policies. His leadership in the reinvention of *la raza* as an American socio-economic institution will be his primary legacy. More than any other leader I know in our generation of Chicano activists, Raul achieved the mission and dreams of our generation."

Roberto Reveles describes Yzaguirre's leadership skills as a unique "ability to organize on a mega scale, responding to reality yet having the courage of a visionary." In Reveles's opinion, Yzaguirre grew the presence of Latinos through NCLR to a national audience. NCLR's growing strength as an institution, over the years, reflected his determination to build something of substance, something that would endure in spite of America's turbulent political climate, creating a new identity for Latinos who often felt fragmented from mainstream America. "We had to understand who we were," Yzaguirre reflects. "We had to know what our power was, and how to use that power to affect change for our communities. We had to take hold of the reins of where we were going."

THE ARTISTIC TAPESTRY

Institutions build rapport with the media, and part of this includes showcasing the arts, music, film, literature and culture. Conscious of this, Yzaguirre turned his attention to something he had failed to recognize. It took him a while to understand the deep significance of the arts as a way to form identity and explore cultural themes, but once he grasped their importance, he advanced with gusto to fulfill another legacy: his love affair with the arts. "Arts and culture define who we were, what we are now, and who we can be.

We can only achieve what we can conceive. The arts enable us to conceive a more meaningful life."

Echoing his theme, fellow activist, Ronnie Lopez, adds, "I never paid attention to the arts as Raul did. If I had to do it over again, I would use the arts as a tapestry of social change. Arts are a way to sustain our culture and values, and Latino artists are as much a part of the American tapestry as anyone else."

Beginning with NCLR's sponsorship of Moctesuma Esparza's dynamic film, *The Ballad of Gregorio Cortez*, followed by Esparza's production of the original screenplay for *The Milagro Beanfield War*, directed by Robert Redford, NCLR turned a corner in establishing itself as an advocate for the arts. These were among the first English-language, Latino-themed, and widely distributed films in U.S. history. In 2004, NCLR launched SíTV, the nation's first English-language, Hispanic-themed cable and satellite television channel. By 1994, NCLR released *Out of the Picture*, which depicted negative prime-time portrayals of Latinos, and a severe lack of Latino artists in films and television. By 1995, FOX aired NCLR's Bravo Awards, one of Yzaguirre's personal projects, honoring talented Latino artists of music, film and television, which would later be named the ALMA Awards. Latino stars, too numerous to name have walked on stage at the ALMA Awards. Among a long list of artists who have been honored are: Anthony Quinn, Ricardo Montalbán, Edward James Olmos, Salma Hayek, Antonio Banderas, Christina Aguilera, Cheech Marin, Lupe Ontiveros, Penélope Cruz, Paul Rodriguez, Selena, Carlos Santana, George Lopez, and Eva Longoria.

"We needed to find ways to create our own media that gave our folks the right role models. One of the biggest problems was a negative self-concept we've derived from watching TV and movies which portray us negatively, and we internalize that image. Media advocacy was needed. We did some studies and found out Latinos were least visible in prime time. We were portrayed less than any other group, and when present, we were negatively portrayed more than any other group in the nation. I didn't see myself necessarily being a role model directly in this. What I saw myself doing was causing things to happen. I created the ALMA Awards putting in process a system that began to look at the media. I became active in the National Hispanic Media Coalition and the National Association of Latino Independent Producers. NCLR helped them get started. We also helped Moctesuma Esparza and his empire get started. Moctesuma shared my passion for the media. I wanted to influence the systems used by the media, as opposed to being a practitioner or going on the road and giving speeches, which I feel comfortable doing, but I got more bang out of my efforts if I created the institutions and if I could get the processes going."

"Together, we created the National Hispanic Media Coalition," Esparza says. "Raul was willing to get together with Alex Nogales and myself to continue a boycott of networks that misrepresented people of color or excluded them entirely. Many of these ideas were incubated in the Encuentros where NCLR members and others would meet with our *padrinos*, Raul and Henry Cisneros."

In another effort to build up Latino arts in the U.S., Yzaguirre joined forces with past associates from OEO to begin the complex process of investigating and drawing Latino entrepreneurs, artists, and art lovers from all over the nation to begin the tedious and time-consuming process of building a national Latino museum.

"I created a task force for the Smithsonian Institute and wrote a report called "Willful Neglect." Emily McKay wrote it, but I gave her all the substance. She followed my ideas very closely. The report was the basis for a congressional law that created a commission to study the feasibility of a Latino museum—the American Latino Museum. That's what I do best. I start with an idea, and get it off the ground, but after that I turn it over to others. I was the chairman of the committee. It was hard to get the report done. It had to be factual to get folks interested in it, and it had to have a sense of longevity, so they would follow up on the report and know it could be done. We concluded that there was neglect of our community and recommended the creation of a Latino museum."

"Congressman Xavier Becerra of California got a law passed through Congress, creating a commission to study the need for a Latino museum. The commission was supposed to be in existence for two years. Later, the commission's advisory committee was chaired by a prominent activist and businessman from San Antonio, Henry Muñoz. The commission came up with a report and we began to raise funds. 175 million dollars were needed and the community had to raise at least a third of it. It's a work in progress, but I'm very optimistic about it, that the vision we presented with the task force in the beginning is taking shape. Finally, we are going to have a way of capturing our own history and presenting our art and the role models of our community to the American public."

On May 5, 2011, the National Museum of the American Latino Commission submitted its final report to Congress and to President Barack Obama. Once built, the Smithsonian American Latino Museum will be the 20th museum erected along the prestigious National Mall complex.

BRUSHES WITH GOLIATH

Leading NCLR's upward climb as an American institution, Yzaguirre often finds that he is at odds with U.S. presidents. One such face-off occurs on April 27, 1994 at a town hall meeting in Arkansas with President Bill Clinton. In a show of solidarity with Latinos, President Clinton asks Yzaguirre to come up on the stage and join him as he signs the Educational Excellence for Hispanic Americans Executive Order. It's a proud moment, and many there will never forget it. Raul, Jr., recalls it as one of the proudest moments of his life, watching his dad shake hands with the president of the United States. "The president asked me to come on stage, and gave me the pen he used to sign the order," Yzaguirre says.

It doesn't take long for Yzaguirre to realize that the Executive Order, although signed amid "pomp and circumstance," will remain, for the most part, one that has no teeth and no real power to initiate change. Federal agencies are not complying with the Order's demand for reports on how their agency is addressing the educational needs of Latino students. Resigning in 1996 during his second term as Chair of the Commission on Education, Yzaguirre cites lack of implementation of the Order as the reason. He then turns his attention to building NCLR's educational agenda—one that will effectively document the needs of America's growing Latino student population.

But his run-ins with President Clinton are not yet over. Responding in 1995 via satellite at one of NCLR's annual conferences, the president is hardly amused when Yzaguirre asks him a "hard ball" question. "I guess the misunderstanding was that the White House accepted soft ball questions, and I had a hard ball question. I brought up the fact that he had not appointed Hispanics in positions of leadership in the White House and Executive Branch. What are you going to do about these appointments? I asked him. The administration was very annoyed by that tough question in front of the convention. Our relationship cooled for a while, and the next year, the president refused to speak at our annual conference."

The Council's switch to state-driven, grassroots efforts clashes in 1996 with Clinton's decision to sign the Personal Responsibility and Work Opportunity Reconciliation Act (PRWORA) also referred to as the Welfare Reform Law (Act). Signed by the president on August 22, 1996, its goal was to change the way welfare had been traditionally administered, eliminating dependency on the system. The law gave states the responsibility of deciding how to administer federal and state funds for an array of public services, which included temporary cash assistance to needy families (AFDC) and health insurance (Medicaid). It increased funding for child care, created a block grant for the care of children of low-income families, and enforced federal and state regulations for collection of child support. However, the law also imposed a citizenship requirement for many benefits, while reducing funding for food stamps, social security income, and child nutrition programs.

"We didn't oppose the Welfare Reform Law," Yzaguirre explains. "We opposed parts of it along with many of the technical changes it proposed. But we supported the goal of keeping welfare available to those who needed the services. The fact that the law denied benefits to newly arrived immigrants and allowed funding only to refugees or those seeking asylum became a source of great concern. So our stance was a bit complicated. We had to move to do advocacy at the state level where decisions were being made on how federal and state funds would be spent."

Drafted during President George H.W. Bush's administration, but actually revised and signed into law in 1993 during President Clinton's administration, the North American Free Trade Agreement (NAFTA) leads Yzaguirre down another controversial path, one that will cause a stir among the nation's Latinos, and disappointment for NCLR's support of NAFTA in the first place.

"Mexico had a closed economy and was unable to compete effectively with the world market." Yzaguirre explains. "NAFTA established rules of engagement between Canada, Mexico and the U.S. Mexico was getting deeper into debt, and had no choice but to join in the effort. Once Mexico decided to open its doors to the competition, it meant that a certain sector of Mexico's economy could not compete and that was subsistence living—the corn crop. All of a sudden it was costing more to produce the corn in small plots, than to put it into the larger labor stream. The process was ongoing before NAFTA, but NAFTA accelerated it and there were requirements that brought many Mexican farmers to ruin. Misery would have come but it would have taken longer without NAFTA. NAFTA and competition with Asian outsourcing brought on more problems. Investments and the world bank that was promised were never implemented, and we had to re-evaluate our position."

In July 1996, Roberto Rodriguez wrote an article in *Hispanic Magazine*, encouraging Latinos to attend a national forum in Washington D.C. on October 12, Día de la Raza, to march against anti-Latino legislation. Yzaguirre attended, but not in his official role as CEO of NCLR. Instead, he spoke on his own personal views of NAFTA. Protestors supported open borders and were against NAFTA. "I spoke as an individual that day, but still aligned with NCLR's position. We were concerned about how NAFTA was being implemented, and wanted to see fair labor laws and trade established that didn't cause undue suffering to Mexico's poor. Controversy continues to this day over how NAFTA was implemented, and new agreements are pending."

Open borders, backed up by NCLR, brings on new opposition from the administration of George W. Bush, as he takes office in 2001, amid growing unrest along America's border with Mexico.

"The president I had most dialogue with on a personal level was George W. Bush, the younger. Because he was Governor of Texas, I got to visit him there and we talked a lot. He visited one of the schools named after me in Texas, a charter school in 1998. After he got elected, and before he took office, he asked some fifteen or so Latino leaders, all Republicans, except me, to come meet and dialogue with him in Austin, Texas. Then he turns to me and says, 'Why don't you start out the conversation.' So, I took off and started telling them of the importance of Latinos in fulfilling what democracy is all about in America. We've been here for centuries and still many consider us foreigners, and that has to stop. We've contributed to America at every level, and we needed his presidential administration to give us places of influence and power so we could move forward, and continue to affect change for the better. I explained that we weren't divided, we were one group, under the banner, Latinos, and there were over fifty million of us, and counting. We were now in the big leagues, and we were not afraid to take on leadership positions. That's only the beginning of what I said."

In spite of his relationship with George W. Bush, and his on-going dialogue with him, NCLR's federal funds were cut, as the Council pressed forward, resisting the Patriot Act, and state laws that gave power to local police to act as federal immigration officers. NCLR opposed the "Secure Fence Act of 2006," brought about by George W.'s administration, one of hundreds of legislative acts that La Raza would solidly oppose over the years. The Act authorized over 700 miles of fencing along Mexico's border with the U.S. Pressing forward for a comprehensive immigration law, NCLR, over the years, has tackled numerous civil rights issues through its Policy Analysis Center, never backing down in advocating for millions of Latinos forced to live under unfair laws and blatant discriminatory policies.

In 2010, President Barack Obama nominated Raul Yzaguirre as U.S. Ambassador to the Dominican Republic, although NCLR had named him the "Deporter-in-Chief" of immigrants, surpassing previous presidents. NCLR continues to call for accountability for immigrants separated from their families, and has stood for the DREAM Act and immigration policies that bring families together and create a pathway for citizenship. President Obama, in the midst of great Congressional opposition, and nationwide controversy, has pledged anew his support of comprehensive immigration. "The road is a long one," Yzaguirre says, "but we must stay the course. We must live up to America's promise for all generations—indeed, we are a nation of immigrants."

SERVANT LEADERSHIP

"Raul's management style was unusual at all levels," says Charles Kamasaki. "He gave you as much rope as you needed to hang yourself, or move ahead. He didn't micro-manage. Some criticized him for being too loose, too tolerant at times, but he was wonderful to work with, and more persistent than anyone else I've ever known. He didn't interfere in the day-to-day judgments we had to make."

Armed with skills set in stone since his high school days by Ms. Laura Pollard, on how to confront problems as a debater, how to think things through in a logical manner, and reared by his father, Rubén Yzaguirre, who helped him see through the mesh of twisted truths, to find real answers, Yzaguirre learned to thrive on challenges and confrontation, under the lash of his age-old adversary—chaos. He wanted staff members who were not afraid to voice their opinions, and could think "outside the box." Kamasaki was a prime example of someone who took Yzaguirre to task, questioning his important decisions and making him see his own views through the lens of his opponents.

"Charles Kamasaki kept things together," Yzaguirre says. "Besides playing devil's advocate he would remind me when we needed to recognize someone for good work, or if someone was having problems. Helen Coronado did the same, and both helped me understand things I might not have been aware of."

Yzaguirre believes that founding institutions attracts leaders of all shapes, sizes and colors who are often prompted by chance, a volatile situation, passion and commitment to become leaders. His childhood vision of a *cacique*, or knight in shining armor riding to the rescue was replaced over the years, by a "roll-up-your-sleeves" mentality of leadership. "My friend and mentor, John Gardner, was a tower of intellectual strength, organizing structures and ideas in response to psychological percepts. On the other hand, Bill Clinton was a doer, putting his ideas on the line, risking rejection. Their styles were different, but they were both effective leaders. The most important thing for me was having a vision and a sense of what we needed. It's important to diagnose a situation. We did not have institutions early on to make us strong, so I started to think what our institutions would look like. We needed to have a constitution, mobilize folks, and we needed the capacity to frame our issues.

To oppose something is not enough; you have to offer solutions. I carried away the lesson that you have to let people define their goals and let them help you lead. Sometimes being a leader simply means being a servant. You articulate a vision of what can be or what should be and if it's real enough, you convince people it's attainable and you move forward. One thing that disappoints me is that although protests, marches and strategies have been used by Latino leaders to effect change, for the most part, our people don't complain. That is, they often don't voice their complaints to legislators and others in authority—that's changing and I hope the momentum continues."

Following Yzaguirre's lead in anchoring the Council as a lasting institution, NCLR created a new component, the Office of Institutional Development in 1990 led by Emily Gantz McKay. Charles Kamasaki was in charge of the Office of Research, Advocacy and Legislation at the time, while Dr. René F. Cardenas headed the office of Technical Assistance and Constituency Support, and Norma Y. López took charge of the Office of Development and Special Events. Yzaguirre's enthusiastic style of leadership was "contagious," as described by many staff members. Naming him the top nonprofit Latino CEO in the nation, Emily McKay, herself, blossomed into a dynamic leader who propelled the Council forward. "Emily matched my own workaholic style," Yzaguirre says. "She set the pace, for me and Charles, getting important reports written in a way that made us the national 'think tank' everybody depended on."

"All my staff had access to me, so it was fair," Yzaguirre says. "Also, if a person came in and asked me to do something that involved other NCLR units, I could not undercut their supervisors. It was their responsibility to inform the others that a decision had been made or was being discussed. Transparency was important, not only to know my decisions but the reasoning behind them."

"Five goals that were very important were: (1) financial security; (2) critical mass of resources; (3) clarity of purpose and mission; (4) clear understanding of our constituency; and (5) clarity of Board functions procedures, accountability and stability. Larger organizations die because they are not accountable to their community. We turned over two or three Board members a year to bring in some new blood. Genders were equally represented. It was a complicated formula, but it worked."

"We made sure our affiliates had a seat or seats on our Board. We needed people who helped with policies, people who understood the movement, people who understand organizations, people who helped find money, and our constituency had to feel a sense of ownership. This put us into a complicated selection process for our Board. Our relationship with our affiliates has been good over the years. There tends to be no competition among affiliates or if there is, it is rare. Our problem with affiliates is that we are pushing them to be more active in advocacy. Lots of times we are dealing with children in our communities, students, their educational needs and their safety. We worry about service delivery, but we have to be a change institution and take on school boards. We have to look at school board elections, and get Latinos elected to make a difference in school districts. We have to push our affiliates to do advocacy for our communities and not just service delivery. And we have to remain non-partisan."

"Every three years the NCLR Board went on a retreat, and every year, the staff had an annual retreat besides the yearly conference open to everyone. We looked at ourselves critically at the retreats, "Yzaguirre relates. "We zeroed in on things we needed to develop to more capacity."

One of the staff's complaints about Yzaguirre was that he didn't give compliments easily. Over the years, he says he's learned how to look at the achievements of others and recognize their worth. "I guess it didn't matter to me if someone complimented me on what I was doing, but that didn't fit everyone else. Over the years, I've learned to compliment the efforts of others."

"We pioneered advocacy and lobbying, and we used that term. I was a registered lobbyist for the organization. And having the think tank for policy analysis and capacity with our constituency behind us helped. We knew what we were doing, we had our technicians on board as well. We could prepare an analysis on time. So we went from being invisible to being very visible and assertive."

Amassing a huge following of mentees over the years, Yzaguirre's energetic ways of managing the affairs of a complex institution, led many to build life-long careers that would create new organizations and more opportunities for millions of Latinos. "Raul was instrumental in helping others engage in leadership on behalf of the Latino community," Ramon Murguia relates. "Two individuals that I know benefitted immensely from their connection with him were my sister, Janet Murguia. and Tony Salazar. Janet is now the President and CEO of NCLR. She was able to interact with Raul in Washington D.C. on various advocacy issues when she worked for the Clinton White House. She was impressed with Raul's commitment to community and strength of character. Having the opportunity to serve with him on the NCLR staff was tremendous training for her. Tony Salazar was a former Board Chair for NCLR. He too learned so much from Raul and went on to accomplish great things in the field of community development."

In reflecting on her boss' influence on her life, Helen Coronado remarks, "Raul changed my life in many different ways. Through NCLR I met many dignitaries and politicians who opened my eyes to a whole new world. Raul also renewed and invigorated my commitment to the Hispanic community."

Cecilia Muñoz firmly echoes Helen Coronado's views, noting Yzaguirre as one who can say no as easily as yes, when the stakes are high for NCLR. "In a town full of leaders who start with good intentions but are often knocked off course by the necessity to secure funding or influence, or the attractions of their own personal visibility, Raul never lost sight of what it was all for. This gave him the capacity to make good decisions—to say no when it mattered—even when it cost him or the institution. He will be remembered as a trailblazer, and an institution builder. His career spans a time in our country's history in which we were invisible outside of the Southwest, Miami and New York and we became not only highly visible but a potent force shaping the country's future. There are a host of organizations that owe their existence to his work."

"People like Raul, every day, they think community," Danny Ortega relates in describing the type of leadership exemplified by Yzaguirre in evolving his plan for building institutions. "His humility, at times, kept him in the background, but at the end of the day, all his work and influence ended up in our living rooms. Issues on immigration, education, health, tax reform, everything that counted—Raul didn't turn away from any of it. His style was to face things head-on. Raul's influence in our lives helped mold our communities. He created a model of leadership for others to follow, and taught me that to lift others, is to lift up the community."

NCLR's fame as the largest constituency-based advocate for Latinos in U.S. history, became a reality through Yzaguirre's leadership, the hard work of his staff and the dedication of numerous affiliate directors who saw in him the promise of an enduring vision. America's Latinos are a viable force in our nation. They are history makers, institutions builders, and inventors of a new future.

"Institution building is a way to anoint new leaders, to give them credibility," Yzaguirre explains. "If you don't have institutions you can't develop effective leaders. We need to know where we want to be as a community and how we will get there. Institutions inspire up-and-coming leaders to say, yes, I want to buy into that."

In 2008, NCLR celebrated its 40th anniversary, a year-long celebration beginning in March with the official grand opening of the Raul Yzaguirre Building and dedication of the new Plaza de los Afiliados. NCLR's headquarters in D.C. is only a few blocks away from the White House, at 1126 16th St. NW and stands as a living memorial to the man who Cecilia Muñoz aptly describes as a builder of institutions. "Raul has played a huge role in shaping who we are as Latinos, and what we contribute to the nation we love. Because of his work, we have strong institutions that provide opportunity and assistance to those in need, and strong leaders in communities all across the country who are linked in a common purpose on critical issues that affect us all, like immigration reform, education, health care, and economic issues. His contributions are extraordinary."

FROM HIS INITIAL ELECTION IN 1974 as President and CEO of NCLR, Yzaguirre emerged as a national success, something he could have never dreamed possible. His words caught the attention of every major newspaper and media source in the nation and abroad, both in English and Spanish. He was followed around routinely by reporters and photographers expecting a word from him, or perhaps an interview. His name became synonymous with what it meant to be a powerful Latino in America. Yzaguirre now looked to many more years of leadership at NCLR, but life would speak a louder, more vicious verdict over him—something unmerciful and unrelenting. The chaos he had contended with for so long had a mind of its own. Lurking in the shadows, it waited, planning its next move. Everything he thought he had would be up for grabs as, unbeknownst to him, he positioned himself to face the darkest time in his life. This time, chaos would strike and not let go, nor would it be persuaded to leave. This time, above all others, would reveal his character, the inner heart of the boy that still beat strong and sure—the beloved grandson of Gavino and Elisa Morin.

24

THE PACKAGE

Once when arriving at Dulles Airport, I felt as if I was an inanimate package. I represented NCLR. When people saw me, they saw the organization. Some people couldn't see past the Parkinson's and saw me only as incapacitated.

—Raul Yzaguirre

FROM OUT OF CHAOS

T'S 2001, AND YZAGUIRRE FACES A DEADLY DIAGNOSIS from his doctors. It's one that will stop him in his tracks, for it must be dealt with. There have been signs that are unclear at first. Then more symptoms appear that some doctors felt might be stress related, or might be tied to a dysfunction of neck muscles. But it turns out to be much more than that. "It started in 1999 with the thumb on my right hand twitching. I went to a neurosurgeon and he did a couple of MRIs and concluded that I had ruptured vertebrae in my neck. He said surgery would be my best option, but just prior to the surgery my doctor referred me to a neurologist and he gave me the diagnosis that I had Parkinson's disease."

Initially, doctors thought Yzaguirre's symptoms were part of Lyme disease, contracted by a tick bite he suffered, perhaps during a camping trip. Lyme disease symptoms often resemble the signs of Parkinson's—a disease of the nervous system, beginning with joint pain, fatigue, loss of coordination, sleeplessness, depression and problems with speech. But if it's Parkinson's a slow, steady devastation will continue in the body as the brain loses its ability to control muscles and the body becomes a prison for a mind that can still reason and understand, but cannot respond in speech or writing.

"A person's muscles begin to atrophy," Yzaguirre explains. "The mind stays clear but the body doesn't respond. It's an auto-immune disease affecting the brain's neurotransmitters. The brain's transmitters are being killed off and it takes a complicated chemical and hormonal treatment to help mitigate the process. The immediate response is lack of emotions and the worst prospect is becoming a vegetable before you die. A person goes through a process first of denial—maybe a mistake was made in the diagnosis, then the person starts grabbing at straws. The second phase is 'Why me oh, God,' a sense of despair and self-pity. The third phase is anger at what's happening, and the fourth phase is acceptance. All along the way there's always hope that something miraculous will happen. Over time, I became more sensitive to people's feelings and limitations. Now I understand how to look at my abilities and not my disabilities."

The whole process awakens Yzaguirre to a new person; someone he didn't expect would come to life. It's his life-long adversary—chaos—now standing by, grizzly in appearance, arrogant and cruel, extending one last wave, one last goodbye to the man Raul used to be—as it creates him anew in the grip of its own distorted madness. Now chaos occupies his body. It's not a problem he can handle in the external world—this is personal. Little by little, he experiences problems with coordination as he struggles with the ever-present tremors—Parkinson's trademark. Then he loses control of his speech and his ability to write. Slowly, the disease takes over his entire body, and is only subdued by medications that rob him of alertness and play on his tired mind, threatening even the stability of his own soul. His vigor and power, his ability to work fifteen hour days, to address tens of thousands at an annual conference, to travel non-stop coast to coast, to sit beside presidents and legislators working out policy issues, and do all the complex things that once defined him, in his mind, as the "NCLR package," a commanding image as one of the nation's most influential Latino leaders, is now distorted and off-kilter.

"As the CEO of NCLR I needed to project a healthy, upbeat personality. I felt I would be limited in my ability to do that. I was worried about being a distraction. People's opinions are often based on how you look and act, before they even hear you speak. I was used to speaking before a large audience, but with Parkinson's I didn't know if I would start trembling in the middle of the speech. If I took a pill, I could lower that risk, but the medication made my mouth so dry, I couldn't speak."

Lisa Navarette, recalls the time they kidded Yzaguirre at the airport about being the NCLR package, as they made plans for one of his numerous trips. "We'll just send you on the road like a UPS package someone said and Raul thought that was funny. He had a dry humor that made us all feel comfortable even in the worst situations."

Sensing the Parkinson's advancing, Yzaguirre relates, "Being president of an organization like NCLR imposes many obligations. I had to attend numerous meetings and events; every day was intense and filled with things to do. I had to testify before Congress, and was often interviewed by numerous news media. You lose control of your life at that level, and become in some ways an inanimate object. Once when arriving at Dulles Airport, I felt as if I was an inanimate package. I represented NCLR. When people saw me, they saw the organization. Some people couldn't see past the Parkinson's and saw me only as incapacitated. Even those who knew me got focused on my disability, more than our conversation. Empathy was there and caring, but I felt I could not be the NCLR package anymore, they needed vigor, power and strength."

Bewildered and frightened by the diagnosis, the Yzaguirre family stood by, watching, praying and giving him support. His oldest living aunt, Guillermina "Mina" Morin, wife of his late uncle, Pedro Morin, relates the hardships experienced and overcome by her nephew in the racially segregated community of San Juan, and now as he faced Parkinson's, his courage remained just as strong. "*Es un gran orgullo para nuestra familia.* (He has brought honor to our family). *Con todos sus problemas físicos, siempre es muy valiente.* (In spite of all his physical problems, he remains a valiant man.)

Raul, Jr. recalls trying to discuss his father's diagnosis when he first found out about it, and recounts a telephone conversation in which he questioned his father, trying to find out exactly what the diagnosis meant, and was stopped abruptly by his father's insistence that it wasn't life threatening, "Here, talk to your mother," his father said casually, handing the phone to Audrey. As the symptoms of the disease have progressed, Yzaguirre, admits the tremors have taken their toll on his body and his speech is for the most part, inarticulate. Medications and recent treatments for Parkinson's have helped to subdue the tremors, and his mind remains clear.

Little by little, led by Raul's courage, uncomplaining stance, and his ability to make light at times of his condition, things begin to ease up. "He doesn't try to hide it," his friend, Hilario Diaz from South Texas relates. "He told me at an event in Texas that he might start slurring a little bit, but that's the way it was."

"I didn't want my family or friends to treat me differently. We still own five acres in Maryland, and I wanted to stay busy, taking care of the lawn and everything that went with it as I've always tried to do—being a family man. Audrey nags me, but in a good way. She wants me to take my meds and eat healthy foods. I even accept help now when I need it, like on a train ride from New York to D.C. I had to carry two suitcases upstairs. Someone asked if I needed help and I accepted their offer. There's an urgency to my life now. I don't know how much time I have left, but I want to stay involved in life. I'd like to see places I've been too busy to visit. A thought keeps reoccurring in my mind that there is one more, big project I must do, like the New America Alliance that Henry Cisneros and I founded. When I visited the organization eight years later, President Clinton had also been invited to speak at their conference. They had contributed one million dollars in dues to charity. So the idea took root. You don't understand how important something is until after the fact. I believe there is one more, big project I must do. One more big ride."

Part of the "big project," Yzaguirre envisioned is the establishment of the Raul Yzaguirre Annual Symposium in 2008, now an established yearly event at the Muhammad Ali Parkinson's Center at the Barrow Neurological Institute at St. Joseph's Hospital Medical Center in Phoenix. The symposium is now the largest gathering of Spanish speakers in the nation who convene to learn the latest information on Parkinson's disease, and ways to keep healthy in body, mind and spirit. "We want to give Hispanics the opportunity to find answers for PD related questions they might have, inform them about resources available in the community and let them know that they are not alone in their fight against Parkinson's," says Claudia Martinez, Outreach Coordinator for the Center.

Working with Yzaguirre since his high school days, Alex Perilla recalls *el jefe's* passionate response to the Latino community, even as Parkinson's took its toll on him. Attending an NCLR conference in Miami, he remembers when Senator Hillary Clinton, an invited speaker at the event, offered Yzaguirre a memorable gift. "Hillary Clinton gave him a painting by a Cuban artist with the inscription, *Keep beating the drums for our community*." I thought it was an appropriate way to describe what he was doing. He brought our community together. His legacy lacks the popular appeal that some leaders have, but it is just as solid. It's not an easily packaged legacy and part of this is because Raul is a modest man, and not one who seeks personal recognition."

Feeling frustrated at times around his boss, Perilla confesses he couldn't put his finger on exactly why he felt that way, until he identified what was going on inside him. "I was near Raul almost daily, but I wasn't sure what our relationship was until I heard Jay Leno talk about Johnny Carson. He said, 'Johnny and I aren't friends, he's a legend, I'm not.' That was my relationship with Raul. He was on another sphere, far ahead of all of us."

Legends like Carson and Yzaguirre aren't created overnight—it's a lifelong process. So often it takes an adversary to create the hero we know and love. Raul's war-bitten adversary, chaos, served a genuine purpose in his life.

It tested him through warring years of blood, sweat and tears, and somewhere along the line, the "package" chaos had sought to destroy, became a legend, and chaos was vanquished.

SMOOTH TRANSITION

At headquarters, the NCLR staff takes a closer look at the ominous signs—they will soon lose their CEO, the handwriting's on the wall. By the time of his retirement in 2004, the symptoms of Parkinson's are prevalent. Staff and thousands of affiliate members are beginning to accept the inevitable, but are still worried. The thought of losing an icon, a man of passion and vision is more than many can endure. Confusion, despair and a sense of wanting to keep him at all costs, begins another wave of anguish among staff members. There is no way Yzaguirre will want to stay at the helm of NCLR, of this, they are sure. But the thought of turning over La Raza to someone else, after thirty years of his leadership, brings questions, long discussions and anxiety of what it will all mean for an organization that rests on his shoulders. Some cannot bear to think of someone else taking over, and go into denial—perhaps something will happen and he'll get better. But as the days go by, nothing changes and Yzaguirre's robust energy is compromised by the devastating symptoms.

"Parkinson's full regiment of meds slowed him down mentally," says Charles Kamasaki, describing his boss's slow decline. "He didn't feel as lively. The tremors could be controlled by meds, and he could walk more easily, but when he wanted to be sharp mentally, he stretched out the meds, and this slowed down his speech, and the tremors got worse."

It was a no-win situation. By the end of Yzaguirre's thirty-year tenure, the number of NCLR affiliates had increased from 15 to 300 service providers, making NCLR the largest constituency-based Latino organization in the nation, impacting the lives of millions of Latinos yearly. Now, for the replacement. Who would be able to follow that kind of success? Names came up as staff members discussed various leaders, and began to critically think about who could continue Yzaguirre's work.

"I met Janet Murguia through her brother, Ramon, who was on our Board," Yzaguirre recalls. "Ramon's an attorney from Kansas City, a very decent human being and dedicated activist. He's on the board of major national philanthropic foundations and works to advance important causes. The Murguia's are a big family and they are all involved in the community in one way or another. Janet worked on the Hill with a congressman from Kansas. Eventually she made it to the White House to work on legislative affairs during Clinton's administration. This was also during the time she began serving as a member of the NCLR Board. We had the opportunity to work together on important issues before we knew that someday she would take over. She also went on the election campaign for Al Gore. Later she worked as a chancellor for the University of Kansas. When I decided to leave, we formed a search committee, and asked her to apply and she was elected my successor. The selection committee then formulated a plan to hire her as executive vice-president and after a year I would resign and she would apply for the job as President and CEO, and she would get it. That's the way it happened."

"Raul was careful about his role during the selection of a new CEO," Lisa Navarette recalls. "Clearly, the selection committee came to the final decision. Raul didn't share that Janet was his choice. He didn't want to disrupt the process by anointing a successor."

Reflecting on the transition that caused a stir among the Council's vast membership, Charles Kamasaki relates, "Janet was an excellent choice. She reinforced quite remarkably, the enduring institution Raul had worked so hard to establish. By the standards of the world, the transition from Raul to Janet was a smooth one. While other nonprofits went through various CEO's, NCLR had a lot of continuity in its senior leadership because of Raul."

As a high school student, Janet Murguia recalls catching her first glimpse of Washington, D.C. through her participation in Girls' State, not realizing that one day she would return to play a major role in the nation's capital. "Every year, the American Legion Auxiliary chose fifty girls from every state to learn how state government worked. I was chosen from Kansas, and participated in trips to our state capitol where we were introduced to legislators and got to see the Kansas state government in action. From Girls' State, two girls, per state, were chosen to become part of Girls' Nation. I was chosen as one of the hundred girls and went on a trip to D.C. to learn how our federal government worked including Congress, the Senate, and government agencies. I shadowed Stuart Eizenstat, head of the Domestic Policy Office during Carter's administration. This experience opened my eyes to the various roles that support the functioning of our government. As I shadowed Stuart, I got to see how the White House worked, and all around it, how the many platforms, entities and agencies served to influence important government outcomes. This was a real eye opener for me. Later, I ended up working near Stuart Eizenstat's office when I worked for the Clinton administration. This experience made me a believer in internship programs for youth that allow them a similar experience, and through NCLR I have advocated for these programs nationwide."

Fully aware of the struggles Latinos faced in attaining the American Dream, Janet Murguia, an outstanding student and budding community activist, did not spare herself as she made her way through the University of Kansas, earning a BS degree in Journalism (1982), a BA degree in Spanish (1982), and a JD degree (1985) from the School of Law. Her high intellect, abounding energy and passion quickly brought her to the attention of former Kansas Congressman Jim Slattery. Working as Slattery's legislative counsel in D.C. brought her into the heart of U.S. politics. Attracting the attention of President Clinton's administration, Murguia served at the White House as his deputy assistant from 1994 to 2000, adding her expertise on Latino issues. Earning the trust and respect of those around her, she also served as deputy director of legislative affairs, taking a hand in managing legislative staff and acting as a senior White House liaison to Congress. Stepping into the spotlight of political campaigning, Murguia led the Gore/Lieberman 2000 ticket as deputy campaign manager and director of constituency outreach. In 2001, she found herself back at her alma mater, now in the position as Executive Vice Chancellor for University Relations.

Initially meeting Yzaguirre through events she attended as part of her brother, Ramon's, work with NCLR's Board, Murguia's first impression of the man she would succeed was one that led her to form a positive and open relationship with him. "I saw him as intelligent, astute, a strong person and very gracious." Later, she was to describe one of the most valuable lessons she learned from Yzaguirre's management style. "I learned how important it is to listen and get the views of everyone at the table. Let everyone show their perspectives first, before making a decision. Raul didn't think he had all the answers; he could step back and listen. He never felt he had to fill the silence with words. Around him, you learned to tolerate silence. It was a very important lesson for me."

Not realizing that Yzaguirre was used to battling chaos, Murguia was to learn another lesson, and one that would demonstrate Yzaguirre's cool composure under pressure. "Early on in my term as CEO. Raul and I were at an NCLR conference in Philadelphia, and we were to join a group of locals at a park. They had plans to renovate the park as part of a community project. Suddenly two busloads of protestors showed up with signs, drums and loud chanting against one of the city council members. The media came out in force, and the scene became chaotic. I looked at Raul and said, "I'm sorry this is happening." I felt myself getting more anxious by the minute, but Raul sat on a bench with a big smile. 'This is great!' he said. 'If people have issues this is a democracy and they have the right to air out their grievances.' I learned a lesson that day, that I shouldn't be afraid of conflict. Letting people voice their concerns is part of getting to the solution. If discord is resisted, and things are too repressed, that probably means we're not getting to the root of the problem."

Unanimously elected in 2004 by the NCLR Board as President and CEO of La Raza, Murguia realized the importance of what she would undertake. "I am honored and humbled that the Board of Directors has selected me to succeed a man for whom I have the utmost respect, admiration and affection. I look forward to building on his great legacy in the years to come as we continue the critically important work of NCLR." On reflecting further on the characteristics she shared with Yzaguirre, she relates, "One thing Raul and I brought to NCLR is that we both leaned into our best values. We both put NCLR and the interests of our community first. When someone steps away from an organization they have served for so long, there can be tension, even if both are working for a smooth transition. But Raul did something very different, he knew how important it is not to look back, not to be a fixture. And how important it is to allow unencumbered time for a new leader to make his or her own mark on the organization, and allow for a good start. Emotionally, these are hard things to do. Raul's values were really important, and his sense of duty to the community was always above his own interests. Some organizations might shut down when someone like Raul leaves, but he was determined that the institution would last long after he was no longer CEO, and that has become a reality. NCLR has continued to successfully serve Latinos with great staying power."

For his part, Yzaguirre felt the choice was a step in the right direction. "She is the kind of leader we need working with us, not only for the future of the organization, but also for the future of the Latino community."

Former Board Chair, José Villareal commented, "We are fortunate to have such a dynamic and respected Latina leader as Janet Murguia. Her experience, passion for excellence, and long history of commitment in addressing issues of our community will help us ensure NCLR's continued growth and progress."

HOLDING THE REINS OF POWER

Murguia's leadership has increased NCLR's participation in issues vital to the nation's 50 million, plus Latinos. Her voice and charisma lead the way in immigration, education, health care, women's issues, housing, civil rights, and against the rhetoric of hate crimes aimed at Latino communities. Her interest in voting rights inspired NCLR's collaboration with other community groups in efforts to register nearly 200,000 Latino voters for the 2008 presidential election. Always conscious of her sister organizations, LULAC, NAACP, Urban League, MALDEF, and many others, she presses forward, cultivating close collaborations. Partnering with other nonprofits, NCLR helped more than 1.5 million eligible immigrants apply for citizenship. Commenting on NCLR's work, President Obama applauded the Council's extraordinary work on behalf of Latinos, in spite of criticism leveled at him by La Raza, as they demanded that he use his executive authority to secure comprehensive immigration reform.

"As Executive Director for nine months, before officially becoming CEO, I went on a listening tour," Murguia says. "It was important to address NCLR's relationship with its affiliate network. I heard from affiliates, listening to the strengths and weaknesses they identified. I listened to the Corporate Board of Advisors to understand how they viewed NCLR and how they felt we could do better. Programs and funders were changing. We had charter schools with sound curriculums, but there was a shift beginning from charter schools to other ways to strengthen education. Housing counseling that led to home ownership was identified as important, along with civic engagement, voter mobilization, citizenship and naturalization issues and NCLR's leadership in working for comprehensive immigration legislation. Communication was viewed as highly important. How did we communicate to the nation who we were? How did we tell our story? Branding NCLR with its own distinct logo would make our involvement with other organizations stronger. There were different components of NCLR using different logos, and not all the components realized they were part of NCLR. We needed to know the interconnections between the components, and through a branding process emerge with strong priorities and moving together in the same direction as NCLR."

The choice was an excellent match for NCLR. Murguia's leadership has turned a new corner, attracting an assortment of high-level Latino leaders and students engaged in the dynamics of searching out the American Dream. Twice selected as one of *Washingtonian* magazine's "100 Most Powerful Women in Washington," she has been featured in every major news media, and selected as one of *Hispanic Business* magazine's "100 Most Influential Hispanics." Murguia has garnered a long list of accolades and distinctions mirroring Yzaguirre's own illustrious career. "She reflects a new era for the Council," Danny Ortega relates in describing Murguia's work at the helm of NCLR. "Her leadership is different from Raul's, but it's just as effective."

BY THE TIME HE GETS TO PHOENIX

By the time Raul Yzaguirre gets to Phoenix in 2004, the entire NCLR family is waiting for him. Phoenix in June isn't a place people normally visit. The heat is stifling, the sun relentless and temperatures rise over 100 degrees by noon; but it's the birthplace of NCLR when it was the Southwest Council of La Raza and had its headquarters in the old Luhrs Building. Phoenix is the only place, albeit the heat, that makes a fitting location for Yzaguirre to say farewell to those he has loved so well over the years—the NCLR family.

The 2004 conference agenda is packed as usual with presenters, performances, workshops, meetings, luncheons, dinners, and everywhere the rush and excitement of over 23,000 attendees, the largest audience yet in attendance. Senator John McCain (R-AZ) is the keynote speaker, and Senator John Kerry (D-MA) is scheduled to lead a Town Hall. But the huge crowd has gathered for one specific reason in particular—to bid farewell to Raul Yzaguirre, to honor him and pay tribute to what it has meant to have him as their leader for three decades. Attendees know what to expect; there will be an official public exchange of power from Raul Yzaguirre to Janet Murguia.

On statements shared in NCLR's 2004 Annual Report, Janet Murguia reflects, "I was fortunate to serve on NCLR's Board of Directors for a year and a half before being offered a tremendous opportunity to serve as Executive Director. This experience has offered me the unique opportunity to watch and learn from an icon in the Hispanic community, an individual who has dedicated his entire life to service. Through his leadership and resolve, Raul has built NCLR into one of the most respected Hispanic organizations in the country."

Reflecting on Yzaguirre's determination to continue firm alliances with NCLR affiliates she comments. "In my role as President and CEO, my highest priority is to work on strengthening the relationship NCLR has with its affiliates. It is important for us to reassess and reevaluate that relationship and make sure we are doing everything we can to strengthen that bond, allowing for a more profound impact in the community."

Monica Lozano, 2004 Board Chair, joined in expressing her thoughts on the importance of the family at the conference. "We have dedicated our 2004 Annual Report in celebration of 'La Familia.' The NCLR family extends beyond our offices—from our dedicated staff to our affiliate partners and the communities they serve, to our generous funders, and ultimately to every Hispanic in our nation."

Echoing her words, Murguia's support of what NCLR is all about—a family—something Yzaguirre readily identifies with—reveals her own passionate desire to raise up the cultural and ethnic pride Latinos feel about family. "We need to let everyone know that America's most cherished values—family, a strong work ethic, sacrifice, faith and patriotism are the same ones that my family and millions of other Hispanic families have passed down from generation to generation."

In considering Yzaguirre's own dedication to family, Murguia credits Audrey for her steadfast allegiance to her husband's career. "Audrey demonstrated incredible support over the years, unselfishly contributing to Raul's mission, and to NCLR. She survived great challenges, as when Raul faced reduced salaries to keep NCLR going, and she helped by working and making do with what they had. Perhaps, if she had not been such a strong source of support, Raul's work with NCLR might have faced even greater challenges. Although remaining in the background, Audrey has been instrumental in supporting NCLR, and is a great part of Raul's success story."

Yzaguirre's words in the 2004 Annual Report leave no doubt that his confidence for NCLR's future success rests on his successor. "Janet Murguia will continue to break new ground, as she did in her previous positions on Capitol Hill, at the White House, and at the University of Kansas, and will serve as a tremendous example to young Latinos and Latinas. I believe that, while building upon NCLR's solid foundations, she will make her own mark in continuing the critically important work of the institution."

Considering NCLR's progress under his leadership, Yzaguirre comments, "NCLR increased its net worth by $6.6 million, including contributions to the Capital Campaign and on a consolidated basis we increased our net worth by close to $17 million. Our total assets now amount to about $100 million and our net worth is approximately $80 million."

In his comments at the conference, Yzaguirre acknowledged the hard work of NCLR staff, and the leaders who served on the Board and "worked above and beyond the call of duty" as crucial to La Raza's success. In particular he mentioned Ed Pastor, Rita DiMartino, Gil Vasquez and Irma Flores Gonzalez for steering the Board through treacherous waters. He pointed to former Board Chairs Ramon Murguia, "an unassuming, courageous leader who gave generously of his time," and José Villareal "who sought above all, the financial stability of NCLR," as two examples, among many, of loyalty and dedication to NCLR's purpose and goals.

In further written reflections, Yzaguirre thanked the Corporate Board of Advisors (CBA) for their dedication in building up the Hispanic community. And finally, he expressed his gratitude to NCLR affiliates "for the work they do for our people. They are the lifeblood of the community, working on the frontlines to secure a more humane and just society. I have been motivated since the age of fifteen by the dream of creating an institution that would have the power to make a difference for our community. At last this is a reality."

LOVE BATH IN 2004

Poised and ready on stage, Yzaguirre approaches the eager crowd at the Phoenix Convention Center in the midst of explosive applause at the sight of him at the podium. His thoughts are clear on the magnitude of what is about to happen. The institution he has labored so hard to build will pass on to other hands. Ending his long tenure is made easier by the thought that NCLR's new leader is capable, talented, passionate and ready to assume all responsibilities. She's a perfect fit.

Yzaguirre's talk is about to make history. It is an extraordinary, heartfelt and eloquent speech that will be cherished by thousands and go down in American history as one of the clearest declarations of what America's Latinos are all about.

His speech "The Values We Live By," is divided into five sections: (1) Thank you Phoenix; (2) Our Shared History; (3) Our Shared Beliefs; (4) Our Shared Future; and (5) Conclusion.

Yzaguirre's a master orator, skilled in debate and in presenting facts and arguments since his high school days, trained by Ms. Laura Pollard, who left no stone unturned in getting the Valley kid, captain of the debate team, to learn how to express his inmost thoughts in a way that would not only be clear, concise and logical, but would profoundly touch his listeners. All who have had the privilege of listening to Yzaguirre's speeches over the years, make the same comments—he is a most profound and unique orator, unmatched in his ability to clearly communicate his ideas.

The entire Yzaguirre family is present, anticipating with great excitement the last speech Raul will deliver as outgoing President and CEO of NCLR. "It was extremely emotional," Alma Yzaguirre recalls. "His words sent chills down my back. He touched every heart in the place. In spite of the Parkinson's, and many other negative things my brother has faced through the years, there's always been a silver lining waiting around the corner for him."

Longtime Arizona LULAC member and community activist, Frank Barrios, poignantly describes Yzaguirre's skills as an orator. "There are very few people that I elevate to the status of a hero, and Raul Yzaguirre, hands-down, is one of them. He is one in a million, a speaker who can get on his feet and weave ideas together, flawlessly, making marvelous statements that would take ordinary people hours to write down. The things Raul states so eloquently, other speakers could never improve on—they are perfect just the way he says them."

A hush falls on the vast crowd filling the Phoenix Convention Center as Yzaguirre begins his opening statements. They know him. They know that every word he will say is meant especially for them…and his words will live on, long after the conference is over. He holds the audience in the palm of his hand as he begins.

"We chose to bring our Annual Conference to Phoenix for the first time not only because the Convention Bureau promised us 70 degree weather in June, but also, more importantly, because this is our birthplace. When the Southwest Council of La Raza opened its doors for business in 1968, our Board of Directors chose Phoenix as our headquarters. Since then, in good times and in bad, we have had a continuous presence in this great city. It feels good to be home."

And with this opening, Yzaguirre begins his own manifesto, an unforgettable sharing of history, beliefs and values that describe the creation of a vibrant, vivacious and powerful people within a great nation: America's Latinos.

"For Latinos, it is not the color of one's skin that determines a person's worth, it is the quality of his or her values, culture, ethics and manners. For ours is a welcoming and inclusive culture that is ever open to enrichment."

Strengthening his enthusiastic listeners, he challenges, "You and I love this country warts and all. The true patriot accepts the truth about his or her country and loves it enough to work to make it as close to perfection as possible. Therefore, the slogan, should not be 'America, love it or leave it.' It should be: 'America, love it, fix it, or lose it.'"

Yzaguirre takes his time and presents beliefs that are part of his own personal credo. Among them is one that is like a firecracker shot into the air, a burst of energy striking the ceiling at the convention center: "We believe in a nation where people are judged by their actions, not by their accents." Continuing in the same distinctive voice he adds. "We believe that civil rights are the birthright of all Americans and not the exclusive domain of any one group. Justice does not mean 'just us.'"

In sharing his vision of the future he affirms. "Hispanics believe in the American dream, and we want to make it real for *all* Americans We have an unshakeable faith that this nation's best days are yet to come. We have a deep conviction that this nation will continue to come ever closer to the ideal society, which others have labeled that 'shining city on the hill.'"

Not forgetting the words his grandmother, Elisa "Licha" Morin drummed into his head as a child, he states. "And my favorite one from my grandmother, *lo cortés no quita lo valiente*, being courteous and having good manners signify strength and sound character, and should never be confused with weakness."

His reasons for staying 30 years at NCLR are crystal clear to him. His wish to be remembered as an institution builder, were all part of the plan. "In accepting this job I did promise one thing. I pledged that I would stay for as long as it took for the National Council of La Raza to become an institution that would make a significant difference in the lives of our community. It's taken a little longer than five years, but I hope you will agree that I have kept my end of the bargain."

Looking out at the packed convention center, Yzaguirre sees tears and smiles everywhere, and then he observes people rising to their feet in a standing ovation. He ends his talk with these words: "I am a very fortunate man. I have had the singular honor of fighting for our people for half a century. I have been blessed with a loving and supportive family. I have followed my passion as an advocate for my community. These things have given meaning to my life, and for that I am eternally grateful. Gracias, y que viva La Raza Cósmica!"

The applause is thunderous. The sense is one of being bathed in love, everyone, at the same time, bathed in a rich flow of exhilarating energy. Here is, *el jefe*, the father figure who has risked so much for all of them, saying goodbye, and they don't know how to let him go. "I thanked them over and over again, and bowed, and exited to left stage, and still the clapping went on. They wouldn't stop clapping. I had to come out four times. I had no idea it would be like this. It was very emotional for me. Tears were shed by so many—and by me. I looked out at them, as if they were all my children. I felt their love, and I know they felt mine. We didn't want to let each other go."

"He went full circle," Murguia relates, describing the emotional farewell. "I believe that it was in Phoenix at the conference that it dawned on him that he was really stepping down. Phoenix was the birthplace of NCLR, so it was fitting that his term as CEO should end there. His sacrifices for his community can never be counted; there have been too many. The emotion and gratitude that flowed from everyone in attendance filled the convention center. Raul's legacy is that he built NCLR into a strong American institution with staying power. He is a pioneer and trailblazer. He put our community on the map, and made us visible, a once neglected, but very impactful segment of American society is now highly visible and moving forward."

The 2004 NCLR Conference went on as scheduled for the rest of the day, but everyone who was there that day to witness Yzaguirre's farewell address had somehow been changed. Love has a way of doing that. More than an embrace, it is part of the work leaders, like Raul Yzaguirre do. Love reaches between thoughts and jostling for positions, making sense of all the things that occupy the daily grind of being a leader and bearing the responsibility of an institution that is built to last, one that will make a difference, and in Yzaguirre's own words, "Leave the world a better place."

THEIR ICON HAD TURNED OVER THE REINS of power and now he was able to leave the stage at the Phoenix Convention Center, but there was still the world stage, and this one, he would not exit—legends never leave us, they live on in the memories we keep. Ronnie Lopez best captures Raul's meteorite rise to national acclaim. "Raul personifies the best of our community. He accepted all his awards in the name of the real champions, our nanas, tatas, moms and dads, and so many others—humble people we must never forget. Raul is the DNA of our community. He lived community day in and day out. His life story is really about all of us."

25

KEEP BEATING THE DRUMS

Raul changed the perception of how we {Latinos} see ourselves. We are not second-class citizens. We can achieve anything in this country.

—Jorge Ramos

WHY THE DRUMS MUST BEAT

THE DRUMMING IS HYPNOTIC. Long into the night it communicates to the band of Mexica warriors—that they will be victorious, the battle is theirs, the gods have declared it so. The sound of their drums travels for several miles, awakening fear in their enemies who also beat their drums, as they answer the voices of the Mexica drums. Why should the gods favor you? Why should you be victorious, heaven is for us too...but it is to no avail. The drums argue back and forth until sunrise, and as Tonatiuh rises, a bright white globe in the eastern sky, the drums stop. Then they start again, this time, with urgency. The drums will now go into battle, their voices will rage on both sides, until the battle is won.

Communication by drums had its own deep, sonorous language to share among Native tribes throughout the Americas. But how has that communication changed for their descendants centuries later in the modern world? What about the billions of Latinos scattered throughout every continent on earth—*la raza cósmica*, people of the fifth sun—living in earth's final age? Claims of bloodlines spring up for them in the midst of corporate meetings, legislative sessions, schools and community centers—secret pathways open before the modern descendants of the Native tribes, unknown twists and turns in a journey that's taken them far away from where they began, a race of emperors and builders of splendid cities, oppressed by one conqueror or another.

Now it's time to beat the drums again, and this time for life-giving necessities, not for the worship of Tonatiuh, but to build up a world community, to make things matter in a world that often forgets that family is the core of our existence. The stability of our communities depends on how we communicate our love, faith and hope, and how we teach our sons and daughters to interpret the modern-day drums...a world of global voices speaking at the same time through sophisticated technical machines, and the voices must be answered and the people, the Latinos, must remain one.

The inscription on the painting by the Cuban artist, *Keep beating the drums for our community*, presented to Yzaguirre by Hillary Clinton, took on human form. Yzaguirre always knew, above all other things, that *la raza* had to remain one, and NCLR had to remain a pan-Latino institution open to all Latino ethnicities, and to others throughout the world who seek justice and an end to hostility based on skin color and racial differences.

The world stage was set for Yzaguirre. NCLR was in the hands of someone he trusted, but there were other tasks ahead of him that would increase his stature, creating his legacy as a global leader. The drums had to go on beating day and night, not for the sake of one tribe, but for everyone.

THE RIGHTEOUS PATH

It's November 8, 2004, and Yzaguirre is again facing a huge audience, this time in Chicago, Illinois. It's the annual conference of the Independent Sector, and he is about to receive the John W. Gardner Leadership Award. Before the event, he's surprised to find that his acceptance speech keeps changing, even as he writes it. The focus becomes Christian values.

"I am proud of the speech given when I won the John Gardner Leadership Award. Elections had just been held in the U.S., an election based on Christian values. I had a speech which was pretty much what you would expect, telling of John Gardner's leadership and how much he influenced my life. At a conference in D.C. before the event, I found everyone talking about Christian values, and how they would determine the election to be held on November 2. So, I went back to my hotel room and got out the Gideon Bible and started looking up chapters for my speech. The main one was 'Give unto Cesar what is Cesar's and unto the Lord what is the Lord's.' Those words guided my speech. The $10,000 dollar prize that went along with the award, I gave away to charity."

The memory of John Gardner's ability to bring together groups with differing goals and agendas to form working coalitions, and Yzaguirre's own insistence that our moral values in America must be worked out in a secular environment, rather than one dictated by one religious principle, begins to draw from him a speech that will become another manifesto, "The Righteous Path."

"Secular government is the only liberating way to enjoy liberty," Yzaguirre says, declaring his solid stance on separation of Church and State. "Black leaders have had their religious institutions over the years, and they helped in the civil rights struggle, but Hispanics could never count on the Catholic Church. Maybe that worked out for the best. We had to form our own institutions, and this turned out to be nonprofits that would create the leaders we needed."

"The Catholic Church said, just have kids," says Ronnie Lopez. "When I was growing up, they didn't worry about us socially or how we were doing politically. There was little concern for social injustice, the role of women in society; the list is a long one. The Church was silent on walkouts and protests. Back then, many of us were still treating ourselves as if we were immigrants, instead of American citizens."

Grappling with moral values brought up in the campaign rhetoric of George W. Bush and his Democratic contender, John Kerry, Yzaguirre is able to decipher, step-by-step, where America is in confronting right wing religious zealots who believe that their brand of religion is the one that should guide our entire nation.

In his acceptance speech, he writes: "How do we reconcile a government that proclaims on its official currency 'In God We Trust' and which begins each legislative session with a prayer from a government-paid chaplain; a nation that requires children in public schools to pledge allegiance to a nation 'under God'? How do we square these realities with our Constitution, which prohibits the establishment or support of religion in any form? In case we have forgotten our civics lesson on the Bill of Rights, let us recall those resounding words in our Constitution: 'Congress shall make no law respecting the establishment of religion, or prohibiting the free exercise thereof.'"

"History tells that the earlier version of the establishment clause was written by two of our founding fathers, Madison and Jefferson, who passed a similar law in Virginia. Jefferson wrote that the clause was meant to set 'a wall of separation between Church and State.' Well, folks, that wall is showing some disrepair lately; some holes have been poked in the wall, and the holes are likely to get bigger. The irony is that the separation of Church and State was articulated by Jesus himself. Recall your Bible readings about the time when the enemies of Jesus were trying to trap him into speaking against Rome. Jesus was clear and unequivocal. Allow me to quote the New Testament in

Luke, Chapter 20: verse 25: 'And Jesus said unto them, Render therefore unto Caesar the things which are Caesar's and unto God the things which belong to God.' Yet, in Jesus' name, there are those who believe that God has told them, through a network of ministers and priests, who to vote for. I would venture to say that most Americans understand the establishment clause as a way of protecting religion from the State. But I assert that the greater concern is in the protection of the State from religion, for theocracies are the proven enemies of liberty and freedom."

Naming his four pillars of faith and moral values, he lists: (1) Separation of Church and State; (2) Tolerance for the "other"; (3) Social justice and good works; and (4) Love of God and love of others. He bares his conscience by going a step further and confronting his own demons and contradictions. "I have a confession to make. I—and perhaps others—have not been very tolerant of those among us who are intolerant. Indeed, in moments of weakness and with feelings of moral superiority, I have stereotyped the 'gun-toting,' 'gay-bashing,' 'Dixie flag-waving' folks – those folks that I view as intolerant, ignorant rednecks or worse. And, undoubtedly, they view some of us as the amoral liberal elite who espouse libertine and un-American values. Although others may articulate their values differently, I believe that my values are shared values—in other words, 'moral values' are not the sole domain of Christians. For me these values emanate from my religious upbringing, but I dare say that something akin to these values resides in the hearts of decent Americans everywhere who are nonbelievers. The religious right has labeled itself the 'moral majority.' I guess that makes the rest of us the 'immoral minority.' But what is immoral about that segment of America who cares about poor people, who worries about the environment, who is deeply troubled about passing on a crushing national debt to our children and our grandchildren, who feels the pain of the loss of life in a war which is based, at best, on questionable legality and discredited intelligence? Are these not moral values?"

Yzaguirre's questions raise age-old debates about the right and wrong of holding over someone else's head personal beliefs that, if not adhered to, make the "other" an enemy. He ends his talk with a plea for the common ground, a theme fundamental to the work of John Gardner. "Let us enter the fray of this great debate strengthened by intellectual and moral principles that are unassailable, and let us be humble and respectful enough to listen to the other side. Let us assume that we do not have all the answers, and maybe others will come to believe that they do not have a monopoly on truth and righteousness. That is the American way. This is the righteous path."

Breaking into wild applause, the conference attendees of the Independent Sector, touched by Yzaguirre's words, commented during the conference, that his speech would have made John Gardner proud—a fitting tribute to their founder's memory and Yzaguirre's own desire to make a lasting difference in the things that mattered most in America.

EDUCATION ON HIS MIND

By the end of 2004, Dr. Michael Crow, President of Arizona State University, is in search of an executive director for the Center for Community Development and Civil Rights (CDCR) at the New American University in downtown Phoenix. Meeting Yzaguirre over the years, he's been impressed by his knowledge of the community, his remarkable leadership skills, the high-profile people he attracts, and his ability to successfully collaborate with national organizations, using his influence to strengthen local and national groups in their efforts to innovate programs and back up legislation that will benefit the community.

Dr. Crow takes his time to listen to the advice of notable community leaders as he makes up his mind. Yzaguirre's name keeps coming up as the number one candidate who can serve as the first executive director of the Center and build a bridge between university resources and community needs. Part of the job description also includes serving as a professor of practice in ASU's College of Public Programs and also serving on the Board of the North American Center of Transborder Studies (NACTS), which engages university professionals in educational and business-related endeavors with an emphasis on incorporating North American content into college and university courses. The Center's focus will be one of implementing projects on community development, civil rights, leadership, education, media, and one of Yzaguirre's favorite subjects, the mentoring of young Latino males. Dr. Crow is certain he has the right man in his sights. Then Governor of Arizona, Janet Napolitano, a staunch believer in Yzaguirre's commitment and dedication to the community also expressed approval of President Crow's choice.

"ASU is one of the premier metropolitan public research universities in the nation," relates Crow in an ASU press release. "Raul's innovative thinking and strong connections with state and national Hispanic assemblies will continue to promote efforts and create numerous opportunities for collaboration."

Among those assisting President Crow in confirming the best candidate to head the CDCR is a group of influential local leaders among them, Nancy Jordan ASU's associate vice president of community development in the Office of Public Affairs; Tommy Espinoza, CEO and President of Raza

Development Fund; Roberto Reveles, Founder of Somos America and past Board President of the American Civil Liberties Union of Arizona (ACLU); and Erlinda Tórres, former President and CEO of the Arizona Latino/a Arts and Cultural Center (ALAC).

"Raul has the expertise to help establish ASU as the nexus of dialogue for Latino community development professionals, policy actors and academic experts," says Nancy Jordan upon Yzaguirre's appointment as executive director. She notes the importance of developing strong alliances with the Hispanic community that will prompt innovative ways to establish new working relationships. "Raul provides the leadership we need to achieve this."

Yzaguirre is notified of their decision and travels to Phoenix for a final interview. This is where, according to Tommy Espinoza, Yzaguirre's true colors show up. Always a humble man, he doesn't realize that his name alone speaks volumes to the community. His expertise and servant leadership have been tested to perfection over the years, inspiring awe in President Crow, who is somewhat surprised when he comes face to face with the other side of Yzaguirre.

"Raul never made any money from NCLR," says Espinoza. "It only makes sense to line up a contract and negotiate the terms of your retirement before you retire. You have to take care of yourself and your family, and spiritually get yourself together. Retirement is a huge loss, like a death or a divorce. Raul did nothing to secure himself after retirement. He wasn't going to cut a deal. He was still the same guy who wouldn't pay himself in the early years of NCLR, until his staff was paid."

"We set up a meeting with Raul and President Crow to discuss the new Center. 'We'd like to bring you on to head the Center for Community Development and Civil Rights,' the president said to him. Raul looked at him, and asked, 'What are my responsibilities? Will I be teaching classes?' The president told him he could do that if he wanted to, and once again Raul asked, 'What are my responsibilities?' President Crow explained if he brought in top leaders to interact with students that would be part of it, and any other ideas he had on how to reach the community and strengthen higher education for Hispanics would also be notable. But, once again, Raul asked about his responsibilities. At the end of the day, Raul wanted to deliver. He wasn't power hungry. To say the least, he didn't sell himself very well," Espinoza explains, humorously.

Erlinda Tórres, serving as Yzaguirre's assistant upon his arrival in Phoenix, relates that working with higher education for Latinos was a perfect fit for him, as one of his greatest concerns has always been education. Roberto

Reveles saw Yzaguirre's position as executive director of the Center as a prime opportunity to make some critical changes and stop the negative "pipe line" that often occurred for young Latino males who got caught up in the criminal justice system and ended up serving time in prison.

Yzaguirre's life as an advocate for education had begun at age 16 when he had confronted the PSJA School District with 500 signatures, citing a District law that made a preschool possible with only 50 signatures. His goal was to end the segregation of early learners on the premise that they didn't speak fluent English. Of course, he lost his case, only to renew his commitment under President Johnson's administration with formation of the Head Start Program. "Lack of preschool exposure is often a predictor of poor success in school," Yzaguirre relates. "The pipe line to higher education begins early. Even though there are many Latino students in the top percentile of their high school graduating class, it has been observed that many of them will not complete four-year programs of study. There are many factors, including lack of money, and need to work, lack of guidance at the high school level, ignorance of the world of higher education, and parents who do not know how to help their children get through the system. Tests have to be unbiased, and that has been a huge battle at all levels—elementary through college. High teacher expectations have to be in place. Teachers have to believe all students can learn. At the Center, we did several studies to focus on what good schools did to establish students' success, and how those models could be widely implemented. I decided to focus on parent training and on how to help young Latino males who experienced a much higher drop-out rate than their female counterparts. Our focus at the Center was on getting research done by our collaborators and filtering it through a clearing house, then to civil rights forums. We would then invite community leaders like Reverend Al Sharpton, Linda Chavez, Juan Williams, Johnny Echo Hawk, Congressman Ed Pastor, senators, legislators, corporate leaders and many more for panels and symposiums. The list was quite inclusive."

Sharing Yzaguirre's concern for the educational success of Latinos, Dr. Hector F. Aldape, a fellow Texan, launched a program in 2004 that addressed the whole family in the development of successful students who would pursue a higher education. "I first met Raul at his Washington D.C. offices the year I accepted my position with the Raul Yzaguirre Policy Center. The first thing I noticed about him was his intelligence. I noticed he always provided his opinions in a data-based manner that made logical sense."

Dr. Aldape recalled the movie *Braveheart*, upon meeting Yzaguirre, and relates that like the great Scottish warrior, William Wallace, a disappointment to those he met who expected to see a god-like hero, an enormous warrior who had killed thousands, and instead saw a man who looked like one of them, likewise, Yzaguirre, unassuming in appearance, hid his own bravery, courage and intelligence. Seeing Yzaguirre at an event, walking behind popular political figures, Aldape recalls, "Raul Yzaguirre was walking behind them, and very few knew who he was. He didn't need the spotlight, but he got things done. Raul has taught me to give back to the community. Education is the answer. We have to prepare the next generation for leadership."

Traveling through Texas with Yzaguirre as he sought influential members for the Advisory Council for the Raul Yzaguirre Policy Institute to be housed at the University of Texas-Pan American in the Rio Grande Valley, Aldape was amazed at the illustrious figures Yzaguirre's name attracted. "Even though the Yzaguirre Policy Institute did not move forward over the years, it inspired me to continue my work at my own institution, Abriendo Puertas, in Edinburg that focuses on families and creating an environment for learning." Including a chapter on Yzaguirre in his 2006 dissertation for his doctorate in education, Aldape concluded that the most important issue facing Hispanic parents in the educational process, was to learn how to be participants in their own education and that of their children.

By 2009, Yzaguirre's own focus on parent training reaps national attention, and the American Dream Academy, (ADA) one of the CDCR's most successful programs, wins the regional C. Peter Magrath University Community Award and becomes a finalist for the national award. "This award recognized an extraordinary partnership with ASU and the Phoenix K-12 educational community," Yzaguirre relates. "The program relied on collaboration with area school districts, as well as community leaders and community service organizations to operate and be successful.

The American Dream Academy has been founded with one goal in mind—to empower parents in low-income areas to understand how to help their students achieve success in the educational system. Parents of K-12 students receive a nine-week training program that improves a child's educational environment—at school and at home. The program's focus is on retention, graduation, and academic success. The long-range goal is to reduce high school drop-outs, and ensure a pathway for success to a college or university.

By the 2010-2011 school year, according to a newsletter issued by the CDCR, the American Dream Academy had worked with 19,500 students with 16,203 having graduated from the ADA training program from 239 schools. Over 40,000 students had, by then, been impacted by involvement with ADA, which meant that one of every 14 K-12 students in Maricopa County was the child of an ADA parent graduate.

Mentored by great men—his grandfather, Gavino Morin, Dr. Hector P. García, John Gardner and Dr. David Rammage, to name a few, Yzaguirre's determination to give to others the same encouragement and support he received became a reality with the creation of the Young Latino Male Symposium. "The disparity in graduation rates between Hispanic males and females is close to a twenty-five point differential, with males showing the high drop-out rate. It's important to find causation. Why this disparity? We have to have more Hispanics graduating from high school who believe they can obtain a college degree, both males and females. Young Latino males often get caught up in the criminal justice system, and early on start fathering children. This makes for more households with a single parent and no father figure. It works against our values and beliefs, and many times stops the upward climb to higher education."

Aligning himself with dynamic male leaders, both locally and nationally, Yzaguirre readied himself to do business for young men who were hungry for a purpose in life, and might lack direction. One of the first symposiums included participants representing the White House, academia, foundations, the media and community based organizations from across the nation. Joining with ASU faculty and ten graduate students from the Walter Cronkite School of Journalism and Mass Communication, the first three-day symposium was moderated by ASU Carnegie Professor, Rick Rodriguez.

Reflecting on the male figures he knew as a child, Yzaguirre relates, "When I was growing up, we had male figures who were not necessarily violent and who contributed to our identity as strong men or *machos*, without the negative connotation. Over the years, many young men who lack fathers in the home, or other significant male figures, suffer loss of identity and don't recognize who they are as men, nor do they establish meaning and purpose in their lives. Often they take on negative behaviors, thinking that this is the mark of a man, and end up in prison. Prison, in my day was something to be ashamed of, but now, it has become a system of over-criminalization and a highly profitable industry, and in some instances it is a rite of passage for those living marginal lives."

With the American Dream Academy and the Young Male Symposium going strong at ASU's New American University, it would seem Yzaguirre's role as the CDCR's first executive director was a smooth one—the drums were beating for everyone, or so it seemed. But when anyone is thrust into the limelight of public opinion, an old adage, used by President Abraham Lincoln comes to mind—*you can't please all the people all the time.* Unbeknownst to him at the time, Yzaguirre was about to become a target for hate-filled rhetoric and bigots of all colors and political persuasions.

El Jefe at ASU

Controversy is another way to describe activism. The two go hand-in-hand. Sparks begin to fly not too far into Yzaguirre's tenure as director of the CDCR. At times, the sparks fanned themselves into a raging fire. A prominent Phoenix attorney, Ernie Calderón, hailing from the mining town of Morenci, found himself on a front row seat during the hotbed of controversy prompted by Yzaguirre's desire to engage ASU students with national leaders who would challenge their perceptions, principles and beliefs. Attending Northern Arizona University, Calderón earned his B.A. then transferred to the University of Arizona to complete studies for his law degree in 1982. Always an advocate for education, he served on the Board of Regents for ASU, and was one of the first to welcome Yzaguirre to ASU's New American University.

"I worked with him, putting together one of the symposiums, and Raul caught a lot of heat over it. He wanted to bring in Reverend Al Sharpton and the regents went after him. They felt Sharpton was an extremist. Some legislators threatened to cut funding to the program because of Sharpton."

Making up his mind to support Yzaguirre, Calderón held his ground. Backing up Yzaguirre's belief in academic freedom, he battled the Board of Regents on behalf of a leader that he saw as one who "walked the walk." He would do the same when Yzaguirre notified him of his decision to bring Linda Chavez, a proponent of English Only programs, to the New American University campus. Bitterly opposed to her, bilingual educators throughout Maricopa County were infuriated.

"When Raul invited Linda Chavez to speak to the faculty and students, once again there was an outcry, this time from the general public as well," Calderón recalls. "There were segments of the Chicanada who hated her. Many Chicanos called her 'Tía Taco.' Some regents didn't have a problem with Linda, but there were legislators who were determined to cut the Center's funding. I believe the students benefited from all the speakers. They heard contrary views, left-wing and right-wing. Raul was showing the complexion of America, not just one side of the picture. He's a scholar, and by his leadership provided diversity of thought. He had a unique skill in bringing together opposing views that challenged students' thinking and drew new ideas. Raul's a treasure for our community. He helped us to keep talking to one another, and keep the detractors quiet. He's someone who spoke for the powerless in such a way that even their enemies would listen."

Arriving in Phoenix in 2005, Alex Perilla, Yzaguirre's faithful intern from the country of Columbia, joined the staff as Yzaguirre's program assistant at the CDCR. "Nothing could stop Raul," Perilla says. "The Parkinson's didn't stop him from working long days at ASU. He was still energetic, strong as a bull and sharp. He knew the isolation of Latinos didn't work. He wanted to weave interests together. He had a great relationship with his opponents, and knew how to find the common ground."

Standing in the line of fire with *el jefe*, Perilla relates he often saw opponents arm themselves against him. "I received hate mail sent to Raul. They misunderstood him. They thought he was a separatist who was concerned only about Mexican Americans. Others thought he had sold out to corporate America. They thought he was wishy-washy. In my opinion, he's always been a man of ideas. He frustrated people because he was not impeded in his thinking by any obstacles. Rather, he focused on what could be, not in Pollyanna thinking. He was about making the possible, probable. He could dream about something, pour energy into it, and coalese people into doing big projects. It wasn't just being positive, it was more than that. Raul has an extraordinary talent to make things happen, and those who limited their vision had trouble understanding him."

Agreeing with Tommy Espinoza's reflection on Yzaguirre's inability to secure wealth for himself, Perilla adds, "Raul never became a wealthy man. He always looked to the greater interests of the broader community, not of a narrow institution or a self-serving opinion. He liked to help people in business make a lot of money. He knew it would be a benefit for the community, and always kept a high ethical standard. Great organizations cease to be credible when leadership fails from an ethical standpoint. Raul's vision for leadership went beyond being a good leader."

Pat Bonn, Yzaguirre's Executive Assistant, had been working for ASU for five years before *el jefe's* arrival in Phoenix. She was acquainted with ASU procedures and the chain of command. She knew local leaders and community activists, and as a historian was acquainted with the history of the Southwest, but as Yzaguirre's assistant, a whole new world opened up for her. "My first impression of Raul, was that he was very humble and unassuming. He was casual with all of us and enjoyed spending time at lunch telling stories and conversing. His ability to set up ideas in a clear and concise manner was done in a casual format, yet his ideas were expansive and far-reaching. At times his fifteen-minute discussions would turn into months or years of research by NCLR members and others who would put into action his vision-ary plans."

"I soon found out that Raul was sought out by high-profile leaders such as Bill Richardson, Secretary Clinton, senators, and legislators, activists and community leaders of all ethnicities, Mexican presidents, famous athletes, and many more. It wasn't unusual to get a call from the White House from one of President Obama's staffers who wanted to talk to him. Sometimes the phone was ringing off the hook. He took each call, and never complained. He was definitely in touch with the movers and shakers of the nation, and they relied on him for his expert advice on many issues. His network of people was extensive—it spanned the globe."

Sharing Yzaguirre's love of writing, Bonn relates she also shared his opti-mism in the way he viewed Latinos. "He was optimistic, but also a realistic. Raul didn't want to victimize Latinos. He wanted to attack the things that were blocking their progress."

One humorous story she recalls hearing *el jefe* share was the time he was arrested in D.C. for protesting in front of the South African Embassy against apartheid. "He called home to tell his mother, but didn't want her to get upset in case the story of his arrest came out in the news. Instead he told her he was in a protestation event, and his mother thought he had said 'prostitution,' and was alarmed."

Bonn credits Yzaguirre for inspiring her to set new goals in her life. "He encouraged me to pursue my degrees, finish my BA and my masters in my mid-fifties. He gave me confidence and he shared with me that if you limit yourself, you'll meet your own low expectations. He always assumed things could be done, and his ideas inspired me to get things done in my life."

Meeting Yzaguirre in 2006 at the Center, Leticia de la Vara's career in community activism blossomed under his mentorship. The daughter of Jose de la Vara, a criminal defense attorney, and native of Yuma, and Elisa de la Vara, who became the first woman VP for Chicanos Por la Causa, and directed Congressman Ed Pastor's District 7 Office in Phoenix until his retirement in 2007, Leticia had been surrounded by community leaders all her life, but never realized she'd work close to one of America's most influential leaders. Applying for a position at the CDCR, she relates, "At first I was intimated about working with Raul because of his reputation as a national leader. But I found him to be very humble, a quiet man, and very approachable. Once I got over the fact that he's one of our icons, I got to know him, and saw how he mentored many young people. He lived and breathed to lift up others and teach us that we weren't victims—we needed to keep moving forward. He's an intellect by nature and can piece together civil rights in history, but he's also in touch with what's going on now. He's so revered, but you can talk to him about blockbuster movies, pop culture, T.V. and films. Everything seems to interest him. I asked him many questions and was awed by his knowledge of history and complex issues. It's not often you have an icon two doors from your office—but I did!"

Also following in the same family path, Leticia's sister, Delia de la Vara, joined NCLR in 1998 working at one of the Council's regional offices in California. "When I started with NCLR there were 180 affiliates, and it grew to 275 over the years. The affiliates had to be Latino-led and Latino-serving nonprofits. They all had to be 501(c)(3) designated and needed to engage with NCLR. We focused on the best serving Latino organizations, and tried to find quality Latino talent in organizations and corporations."

Delia de la Vara's first introduction to Yzaguirre was when she read about him in a book while a sophomore at the University of Arizona in 1994. "My mom told me to come to Phoenix for a reception for Raul. I was impressed with him. I knew Ronnie Lopez, Ed Pastor and other leaders through my mom, and everyone there had come to greet Raul. There was a who's who of Latino leaders at the event—tons of people. I was shy and was struck by everything. I found there was a connection to the D.C. office from Arizona and other parts of the nation. Later I went to D.C. as an intern, and met an Arizona friend there, Tommy Espinoza. I learned so much. I wanted to be a fly on the wall at meetings. I went to different NCLR meetings and learned from Raul how committed they were to their affiliates. There was a lot of personal engagement with affiliates from Raul and Charles Kamasaki."

Delia's first job as a coordinator put her in close connection with Yzaguirre. "Raul was accessible and highly respected by all. He had command of the issues and was down-to-earth, not distant or elite. Raul has a vision of where our community is going. I had never thought of the word 'vision.' I worked with him during the last five years of his tenure and the word 'vision,' gave me the idea that we should be looking forward to where we are going, learn how to navigate the journey and not be distracted from reaching our goals. More is revealed as we move ahead."

Meeting him at the CDCR, Delia reflects on Yzaguirre's continued concern about education for Latinos, and her own experience with high school counselors who, as in Yzaguirre's life, discouraged her, instead of directing her to higher education. "The counselors at my high school were not supportive of us moving on to higher education. We got little help. I had thought I wanted to be a counselor, but now I know I can touch others' lives by working with NCLR and attracting community activists from the White House, television and the media, people from all over the nation."

Delia de la Vara and her sister, Leticia, shared numerous experiences with famous community activists over the years, although at times, like Yzaguirre's children, they didn't see much of their parents. "We didn't realize that other kids didn't experience what we were going through," Delia recalls. "But even though we were apart at times, we recognized touching moments as a family. At the 2004 NCLR Conference, I remember, Bobby, Raul's son, saying he had come to terms with his father's time away from home. Our parents had also sacrificed for the good of the community. We were fortunate to see them in their roles as leaders."

Cecilia Muñoz vividly remembers a video made for Yzaguirre's 25th year at NCLR. "One of the interviewees was his son, Bobby, who spoke very personally and eloquently of how much it cost him that his dad was on the road so much. He recounted that he would hear his dad talk about everything he was doing and think, 'What about me?' And through tears, Bobby concluded by saying, 'and now I understand that he was doing it for me.'"

A role model in loving his family and serving his community, Leticia de la Vara recalls one of Yzaguirre's mottos—words he often shared with the staff at the CDCR office, "Just do the right thing." The words rang true when opposition and confusion brought conflicts that were hard to resolve. One national leader, Jorge Ramos, journalist and prominent anchor for Noticiero Univision, took Yzaguirre's words to heart. Resisting life's obstacles, he embarked on his own journey to fulfill his destiny in the U.S.

Born in Mexico City in 1958, Ramos suffered poverty and hardships, and eventually made his way to the U.S. on a visa in 1983. A graduate of the Universidad Iberoamericana in Mexico City, he continued his studies in communications in the U.S., earning a Master's Degree in International Studies from the University of Miami. During an interview with Brian Lamb of C-SPAN on the talk show Q & A on July 6, 2010, Ramos identified Raul Yzaguirre as one of three people who had deeply influenced his life, describing him as the "Father of the Latinos."

Considering how el jefe has been seen as a father figure by thousands, Ramos is very close to the truth. A real father nurtures those under his care, and inspires them to greatness. In Ramos's own words: "Raul changed the perception of how we {Latinos} see ourselves. We are not second-class citizens. We can achieve anything in this country."

ON THE WORLD STAGE, Yzaguirre was soon to embark on another "big ride." This one would lead him to an ancient island, Hispaniola, the first European settlement of the Americas, founded by Christopher Columbus in his travels in 1492 and 1493. Spanish conquistadores flourished there for centuries, and this was where Yzaguirre, himself a Basque of northern Spain, would soon find that life on an island divided by racism, war, poverty, international drug cartels and the explosive daily problems of a third world country would thrust him into the center of international politics. He would now journey across the sea with Audrey at his side, to the Dominican Republic—and his job as ambassador there would, in his own words be, "more than I could have ever imagined."

But before he made his lengthy journey abroad, Yzaguirre would again cross paths with then Senator Hillary Clinton, and she would ask a favor of him—something he could not refuse.

The drums were about to start a new rhythm.

26

PRESIDENT'S CHOICE

I understand that your hold of Raul's nomination has been prompted by your concern over implementation of sanctions under the Iran Sanctions Act (ISA). In the meantime, preventing Raul's confirmation from moving forward damages U.S. interests in a critically important region of the world. It is my continuing hope that you {Jon Kyl} will release your hold on Raul Yzaguirre's nomination without further delay.

—Hillary Clinton, Secretary of State

AN OFFER HE COULDN'T REFUSE

AN ELECTRIFYING YEAR IS 2008. It's the year two powerful candidates engage in a struggle for the Democratic nomination for president. Hillary Clinton and Barack Obama are history-makers. Either one in the White House will be a first for the U.S. Millions of American voters are impressed with the idea that perhaps something new and unexpected will suddenly appear: an African American, or a woman may soon occupy the Oval Office—something never seen before.

Having met Yzaguirre in the past, and acutely aware of his power and influence as a Latino leader, Hillary Clinton wastes no time in seeking his endorsement for her bid as the nominee for the Democratic Party. She knows Yzaguirre's been critical of her husband when he was president. The Educational Excellence for Hispanic Americans Executive Order, initiated by President George H.W. Bush, and signed anew by President Clinton in 1994, went nowhere, according to Yzaguirre, and this was troubling to him as millions of Latinos struggled nationwide with an educational system that lacked understanding of their needs as students.

She also knew Yzaguirre had faced-off with her husband during a satellite visit at one of NCLR's conferences, accusing him of not appointing Hispanics for important positions in his administration. This came as an unwelcome surprise for the president and the effect of Yzaguirre's "hard ball," question roused the ire of thousands of Conference attendees. Caught on camera and beaming down on the Conference there was nothing for the president to do but address Yzaguirre's insistent questions. She knew Yzaguirre had also criticized part of the Welfare Reform Law, enacted by her husband, citing concerns on how immigrants would be treated under its rules and sanctions. Then, in 1993 NAFTA, another signatory piece of legislation begun in George H.W. Bush's administration and signed into law by President Clinton, became a bone of contention between the two, once Yzaguirre realized that it would not be implemented as planned.

But let bygones be bygones. Over the years, President Clinton switches gears, and appoints top Latino leaders for influential positions in his administration, including Janet Murguia, whom he appoints as a staff counsel. Time has a way of resolving political differences, and the rise in numbers of Latino voters isn't something the Clintons, or anyone else can long ignore. Joining her husband, wholeheartedly, in his efforts to address numerous issues facing America's Latinos, Senator Clinton, a shrewd politician herself, begins to create a pathway of trust and confidence, forging positive links with the nation's Latinos. One of her plans includes calling Raul Yzaguirre to ask for his help in her campaign. Her hope is that he will accept her offer.

On April 12, 2007, Senator Clinton happily announces that Yzaguirre will join her campaign as her national co-chair, and chair of her Hispanic outreach. "Throughout his life, Raul Yzaguirre has worked tirelessly to expand civil rights and create opportunity for working Americans. I'm delighted that Raul will play a leadership role in this campaign as we reach out to all Americans and ask them to join our effort."

A staunch believer in women leaders, Yzaguirre viewed Hillary Clinton's bid for president as far-reaching, and something long over-due in America. In a news article for the *Arizona Republic* (November 2, 2008), as the election closed in on the candidates, he reflected. "When I agreed to lead Senator Clinton's efforts to attract Latino voters during the presidential primaries, I believed she was the most qualified candidate, in part, because she had built a profound and lasting relationship with our community. Most Latino primary voters agreed in state after state, as Clinton routinely attracted sixty to seventy percent of the Latino vote. Bill and Hillary have long been among the Latino community's greatest advocates."

"In 2008, I was courted by both Senator Clinton and Senator John McCain to endorse them," Yzaguirre recalls. "Though I had a great deal of respect and affection for McCain, my political views were, and are closer to Hillary Clinton's. I agreed to lead her Hispanic campaign."

Understanding the weight upon the nation of a general election that would challenge allegiances between people of color, and Anglos, and cause deep clashes with right-wing White supremacists, Yzaguirre walked a thin line. In contact with both Obama and Clinton throughout the election process, he was always ready to seek common ground. He fortified his efforts in building understanding between warring factions as election day drew near and many who bitterly opposed Obama's election spent millions on publicity to slander his campaign.

In spite of considering Obama "smart and well-intentioned," Yzaguirre worried that he "didn't have a track record with us {Latinos}." As for Senator McCain, whom Yzaguirre regards as a friend, he also saw limitations. "Most Latinos disagree with much of the GOP platform. The Latino community was also disappointed by McCain's shift in recent months to placate his party's extreme right-wing, which many of us view as antagonistic to immigrants and people of color."

Facing the final electoral votes, Hillary Clinton's bid for the nomination came to a close. "When Hillary withdrew from the campaign I called for a meeting of the Clinton and Obama Latino supporters for a unity meeting. We had then Senators Obama and Clinton in attendance along with some two hundred or so leaders at a meeting in Washington D.C. I began the dialogue, and in spite of divisions and concerns, we were able to unite."

In a prophetic comment he reflected, "Like Obama, many of our nation's most successful Hispanic politicians got their start as community activists. I'm convinced there's a future presidential candidate in our midst."

Working with Yzaguirre on Hillary Clinton's campaign, Fabiola Rodriguez-Ciampoli, came to realize the depth of his passion in keeping his word and in charting out far-reaching goals for Clinton's campaign. First meeting him in 1996 in D.C. when she participated for an event of the Democratic National Committee (DNC), the organizing arm of the Democratic Party, she relates, "I was a graduate student and volunteering hours to the Democratic National Committee, and Raul was at the event. I had heard a lot about him from NCLR members. He impressed me as being a humble man, no ego, but one who was also very decisive."

A staff member of House Majority Leader, Dick Gephardt (D-MO), Rodriguez-Ciampoli specialized in immigration issues, and often met with Raul who represented NCLR as a non-partisan member. When she went to Texas as a young lawyer to register voters, she credits Yzaguirre for introducing her to

Latino communities in his home state. "Raul was a roll-up-your-sleeves kind of campaign worker. He spoke to multiple leaders in Latino communities. He was glad he could now be partisan and work openly with Democrats. His tenacity left a huge impression on me. The Parkinson's disease never stopped him. He never thought he was above anyone else because of his position as a leader. He's always been a great mentor and adviser to many."

Arriving in Iowa on a cold winter's day, Fabiola, will never forget how Yzaguirre's determination to solicit votes for Hillary Clinton left her an indelible image of his persistence and resolve. "There was a horrible snow storm and Raul was stuck in the airport for hours. When he finally got to the city, he started walking the neighborhood, knocking on doors and campaigning for Senator Clinton. We were concerned about him, but he just kept going on. His energy and passion were amazing."

Rodriguez-Ciampoli applauds Yzaguirre's work with Latino organizations, both big and small. "He gave them a voice in Congress. Raul put Latinos on the map in terms of policy making. He's been like a father to so many of us and gave us that wake-up call, that demographically, Latinos will one day be the majority and that the future of the U.S. works hand-in-hand with the Latino community, which is why we need educated, empowered Latino leaders."

LIFETIME MEMBER

"I've always been interested in foreign affairs, and wanted to work on foreign policy at NCLR. At first, they didn't want me to do anything with foreign policy, but I told them you have to give me some leeway. I had one staff person working in national affairs in my last years of tenure with NCLR. I was on the Board of the National Democratic Institute [NDI] for a long time, and head of the Pan-American committee. I also worked in South Africa with the African National Congress [ANC], which was the guerilla operation that became outlawed, then became legal again. I went down there for a week and trained their leadership. As part of an international campaign with the NDI, I went to Guatemala, El Salvador and Mexico, but it didn't become a big part of my life at the time. When Madeleine Albright became chairman of the Board I left because I did not like her style. I gave my seat to Arturo Valenzuela who was my boss for a while, and Assistant Secretary of State under Clinton's White House for national security."

"It's a funny situation, the Institute is supposed to foster democratic principles throughout the world. The chairman is democratic, but members are mixed. To work outside the U.S. the Institute gets a core funding amount, then they compete for contract work with the State Department. They do observations of elections, under contract with the State Department, and work to strengthen political and civic organizations. The Institute's goals include promoting citizens' participation in voting and empowering citizens to demand government accountability."

Yzaguirre's interest in foreign relations results in his being selected as a lifetime member of the Council on Foreign Affairs (CFR), an elitist organization of scholars and political movers and shakers, many of them presidents, senators, secretaries of state, business executives, journalists, educators, members of the intelligence and foreign policy community, economists, high-profile leaders and students who study current foreign issues, often writing their views in scholarly articles which reflect the Council's role as a vital resource in understanding foreign policy. The CFR is noncommercial and nonpolitical, and is not a policy-making body. It is bipartisan and open to an array of multicultural ethnicities. It offers fuel for debate on vital issues facing U.S. foreign policy and through the David Rockefeller Studies Program influences presidential administrations and the diplomatic community by making recommendations on foreign policy, testifying before Congress, responding to the media on foreign issues, and publishing scholarly works.

"Becoming a member is an honor," Yzaguirre relates. "It's an individual process, and it's not unusual for a cabinet secretary to be turned down. Meetings and conferences can be held by telephone, and members join in on the conversation throughout the U.S. or abroad. The Council publishes a great bi-monthly journal on foreign affairs, and it is a way of keeping the public informed on what's happening in foreign policy. Members participate in task forces. NAFTA was part of a task force. Sometimes a president will come in and make a speech, and this gets published. Members get plugged into other members of the Council functioning at very high levels. The Council is a think tank on foreign affairs."

"Council members are very influential in foreign policy, and are often asked by the media to render opinions in a nonpartisan manner. They are knowledgeable of factual and technical questions that the public may not be aware of. The way you get chosen, is that you must be solicited by a current member. I was solicited, and a member recommended me. Then I filled out an application, and had to get members to support my nomination. Then, they asked a series of questions related to my knowledge of foreign affairs. They asked what I had done with foreign affairs over the years. I was in the National Democratic Institute, and also part of the African National Congress besides working on immigration issues regarding Mexico and Latin America through NCLR's Policy Analysis Center. So I had a lot of experience there and that helped me, but I had yet to be an ambassador."

Concerned about the under-representation of Latinos on the CFR, Yzaguirre begins his own brand of recruiting. "I was on the membership committee, and helped select who got to be a lifetime member. I called and did a lot of work on identifying potential members. I brought in the head of the Council to explain to potential members what it would mean for them to become members and inspire them to apply. I made a special effort to recruit Latinos and gathered about thirty potential members, but most of them did not apply. I believe there may be one thousand Council members, throughout the whole world, many from the New York and D.C. area, but the proportion of Latinos is very small."

Yzaguirre's interest in international affairs related to Mexico brings him into contact with Mexican presidents, among them Carlos Salinas, Ernesto Zedillo and Vicente Fox. His allegiance to the concept of *ascercamiento* becomes a base for how he will do business as the ambassador to the Dominican Republic.

"*Ascercamiento* was a way to get better acquainted with the Mexican American diaspora in the U.S. and the Mexican government. It's a concept of trying to be mutually supportive of each other. There was lots of interest in *ascercamiento* when I met Carlos Salinas, before he took office as president. He ended up at Harvard while I was still there and we started to correspond through fax machines in the library after he became President of Mexico in 1988. Folks were surprised that the President of Mexico was corresponding with me at Harvard. When he came to Washington, I put together organizations from around the country and we would have a dialogue in D.C. and we asked that he institutionalize the process of creating a unit within his foreign relations ministry. He appointed a whole office and every single Mexican President has maintained a process of staff dedicated solely to improve relations with Mexican Americans in the U.S. It involved the consuls of Mexico, and grew to actually selecting regional representatives, through local consulates."

In 1993, invited by President Salinas to attend an elaborate celebration in Mexico City's presidential palace, Yzaguirre was awarded the Order of the Aztec Eagle, the highest honor that Mexico bestows on a person not a citizen of Mexico. "I was humbled by the award, recognizing that it represented years of engagement with the Mexican diaspora in the U.S. People on both sides of the border had made the work successful," Yzaguirre relates.

Forging ahead to strengthen ties with Spanish speaking countries, Yzaguirre extended an invitation to President Ernesto Zedillo to speak at an NCLR

Conference on July 23, 1997 at the Old Navy Pier in Chicago. Zedillo spoke on electoral reform in Mexico. "He was a big hit," Yzaguirre recalls, "well-received, a very energizing and charismatic leader. He's a wonderful human being, and we're still good friends."

At one point, Yzaguirre challenged President Vicente Fox over the use of terminology related to Mexican immigrants, revealing another layer of concern he would face as ambassador to the Dominican Republic (DR), taking to task the country's often racist and oppressive relationship with immigrants from neighboring Haiti.

"Words are powerful," Yzaguirre relates. "They can build up a community or tear it down." Focusing on the word *amnesty*—defined as an official pardon for those convicted of political offenses, or a reprieve offered to offenders for a specific time as designated by authorities, Yzaguirre insisted that President Fox instead use terms such as: regularization, legalization, normalization, permanence or earned adjustment, instead of "amnesty" which incited the ire of White supremacists. "Illegal aliens is another term that needs to be eliminated. Immigrants are hardworking people who are paying taxes and supporting the American economy. They're creating jobs, not taking them away."

Setting his face like flint against discrimination of immigrants coming from Spanish-speaking countries, Yzaguirre, unknowingly, was preparing himself to take on international immigration issues not very different from those he had faced all his life along the Mexican border in the Rio Grande Valley. The word *ascercamiento* would soon take on global proportions, as Yzaguirre stood on the precipice of another journey, one that would lead him far from the shores of America.

OBAMA'S CHOICE

The President-elect places his hand on one of the most famous Bibles in American history—President Abraham Lincoln's Bible, used at his own inaugural ceremonies. Obama's left hand rests lightly on the Bible's burgundy red velvet cover, the gilt-edged pages within bearing Lincoln's own invisible fingerprints. His wife Michelle and their daughters Malia and Sasha, stand proudly, close by. Chief Justice John Roberts is ready to begin the swearing-in ceremony. The day is traditionally cold, 28°F light winds, and a bright sun. Obama stands on the West Front of the United States Capitol, looking across the National Mall to the Lincoln Memorial in the distance. The crowd of 1.8 million is the largest ever gathered in the history of Washington DC. There's never been such a moment in American history. America's first African

American President is about to be sworn in as the 44th President of the United States, a climactic moment for the world, and only a few short weeks away from the 200th celebration of the birth of America's 16th President on February 12, 1809. Lincoln's renown for leading the nation through the Civil War and enduring overwhelming opposition from slave owners, and in the end losing his life to save the Union, is etched in the minds of all Americans and freedom-loving people in all corners of the globe. Through the Emancipation Proclamation of 1862, he set free Black slaves held in states that seceded from the Union. In the end, the 13th Amendment, adopted by Congress in 1865 would forever ban slavery from the U.S.

No one will ever know what might have been President Lincoln's thoughts at the moment when Barack Obama's hand rests on Lincoln's own personal Bible, and his right hand is raised to recite the famous oath of the office of President of the United States..."I, Barack Hussein Obama do solemnly swear that I will faithfully execute the Office of President of the United States, and will to the best of my ability, preserve, protect and defend the Constitution of the United States. So help me God."

In spite of a rearrangement of words, by Chief Justice Roberts, and a do-over later in his chambers, the oath is accepted, and the crowd bursts into thunderous applause. It will be a moment set into the memory of billions who walked the earth on that day.

"The day Obama was sworn in was like no other I have ever witnessed," Yzaguirre says. "There was this impossible dream that had just been accomplished, a Black man would occupy the Oval Office. America had leaped forward—and for myself and everyone else who witnessed this historic moment, it was something we would never forget. America was living up to its promise, that all are created equal."

It isn't long after the breathtaking ceremony and all the festivities of the inauguration are over that President Obama approaches Yzaguirre with a request. "Right after he was inaugurated, the president asked me if I was interested in any government positions. Nothing really interested me at the time, as I had worked on several commissions and agencies and with many members of Congress over the years, so I thanked him and told him I would think about it. Then someone from his staff called me, and asked me if I would be interested in an ambassadorship. He said I could have my choice of countries that were available. Mexico was my first choice but it wasn't available. Then I thought of El Salvador, but it wasn't available either. Then the Dominican Republic came up. We talked for a while longer, and I told him the Dominican Republic would be a good choice for me. Later, he called back and said the president had signed off on assigning me as ambassador to the Dominican Republic."

Unbeknownst to Yzaguirre at the time, the nomination process would prove to be a grueling, intrusive ordeal, as every aspect of his life would be investigated. "It was very burdensome to go through the nomination process. I had to spend a lot of time, money and energy. As part of my finances, I had to find out and identify all my interests, pension funds, and mutual funds, and that might include a thousand companies, and they wanted to know every one of the companies, how I bought and sold stocks and bonds, etcetera. Just to find out where everything was over my entire lifetime was an enormous task, stocks and bonds bought and sold, everything that I owned, my wife owned, and my kids owned. They wanted to know what contributions I made politically, what contributions my brothers and sisters made and their spouses. Was anyone living abroad? That's how Audrey found out she had a cousin in Australia so they had to investigate him. The process is very intrusive into your personal life. To locate all the boards I had ever been on, hundreds of them, and all the contributions made, I had to hire a CPA to put everything together. The same questions would be asked again in different ways. In the past five years, then past fifteen years, the questions would go on and on. The Senate Foreign Relations Committee had one set of rules and questions, and the State Department had another set of questions and time spans. So it was hell—extremely complicated. Then I had to go to ambassador school for two weeks, then off and on for another two weeks. I had to make a solid commitment."

In his address before the Senate Foreign Relations Committee during confirmation proceedings in March 2010, Yzaguirre noted America's strong links to the DR in business, trade, sports and culture, emphasizing the importance of individual relationships as the most important of these links. He cited the example of Secretary of State Clinton and Dominican President Leonel Fernandez, uniting to help Haiti's earthquake victims.

"Family ties between the United States and the Dominican Republic are another important link connecting our two countries," Yzaguirre stated, making direct reference to the Dominican diaspora in the U.S. "I have heard anecdotal evidence that Dominicans here in the United States under-invest back in their home country. I would like to engage this community to get a sense of what their concerns are, show them the work our mission is doing in the DR, and determine how we can work together to solve problems of mutual concern."

America's pledge to secure regional security in the Caribbean under the goals of the Caribbean Basin Security Initiative (CBSI) was foremost in

Yzaguirre's mind. "One of my primary concerns, if confirmed, will be that of public safety, and the efforts to cooperate with Dominican authorities on anticorruption and counter-narcotics programs." Always, thinking ahead as a civil rights advocate, he stressed his desire, "to advocate for policies that foster economic and social justice," adding, "I want to help the Dominicans improve their education and medical systems to ensure that the poor are not left behind as the Dominican Republic's economy grows."

Always a proponent of human rights, Yzaguirre asserted his desire to work on civil rights issues pertinent to the DR. "If confirmed, I hope to advance a dialogue to address the problems and issues of long-time residents {Haitians} whose immigration status is unresolved." Lastly, Yzaguirre planned to collaborate with NGOs (Non-governmental organizations) as a way to advance economic goals in the DR, citing his long-term relationship with U.S. foundations, and a large network of business and nonprofit organizations.

"Once I was appointed as ambassador, I couldn't have an affiliation with ASU, I couldn't take a leave of absence from my post as ambassador, I would have to resign instead," Yzaguirre recalls. "I couldn't lobby the government for so many years...all this stuff, all this before I got officially nominated. Then I had to do all this again with the Senate Committee once I was nominated. I had to sit before a committee, almost a year and a half, and in the end, some senator, for reasons not set up by me, put a hold on my nomination, and in the meantime I couldn't plan anything nor could I commit to anything. I was asked to speak at an event a few months into the process with a nice honorarium but had to turn it down because it would be a conflict of interests. I had to resign from all boards that were compensated. The only one I could stay on was the Council of Foreign Relations. They didn't want a conflict of interests. They allowed me to hold onto any property I owned; I could rent it out. The number of years as an ambassador is determined at the pleasure of the president."

The senator who adamantly objected to Yzaguirre's nomination turned out to be John Kyl (R-AZ). Kyle's resistance to Yzaguirre's nomination caused delay after delay, and in that time span, Yzaguirre hung in limbo, not able to move one way or another. By 2010, Hillary Clinton had been nominated and confirmed as Secretary of State, and it was in that role that she sent Senator Kyl a letter asking him to end his hold on Yzaguirre's nomination. "I understand that your hold of Raul's nomination has been prompted by your concern over implementation of sanctions under the Iran Sanctions Act (ISA)." She assured the senator that the extensive sanctions placed on Iran with the goal of constraining its nuclear ambitions, would be fully implemented. "In the meantime, preventing Raul's confirmation from moving forward damages

U.S. interests in a critically important region of the world. It is my continuing hope that you will release your hold on Raul Yzaguirre's nomination without further delay."

Recognizing the Dominican Republic as a major player in U.S. relations in the Caribbean, Clinton described the island as "a significant trading partner" and "a major hub for our relief and reconstruction efforts in neighboring Haiti." Senator Harry Reid (D-NV) noted the urgency of Yzaguirre's nomination, citing the fact that if the nomination did not go through, a delay of five weeks due to congressional recess would further delay the process.

Senator Kyl finally conceded, and the people of the American embassy in the Dominican Republic, who had waited for a new ambassador for 18 months, finally had their American diplomat. On September 29, 2010, Yzaguirre was confirmed by the Senate as Ambassador Extraordinary and Plenipotentiary of the United States to the Dominican Republic. The following month on October 25, Hillary Clinton proudly presided over Yzaguirre's swearing-in ceremony in the Treaty Room of the Department of State in D.C. A packed crowd attended, including Yzaguirre's family, friends, colleagues, and numerous well-wishers.

Reflecting on Yzaguirre's role as ambassador, Janet Murguia relates, "Ambassador Yzaguirre is well recognized and deeply respected by U.S. presidents and international heads of state as a civil rights leader with more than fifty years of service to our country. He is a perfect choice to represent the very best ideals and values of the American people on the international stage. His legacy of building strong American institutions that have advanced the Latino community in the U.S., of which Dominican Americans are a growing segment, make his confirmation as U.S. Chief of Mission to the Dominican Republic particularly fitting."

Having attended ambassador's school with Yzaguirre, Mari Carmen Aponte, Ambassador of El Salvador recalls. "Although I remember meeting Audrey at some point in the 1990's, I got to know her better when Raul, Audrey and I attended the State Department's Ambassadorial Seminar in the fall of 2009. During the course of the seminar, we needed to do certain press "training," as if Raul needed any! Audrey had to do the press training as well. As I recall, the exercise was for the Ambassador's spouse to discuss a project which had been important to her. Audrey chose to speak about a project she undertook to find a long lost relative using technology. I remember being very moved by the description of how she consistently followed every clue on the Internet, using social media as well as other tools. She spoke of what drove her to find the relative and her desire to dig into her own roots, especially since Raul was so much in touch with his. Of the entire ambassador spouse's projects, it was Audrey who most poignantly presented in a way that provided a window of what has been most important to her during her life—her family."

During the weeks spent together at ambassador's school, Aponte had a unique opportunity to see the depth of Yzaguirres' commitment and sacrifice for his family and country. "While attending the State Department Ambassadorial Seminar we were asked to talk about challenges and/or difficult times in our lives. Raul spoke openly and honestly about a time in his life when he declared bankruptcy, and described how it was a very strong Audrey who had gone to work to support their family, who kept the family together, emotionally and economically. Raul spoke about that time softly, haltingly, fighting back tears. After all the years hearing about his strength and knowing first hand his contributions to our community, I saw a deeply committed family man, loyal to his values, and unafraid to acknowledge the contributions of others to his life."

Sharing Ambassador Aponte's remarks about Yzaguirre's faithfulness to his family, the entire Yzaguirre family stood at his side, proud to have among them, the father figure his siblings could count on, the Dad who adored his children even though many times his obligations kept him away, and lastly the husband, loved by his wife Audrey—the one woman who had "listened to his dreams," when his dreams were still pinpoints of hope in his mind. But, at the end of the day, Yzaguirre wanted to be who he was, the man they had known all their lives.

On November 17, 2010, Yzaguirre presented his credentials before the President of the Dominican Republic, Dr. Leonel Fernandez. Another "ride" was scheduled for him, one he did not expect would be so engrossing, challenging, and filled with welcoming Dominicans and hundreds of world figures he would never forget. Leaving ASU's CDCR Center in the hands of his co-director, Alex Perilla, and the Center's Administrative Assistant, Pat Bonn, Yzaguirre readied himself to take on his new duties as ambassador. His presence on the island would form life-long bonds of trust for both he and Audrey as they left U.S. shores to spend time abroad, sacrificing family and their home in America to do what Yzaguirre had decided to do when he was fifteen years old—serve others.

27

HISPANIOLA

*People often say I'm a maverick, well that name really fits my friend
Raul Yzaguirre. He's an original maverick. Raul is his own person who
believes in doing the right things regardless of public opinion.*

—Senator John McCain

LITTLE SPAIN

Hispaniola, also known as "Little Spain," and in modern times—divided into two countries—the Dominican Republic and Haiti, lies in a strategic position, between Cuba and Puerto Rico, on the Caribbean Sea. The island's legendary history begins with the landing of Christopher Columbus in 1492, and his first contact with the Taíno people, one of the numerous tribes that once inhabited the Americas. Occupying the island since the 7th century, tribal members had no way of knowing that they would one day fall prey to Spanish conquest.

Santo Domingo, the oldest continuously inhabited city in the Americas and the first seat of Spanish government in "Little Spain," becomes Raul Yzaguirre's new destination. The American Embassy, set in the heart of the city's bustling streets, is not far from a panoramic view of the Caribbean Sea. The ambassador's mansion, surrounded by lush green lawns, gardens and stately trees, boasts tennis courts, a pool and official buildings, creating a respite for visiting dignitaries, embassy employees, their families and friends. Marines in charge of the embassy, abide by strict security codes. "I had to get used to military escorts," Yzaguirre says, "Everything was checked for possible explosives, and the cars that accompanied us were equipped with military weapons in case of an attack."

Historically, life in the DR has been one of strife and war, and after three centuries of battles against Spanish, French and Haitian rule, the DR established its own independence in 1821, the same year Mexico gained its independence from Spain. Not free for long from unrest, the DR had its problems with Haitian slave revolts, as Haiti fought for its own independence from the super powers, Britain, France and Spain, eventually becoming the first independent nation in 1804 led by slaves. At one point the DR actually returned to colonial government, but soon came to its senses, and ended Spanish rule once-and-for-all in 1865. The DR's volatile history includes an occupation by the U.S. (1916-1924), culminating in the end of the dictatorship of Rafael Leónidas Trujillo. U.S. intervention in the country's last civil war in 1965 led the way for the establishment of what is now the DR's modern democratic government. Initially, the island's magical appearance hides age-old problems, conflicts between the more prosperous Dominicans and the poverty-stricken Haitians. Yzaguirre soon discovers that the *ascercamiento* he longs for, that will strengthen the diaspora of Dominicans in the U.S, is a work in progress.

"America invaded the DR in 1965, so the heroes of this country are those who fought against us during the invasion, yet Americans have close to a ninety percent approval rate in the DR, which is one of the highest in the world," Yzaguirre relates. "Now, how do you explain that? Well, one of the reasons is baseball, and the other is that there are a million and a half Dominicans in the U.S., so almost everyone in the country has family or close friends in the U.S. Another factor is tourism, which is a third of the country's economy and a large portion of that is from America. Driving down the streets, you see McDonald's and Wendy's, and think you're in Puerto Rico. Contradictions like this exist. On one hand many resent us, yet on the other hand the population is very Americanized. America is well-respected, yet there are lots of grievances against us and one is the enormous trade surplus. We export more than we buy from the DR."

Offsetting the odds set up like dominoes against him as he embarks on his journey to the DR, is the staff at the ambassador's mansion, led by Kiko, an aging Dominican who has faithfully served DR's ambassadors since his youth. It didn't take long for Raul and Audrey to become staff favorites. "They were very dedicated to us," Yzaguirre recalls. "Kiko led the staff and was as gracious a host as any on the planet. They were totally committed to us, and went out of their way to please us. Audrey planted an herb garden with their help, and they often used the herbs to spice up our dishes. I could count on the staff for simple things, and for difficult engagements, as when we had a senator, president or other dignitary coming for a visit. I knew everything would run smooth, and I had nothing to worry about. We were more like a family than an ambassador and staff."

Lapping at his heels, Yzaguirre's nemesis makes its way to the DR, under the disguise of Parkinson's disease. Overcoming the chaotic symptoms as he performs his duties as ambassador will be one of his greatest challenges. Upon assuming his post, surprising facts begin to surface, prompting him to come up with new perspectives and move in unforeseen directions as his vision for the country quickly takes on several unexpected twists and turns.

"It was a much bigger job than I had expected. I had a sense of what it meant because I've been around ambassadors all my adult life and had interaction with ambassadors abroad and stayed at the embassy offices before, so I had a sense of what it was, but never understood the depth of the responsibility before I got to the DR. The breadth of the work is very hard to deal with, and a great amount of energy is required. I had to deal with trafficking issues, copyright issues, extraditions, visas, and a large number of bilateral issues between us and Cuba, Venezuela and other countries around the world. So it was an enormously complicated job. I've been fortunate because I've been around Washington all my life, so most of the work was very familiar. I knew the DR trade agreements, including the CBSI related to Caribbean security and free trade agreements. What was unfamiliar to me was the visa process, which I found enormously complicated. A simple question turned out to be much more complicated, and much more of an issue here than I expected it to be. The DR is one of the largest visa issuing embassies in the world, and second in problems related to fraud. The Embassy had the advantage of being able to set reasonable expectations, or reasonable doubt without a hearing and we could deny a visa, because it's a privilege, not a right. Given the narcotrafficking that passes through this country, we knew that there were a lot more people involved than we had been able to identify, so we were under pressure to bring this information into some kind of relationship between the drug trafficking and the number of visas we denied."

"Another surprise was the number of visas issued per day. Almost daily, I would have a senator or congressman or influential person asking me to intervene on behalf of a constituent or friend who needed a visa. Most of the time, there was nothing we could do, besides making judgment calls. There are some absolutes to this process. For instance, if a person is convicted of a crime then it's automatic they will be denied a visa, or if they've falsified papers they have to wait an extended period of time, so there are certain things that are very clear but the module of expression is very significant."

President Fernandez proves to be a positive force, for the most part, working in collaboration with the U.S. Embassy; however, there are times when goals don't move forward, and this proves to be a frustrating impasse for Yzaguirre, and one that will, at times, dismantle his plans for progress.

"We had a number of meetings, twice a week on one topic or another and the president was very friendly, very accessible. Every time I asked for a meeting, he immediately responded in a positive way. He's enormously intelligent and has a sense of history, almost professorial, in the way he talked to me and to an audience. He dissects the evolution of any topic in a given situation. In spite of the fact that overall my relationship with the president was good, at the same time I have to say that many times he didn't follow through on what we had agreed on, and that became a continuing problem. I couldn't take his 'yes' for an answer. His administration would say yes, but I didn't know if they would go through with what we had agreed to do. The first lady was also very influential and we were on friendly terms. She asked for minor things that were important to her. One of these concerned her autistic child. She wanted us to bring in some experts to teach caregivers how to treat autistic children. We did that, and she was very pleased with the result."

Moving closer to the themes most important to him, Yzaguirre turns his attention to education, the Dominican diaspora in America, drug enforcement, Haitian immigration issues, fair election campaigns, and the need to bridge the gap between the "haves and have-nots" noting the country's ongoing struggle with enormous disparities between the rich and poor in both rural and urban communities.

Taking on age-old issues and creating new frameworks for realizing goals is something Yzaguirre has successfully tackled throughout his career, similar to the ride on the bucking bronco he took so long ago in Cheyenne, Wyoming, proof of his willingness to take on impossible tasks even as a young leader. Now the odds will be greater and a blaring contest horn won't signal a successful ride, as much as sheer stamina, perseverance and determination, something he learned in his earliest days, maneuvering the pick-up truck at seven years old down the streets of San Juan at the break of dawn so his grandfather, Gavino Morin, could make his ice deliveries on time.

147 of 147: Education in Need of Repair

"Education was the first big issue I focused on, and I started by doing some minor things, with the hope of doing more before my term was over. The DR was 147 out of 147 countries, tied for last in education. I think it was Slovenia or some other very small country that came in tied with the DR. The average child in the DR got two to four hours of education per day in many places where there were no schools whatsoever and a local person had to teach, and in other places where the schoolhouse was under a tree. The teacher's union was a very significant problem there, adding more demands that required additional funding. I heard a story that I think was true that the government had commissioned a study on ways to improve higher education and make it available to more students. The government formed a ministry for higher education and one for K-12. The people who were responsible for the study said there was nothing they could do to improve higher education because the major problem was basic education. The pipeline started in K-12, and unless that was fixed, it was a waste of time trying to fix anything else."

"The DR's constitution required that the government spend four percent of the GDP, (Gross Domestic Product) on education. At the time I served, the government was spending slightly under two percent and that was actually an increase of what it had been in the past. This discrepancy looked as if it was a violation of the constitution, so there was a growing movement called the 'Four Percent Movement.' Both candidates, running for president, Danilo Medina representing the Dominican Liberation Party (PLD) and Hipólito Mejia of the Revolutionary Dominican Party (PRD) agreed to do all they could to increase funding for education."

Brainstorming ideas on how to begin to remedy the extremely low government funding for education, Yzaguirre plugged into his skills as the former President and CEO of NCLR, banking on his past experiences in bringing together hundreds of service providers, foundations, and corporations to collaborate on goals that advanced the needs of America's growing Latino population. "I got a lot of the funding sources together, the World Bank and some of the other embassies that had programs in the DR, to agree to fund a coalition of private sector organizations to create a commission that would be the initial active phase. The commission would be charged with putting together a plan, not a study, but what needed to be done in a detailed plan, specifically identifying who was involved, what the scope of the program was, and what timelines would be observed. We presented that plan to both candidates for presidency and they agreed to work with us on the commission. I was very impressed with their positive attitudes and quick response. Also, I began to create a funding source, tapping into the Dominican diaspora in the U.S. to fund educational programs. I started specifically with orphanages that had educational programs going on, and that was lots of them. A large number of children, due to poverty and many other issues, were homeless with no close relatives to take them in so they ended up in orphanages. The Catholic

Church had been fairly aggressive in dealing with the problem, so I decided to start with the orphanages to get some funding going. Another thing we did was engage the local university to train a new core of political leaders of all parties, and the commitment we put into the training process for honest and accountable government was increased enormously by young people, whom we strongly supported."

The plight of women, especially in poverty stricken areas of the DR, was something Yzaguirre could not avoid addressing. "I brought it up routinely, education favors females. But it's the worst outcome here in the DR, males consistently assaulting or killing females. The theory is that as jobs are more open to women, and more women become heads of household, the male feels very threatened and has no role in the family. Some women enter into careers and become more independent. The man gets jealous and ends up killing the woman and himself. One of the women working at the Embassy was killed by her ex-husband. Hundreds of women are killed by their husbands, boyfriends or ex-husbands. It hasn't gotten to that extreme in the U.S. but I see the problem growing in other countries. This destructive lifestyle is happening to more males, acutely, and more to minority males."

Yzaguirre, backed up women in the DR, setting up a time to showcase successful women and tell their stories. "In the DR we had Women's Recognition Day, a time when we honored women leaders. One of the young women who came to our attention had graduated from law school at seventeen and was serving as a local prosecutor. Myself and the First Lady were very supportive of her."

Meeting the needs of students and families in the DR brings Yzaguirre face-to-face with a number of highly successful Dominicans living in the U.S., and some who have made their mark in America then returned to the DR. The diaspora he hopes to plug into becomes a viable network of Dominican leaders in business, sports, social issues, community related enterprises, television and film, government agencies, and some he knows personally—past and present members of NCLR. One in particular, is to make his presence felt, touching the hearts of two of Raul's friends from Arizona—Ernie Calderon and his son, Steven.

CARIBBEAN TREASURE

The evening begins with a crowd gathering on the lawn of the ambassador's mansion. The lush, green lawn is elaborately set with chairs facing a small stage for listening to speeches, and tables scattered throughout the lawn covered in white linen with flowers and small twinkling table lights as center-pieces. The night is balmy, the moon barely visible as clouds and city lights mask stars shining in the dark, Caribbean sky. Raul and Audrey stand inside the mansion's foyer, flanked by the U.S. flag and the Dominican flag in the background both in semi-casual dress, Yzaguirre sporting one of his Guayabera style shirts. They warmly greet guests as they enter through the mansion's huge carved door.

"Raul and Audrey made everybody feel special," says Ernie Calderon, formerly on the ASU Board of Regents when Yzaguirre became Executive Director of the CDCR Center. He and his son, Steven, a college student at the time, were visiting the DR, and at Raul's insistence were given lodging at the mansion and invited to a dinner on the mansion lawn.

"Raul is a lesson in walking and talking humbly," Calderon reflects. "He didn't like the title 'Your Excellency,' although as ambassador, that was one of his titles. That night it was a who's who of leaders of the Dominican Republic, and many other countries as well on the night my son, Steven, and I were present for dinner at the ambassador's mansion. We were told not to discuss politics. This was when Obama was up for re-election in 2012 and some folks there knew we were from the U.S. One man said to my son, 'What a tragedy if Obama doesn't get re-elected,' and my son, remembering what we had been warned about, answered casually, 'Interesting,' so he stayed neutral, and clear of politics. Then someone else asked him if he thought Mitt Romney would be the Republican nominee. 'A better question is who is the best Dominican baseball player,' was my son's answer. A discussion began about the subject. Manny Mota's name came up, and I said he had the best pinch-hitting record in the Los Angeles Dodgers, besides being one of their coaches. The Mayor of Santo Domingo was sitting next to Raul, and he said, 'lo conozco' (I know him). I told them he was my hero. He'd get a hit even if not playing regularly. Raul was quietly listening to all this. The next day Raul told my son and I to be at the front door of the mansion at 2:30 PM, but gave no further information. An Embassy car picked us up promptly at 2:30 and we were driven to an unknown location. We ended up in one of the poorest barrios in the city. As we approached the location, a big gate opened and we saw a baseball stadium, and a building with classrooms, computers and a place to eat. Then, out comes Manny Mota to meet us, and he says, 'I want to meet my fan Ernie Calderon and his son.' My son and I were shocked that we were actually meeting Manny Mota. It turned out that Manny runs a program for street children, boys, he feeds and cares for. The boys take an hour or two of computer classes, then they go to the chapel for religious services. Then the kids play baseball and Manny brings in other famous players to talk to them and help mentor them. He is the hope of that barrio. Raul led us to Manny Mota."

Inducted to the Hispanic Heritage Baseball Museum Hall of Fame on August 23, 2003 in a ceremony at Dodger Stadium, Mota's career reflects his skills as one of the best Dominican baseball players in the U.S., as well as one who has successfully launched a second career as a sports broadcaster. Mota and his wife, Margarita, reside in the DR where they have established the Manny Mota International Foundation, now over thirty years old. The foundation offers assistance and schooling to disadvantaged youth and their families in both the DR, and the U.S. In 2014, Yzaguirre and Calderon nominated Mota for the NCLR Roberto Clemente Humanitarian Award, which was presented to him at the annual NCLR conference.

For Yzaguirre, Manny Mota became a symbol of what it meant to fire up the Dominican diaspora in the U.S. and tap into the wealth and expertise of those who had been privileged to take on leadership roles in both countries; however, he quickly found out there was a catch-22 to how the system actually worked. "One problem we encountered was that the diaspora in the U.S. does not trust a lot of the nonprofits to spend the money in a way they feel it should be spent. So what I was trying to do was create a mechanism that gave donors a sense of confidence that the money would be allocated in the right way. Originally, my idea was to get the money and distribute it to a central entity, so I did a sort of personal visibility study by going to meet with all the groups I could identify in the U.S. I spent a week going from city to city and arranging meetings with folks from the Dominican Republic. They were very interested in investing in the DR and contributing, but they didn't trust anybody, and especially, they didn't trust the government. Also, they weren't interested in giving to a cause, they were interested in giving to a specific thing, like a school or an orphanage or some economic development agency that focused on a specific area. They wanted to support things they really cared about, things close to their hearts, like education or the environment or certain geographical locations, neighborhoods and cities they knew firsthand. That's what they wanted. So I figured if I could create the environment where they could identify and get the information they needed, at least they could have some sense that the money was being put to good use. I got the American Chamber of Commerce to set up that entity, and create a catalog of organizations and give them their blessing in the sense that they'd describe them as having annual audits, and whether they had a functioning board or not. So, while we couldn't guarantee absolute legitimacy, at least we could guarantee the process was in place for there to be some accountability.

I looked to the fact that Singapore had made great economic strides within this century with exactly the same economic characteristics as the DR. Yet they had gone far ahead of the DR, and the question was, why when both are island countries and had started out the same way. Singapore was at one time a third world country, but has come a long way and is now one of the richest countries in Southeast Asia, so we had to assert ourselves to the diaspora in America and say we can do the same, pay attention to us, help us get there."

DARK ELEMENTS, BORDER MADNESS

Drug trafficking is a term associated with familiar words—black market, the underground, illicit drug trade, drug seizures, cartels, and perhaps the two words that keep the world of drugs in business—high profits. There are high profits for growers, manufacturers, cartels, dealers, smugglers, and wages earned by millions who harvest, manufacture and ship the drugs to connection sites that span the globe. The dangerous cat-and-mouse game played by drug enforcement agencies are no match for the relentless buying, selling and demand for addictive drugs that nets trillions in world markets, yearly.

The U.S., working along with 14 Central and South American countries, including the United Kingdom and the Netherlands, operates an anti-drug effort through a multinational detection operation called Operation Martillo (hammer). Contributing U.S. Navy, Coast Guard, aircraft, military and law enforcement agencies, the U.S., along with its partners, aggressively campaign against the movement of illicit drugs, precursor chemicals, bulk cash and weapons. In a similar fashion, the CBSI addresses the DR and the Caribbean community with the same program objectives.

"The CBSI mostly has to do with anti-drug trafficking, but it hasn't had the effect of Operation Martillo," Yzaguirre explains. "It didn't have the kind of funding we hoped for. Much of the money was diverted, so the effect we had hoped for wasn't realized. Cocaine drug trafficking is such an insidious phenomenon from the highest levels to the lowest. It is penetrated at many levels by the drug lords. We had various agencies working with DR agents, the DEA (Drug Enforcement Agency) and the NAS (Narcotic Assisted System)."

"One of the success stories we had involved DR police. There had been problems with them long before I became ambassador and most Dominicans felt they couldn't be trusted. My suggestion was to create a unit within the various law enforcement agencies that would have a vetting process, which meant that workers would be screened more thoroughly. They would be administered a lie detector test once a week. They would be trained more intensely and given a bonus, paid by the U.S. government to stop the temptations to steal, accept bribes, etcetera. Wages for the employees were very low. They couldn't raise a family with the wages they were paid, so we were trying to make it possible for them to do the right thing and stay on as honest police officers. We gave them the tools and backup with the bonus money; unfortunately, the program was very limited and I had all kinds of problems trying to get it implemented. I wanted to expand the program but that never materialized. Although President Obama did all he could to promote the program, it lacked commitment from other parts of U.S. drug enforcement. We put pressure on President Obama to keep an honest man in charge of the effort, while we worked to keep the DR Navy aligned with our goals. We helped to get U.S. planes and helicopters onboard and pretty much stopped trafficking by air, but it increased by sea maritime. Drug traffickers are very sophisticated and use submarines to smuggle drugs, most of them coming from South America."

At the root of the complicated problems Yzaguirre faced with drug trafficking, low wages, and the lack of a viable educational system, was the country's poverty and on-going border issues with Haiti. "Rural poverty was more extreme, but urban poverty was more prevalent," Yzaguirre explains. "The Embassy had more success helping small villages with major needs. We took some villages where there was no water, no sewage and no new jobs, and helped them create sustainable resources. For instance, in a village that had water that flowed downstream but no electricity, we helped build a hydro-electric plant so they could manage their own needs. One of the problems in the country is that many don't pay electricity bills. Instead they destroy lines and want to maintain their own plants. As a result, there are blackouts and when that happens, a generator will click in, if there is one, otherwise people have to wait several hours to gain power again. Folks who have more constant electricity use water flowing down stream and build cooperatives and community centers that create jobs. It shows what people can do when they are willing, and many are willing in the DR but often hindered by government restrictions."

Raised along the Rio Grande Valley, immigration issues and volatile border confrontations were well known to Yzaguirre. The DR's border with Haiti seemed to him a close analogy of what he had seen along the border with Mexico. And, although, there were no Texas Rangers on the loose, the anti-Haitian sentiment often exploded in fierce protests and outright acts of racism and discrimination.

"There is an inferiority complex among the Haitians and immigration issues similar to those faced at the U.S. border with Mexico. What is very different and very troublesome is the fact that according to the DR's new constitution if a person is Haitian, but was born in the DR, they would still be considered a Haitian. The DR does not grant citizenship because a person is born in the country. The government also took away national identity cards from Haitians. Groups of people formed members of a pro-Haitian, Dominican effort led by Sonia Pier, a Black Haitian whose efforts we supported; unfortunately, she died at a young age."

Long-term deforestation issues escalated tensions along the Haitian/Dominican border. Dominicans blamed Haitians for deforestation of their island and chopping down trees to be used as charcoal for heating. However, when Yzaguirre took a closer look at the problem, he discovered that the deforestation done in the DR by Haitians was for use of Dominicans who were buying and selling goods made from trees and forest byproducts. It was not a matter of good guys vs. bad guys, because deforestation occurred on both sides of the border.

"We had some very frank conversations with the authorities who made the point that the U.S. is a big country and can afford to have minorities, whereas, the DR is a smaller, poorer country that can't afford minorities. Their goal is to be united, so there's a racial ethnic element to the argument. They spend lots of money, and have the same kinds of pressures as the U.S. in taking care of immigrant Haitians, providing HIV/AIDS treatment, school, and so forth. But, as in the U.S. the construction industry is dependent on Haitians, as is the service industry, and their labor has also traditionally been used in the sugar cane industry. Although the sugar cane industry is now more mechanized, in the past, Haitians were treated as brutally as Black slaves on southern plantations. Shanty towns exist to this day, housing the poorest Haitians, yet this does not receive much attention."

The rise of Barack Obama as U.S. President brought new questions about race, and Black ancestry in the DR and Haiti. Although the Dominicans applauded Obama for his big win, personally they chose to align themselves with indigenous ethnicities. "Race is a big issue in the DR," Yzaguirre explains. "Most Dominicans have African blood, but they want to emphasize their Indian ancestry, which is almost non-existent. This is a complicated issue as they refer to themselves as being Black, but consider themselves different from Black Haitians. This is part of the racial tension that goes on between the two countries. Dominicans use Haitian labor, but they also want them to be responsible for their own country and not be dependent on the DR for handouts."

On the go, from dawn to dusk on most days, then attending evening events, and often hosting important functions at the mansion with dignitaries from around the globe take their toll on Yzaguirre's declining health. "I had to remind him daily to take his meds," Audrey says. "I would say goodbye to him early in the morning, and might not see him until the evening, although he often stopped by for lunch, especially when we were hosting visiting dignitaries, family or friends." The pace becomes unbearable, and gets to the point where Yzaguirre makes only brief statements in public as Parkinson's disease takes a stronger hold on his waning strength and his ability to articulate speech. He knows that without a doubt, he must make a decision about his service as ambassador, and the sooner, the better.

THE MAVERICK

The opulent ambassador's mansion, part of the American Embassy in the DR, became a magnet for Yzaguirre's family and close friends. Everyone knew it was where Raul and Audrey were serving their country as President Barack Obama's representatives; but it was Yzaguirre's relaxed, open-hearted manner, and Audrey's gracious, kind hospitality that kept everybody coming back.

"I loved to cook at the mansion for my brother," Alma recalls. "The kitchen was stocked with everything I needed, and the staff were always willing to help. I made his favorite Mexican dishes, and everybody got a chance to sample our home cooked meals."

Knowing his brother hated the titles, "Excellency," or "Ambassador Extraordinary and Plenipotentiary," and other official designations, Ruben's visit to the DR with his wife Vicky, took on a humorous turn, even before they reached the mansion. "The first time I visited at the mansion, I remember I had on my baseball cap. As my wife and I got off the plane we were escorted to a special reception room at the airport where Raul and Audrey were waiting for us. We didn't have to pick up our luggage or do anything else; Raul's staff did all that for us. Right before we entered the reception room, one of the staff members told me to take off my cap. I said to him, but he's my brother, and the staff member just looked at me and said, 'Sir, please remove your hat in the presence of the ambassador.' Raul got a good laugh over that."

As Secretary of State, Hillary Clinton spent time in the DR, vacationing there with President Clinton. "Hillary visited me at the mansion, and more important she came on her own dime to spend Christmas and New Year's," Yzaguirre recalls. "I admired her work ethics. She got more done in twenty-four hours than most people do in two weeks. At one visit, I met her in the mansion's entryway with the press waiting right outside the door. I gave her four or five points to cover. She not only knew the points, she enlarged on them. She can take information and adjust it, and spit it out in ways that make sense. She can take complicated issues and make sense of them, very much like Bill. At another time the Clintons vacationed at the home of Oscar de la Renta at the DR. I spent time at the party with Henry Kissinger and his wife, Charlie Rose, Barbara Walters and other celebrity figures. After a lovely lunch, the Clintons invited me for a chat and stroll in the gardens. I recall that our respective security personnel were having some anxious dialogues. I didn't ask for details."

President George W. Bush threw a party in the DR during Yzaguirre's term as ambassador, and Yzaguirre got to see a more relaxed man than he remembered in Texas. "President Bush, his wife, his mother and father, former President H.W. Bush, a sister I never even knew existed, the former president of Spain and numerous dignitaries all came together for a party. We had fun, not talking politics, and towards the end of the evening we sang Mexican songs."

These light-hearted moments, among many, the quiet times, the times of comradeship among friends, family and the mansion staff, and the lonely times away from loved ones in the U.S., the constant appearance of dignitaries from around the world, the charming and not-so-charming visits from leaders who presented complex problems related to global trade, drug trafficking, volatile issues along the border with Haiti, and the poverty that plagued so much of the country made for challenging and intriguing times for Yzaguirre. All of it, the laughter, worry, constant meetings, and confidential information handled by his secretary Rachel Griego, an astute and knowledgeable young woman who had worked with Raul at NCLR, revealed a compelling mosaic of constant duties that fell into place like clock-work for *el jefe*. Nothing should be allowed to cloud Yzaguirre's service in the DR; everything had to be transparent, and U.S. interests had to be honored. Personal interests were set aside, something Yzaguirre was an expert at doing. That was the sacrifice that went along with his post as ambassador.

Always astute about foreign relations, and a man well-versed as a member of the NDI, whose purpose is to focus on elections around the world, encouraging democratic representation and free expression of voting rights, Yzaguirre's role in the DR's 2012 presidential election, drew both positive and negative responses from Dominicans. Some felt America had no business getting involved in their country's elections, and others were grateful for U.S. back-up in the democratic process. The presidential elections completed on May 21, 2012 in the Dominican Republic are an example of how Yzaguirre had to face the Dominican population, and inspire trust and faith between their country and the U.S. Danilo Medina from the governing party for Dominican Liberation (PLD) received 51% of the vote winning over his rival, Hipólito Mejía, at 46%, former president of the DR from the Revolutionary Dominican Party (PRD). Yzaguirre hailed the election with the words, "Long live democracy," saluting the Organization of American States (OAS) for their work in following through on the voting process.

Through all the hopes and plans, failures, successes and work in progress in his role as ambassador, one nagging question remained for Yzaguirre. How did someone end a life of service, a time when "making the world a better place," had been one's mantra? But the day came too quickly for him. Parkinson's would not let go, and he knew, as everyone around him knew, that the treatments, although, easing some of the symptoms, were not the answer. He and Audrey would have to go back to the U.S. to try some new procedures, new medical cures that might hold out some hope that the disease would be halted, or at least stalled.

On May 6, 2013, Yzaguirre met with Foreign Minister Carlos Morales Troncoso in Santo Domingo to inform him that he would be resigning by the end of the month. For several years he had been cradled on an island adrift on the blue waters of the Caribbean Sea, amidst the bustling streets of one of the oldest cities on Earth—Santo Domingo. More importantly, the Dominicans, themselves, had become a people he deeply respected—interpreters of a new world, birthed from an ancient one that spoke its own mythical language in symbols and visions, always pointing to something more splendid. The Dominicans are brave people, who over the years, have met war and death with exceptional courage. Bright, new faces of young Dominicans remain etched in Yzaguirre's mind as he and Audrey make their departure to the U.S. Standing on the shoulders of those who have forged ahead, creating new pathways, young Dominicans are the promise that the country will come into its own, in its own time, and in its own way.

Reflecting on Yzaguirre's life and contributions to the world community, fellow Texan, and State Senator, Rodney Ellis (D-TX), relates, "Raul Yzaguirre is a person who showed many young people how to stand up and move ahead in building on the success of our ancestors, those who paved the way to get us where we are today."

Senator John McCain (R-AZ) notes Yzaguirre's stance, over the years, for doing the right thing no matter what the cost—and his constant desire to put his community first, above personal interests. "People often say I'm a maverick, well that name really fits my friend Raul Yzaguirre. He's an original maverick. Raul is his own person who believes in doing the right things regardless of public opinion." McCain, further reflects, "Raul's passion and commitment for the continued success of the Hispanic community inspire me. Raul's love for his community and country is clear because my friend knows that as the Hispanic community makes strides, so does our entire nation."

Former Arizona Congressman Ed Pastor, active as Chairman of the Board of NCLR in its early days, describes Yzaguirre as someone who, "advocated for Latinos, inclusive of all groups. He stayed the course and has taken us to places we've never been to before."

Poignantly summarizing his father's legacy, Raul, Jr., reflects, "When we talk about what a hero means to me, it is someone who protects and defends those folks that need it the most, and for me that's always been my dad, my hero."

ONCE ON AMERICAN SOIL, Yzaguirre's new "ride" begins, in the face of his adversary's progressive march, the endless battle with Parkinson's, the meds, treatments, sleepless nights, and the symptoms that rob him of all he once personally valued. He lives in his own private world, set up by Parkinson's rigid distortions, loving others as he always has, and being loved in return, first by his wife, children and family, and then by thousands throughout the world whose lives he has touched. He still reaches out to others and does not absent himself from conferences, activism and important events that affect his beloved community. He possesses what no disease can ever claim—freedom. Raul Yzaguirre remains a free man, one who has diligently answered the call, "to leave the world a better place."

28

LESSONS LEARNED
AT THE TABLE

*I want the world to know of Raul's bravery and courage in lifting up
the Latino community as a political force, and in creating a space
for the Latino community at the table. He took risks and never
backed down in fighting for fairness for our community.*

—Ramon Murguia

THE TABLE IS SET. Mama Licha is ready to serve dinner. Her husband,
Gavino, is sitting in one of the plush, velvet chairs in the living room,
watching T.V. But as soon as Raul comes in and washes up, they'll
sit together at the table for their evening meal. All day long Mama Licha has
scrubbed and scoured the house—every corner dusted, swept and mopped.
The wooden floors are polished to perfection, and the kitchen walls gleam,
spotlessly clean. Today, she washed their clothes, sterilizing them in boiling
water. No telling what dirt the clothes harbored. She wears her gray hair up in
a bun, and glances anxiously at the clock as she sets the silverware and dishes
on the white linen tablecloth. Where is he? That grandson of hers. He had to
make some late ice deliveries, but now she's worried he's gone off to another
meeting. He's busy organizing, although she doesn't know exactly what he's
organizing. She knows her husband and Raul talk about everything, and she
could ask him. But all she wants is to serve dinner—the spicy, savory meat
dish, beans, rice, warm tortillas, the creamed carrots Gavino loves, and for
dessert his favorite—pineapple upside down cake.

She hears footsteps on the wooden porch, and knows its Raul. She hears
his voice greeting his grandfather, calling him Papa, and yes, she is Mama.

He's lived with them since he was five years old; he belongs to them. She glances adoringly at him as he walks into the kitchen, and in a gruff voice orders him to wash up and come to the table. Already, Gavino is sitting at the head, and she pauses to look at him, happy to see the man she loves ready to enjoy the food she's cooked, but she won't let him know that. Her affection is hidden, but it's real. Raul walks to his place at the table, smiling, teasing his grandmother, telling her maybe he'll go off to sea again, and his grandfather asks him, "You haven't gotten it out of your system yet?" They all laugh, remembering what happened the last time he ran off. They sit together at the table, ready to enjoy Mama Licha's delicious food, and that's when the stories begin—stories that will become lessons their grandson will never forget.

There will be many tables over the years for Raul, and many lessons to be learned—power to be realized, visions to be birthed and hopes that will become real. But for tonight, it's the three of them, and the food is tasty, truly fit for a king. The real power of the table is love, something Raul will discover all by himself as the years go by, and he brings Latinos to tables, some in America, some set in foreign countries beyond America's borders. He'll sit Latinos in places undreamed of before—tables of power. There, they will sit at their rightful places, their voices finally heard. They will no longer be considered foreigners in America—their invisibility will be a thing of the past.

WORDS OF WISDOM FROM A LIFE WELL-LIVED

Lo cortes no quita lo valiente. My grandmother used to say that. That's a concept that inspires us to be valiant while being courteous; the two go together. You're a man when you do the right thing, not when you abuse someone.

MACHO AND EMBRA

What is *macho*? First of all, we took a word that was once positive and made it negative. To me what *macho* was when I was growing up was somebody who was responsible *una persona que tenia palabra* (a person true to his word). He was a man who was not afraid to do the right thing. Later, it became someone who was a womanizer, a drunkard, and violent with women. This kind of man was a sexist. To me it's the opposite of *embra*, a woman who is courageous who has *palabra*, who takes responsibility for her life. That's a woman, a real woman. She stands equal to the *macho*, I knew as a child, both of them having the same qualities for keeping their word and being fully responsible for their lives.

DEFINING EDUCATION

Education is intellectual growth and understanding. It's about a life examined. A good education inspires a person to be introspective and to seek to understand life and make connections between different disciplines: science, civics, sociology, history, economics, philosophy and cultural and political systems, which argue for a liberal arts education. Education connects the dots and begins to give some semblance of cohesion, forming a basis for universal thought. It's not about learning a skill, that's training. Education is about understanding relationships between human beings and the world they live in. Latino stories, history and culture have not traditionally been reinforced in schools, and this makes for a distorted view of who we are. Good education connects students with the real world.

GENDER DISCREPANCIES

Latino students continue to have high drop out rates. What's missing? First of all there is a gender difference. Latina students are doing reasonably well, far out-pacing Latino males. So we have a problem with getting more Latino males through higher education. Many young Latinos lack male role models and don't grow up with a good self-concept. They can't see themselves as winners or successful people. Unfortunately, some get in trouble with the criminal justice system and become part of the over-criminalization done in this country. Others are forced to leave school due to financial pressures. Also, a misguided concept that really scares me is something called 'acting White.' It's part of a Harvard study. Students who study and work hard to get good grades and make something of themselves, may be described as 'acting White' by their peers. They equate studying with being White, which causes young Latinos to down-play their academic success.

TEACHER AS THE DIFFERENCE

Educational problems begin early on. Many times, educators don't adopt their teaching methods to the realities of life. Kids particularly boys, don't necessarily learn by observing and listening, and the theory is you've got an empty head, sit down comport yourself, and I will pour my knowledge into your head. That's not the way it works. Students learn by asking, they learn by doing and by having a theory, a framework presented to them. More than anything else there is the need for the right curriculum and the right attitude. Teacher attitudes and expectations are two of the biggest predictors for success. Whatever the teacher thinks students can do, they will do. If a teacher thinks students are smart, they'll get good grades, and will be smarter because they're interested and engaged. Success is step-by-step, answering one question correctly, motivates students to want to do more. It's all part of connecting the dots and developing cohesiveness.

BILINGUALISM

I favor programs that allow for growth in language and a sense of identity. Evidence shows that bilingual programs not only help students maintain fluency in two languages, they also help them learn English faster. Learning another language, in and of itself, makes a student a smarter person, not only because they know a different language, but because they gain content that increases synapses in the brain allowing them to learn and make connections with information at a faster pace. That's a proven physiological fact. Bilingual and maintenance language programs are highly successful and do not pose a problem for learning English.

MALE GANG MENTALITY

There is a group mentality of rebellion in youth who join gangs. Those who end up in prison continue their rebellion there. Going to jail, at times, becomes a rite of passage for young men. It reaffirms their manhood. I think the basis for all this dysfunction has to do with boys not feeling or becoming a part of something bigger. They may feel lonely and lack a personal identity. They have no scripts to follow and may have few, if any, positive role models. The gang gives them an identity, and protects them. It's a strange kind of love that develops which makes sense to them. It forms a core of beliefs that gang members subscribe to. Belonging is an important part of evolving. It's a universal human need, and the gang offers that opportunity. It meets the psychological needs for belonging not met in a family.

DRUG PIPELINE

One thing we have to seriously consider is the over-criminalizing of offences related to drug abuse. Society pays big money to keep drug abusers behind bars. The price of cocaine can often be twice the price of gold. People can find themselves in jail for a drug transaction that involved ten or twenty dollars that will cost society hundreds of thousands of dollars in maintenance of the convicted person. No one but the perpetrator is a victim, yet society pays big money. We need to construct fewer prisons and build more classrooms.

CRIME AND PUNISHMENT

Given the same circumstances and the same crime, Latinos often get charged more often than their Anglo peers, and once charged, they're liable to get indicted with a higher level of charges. Once charged, they're less able to make bail, or bail is much higher. Once they get to court, their chances of getting convicted are higher for the same crime. Once convicted, they get longer sentences and harsher punishment, and are more apt to serve the time, than get parole. Empirically, the system is geared against Latinos, and as a society, we haven't made up our minds on how to deal with crime. There are two concepts, one is punishment, and the other one is rehabilitation, and the latter is often not in place due to shortage of staff, finances, and other problems. Sometimes the rate of those staying in is so high, you might as well keep them locked up because they'll go right back in. It becomes a pattern. The unfairness of the justice system is easily seen, for example crack cocaine, vs. powder cocaine. It's the same substance in different forms. One of them is cheap, crack cocaine, and the other is pure and more costly and is for those who can afford it. For the same amount of substance, users of powder cocaine get a lesser sentence. A critical point in the criminal justice system is whether a person can make bail, if not, the chances of coming out whole are very low. You are looked at differently by a jury and judge if you make bail. Many Latinos lack funds to make bail, and suffer the consequences. We need to rethink the whole criminal justice system.

POLICE BRUTALITY

Police officers risk their lives to serve the community, that's the ideal. However, the difficulty of the job can desensitize them, for instance, if an officer's partner is killed the officer can build up anger and take it out on the weakest people. I've been aware of police brutality growing up in the Rio Grande Valley and know it's a big problem, especially for people of color. Counseling, screening, training, and psychological evaluations should be givens in the hiring process.

MENTORING

Giving back to the community means mentoring youth. Experienced leaders must take responsibility for forming new leaders. I learned how to care about my community by watching experienced activists do their work and learning how I could participate. Especially young Latino males, need to see successful Latino men dressed in business suits at schools and conferences. One of the most powerful ways to teach success to youth is to show them someone who looks like they do, and is in a position of power and influence.

LIBERATION OF WOMEN

Latina women are doing very well. Their educational level is now higher. Many have college degrees, and post-graduate degrees as well. What I think needs to happen is we need to have non-stereotypical roles, we need more women to become doctors, astronauts, judges, scientists, and join other professions that tend to be dominated by men. I'm glad to see more women moving into higher leadership roles, they inspire young women to follow the same path. Women I have most admired in my life are: Hillary Clinton, Golda Meir, Joan of Arc, Mother Teresa, Margaret Thatcher, Eleanor Roosevelt, my mother and my grandmother.

LEARNING FROM FAILURE

When I experience failure, I go back and analyze the situation and learn from it. But there was a period of time at NCLR when I found myself feeling very negative about failure, feeling very disenchanted and uptight about it, but on the other hand, not feeling really joyous about victory. It's natural to feel bad about a failure, but usually you feel good about a victory. I was taking victory for granted it was almost like I needed a bigger high, similar to a drug addict who needs a bigger high, that's the way I can explain it. I needed to do something bigger and better and more transformative. It got to be a part of my character. I needed to manage my own psyche and the feelings of those around me. I had to learn to celebrate other people's victories for their own satisfaction and motivation, even though I didn't feel much emotion about it. In some ways failure was more motivating for me than success. Failure made me work harder, but the hardest part was when someone I trusted failed me. There's a tendency to want to generalize, 'Damn, all people are no good,' based on the actions of one person. I realized that carrying the hurt and the sense of being a victim of someone behaving in an unjust way towards me was something I had to get rid of. There have been times I've tried to exclude someone from my life over past hurts, but then, I take it all back and my enemy can sometimes become my friend again.

LEARNING TO COMPLAIN

I have found that members of our community, although making progress in asserting their rights over the years, in many instances, don't complain, and don't file grievances. I can't reconcile the fact that we're the bravest of the brave when it comes to war, risking our lives, yet we can often be timid when it comes to fighting for relief of discrimination. For example, at NCLR we were able to prove, and convincingly so, civil rights violations in terms of job discrimination. The policy was to look at individual complaints, but this was not working because Latinos weren't complaining. So we were forcing civil rights issues, but with no substance from employees. We then shifted our approach and began to analyze the company's workforce, managers, and technicians. What was the percentage of Latinos in the workforce in these areas? We compared that to the company's business profile. Were Latinos also a good part of their consumers? We contacted those who had applied for work there. Who had the company attracted and who was discouraged from applying? If the results showed a poor ratio of Latinos hired, then the company had to come up with a plan to fix the problem, perhaps by advertising in Spanish language TV, newspaper, radio, etc. Another way was to offer job fairs at colleges and universities and places in the community where Latinos and other people of color were predominant. We worked with OEO and other equal opportunity agencies. That level of detail was something new for our community.

ADVICE TO LATINO LEADERS

Be very clear about who you are, and what you want to accomplish. Communicate that to your staff and to your board, so your board and staff and constituency are appropriately aligned, or as closely aligned as you can get them in understanding your goals. To be defined one way and then become something very different creates a lot of problems. Know that genuine leaders are servant leaders, willing to serve the community first, before their personal interests. One question I often asked during heated debates, was: Who are you doing it for? The answer was obvious. Take everything seriously, and be careful with money. One thing that hurts an organization is a scandal over money. That can tear down an organization overnight. We went the extra mile at NCLR so no one questioned our finances. We had every penny we ever spent audited, and this remains the policy.

MAKING JUDGMENT CALLS

Leadership is also about making judgment calls. It's good for leaders to surround themselves with people who challenge their ideas, likeminded people with tenacity and determination who are not afraid to bring up the flaws in a given situation. I've got three great ideas, but only one of them may be something we can implement. I tried to create an environment where people felt comfortable challenging me, and bringing up opposing views, but sometimes I had to go ahead with what I conceived was best, in spite of opposition. Leadership is not always a democratic process and calling the shots is part of the risks a leader has to take.

Maintaining a Family Atmosphere

It's important to take time to relax together, laugh, and spend time getting to know one another away from an office environment. We used the Encuentros to meet together in family style for several years at NCLR, and that's where some real decisions were made about policies that were only visions at the time. The annual conferences also served that purpose. The Morin side of my family was more humorous, especially my grandfather, uncle and mother. I learned that taking time to laugh keeps you from becoming caught up in your own importance.

Meaning of Success

I realized that what I thought was success had no meaning for me. When I worked on the ship at the age of fourteen, I had freedom and adventure. So what was next? After I ate all the hamburgers I wanted, and went to all the movies I wanted, I still had some money left over, and I thought to myself there has to be more to life than this. So, somehow I formed an idea in my mind, a script. I think all of us write scripts in our minds. And my script is: You leave this world a little better place than you found it. That's success. Kids get lost because they don't have a script, something that tells them what their purpose is.

Obstacles and Hope

One of the greatest obstacles facing Latinos in this nation is the lack of a positive self-concept. Our future is in our hands. We can do anything if we really believe in ourselves. If my people could see themselves as I see them, it would be great. I see them as very loving, caring, and patriotic, and if I could make everybody believe that is true, we wouldn't need government programs to do the job for us, if we just believed in ourselves.

911 Changes

911 changed America. It changed it for generations to come. We need to understand how organized religion works, its worth and its negative impact

on society. Radical Islamists who caused the attack on America claimed their religious beliefs as the law of the land. Religion cannot be equal to state law. Secular government is the only liberating way to enjoy liberty. The minute you start getting into religious precepts, all your principles become linked to universal religious thought. If I was the president, I wouldn't let any church form my opinion on abortion, capital punishment or any other issue. The Catholic Church, for instance, has the right to believe what it wants to, but it cannot be the law of the land. People lose everything when a religious belief takes over. 911 is a prime example of this.

COMMON GROUND

African Americans have experienced more common ground in the U.S. than Latinos. The experience of being slaves, the civil war, segregation and desegregation and many other social issues have been their common ground. Our existence in America begins even before the pilgrims landed on Plymouth Rock, and our experiences differ widely. The Cuban experience is different from what Puerto Ricans experience, or what Mexican Americans in the Southwest have gone through, or what South Americans experience in coming to America. No one ethnic group can speak for all 50 million Latinos in America because all have different historical perspectives, however, we do share many successful immigration stories of pursuing the American dream, common civil rights struggles, a common language, and we share common values, beliefs, customs and traditions that unite us. It is this unity that is our strength; that is our common ground.

THE OLD GUARD

The old guard, that is leaders who have been in power for years, have to be aware of new leaders and be willing to mentor them. Some in the old guard are comfortable in their positions, but often do not let aspiring leaders move into influential positions. We are still working to put people through the process of retiring with dignity and prosperity. Once a member of the old guard moves on in a positive way, there is no looking back. Trust must be put in the new leadership,

LOVE

There are different kinds of love and different stages of love. When we think of love we sometimes mean romantic love, and the love for my wife comes to mind. But love also has a lot to do with giving and trusting, and a deep sense of commitment and responsibility, which is another kind of love. There is also parental love, love of friends, love of nature, of country, of God, and all bring up strong feelings and emotions. I try not to dwell too much on emotions. I try to keep my emotions to myself. I don't wear them on my sleeve but sometimes they come out. I can be emotional when I am trying to move a crowd to believe something. I don't usually talk about love, but I've gotten better. My kids say, "Love you," and I've learned how to say, "I love you much more." The words don't come easy for me. Primordial emotions are hard for me to express, and also hard to conceal because I can get very emotional at times. I deliberately stay away from using emotions when I speak to people because emotions are so powerful. Love is a sense of caring for someone's welfare, trying to put yourself in that person's shoes. What does my beloved want? Also, important is love of my people. I needed to feel very good about my people, to respect those I served. I needed to understand the good and bad about our community. I had to be motivated by that love in order to sustain. I think when I first started I didn't have it. I think it was more like I needed to set things right. It was that kind of motivation. It wasn't love; it was more a sense of doing the right thing. With time, I found out that having a sense of right and wrong is not enough. You've got to really love the people you serve.

Marriage

I would advise those who want to get married to check their assumptions. Ask themselves why they want to get married. Try to project twenty-five years from now. Is this the person you want to be with for the rest of your life? How would you look at her or him in thirty-five or fifty years from now? Would you wash your loved one's underwear? If you can do intimate things like that and have no sense of aversion, that's love. Suffering is also part of love. My grandparents lost four of their kids, three when they were children, and one as an adult. Yet they never felt bitter, nor felt God had betrayed them. They demonstrated a lot of love for each other. It was so beautiful to watch them, a delight.

Parkinson's Disease

Through suffering Parkinson's disease, I have learned how to be sensitive to people with disabilities. I have learned a little bit of the psychology of what it means to lose one's physical abilities. We want to be helped when we absolutely want to be helped and we want to do things on our own as well. I learned to embrace my condition and have tried not to think of it as negative.

I appreciate life and good health, and don't take anything for granted. Parkinson's made me understand that I can fight back I'm not simply a victim. I have my own destiny. Why me God, why did you make me a victim? If you can get over that feeling and know you're not a victim, you can take charge. I've learned that we need to value what we have and appreciate it. For me, that is part of humility and servant leadership.

MEANING OF DEATH

Death means different things at different times. I was always afraid of living my life and not accomplishing anything; that would have been a death for me. Now I feel I've accomplished some things—there is no longer a fear of not doing anything. The thing that still frightens me is saying goodbye to people I have loved. There are some people who retire and become hermits and isolate themselves. They're as good as dead, but just don't know it. They've chosen to leave the world. If I could choose a death I'd like to be shot at the age of one hundred-two by a jealous husband, but that's just a joke. I'd really like to die in my own bed, in my own home, with those whom I love around me, Audrey and my children and family members. I'd like to say goodbye to them, shut my eyes and move on. In the end, it's all about love, that's the only thing that really matters.

BIBLIOGRAPHY

PRINTED SOURCES

Berg, Scott W. *Grand Avenues: The Story of the French Visionary Who Designed Washington D.C.* New York: Pantheon Books, 2007.

Cisneros, Henry G. ed., with John Rosales. *Latinos and the Nation's Future.* Houston: Arte Publico Press, 2009.

Chipman, Donald E. *Spanish Texas, 1519-1821,* Austin: University of Texas Press, 1992.

Crutchfield, Leslie R., and Heather M. Grant. *Forces for Good: The Six Practices of High-Impact Nonprofits.* San Francisco: Jossey-Bass, 2008.

De León, Arnoldo. *Mexican Americans in Texas: A Brief History.* 3rd ed. Wheeling, IL: Harlan Davidson, Inc., 2009.

Galarza, Ernesto, Gallegos, Herman and Julian Samora. *Mexicans Americans in the Southwest.* 2nd ed. Santa Barbara: McNalley & Loftin Publishers, 1970.

Garcîa, Ignacio M. *Hector P. García: In Relentless Pursuit of Justice.* Houston: Arte Publico Press, 2002.

García, Mario T. *Memories of Chicano History: The Life and Narrative of Bert Corona.* Berkeley: University of California Press, 1994.

Kadis, Jennifer. "A New Chapter Begins." *Agenda* (Fall 2004/Winter 2005).

McKay, Emily G. *The National Council of La Raza: The First 25 Years.* D.C.: National Council of La Raza, 1993.

Martinez, Elizabeth, ed. *500 Años del Pueblo Chicano, 500 Years of Chicano History in Pictures.* Albuquerque: Southwest Organizing Project, 1991.

Montejano, David. *Anglos and Mexicans in the Making of Texas, 1836-1986.* Austin: University of Texas Press, 1987.

_____. *Quixote's Soldiers: A Local History of the Chicano Movement, 1966-1981.* Austin: University of Texas Press, 2010.

O'Reilly, Bill and Martin Dugard. *Killing Kennedy: The End of Camelot.* New York: Henry Holt and Company, LLC., 2012.

Paredes, Américo. *With His Pistol in His: A Border Ballad and Its Hero.* Austin: University of Texas, 1958.

Ramos, Henry, A.J. *The American GI Forum: In Pursuit of the Dream, 1948-1983.* Houston: Arte Publico Press, 1998.

Ruiz, Ramon Eduardo. *Triumph and Tragedy: A History of the Mexican People.* New York: W.W. Norton & Company, 1992.

Utley, Robert M. *Lone Star Justice: The First Century of the Texas Rangers.* New York: Oxford University Press, 2002.

Yzaguirre, Raul. "'54 Civil Rights Case Shed Light on Bias Against Mexican Americans." *Arizona Daily Star,* February 23, 2009.

Yzaguirre, Raul. "Ascending Latino Leaders." *Latino Perspectives Magazine,* January 2006.

Yzaguirre, Raul. "Big Chance for Latino Voters." *Arizona Republic,* November 2, 2008.

Yzaguirre, Raul. "Building Bridges Between Brethen." Keynote Address, National Association of Minority Auto Dealers. Detroit, MI: February 3, 2003.

Yzaguirre, Raul. "Mexico's Best Friend, Worst Enemy." *Arizona Republic,* February 22, 2009.

Yzaguirre, Raul. "The Righteous Path." Acceptance Speech, John W. Gardner Leadership Award – Independent Sector. Chicago, IL: November 8, 2004.

Yzaguirre, Raul. "The Values We Live By." Farewell Address 2004 NCLR Annual Conference. Phoenix, AZ: June 29, 2004.

ELECTRONIC SOURCES

Alurista – Wikipedia http://en.wikipedia.orb/wiki/Alurista. Retrieved March 2, 2015.

Ambassador's Speeches Embassy of the United States. *Statement of Raul Yzaguirre –Designate to the Dominican Republic* Senate Foreign Relations Committee. http://santodomingo.usembassy.gov/yzaguirre_statement.html. Retrieved May 8, 2012.

American Experience episode – *A Class Apart*. Retrieved from http://www. pbs.org/wbgh/americanexperience/

ASU Center for Civil Rights and Community Development (CDCR), Spring 2011 Newsletter. *American Dream Academy Wraps up Successful School Year*. Retrieved from http://cdcr.asu.edu.

Baca, Polly. Colorado Legislative Women's Caucus. Retrieved from https:// sites.google.com/site/coloradowomenscaucus.

Brown v. Board of Education – Wikipedia. http://en.wikipedia.org/wiki/ Brown_v._Board_of_Education. Retrieved September 24, 2013.

Burt, Kenneth C. "Henry Santiestevan '40, Mexican American Activist." *Occidental College Magazine 22*, no. 4 (Fall 2000). Retrieved from http://www.kennethburt.com/santiestevan.html.

Castillo, Lionel. Tejano Voices: The University of Texas at Arlington Center for Mexican American Studies Oral History Interview - June 28, 1996. http://library.uta.edu Retrieved June 28, 2014.

Cisneros, Henry G. Secretary of Housing and Urban Development. Retrieved from http://govinfo.library.unt.edu/npr/library/status/bios/ cisneros.htm.

Costello, Rory. *Manny Mota*. Society for American Baseball Research. Retrieved from http://sabr.org.

Dream Act. American Immigration Council. Retrieved from http://www. immigrationpolicy.org/issues/Dream-Act.

Dominican Republic – Wikipedia. https://en.wikipedia.org.wiki/Dominican_ Republic. Retrieved August 21, 2015.

Embassy of the United States Dominican Republic – Raul Yzaguirre. Retrieved from http://santodomingo.usembassy.gov ambassador. html.

Executive Order 12729. Educational Excellence for Hispanic Americans – Wikipedia. http://en.wikisource.org/wiki/Executive_Order_12729. Retrieved July 7, 2014.

Galarza, Ernesto Commemorative Lecture. Retrieved from http://www.chs. stanford.edu/pdfs/1st_Annual_Lecture_1986.pdf

Gallegos, Herman. California Social Welfare Archives Oral History Interview - December 15, 2011. http://digitallibrary.usc.edu. Retrieved March 27. 2014.

Gonzales, Rodolfo "Corky." – Wikipedia. http://en.wikipedia.org/wiki/Rodolfo_Gonzales. Retrieved January 22, 2014.

Gonzalez, Henry B. Retrieved from US House of Representatives http://history.house.gov/People/Detail/13906.

Handbook of Texas Online. Historical facts about Texas and famous Texas figures. Retrieved from http://www.tshaonline.org/handbook/online/articles/usa Published by the Texas State Historical Association.

Immigration Reform and Control Act of 1986 (IRCA) a.k.a. Simpson-Mazzoli Act US Immigration Legislation Online Retrieved from http://library.uwb.edu.

Johnson, Lyndon B. – Wikipedia. http://en.wikipedia.org/wiki/Lyndon_B_Johnson. Retrieved February 11, 2015.

Luhrs Building – Wikipedia. http://en.wikipedia.org/wiki/Luhrs_Building. Retrieved March 14, 2014.

National Council of La Raza Official Site. Overview, history, programs, conferences and media news. *Raul Yzaguirre American Hero* – Parts 1 and 2 - documentary. http://www.nclr.org.

Obama, Barack First Inauguration – Wikipedia. http://en.wikipedia.org/wiki/First_inauguration_of_Barack_Obama. Retrieved August 17, 2015

Olivarez, Graciela H. Retrieved from http://selfrescuingprincesssociety.blogspot.com/2015/03/graciela-olivarez.html.

Overview of Basque Country. Retrieved from http://geography.about.com.

Paredes, Américo. Biography. Retrieved from http://www.lib.utexas.edu/benson/paredes/biography.html.

PR Newswire: *Texas's Raul Yzaguirre School for Success Partners with American Readiness Company to Launch Nation's First ACTION 100 Dual Language Reading Initiative.* (November 8, 2012) Retrieved from http://www.prnewswire.com.

Roosevelt, Franklin D. Retrieved from http://www.whitehouse.gov/about/presidents/franklindroosevelt.

Samora, Julian. – Wikipedia. http://en.wikipedia.org/wiki/Julian_Samora. Retrieved June 5, 2013.

San Juan de los Lagos – Wikipedia. http://en.wikipedia.org/wiki/San_Juan_ de_los_Lagos. Retrieved October 14, 2011.

Sargent Shriver. Retrieved from http://www.sargentshriver.org.

Tax Reform Act of 1969. "Private Foundations and the Tax Reform Act of 1969." Retrieved from http://scholarship.law.duke.edu.

Vasconcelos, José. Biography – Encyclopedia Britannica. Retrieved from http://www.britannica.com/biography/Jose-Vasconselos.

Villa, Pancho – Wikipedia. http://en.wikipedia.org/wiki/Pancho_Villa. Retrieved May 18, 2013.

Voting Rights Act of 1965. Retrieved from http://www.civilrights.org/ voting-rights/vra/.

Yo Soy Joaquin. Retrieved from http://www.latinamericanstudies.org.